THE GREAT POWERS
IN EAST ASIA
1953–1960

The United States and Pacific Asia:
Studies in Social, Economic, and Political Interaction
Carol Gluck and Michael Hunt, General Editors

THE GREAT POWERS
IN EAST ASIA
1953–1960

EDITED BY

Warren I. Cohen and Akira Iriye

COLUMBIA UNIVERSITY PRESS
New York

COLUMBIA UNIVERSITY PRESS
New York   Oxford
Copyright © 1990 Columbia University Press
All rights reserved

Library of Congress Cataloging-in-Publication Data

The Great Powers in East Asia: 1953–1960 / edited by Warren I. Cohen and Akira
   Iriye.
      p.   cm.
   Includes bibliographical references.
   ISBN 0-231-07174-4
   1. East Asia—Foreign relations—United States.   2. United States—
Foreign relations—East Asia.   3. United States—Foreign
relations—1953–1961.   I. Cohen, Warren I.   II. Iriye, Akira.
DS518.8.G69   1990
327.7305′09′045—dc20   89-20981
                            CIP

Casebound editions of Columbia University Press books are Smyth-sewn
and printed on permanent and durable acid-free paper

Printed in the United States of America
c   10 9 8 7 6 5 4 3 2 1

For Dorothy Borg as Usual
AND
In Memory of Our Editor and Friend, Bernard Gronert

CONTENTS

THE GREAT POWERS
IN EAST ASIA
1953–1960

INTRODUCTION

In September 1987, at the Villa Serbelloni in Bellagio, Italy, an extraordinary conference convened under the auspices of the Committee on American-East Asian Relations.* For the first time, Chinese and Soviet scholars joined American, British, and Japanese colleagues to discuss the international relations of East Asia during the Eisenhower era. This volume contains the fruits of that conference: the papers of the participants as revised after an intense week of discussions.

As one expects of an international conference attended by some of the world's leading scholars, several of the essays are written superbly, contain new information, fresh insights, and brilliant analysis. Some readers may be surprised by the understanding of China, Japan, and the United States demonstrated by Soviet scholars and by the perceptiveness of the Chinese analysis of the domestic restraints on American policy. More exciting to most, however, will be the insights offered into decision-making in Beijing, based on documentary evidence and interviews of Chinese participants. It is clear that at least some Chinese scholars have access to materials not yet available to foreigners and many times more valuable than anything yet open to their Soviet counterparts.

Together these essays constitute one approach to the writing of international history. Scholars from five nations, each of whom has specialized in the foreign relations of his or her own country or in the affairs of one or more Asian countries, came together to share their perspectives. The work of each was in some way enhanced by the

*Chaired by Akira Iriye, affiliated with the Society for Historians of American Foreign Relations, supported by the Henry Luce Foundation, and housed at Michigan State University.

1

encounter with minds schooled in different cultures, informed by different national experiences. The threads they weave together create a tapestry far richer in texture than a national or binational approach could ever produce.

A preliminary essay sets the stage by examining three of the Asian revolutions to which American leaders responded. Of the essays that follow, the first series focuses on the evolution of American policy. American historians examine the workings of the Department of State and the Pentagon and the role of the president. Then an American and a Chinese analyze the foreign economic policy of the Eisenhower administration as applied to Asia and especially China. Bureaucrats and diplomats, soldiers and sailors circle an Asia few comprehend, trying to protect their nation's interests from enemies perceived at home and abroad. The president's "hidden hand" appears, waves, and does little to redirect the nation's course along more promising lines. The Chinese and American views are hardly distinguishable. Finally, a British scholar discusses the tensions in Anglo-American relations over policy toward East Asia — more charitably than her subjects judged each other.

The second series of essays is Japan-centered. Japanese, Soviet, British, and American analysts discuss a decade in which Japan tried to reach beyond its troubled alliance with the United States, eager to improve relations with and find markets in China, the Soviet Union, and the rest of Europe. Here Japanese grievances against the super-powers emerge, as does Soviet dissatisfaction with the closeness of the Japanese-American relationship. Only the British, in retreat, indicate fear of a competitor's reentry into the international system.

In the third group, a Chinese scholar offers his perspective on the straits crises of the 1950s and a Soviet scholar looks closely at Chinese-American relations. Mao's design, born of miscalculation and the determination to thwart the American dream of two Chinas, is unfolded before our eyes. And the Soviet view, while critical primarily of the United States, does not attempt to absolve the socialist side of fault.

The last three essays put Southeast Asia in the spotlight. American and British scholars look at their countries' experiences in the 1950s, the road to Vietnam and why the British knew better, and another American, sketching the Soviet role in East Asia, touches heavily on Indonesia and Indochina.

There are a number of subjects which do not receive adequate attention. Korea is missing. A Japanese perspective on Japanese-American relations and Japan's role in Southeast Asia would have been valuable. Chinese and Soviet papers on the Sino-Soviet relationship were desirable. Vietnamese and Indonesian perspectives on the role of the great powers in East Asia might have been fascinating. In some instances, either because of the lack of documentary material or the politically charged nature of the subject, the time was not ripe for scholarly consideration. In others, scholars invited to contribute were unable to. Even on the American side, where the record is fullest, there is much yet to be seen for the late 1950s. But the largest pieces of the puzzle are in place now and most of the others should fall into place over the next decade.

In these essays it is apparent that American and Soviet leaders remained Europe-firsters in the 1950s. With the stabilization of Europe, the superpowers began to grope ineptly toward detente. In East Asia, both Washington and Moscow found conditions which they did not like and over which they had minimal control, which kept satisfactory accommodations out of reach until the 1970s.

The strength of the Japanese-American alliance troubled the Soviet Union and the Sino-Soviet alliance worried American leaders even more. Having been bloodied by the Chinese Communists in Korea, the United States maintained a belligerent posture toward the People's Republic throughout the Eisenhower years, mitigated only by the ambassadorial-level talks which began in 1955. Similarly, the United States responded hostilely to Communist-dominated nationalism in Indochina.

To several of the essayists in this volume, Eisenhower and Dulles reveal a more sophisticated understanding of events in East Asia than has been evident previously. On the other hand, Eisenhower's leadership is less impressive than the Eisenhower "revisionists" would have us believe. He makes little effort to educate the public, to redirect Congress, or even to force his ideas on his administration. Similarly, Dulles is obviously much more deserving of the reputation for wisdom with which he entered office than Townsend Hoopes and others would admit, but the policy successes are few. Neither Eisenhower nor Dulles seemed sufficiently concerned with the provocative military posture the United States assumed in East Asia in the 1950s.

The British, however, were deeply concerned, but depressed by their impotence. Again and again, we see British fears that the United States will precipitate WW III over a minor issue in an area of peripheral importance. Sometimes the Americans are restrained by the desire to alleviate the apprehension of their allies; nonetheless, we are struck by the decline of Britain as a factor in the politics of East Asia.

In none of these essays is there an indication that anyone perceived the imminent remergence of Japan as a major force in world affairs. Eisenhower worries about the Japanese becoming a burden to the

United States if they are not allowed to trade with China. The Soviets ignore opportunities to woo the Japanese away from the American embrace. The Japanese fret about their independence, manipulate the Americans shamelessly, and exhibit no awareness of the greatness ahead.

China emerges as the most independent actor in East Asia. Mao pushes when he pleases and the Soviets and British shiver as they anticipate overreaction by the United States. And, in general, perhaps the most important point to emerge from the Bellagio Conference and these essays is the fact that the initiative had passed to Asia. Chinese, Japanese, and Vietnamese determine the agenda—not Europeans or Americans. As Asians struggle to win their independence from European colonial powers or to maintain it under pressure from the superpowers, Washington and Moscow maneuver ineptly to force them into the calculus of the cold war—without notable success.

In the preliminary essay, Michael H. Hunt and Steven I. Levine explore revolutionary Asia with particular attention to the communist-led revolts in China, the Philippines, and Vietnam. They discuss developments in these revolutions, the American perception of them, and the Soviet role in them. Permeating their argument is the familiar charge that American leaders did not understand events in Asia and were too quick to assume that Soviet inspiration rather than local grievances were responsible for peasant unrest. And they remind those who would write about American policy toward Asia of the need to study the Asian arena as well as the American (or Western) players.

In the lead essay, Nancy Bernkopf Tucker examines the role of the U.S. Department of State in the formation of American policy toward East Asia, using the formulation of policy toward China to reveal how the department functioned and to what end. She notes that although the key appointments—ambassador to the Republic of China, assistant secretary for Far Eastern affairs, director of the China desk— were all given to men deemed friendly to Chiang and acceptable to the likes of Senator William Knowland and Representative Walter Judd, these were not the men to whom Dulles was attentive. His inner circle was comprised of men who shared his skepticism, even contempt for Chiang, and his essentially Europe first orientation. Consequently, on the critical issues of the Eisenhower era, the alleged "unleashing" of Chiang, the Taiwan Straits crises of 1954–55 and 1958, how to drive a wedge between the Soviet Union and the People's Republic of China, Dulles' views reflected the prudent, pragmatic approach of men like Robert Bowie, Douglas MacArthur II, and Livingston Merchant, rather than the ideologically charged confrontational policies advocated by the likes of Karl Rankin and Walter Robertson. Without apologizing for Dulles' failings, Tucker portrays a man less rigid than the images found in most of the literature available in the quarter century after his death. Nonetheless, she concedes readily that Dulles' advice to the president was not the only counsel Eisenhower received—and that Eisenhower rather than anyone in the Department of State was responsible for the major decisions of his administration.

Marc Gallicchio gives the freshest analysis to date of American military perceptions and intentions in East Asia in the 1950s. Using hitherto unseen military records, he reveals the development of a strategy designed to allow the United States to take more aggressive action in Southeast Asia, the next point of confrontation with Communist power.

Gallicchio notes that Eisenhower had chosen Admiral Arthur Radford as chairman of the Joint Chiefs of Staff because of his reputation for budget consciousness and his views on nuclear deterrence and global strategy, but his Asia First views occasionally troubled the president. On the other hand, Eisenhower shared the sense that the containment line was stable in Europe and that it was in Asia that the United States faced its most threatening situations. As a result, the president did little to restrain offense-minded and provocative policies devised by military leaders eager to regain the initiative in Asia, eager for another shot at China. Military advisory groups, alliances, and the basing of various missiles and bombers along the defensive perimeter quickly remedied the deficiencies of the Truman Administration's military posture in the area. Only when the military became overly exuberant about the use of nuclear weapons did Eisenhower exercise any apparent restraint.

In general, the military was more supportive of Chiang's regime than the rest of the administration and perhaps more eager to build up Japanese military power. Military leaders were very much troubled by linkage between China and the Vietminh and Navy strategists wanted to strike at Chinese bases on Hainan before going to the rescue of the French at Dienbienphu. After 1958 they were convinced that the Soviet Union was distancing itself from China and that the PRC was vulnerable to American military power. Through Gallicchio's eyes, it is relatively easy to see how the United States came to commit itself so deeply to an area of peripheral importance in Southeast Asia.

Waldo Heinrichs' Eisenhower will be readily recognizable to readers of pre-revisionist literature on the 1950s. Heinrichs is skeptical of the "new" Eisenhower, prepared to concede the "hidden hand," Eisenhower in command, but unwilling to divine wisdom in the entrails of failed policies. The president saw China as his country's enemy in Indochina, the "head of the snake" and believed it necessary to draw the line there. Although uneasy about the plans for an operation to rescue the French at Dienbienphu, Eisenhower was trying to find a way to make it practicable—rather than toying with Radford, Nixon, and Dulles when he sent them off for British and Congressional support. Heinrichs is unable to find "constructive value" in the administration's Indochina policy. Like Tucker in her analysis of Dulles, Heinrichs finds the president preoccupied with European affairs and tending to be indifferent to Asia.

The economic policy of the United States toward East Asia included an effort to isolate the People's Republic of China in which, according to Burton Kaufman, the president did not believe. Eisenhower initially endorsed the idea of economic pressure on the Chinese as a means of straining the Sino-Soviet alliance, but was soon persuaded that the policy was counter-productive with China and was manifestly straining the Western alliance. Increasingly Eisenhower worried about Japanese trade opportunities and pointed toward China and Southeast Asia as natural outlets for Tokyo. Gradually the president perceived that attempting to strangle China was less important than bolstering the Japanese economy and easing the anxieties of his friends in Europe. If Eisenhower's thoughts on economic foreign policy were sounder than those of men like Walter Robertson, it made little difference. Kaufman notes that the president failed to support his bureaucratic allies. He may have been a wiser president than earlier writers imagined, but Kaufman and Heinrichs are agreed that he was not necessarily a more effective one.

Qing Simei, demonstrating extraordinary insight into American political culture, offers a Chinese analysis of Eisenhower's thought and policies on trade with the People's Republic. She describes a president eager to reduce financial subsidies to his allies and looking to free trade as the answer to European and Japanese economic problems. More than Kaufman, she credits Eisenhower with aggressive support of allied demands to expand trade opportunities with China and notes that he even allowed American subsidiaries in Canada to sell to the Red Chinese. But Qing finds Eisenhower backing away from thoughts of direct trade between the United States and China when confronted by threats to cut Mutual Defense Act appropriations emanating from Chiang's friends in Congress. All too briefly, she indicates Beijing's awareness of Eisenhower's willingness to erase trade restrictions and explains why Chinese leaders were not overly responsive. But clearly, Eisenhower was not seeking to isolate the People's Republic.

Rosemary Foot demonstrates the inability of British and American leaders to achieve a meeting of minds about China. In particular, she documents much that we have suspected about tensions between Anthony Eden and Dulles, long before Suez. Fully appreciative of the American dilemma during the straits crises, the British were nonetheless horrified by the danger of war over the offshore islands.

From the British perspective, there was no movement on the American side in the 1950s. The United States ended the decade as tied to Chiang Kai-shek, the domino theory, and fears of undermining American credibility as it had been at the beginning. Through the new insights Foot provides into British thinking, it is apparent that the British were barely able to paper over their differences with their American allies, especially on the issue of Chinese representation at the United Nations. Here the reader begins to sense the frustrations of men living through and trying to adjust to the decline of British power and influence in Asia, a sometimes subliminal theme that permeates all the British essays.

At the conference, Hiroshi Kimura presented a relentless discussion of what he contended is the abnormality and illegality of the Soviet position on the "northern islands" issue which continues to poison Soviet relations with Japan. When the occupation ended, Japan moved quickly toward the "normalization" of relations with the Soviet Union, but only a limited rapprochement was achieved because of Soviet unwillingness to return islands seized at the end of World War II. Soviet resentment at the close Japanese-American relationship clearly contributed to Soviet rigidity. Kimura noted that the Japanese negotiating position was weakened by domestic factionalism.

Konstantin Sarkisov replied with a straightforward view of Soviet participation in East Asian affairs in the 1950s, with considerable reference to his country's current concerns. He and Kimura have sparred before and Sarkisov left no doubt that Japan and the United States were responsible for whatever tensions remained in that triangular relationship. He indicated regret at the deterioration of Sino-Indian relations in the 1950s and noted the difficulty the Soviet Union had pleasing the comrades in China while attempting to win friends in the most important nation in South Asia. Looking at Soviet-American relations in East Asia, Sarkisov was relatively gentle with Eisenhower, reserving his hardest judgments for Dulles. And, he suggested, Soviet policy after 1953, might be seen as foreshadowing the policies of M. S. Gorbachev.

Roger Buckley's analysis of Anglo-Japanese relations stresses British disinterest in Northeast Asia after World War II, tempered by British dissatisfaction with American dominance in Japan and rigidity elsewhere. British leaders were particularly mistrustful of John Foster Dulles, partly because of his role at the Japanese peace conference when they concluded he had deceived them, and because of his general tendency toward unilateralism. Like Foot, Buckley describes the difficult adjustment of the British to their status as a "middle power," trailing in the wake of a country for whose leaders they had little respect. With the virtual disappearance of their strategic concerns in the region, the British perspective was almost exclusively economic. Japan was perceived primarily as a competitor for trade and the bitter memories of World War II were used by the British to justify their rigid resistance to any resurgence of Japanese power or influence.

To analyze the Japanese-American alliance in the 1950s, Roger Dingman uses the story of the *Lucky Dragon*, the Japanese tunaboat victimized by fallout from the American hydrogen bomb test at Bikini in March 1954. Among other things, he demonstrates Japanese adroitness at manipulating the United States. He leaves little doubt that the alliance was viewed differently by the two partners. The United States, as is evident in most of these papers, was concerned primarily with containing the Soviet Union and China. The Japanese had a more fundamental goal: winning their independence.

He Di's discussion of the offshore island crisis provides insights into the Chinese policy process and into Mao's thought that we have never had. He does this by using materials not yet available to American scholars—and which may never be available to us.

He Di leaves no doubt of Chinese leaders' determination to unite Taiwan with the mainland, but he argues that they understood there was no possibility of achieving that goal in the shortrun. They began shelling the offshore islands in 1954 to signal their unwillingness to abandon Taiwan, their refusal to accept a two Chinas outcome of the civil war. Shortly afterward, they chose to begin attacking the lesser islands both to gather in as many as possible *and* to gain the amphibious warfare experience essential for the eventual conquest of Taiwan. They did not want conflict with the United States and did not anticipate the strong American response which included the threat to use nuclear weapons.

When the United States responded sharply in 1955, Mao and Zhou succeeded in instituting ambassadorial level talks to defuse the issue. When those talks broke down, the Chinese, aware of disagreements between Washington and Taibei, within the United States, and within the Western alliance, played upon these "contradictions" by instituting a new crisis in 1958. Aware that the United States was pressing Chiang to abandon Jinmen (Quemoy) and Mazu (Matsu), Mao preferred to allow Chiang to keep them to preserve the link between Taiwan and the mainland—again to thwart the two China policy toward which Washington had moved.

Although he reflects disparagingly on Soviet support for China during the crisis, He Di stresses China's desire to maneuver independently, its determination not to allow its ally, any more than its adversaries, to restrict its course of action.

Peter Ivanov, on the other hand, stresses the steadfastness of Soviet support for the People's Republic of China, especially on the issue of Taiwan, in contrast with American opposition to the Beijing regime. He sees American hostility to China emerging in the context of the cold war. In Asia, American hostility toward Socialism was focused on China. He argues that the United States entertained exaggerated fears of China, was unwilling to normalize relations, but was not eager for war—as evidenced in particular by the exclusion of the offshore islands from the application of the "Formosa Resolution" of 1955. Although he writes of tension between Chiang Kai-shek and the Eisenhower administration, Ivanov emphasizes the support Washington felt constrained to give the Republic of China. Perhaps most interesting is his suggestion that the Chinese-American relationship was influenced by different political cultures, different internal political contexts, and different levels of political and diplomatic experience, precluding effective communication. Some readers will doubtless be surprised by his use of a construct very much like Richard Hofstadter's "psychic crisis" to explain the irrational American response to communism in China. Noteworthy too is his understated criticism of Chinese actions in 1958.

Tony Short's analysis of British policy toward Southeast Asia returns to the theme that British leaders were as much concerned with restraining the United States as they were with containing communism. As the result of British experience in Malaya and Singapore, Churchill, Eden, and their advisers perceived events in Indochina as a civil war rather than indirect Chinese or Soviet aggression. They discounted American fears of Chinese aggressive intentions and were fearful that the United States would provoke World War III by its actions in Vietnam.

Gary Hess demonstrates that the British succeeded in restraining the United States; that the American government considered its options limited in Asia by the need to retain the confidence of its European allies whose cooperation was vital in the primary theater of

Europe. But clearly American perceptions of China's expansionism and of the danger to follow the loss of Indochina were very different from those of the British. Nonetheless, Hess notes a fundamental ambivalence between the Eisenhower administration's assessment of the tremendous importance of Southeast Asia and its attempt to serve American interests there with a minimal commitment. Like Tucker and others, Hess also concludes that Dulles' approach, in this instance to the nonaligned countries of Asia, was more sophisticated than his rhetoric indicated.

In the last essay, Steven Levine provides a carefully crafted overview of Soviet policy toward Asia. Not surprisingly, his perspective is quite different from that of Kimura, Sarkisov, or Ivanov. Levine establishes the Soviet domestic context after the death of Stalin and then analyzes Khrushchev's policies. In particular, he notes the tension between the Soviet leader's attempts to ease the confrontation with the United States and his desire to meet the aspirations of his Chinese and Vietnamese allies. Like Heinrichs' Eisenhower, Levine's Khrushchev saw Asia as peripheral to his nation's vital interests and was loathe to become deeply involved there. Levine sees China as Khrushchev's greatest failure, but contends that the Soviet "loss" of China, like the American "loss" a decade before, was the result primarily of Chinese domestic affairs. He concludes with a thoughtful comparison of Soviet and American policy in the region.

In sum, this volume examines the international relations of East Asia during the Eisenhower era. The contributors reveal the levels of understanding the major powers had of each other and, in some instances, of the smaller nations of the region. They explain when and why American or British policymakers were driven or restrained by domestic considerations, why the Japanese persist in their efforts to regain the northern islands and why the Soviets remain unyielding. Mao's calculations and miscalculations are put before us for the first time. The essayists leave no doubt that neither the Americans nor the Soviets ever succeeded in controlling their Chinese allies. And it is evident that few Asians served as the dutiful cold war surrogates the super powers sought. Nor did the British have much luck with their efforts to use English brains to direct the use of adolescent American power. But if East Asia was frought with frustration for the Americans, British, and Soviets in the 1950s, Asians did not fare much better. Although Europe and America could no longer dominate East Asia, they retained the power to thwart Asian aspirations, whether it be for a united China or Vietnam — or Japan's northern islands. The Eisenhower years were a time when the United States in particular still approached East Asia as a front in a global cold war. They were also years of transition for the region, as Asians struggled for control of their destiny and attempted to separate their concerns from those of the super powers. This is the story contained in the pages that follow.

Warren I. Cohen

1

The Revolutionary Challenge to Early U.S. Cold War Policy in Asia

MICHAEL H. HUNT
University of North Carolina, Chapel Hill

STEVEN I. LEVINE
Duke University

During the early cold war period, the United States had a deeply troubled relationship with a Pacific Asia undergoing profound revolutionary transformation. This much, at least, emerges clearly from the scholarly literature on the subject.[1] Indeed, scholars of markedly differing persuasions agree that Washington's perceptions of unrest in Asia and of the Soviet connection with that turmoil fundamentally conditioned U.S. policy, defining to a significant degree its contours and contents. It is unfortunate that despite broad agreement on these points, students of U.S. policy for the most part have not done enough to supply an Asian context to their studies of the early cold war in Asia. Lacking that context, one cannot fully understand American actions, provide cogent evaluations of American views, or properly judge American policy and the men who made it.

This paper is intended as a partial remedy to this inadequately developed Asian context for U.S. policy—and as an invitation to others to formulate their own alternative approach or to extend and refine this one. The survey that follows highlights certain central features of revolutionary politics in Asia during the early cold war period that must be borne in mind when examining American policy in the region. The value of the increasingly sophisticated and detailed studies of U.S. Asia policy and of American policy-makers that are now being undertaken will be considerably enhanced if they are grounded in a broad knowledge of Asian conditions, in particular of those aspects of revolutionary politics remote from American historical experiences and cultural values. Without this grounding, such studies run the risk of being U.S.–centered and parochial.

The Asia that American policymakers confronted after World War II was a region in which "regime collapse" was nearly ubiquitous. From India to Japan political structures and elites, some colonial and others indigenous, were under siege. The rise of elite nationalism, the turmoil associated with Japanese victory and occupation, the surge of American power into the region, and the postwar return of colonial authorities combined to create a fluid political situation. The nature of the ensuing political change varied widely.

In India, Burma, and Indonesia, new regimes emerged with relative ease as former colonial masters began to decamp. In the southern half of Korea and in Japan elements of the old political elites, with the cooperation or acquiescence of American proconsuls, established regimes that were fundamentally conservative in orientation even when, as in the case of Japan, a democratic political system was established.[2] Elsewhere, particularly in China, Vietnam, and the Philippines, revolutionary forces grew apace. Of all the regional problems confronting American policy-makers, none more alarmed Washington and more directly and forcefully challenged the American presence in the region than did social revolutions. Focusing our attention upon those three countries, we shall sketch in a picture of this too often neglected Asian revolutionary setting for U.S. policy.

The history of modern Asia and the sociology of revolution suggest some of the pertinent questions. What manner of men embarked on revolutions? How did they build a base of popular support sufficiently strong to bid for power and challenge the American presence? What conditions favored the emergence of revolutionary nationalism? What was the Soviet relationship to Asian revolutionary movements and regimes? How did this relationship change when revolutionary movements came to power? Students of American policy must come to grips with these questions if for no other reason than to establish a benchmark for judging how well U.S. policy-makers themselves understood what was happening in Asia and how appropriate were the policies they devised in response.

REVOLUTIONARY MOVEMENTS

Twentieth-century Asian revolutions have passed through two fundamentally different stages. They have begun as *revolutionary movements*, mobilizing resources and people in the process of struggling for power and legitimacy. If and when they succeeded, then as *revolutionary states* they have devoted themselves to realizing the economic and social transformations that had animated them from the beginning. These two stages, each in its own fashion, challenged the specific postwar policy of containment no less than the broad foundation of American cultural values and political ideology on which that policy rested.

The revolutions in Pacific Asia were in transition from the first to the second stage in 1953 as Harry Truman yielded the White House to Dwight Eisenhower. The Communist revolution in China had triumphed in 1949, and the new state was in the process of consolidating its political control and pursuing its socioeconomic goals. In French Indochina a second revolution, displaying considerable political strength and military tenacity, was preparing for the battle at Dienbienphu that would soon deal the coup de grace to an overextended and war-weary colonial power. In the Philippines a third revolutionary movement, the Huks, had gained momentum in 1950, creating panic in the Filipino government and sudden alarm in Washington.

Revolution in these three countries arose out of long-brewing indigenous political crises that can be understood only by taking a broad and long-term perspective.[3] (The lack of such perspective, we suggest, seriously distorted Washington's view of these revolutions.) Revolution was initially an elite enterprise that developed through several difficult stages and, where successful, commanded a widening circle of supporters and a growing base of resources. We will gain a better grasp of the revolutionary challenge that Washington faced if we look at the three phases through which a successful revolution had to pass before culminating in victory.

First, the initial impetus to revolution arose from a quiet crisis of confidence that took shape in the minds of politically engaged intellectuals. Concern about the traditional states' diminished capacity to meet foreign and domestic responsibilities goaded these leading players in the drama of revolution into undertaking political activity. In China, the crisis of state and society underlying the collapse of the Qing dynasty in 1911 stimulated a search for alternative political forms that might restore China's strength and glory. By the 1920s some leading intellectuals had begun to find in Marxism-Leninism an attractive idiom for expressing their concerns and a vehicle for political organization.[4] In Vietnam the state crisis was even more profound. There a well-entrenched colonial power loomed over the patriotic intellectuals who wished to restore indigenous political authority. Vietnamese intellectuals followed the pattern established by their Chinese counterparts. By the 1920s patriotic and social concerns— couched often in Marxist concepts and categories—gripped a younger generation of intellectuals and political activists.[5]

Second, the fortunes of revolution depended heavily on the ability of nascent revolutionary elites to construct a shared ideology and forge an effective party organization. They had to translate the esoteric language of an elite ideology into a popular vision of a new order accessible to the masses. Equally important was the creation of a unified, disciplined party capable of challenging both local power-holders and the central government.

By the 1920s activists in both China and Vietnam had discovered in the concept of a Leninist party a powerful tool for achieving revolutionary success and in the Soviet experience a model to emulate. The Communist International (Comintern), established in 1919 by the youthful Soviet regime as an instrument of world revolution, recognized a historic opportunity and stepped in to supply nascent Communist parties with funds, schooling, literature, and advisers. The Chinese Communist Party (CCP) took shape in 1920–21 with a mere fifty members.[6] Its Vietnamese counterpart, the Indochina Communist Party, began in 1925 as a nine-man cell and was formally organized in Hong Kong in 1930, when Ho Chi Minh, already an experienced Comintern operative, brought together rival Communist groups.[7]

Third, ultimate victory turned on the successful application of party ideology and organization to the task of mobilizing the resources—manpower, taxes, labor, and intelligence—that revolutionary organization required. Initially, activity began in the cities with an attempt to forge a proletarian spearhead for the revolutionary movement. When the cities proved inhospitable and dangerous, the urban intellectuals qua early revolutionary leaders took refuge in the countryside where four-fifths of their countrymen lived. The CCP took advantage of the rugged Jinggang mountains in the south and then the primitive Yan'an area in the north, while the Vietminh established a secure base in the inaccessible mountains of North Vietnam from whence they penetrated the populous Red River delta.

Perhaps the most difficult as well as the most important task required to make revolution self-sustaining was that of mobilizing peasant support. Translating revolutionary abstractions into political practice in rural areas was a fragile and contingent operation that put a premium on an experimental outlook. Success demanded extraordinary sensitivity to the great variety of conditions existing both within and between different regions. The political consciousness of peasants and, in turn, the degree of peasant activism depended on the nature of those conditions. Only by constructing a revolutionary program flexible and ample enough to accommodate the diversity of peasant experience and needs could the revolution make headway.[8]

Revolutionaries struggling to build a base of support within secure zones of operation faced a formidable and changing set of foes. Local power-holders and the central government, sometimes separately and sometimes in combination, exploited the vulnerability of the peasantry to the assertion of state power or, where the revolutionaries had dug themselves in, to the exercise of counterrevolutionary terror. At times the intrusion of foreign powers dramatically redefined the nature of the conflict. The CCP faced first the Nationalists, then the Japanese, and finally the Nationalists again, this time backed, however ineffectively, by the United States. For the Vietnamese Communists the first foe was the French, then briefly the Japanese, and once more the French, now bolstered by increasing levels of American support.

By the late 1930s the CCP had worked out a viable strategy.[9] The Vietminh for its part solved the riddle of rural mobilization in the course of the early 1940s while organizing resistance to Japan and battling famine.[10] The mark of success in both cases was the establishment of relatively secure rural base areas that gradually evolved into embryonic states containing the seeds of a new social and political order. By 1945, after two decades of struggle against long odds, both the CCP and the Vietminh had created conditions of "multiple sovereignty" (to use Charles Tilly's phrase),[11] raising hopes for an imminent victory.

The ultimate challenge for revolutionary leaders was to identify the moment for decisive action when sufficient resources had been aggregated to meet and master a vulnerable enemy. In China and Vietnam no less than in the Philippines (to be discussed below) World War II set the stage by discrediting the old regime and by weakening its hold on the countryside. During wartime, revolutionary parties firmly seized the chance to extend territorial control and to promote a patriotic united front that appealed to previously uncommitted groups. In 1946 the Chinese Communists drew on the strength accumulated during the anti-Japanese War in meeting the military challenge of their Nationalist foes and then fought their way to victory in a three-year civil war. For the Vietminh the opportune moment had come in 1945. A policy of revolutionary expansion took advantage of

French weakness, the impending defeat of the Japanese, and socially disruptive famine in the north. The Vietminh offensive culminated in August in the seizure of Hanoi and the creation of the Democratic Republic of Vietnam (DRV). This gave the Vietminh at least a tenuous hold on power in the north.

The revolutionary crisis that erupted in the Philippines in the late 1940s and then subsided in the early 1950s departed significantly from the Chinese and Vietnamese patterns. Fundamental to the failure of revolution in the Philippines was the absence of a crisis of the state comparable to that which had proved so troubling to intellectuals in China and Vietnam. Filipinos had known only weak government in Manila. After the ouster of the Spanish in 1898, leading Filipino provincial families ruled in league with American proconsuls. The elite comprised of those families not only lacked a tradition or model of a strong state but was also compromised by a habit of collaboration with foreign masters on a scale unmatched in either China or Vietnam. After briefly resisting the American takeover, the elite had settled into a collaborative relationship with the United States that safeguarded its domestic privileges while promising ultimate political independence. When the Japanese conquered the islands during World War II, the elite again accommodated to foreign rule. Finally, when the Americans returned, the Philippines resumed a dependent relationship with the United States, which continued even after the attainment of formal independence in 1946. Rather than forcefully rejecting external domination, the dependent Filipino elite developed at best a kind of submissive nationalism.

The type of collaboration prevailing in the Philippines served as a model for U.S. policy-makers with regard to other Asian countries. Local elites that deviated from this norm were at the very least viewed with suspicion by Americans who preferred and expected complaisance from their Asian partners. By explicitly and often passionately rejecting the subordinate and dependent position such a model entailed, revolutionary elites directly challenged American political values and presumptions. This conflict was one of the core elements in the confrontation between the United States and Asian revolutionary movements.

In the case of the Philippines, it appears that the Huk crisis arose not from elite disaffection but rather from peasant discontent, which became pronounced in the interwar period. The deterioration of patron-client ties left peasants without economic security. Landlords with whom peasants had once enjoyed a mutually supportive relationship increasingly embraced commercialized agriculture and "rationalized" their use of peasant labor so as to eliminate traditional but costly welfare practices. The catalyst for peasant resistance was a rural order characterized by increasingly high rates of landlessness and tenant debt. In the 1920s sporadic, isolated acts of collective peasant protest threatened the local elites and attracted the attention of the Socialist Party, which helped organize peasant unions. The Philippine Communist Party, established in 1930, also embraced the cause of the peasant, perhaps even before it merged with the Socialists in 1938.

The Japanese occupation of the Philippines in 1941 set the stage for the creation of the People's Anti-Japanese Army, popularly known as the Huks.[12] In March 1942 prominent Socialists and Communists met to organize a united-front, peasant-based force. They put at its head Luis Taruc, a charismatic Socialist from a poor, rural background. The Huks resisted the invaders and punished Filipino collaborators, many of them landlords. But Huk leaders failed to undertake the ideological and organizational work that was in the long run essential if the movement were to be sustained and made cohesive. In this critical respect, the practice of the Huks differed from the CCP and the Vietminh.

As in China and Vietnam, the end of the war brought only a hiatus in the gathering rural crisis. The Huks disbanded, and the initiative in the countryside passed to local forces sponsored by landlords, who were in turn supported by the Roxas government of the newly independent Philippines. As the futility of peaceful peasant organization and protest became apparent between 1946 and 1948 and as wartime gains evaporated, armed Huk units sprang back to life, reestablishing themselves in their stronghold in central Luzon.[13]

In January 1950 the Huk leadership, dominated by the Communist Party, decided to gamble on an all-out offensive to seize power.[14] That decision was prompted in part by Manila's ineffectual response to the Huk challenge and in part by the Communist leaders' conviction that the United States was on the defensive in the cold war and would not be able to save its Filipino allies. However, the general offensive failed and the Huk cause suffered a crushing defeat. Under a series of heavy blows the Huks rapidly declined. At its peak the Huks had boasted 12,000 to 15,000 combatants and 1.5 to 2 million followers, but by the mid-1950s the Huks had disappeared as an organized force.[15]

The defeat had several sources. Among them was a wrong assessment of how the United States would react to a revolutionary upsurge and a serious misreading of the mood of the peasantry. Once the gravity of the Huk threat became clear during the first half of 1950, Washington had rushed assistance to Manila. Communist leaders also erred by stressing the threat of American imperialism but failing to link it to the local grievances and personal aspirations of the peasantry.

In Ramon Magsaysay, moreover, the United States had found an effective Filipino partner in turning back the revolutionary challenge. As the Huks scented victory over the Quirino government in September 1950, Magsaysay was made Secretary of Defense at the urging of the Americans. Bolstered by various kinds of American assistance, he transformed the army into an effective instrument of rural pacification, while himself promising land reform. His success at capturing Huk leaders and at sowing dissension within the movement further blunted the revolutionary thrust.[16]

The failure of the Huks may be interpreted in several ways. The United States had found that it could indeed neutralize rural-based revolutionaries by combining the effective application of force with a program of political inducements and promises of reform. From this experience was born the notion of counterinsurgent warfare. An alternate reading of this experience was that in the Philippines the ingredients for a successful social revolution — a disciplined party able to translate elite discontent into a program that could mobilize and sustain peasant support — had not yet appeared. The Huks arose on the basis of strong peasant grievances, but they never acquired an elite leadership armed with the ideological and organizational tools to harness the peasantry to revolutionary goals. The leadership of the Huks, a heterogeneous lot, lacked a common program, and some among them were still psychyologically oriented to the cities and not attuned to rural conditions and the military potential of armed Huk units. These leaders were responsible for the ill-advised and disastrous all-out offensive of 1950.[17]

Before considering the transformations undertaken by revolutionary Asian states, let us briefly sum up the implications for the United States of our three cases of Asian revolutionary movements. First, at a time when American power was still very much in the ascendant, the successes of Communist revolutionaries in China and Vietnam already foreshadowed the limits of American influence in postwar Asia. The Chinese revolution in particular forced Washington to abandon the idea that China could be a reliable bulwark against a perceived Soviet threat to the stability of postwar Asia. Second, the United States, which prided itself on being different from and better than the European colonial powers, was reviled by the revolutionaries as merely the latest of the Western imperialist powers to seek domination in Asia. Although American leaders naturally denied the charge, it stung nonetheless. Third, the coming to power of revolutionary counterelites who rejected American guidance in no uncertain terms directly challenged the tutelary model of external patron-domestic client relations that Washington favored. This model, first evident in the Philippines' case, was seen by Washington as the way to accelerate political and economic development while blocking Soviet penetration. The successful suppression of the Huk uprising may have strengthened the confidence of policy-makers that they could cope with rural-based insurgencies elsewhere.

REVOLUTIONARY STATES

R evolution in America's Asia entered a new era as triumphant revolutionary movements in China and Vietnam assumed state power. Revolutionary leaders left behind them the heroic and perilous age of the struggle for survival and confronted a new period filled with formidable policy challenges and fresh perplexities. Among their core tasks was that of creating an efficient state apparatus and tackling the yet unrealized goals of the revolution—social transformation, long-term economic development, and strategic security. Here, as in the earlier phase, the United States discerned danger in the ways that revolutionary leaders pursued these goals.

The transition from revolutionary movement to revolutionary state produced considerable tension in the revolution as some leaders adjusted more easily than others to the new tasks at hand. That tension arose out of a basic dilemma: how to build a strong administrative structure and promote development without losing touch with the revolutionary ethos or abandoning the political style promoted over several decades of intense political and military activity. Those gripped primarily by the statist concerns that had initially driven the elite toward revolution placed priority on building up a strong party and government bureaucracy governed by expertise and regulations. While they wanted to preserve and promote the myths of the revolution, which provided legitimacy and fostered national unity, they deemed the improvisational and voluntaristic practices of the movement days unsuitable to the new age. Those of a more populist persuasion, however, saw in the program of the state-builders a threat to the vision of national unity and popular mobilization that had shaped revolutionary strategy and produced victory.

In China this statist-populist tension is evident in the domestic policy pursued during the first decade of the People's Republic. Most of the leadership, including Zhou Enlai, Liu Shaoqi, and Deng Xiaoping, generally favored a prolonged period of domestic stability conducive to state-building and laying the foundation for the later development of an advanced socialist economy. On the other side, Mao Zedong embodied a populist commitment to maintaining revolutionary consciousness and egalitarian values long central to the struggle that he had led. Development would come not through deadening, routinized work but through "storming," directing a burst of energy from the Chinese people against economic obstacles. A period of rest and consolidation would follow, setting the stage for attempting new breakthroughs.[18]

The divergent goals and styles evident in domestic affairs also supply a clue to the tensions at work in the foreign policy realm. Statist concerns made foreign policy an instrument to serve China's concrete development needs once the essential security of the revolution had been attended to. Links to the Soviet Union were important, both in deterring any American-sponsored attack and in guaranteeing economic aid and technological transfers. But links to other states, regardless of their social system, were also valuable for the economic opportunities they might open up and for the diplomatic opportunities and international status such contacts might bestow on China. By contrast, foreign policy initiatives that threatened to embroil China in conflict were unwelcome. China needed to direct its resources into development at home, and it needed a calm and stable international environment to pursue its domestic agenda.

From the populist perspective, most forcefully articulated by Mao, foreign policy was to serve the same essentially revolutionary goals that defined domestic policy. Only an assertive and principled foreign policy could shape a popular revolutionary consciousness, align China with the world's struggling peoples, and isolate ideological backsliders from potential foreign support. Such a foreign policy entailed a vigorous defense against the predictable imperialist attempts to disrupt the revolution and divide the Chinese people against itself. It also meant promoting unity among China's natural allies—the Soviet Union and the weak and oppressed peoples of the world—as a counterpoint to the popular unity Mao sought to promote domestically.

Two issues of particular importance to the United States—the Korean War and Taiwan—illustrate the various concerns that the Chinese leadership brought to foreign policy questions. General Douglas MacArthur's advance up the Korean peninsula in the fall of 1950 appears to have produced considerable agitation within the Chinese leadership. Deeply absorbed in the search for an appropriate response, Mao decided on October 2 in favor of armed intervention. Undaunted by the U.S. military advantage, he contended that China could not meekly acquiesce. If the Americans occupied all of Korea and dealt a heavy blow to the Korean Revolution, "then the American aggressors would run even more wild to the detriment of all of East Asia." On October 8, the day after U.S. troops crossed the thirty-eighth parallel, he gave the orders for Chinese forces to prepare to move across the Yalu River and do battle. Through this period and as late as October 13 Mao had to contend with the doubts his decision raised in the minds of his colleagues. (The identity of the doubters differs from one account to another.) They argued for at least a delay in sending troops to Korea to allow for more time to consolidate state control, complete land reform, stabilize the economy, and prepare the armed forces. They may also have stressed the uncertain nature of Soviet assistance. Time for discussion soon ran out as Chinese troops crossed into Korea on October 19, setting in motion the events that would bring war with the United States late the next month.[19]

The tension between statist and populist outlooks became sharper in the mid-1950s in foreign affairs as in domestic affairs. China's handling of the Taiwan question illustrates how leaders were pulled in different directions. While agreeing on the importance of liberating the Nationalist-held offshore islands, they differed on the urgency of that task and the resources to be devoted to it.

Zhou Enlai seems to have regarded the Taiwan issue warily. As head of the government, he recognized that military confrontation with the United States would drain scarce resources away from socialist development. Zhou, moreover, saw the Taiwan issue within the broader context of China's efforts to break out of the diplomatic isolation that the United States sought to impose and to cultivate friends outside of the Soviet bloc.[20] Zhou and his aides had made quiet overtures to the United States in 1949, established China as a player in great power politics at the 1954 Indochina Conference, proclaimed the outward-looking Bandung spirit in 1955, and in that same year initiated a cautious opening to the United States through the Geneva ambassadorial talks (shifted to Warsaw in 1958). From Zhou's perspective, a diplomatic solution of the Taiwan issue, achieved through an international conference or direct dealings with the United States, made far more sense than did a hazardous military solution with unpredictable international consequences.

Seen through Mao's populist prism, however, the Taiwan question was primarily a test of revolutionary morale and unity. Left unresolved, the Taiwan issue stood as a galling reminder of imperialist intervention in Chinese affairs and of the unfinished business of the civil war. Pursuing a purely diplomatic solution opened the CCP to the very charges of capitulationism that had arisen earlier as a result of the weak Nationalist response to Japanese aggression. A passive stance toward Taiwan might give the lie to Mao's claim that China had stood up in the world. A Taiwan unredeemed, moreover, left Chinese counterrevolutionaries a rallying point and the Americans a base for their strategy of encirclement. On the other hand, a bold initiative leading to the resolution of the Taiwan question would be a major contribution to strengthening the people's revolutionary spirit and consolidating the security of the revolution. In addition, by challenging the American hold on Taiwan, Mao also hoped to drive a wedge between the United States and the nationalist authorities on Taiwan.

Mao set the Taiwan pot to boil in 1954. In July he gave the signal for action, and in September Chinese forces began shelling Jinmen (Quemoy), an island guarding the approach to the port of Xiamen (Amoy). By February they had taken the last two Nationalist strongholds further to the north (Yijiangshan and Dazhen islands right off the Zhejiang coast). As the Eisenhower administration began to threaten reprisals, Zhou stepped forward to offer words of conciliation and suggestions for a diplomatic way out.

When three years of talks with the United States yielded no results, Mao again turned up the heat. The Great Leap Forward provided an appropriately populist domestic setting for another spirited challenge to the Americans, one that would remind them of Chinese determination on the Taiwan question, while at the same time stimulating tensions between Washington and its allies in Taibei and in Western Europe. Mao made his decision in the latter half of August 1958, and bombardment of Jinmen began almost at once. In early September Chinese leaders met again, apparently to rethink Mao's audacious confrontational approach, and by October they had ruled out any further attempt to oust Nationalist forces from the islands.[21]

The revolutionary movement in Vietnam did not enjoy a moment of decisive revolutionary triumph such as the Chinese had savored in 1949. Thus the tension between revolutionary and state-building goals was even sharper there. Vietnamese Communist leaders traversed two crossroads on their way to ultimate victory. Vital decisions about the future of the revolution they had to make on those two occasions engendered prolonged debate, and out of those two debates came the decisions that pointed toward reunification in 1975.

The first crossroads was reached following the August 1945 revolution. On that occasion Ho Chi Minh, convinced that the newly established DRV was too weak to confront the returning French, adopted a policy of moderation that gave priority to building a Vietnamese state. Ho sought to strengthen domestic support by continuing the wartime united-front strategy. The Indochinese Communist Party was (at least on paper) dissolved in November, and the new government promoted domestic policies calculated to appeal to non-Communist patriots. At the same time Ho sought to shield the DRV behind an international united front. He pointedly appealed to the victorious allies for support, expressed goodwill toward his Chinese Nationalist neighbor whose forces occupied the north, and called for French and American support on the basis of a presumed common commitment to the principles of liberty and self-determination. Having set the stage with these domestic and international appeals, Ho tried to convince the French that it was in their own best interests to withdraw gradually from Vietnam.

Ho's "soft" policy, especially his handling of the French, appears to have aroused resistance and criticism from some of his compatriots, if not from party comrades. The French, they suggested, were unlikely to offer acceptable terms, and Ho's effort to avoid a showdown was thus foredoomed and humiliating. Indeed, by the summer of 1946 Ho's negotiations with the French had proven fruitless, as the skeptics had all along predicted. In December the Vietnamese-French conflict began in earnest, pointing the way to the realization of long-term revolutionary goals at the short-term cost of sacrificing Hanoi and the trappings of statehood.[22]

The second turning point occurred in 1954, following the military victory over France at Dienbienphu. Under pressure from its Soviet and Chinese allies, the Vietminh accepted a temporary partition of the country and the promise of reunification through elections within two years. Ho advocated a cautious and flexible policy that gave his forces a consolidated base of operations north of the seventeenth parallel within which state construction could proceed. Rejecting the proposed Geneva settlement would have alienated valuable allies and left a perhaps isolated Vietnam facing an American presence already entrenching itself in the south. Ho deemed it better to accept the half-a-loaf settlement and to concentrate on constructing socialism in the DRV (North Vietnam). If elections were not held, Hanoi would at least be in a better position to pursue a military solution.

Once more Ho managed to overcome arguments in favor of pushing the revolution to a rapid conclusion. Instead, he temporized, leaving the southern problem unresolved and the comrades in the south isolated and vulnerable. But once again events conspired against Ho as the Americans stepped up aid to the anti-Communist regime in the south and supported Ngo Dinh Diem in his refusal to hold national elections. Finally, Diem's attacks against underground Vietminh cadres in the south endangered a valuable revolutionary resource. If Hanoi continued to insist that these beleaguered activists avoid armed struggle, the result might be their liquidation. If the revolutionary cadres adopted an independent course of self-defense, Hanoi risked losing control of the situation in the south.

Hanoi took the first clear step toward reversing Ho's policy as early as 1956, and a January 1959 directive completed the shift. It authorized defensive military measures to support political efforts at reunification, specifically to ensure the safety of activists and the party apparatus.[23] Hanoi took yet another step on the road to full scale civil war the next year with the organization of the National Liberation Front, thereby constituting an anti-Diem united front and a southern government-in-embryo.

Vietnamese and American initiatives now interacted in quick succession to raise the level of conflict and thereby set at risk the gains of socialist construction in the north. The creation of an American military advisory command in 1961–62 was followed in December 1964 by the introduction of the first combat units from the north. American combat units and strategic bombers made their appearance the next year, thus further raising the stakes for Hanoi. The conflict over reunification that Ho had twice tried to avoid was once more joined, and another decade of bloody warfare was required before the United States would finally withdraw from Vietnam and the Vietnamese revolutionary movement would at last reach its nationalist goal.

I n both China and Vietnam, U.S. intervention disrupted the transition from the movement phase to the state-building phase of the revolution. Beginning in the Truman administration, Washington promoted Taiwan ("Free China") as an anti-communist alternative to the People's Republic. The Eisenhower administration made a similar attempt to nurture an anti-communist South Vietnam. These actions in turn justified the arguments of Chinese and Vietnamese Communist leaders who resisted the routinization and bureaucratization of their revolutions. Until American imperialism was defeated, they argued, the unfinished tasks of national unification and the defense of the revolution required popular mobilization and unremitting struggle. Washington for its part interpreted the pursuit of these tasks by Beijing and Hanoi as evidence of Communist bellicosity and aggressiveness that threatened stability and order in Asia. Thus, American actions provoked the behavior that U.S. leaders then condemned and intensified their efforts to oppose.

If the United States abhorred the advent to power of revolutionaries in China and Vietnam, it was no less hostile to their attempts to build socialism once in power. The expropriation of private property, the widespread violence unleashed during land reform, the attacks against religion, "brain-washing" techniques and recurrent campaigns directed against intellectuals, and similar features of revolutionary transformation induced revulsion on the part of most Americans. Moreover, the strident anti-American rhetoric of triumphant Communist revolutionaries and their adherence to the Soviet side in an era of cold war confrontation further strengthened American antipathy and served to justify Washington's efforts to isolate, harass, and destabilize the revolutionary regimes. If pragmatic considerations ultimately suggested the wisdom of dealing with such regimes in the diplomatic arena, this was considered a distasteful and unfortunate necessity. Quite unlike the compliant Filipino elite, which followed America's lead and gratefully hosted American military bases and corporations, revolutionary elites in Beijing and Hanoi were seen as emulating Soviet socialism at home while joining their countries' fortunes to America's cold war adversary in Moscow.

THE SOVIET UNION AND REVOLUTIONS IN ASIA

In Asia, as elsewhere, wherever revolutionary movements threatened the status quo, the United States was inclined to see the hand of the Kremlin.[24] There can be no doubt that in the broadest terms the Soviet Union supported revolutionary change in postwar Asia, but this simple truth masks a complex reality. Indeed, from the very beginning of its involvement in Asia following the October Revolution of 1917, Soviet policy had reflected its own often conflicting revolutionary and statist imperatives. On the one hand, it pursued the traditional statist goal of survival within a hostile international environment. At the same time, as the bearer of the Bolshevik revolutionary tradition, the Soviet state promoted revolutionary change abroad that looked toward the transformation of the international system.

The revolutionary imperative derived initially from Moscow's status as the self-proclaimed center of the "world revolution," the command headquarters of the Comintern. The Comintern assisted in the estabishment of revolutionary Marxist-Leninist parties throughout the world and sought to coordinate and direct their strategies for taking power. Moscow recognized in nationalism a revolutionary force with the potential to undermine colonialism and imperialism in Asia. Unfortunately, the leaders of nationalist movements frequently perceived communism as an alien force that fostered class divisiveness instead of national unity and Communist parties as threats to their own power. When Moscow tried to ride the twin tigers of communism and nationalism simultaneously, as it attempted to in China in the 1920s, the results were disastrous both for the local Communist Party and for Soviet diplomacy. The CCP, which Moscow had forced into a shotgun wedding with the Chinese Nationalists, had been virtually annihilated in 1927, when Chiang Kai-shek turned on his partners in the united front. For good measure, Chiang sent all of his Soviet advisers packing and broke off diplomatic relations with the Soviet Union.

In the late 1920s, concomitant with the onset of the world depression, the Comintern asserted that the new crisis of capitalism was creating the conditions for another revolutionary upsurge. It was in the grip of this apocalyptic mood that the Communist movement in Indochina was consolidated and the Communist Party of the Philippines established. By the 1930s, as Moscow witnessed the rise of fascism in Europe and Japanese militarism in Asia, it directed Communist parties in the service of Soviet foreign policy objectives to enter broad national coalitions of a popular-front type in which Communist revolutionary goals were subordinated to the quest for national unity. National resistance based on national unity took priority over a peasant-worker revolution with its divisive emphasis on class conflict. The Chinese Communists moved toward a second round of cooperation with their Nationalist foes. The Communists' united-front strategy in Vietnam echoed that of the Popular Front government in France and temporarily ceded the class-based revolutionary ground to unreconstructed revolutionaries such as the Trotskyists. As noted above, the formation of the Huks in 1942 expressed the same strategy in the context of a Japanese-occupied Philippines.

Although a post–World War II Asia in turmoil was rife with revolutionary opportunities, the Soviet Union acted with considerable circumspection. While Western leaders anxiously scrutinized Soviet behavior in the region for symptoms of rabid Leninism, Stalin accepted the limits that superior American power imposed on the Soviet Union. Thus, even though he got back southern Sakhalin and the Kuriles at Yalta, he had to abandon his demand for a zone of occupation in Japan. In China, Stalin initially expressed skepticism toward the Communist bid for power and counseled caution. Soviet aid was extended to Chinese Communist forces during the Chinese civil war (in northern Manchuria), but it was carefully shielded from prying Western eyes. In Southeast Asia, Moscow scarcely took notice of the Vietminh and the Huk struggles for power.[25]

If the Bolshevik Revolution still inspired Asian revolutionaries in the 1940s, it was because of what Lenin had written concerning the need for organizational efficiency and ideological coherence and what he had actually accomplished in 1917, not because of what Stalin was doing after World War II. Yet foreign Communists persisted in viewing Stalin as the preeminent leader of world revolutionary forces, and Moscow said nothing to disabuse them of this notion. (The Red Army's "liberation" of Eastern Europe was hardly a model for Asian revolutionaries—with the exception of Kim Il Song in North Korea, who came to power via essentially this same route.)[26]

During the Eisenhower era, American understanding of Soviet policy in postwar Asia lagged considerably behind the evolution of that policy itself. Washington remained fixated with the Kremlin as some sort of corporate headquarters of franchised revolutionaries, actively seeking opportunities to extend its operations. In fact, the Soviet role was actually quite different and far more modest. Soviet policy towards the revolutionary states established in China after 1949 and Vietnam after 1954 clearly demonstrates this point.

In both cases, the post-Stalin leadership escalated the level of Soviet interest in and commitment to the Communist regimes in power. It did so, however, not to nurture Mao's revolutionary romanticism or to encourage the territorial irredentism of Ho's colleagues, but rather to support their statist aspirations for political consolidation and economic development.[27] Moscow regarded the dour party bureaucrats and budding Communist technocrats as its natural partners in the 1950s. The Soviets promoted programs of industrialization via loans and the provision of technical assistance. The growth of these allies' state-run economies would contribute to the overall strengthening of the socialist bloc vis-à-vis the capitalist world while the success of a socialist development model would contribute to the prestige of the Soviet Union, facilitate its entrée into newly independent, nonaligned states, and in general put behind the era of Stalinist isolation in international affairs.

Following Stalin's death in 1953, Nikita Khrushchev brought Moscow's Asian policy full circle, back to its Leninist origins in the early 1920s. This earlier Leninist experience supplied a useful point of reference for Soviet leaders as well as the ideological formulas and the tactical tools to respond creatively to the fluid character of international relations in the 1950s and 1960s. Khrushchev recognized that a historic shift was underway; the accelerating decline of the Western imperium in Asia and Africa was opening the way for some new, yet still undefined, international system. The Soviets believed that what they called the governments of "national democracy"—i.e., the radical nationalist regimes of Fidel Castro in Cuba, Sekou Toure in Guinea, and Kwame Nkrumah in Ghana—were headed toward socialism and that the most radical of these nationalist regimes were worthy of Soviet encouragement and support. By supporting these regimes rather than by instigating revolution, the socialist world could strengthen its "natural alliance" with third world nationalism and more effectively undermine American power and influence. Such support, of course, fed American suspicions of radical nationalism and pushed the third world further into an arena of superpower competition.

CONCLUSION

Our survey of revolutionary change in America's Asia carries an important implication for those who study the history of policy toward that region. Our most urgent task is not that of matching Asian archives with American archives—though that would be a welcome advance. What is needed even more than archives is a broad conception of the Asian stage on which Americans sought to play out their postwar role as defenders of freedom against communism. The tribulations of American policy cannot be understood without also understanding the revolutionary movements that aroused and sometimes frustrated U.S. policy-makers.

Historians of U.S. cold war policy must, then, above all else, be on guard against the natural proclivity to adopt an incessant and incestuous focus on the United States alone, seeing Asia only through the eyes of American leaders, who were themselves (it may be suggested) conceptually hobbled. Historians of U.S. global involvement must by extension be prepared to pose the difficult but potentially revealing questions those leaders found so difficult to ask, let alone answer. To our understanding of revolutionary movements and regimes in America's Asia and of the Soviet role in the region we must bring to bear a historical and sociological consciousness not necessarily to be found either in the minds of American policy-makers or in the abundant records they have left behind. To overlook the rich literature on modern Asian history and the sociology of revolution is to diminish our own work and deprive our readers of global vistas as vital today as they have ever been.

NOTES

1. Robert J. McMahon, "The Cold War in Asia: Toward a New Synthesis," *Diplomatic History* (Summer 1988), 12:307–27. McMahon's survey of the recent literature notes the neglect of the Asian context. (see esp. pp. 318–19, 327.) Gabriel

Kolko, *Anatomy of a War: Vietnam, the United States, and the Modern Historical Experience* (New York: Pantheon, 1985) is a major exception.

2. For treatment of some of these "nonrevolutionary" postwar transfers of power, see Bruce Cumings, *The Origins of the Korean War: Liberation and the Emergence of Separate Regimes, 1945–1947* (Princeton: Princeton University Press, 1981); John Dower, *Empire and Aftermath: Yoshida Shigeru and the Japanese Experience, 1878–1954* (Cambridge: Harvard University Press, 1979); and Robert J. McMahon, *Colonialism and the Cold War: The United States and the Struggle for Indonesian Independence, 1945–49* (Ithaca: Cornell University Press, 1981).

3. For an introduction to the Chinese revolution, see Lucien Bianco, *The Origins of the Chinese Revolution, 1915–1949*, trans. Muriel Bell (Stanford: Stanford University Press, 1971); James P. Harrison, *The Long March to Power: A History of the Chinese Communist Party, 1921–72* (New York: Praeger, 1972); and the relevant chapters in John K. Fairbank and Albert Feuerwerker, eds., *The Cambridge History of China*, vols. 12–13 (Cambridge, U.K., Cambridge University Press, 1983 and 1986). Good starting points for Vietnam are William J. Duiker, *The Communist Road to Power in Vietnam* (Boulder, Colo.: Westview, 1981); James P. Harrison, *The Endless War: Fifty Years of Struggle in Vietnam* (New York: Free Press, 1982); Alexander Woodside, *Community and Revolution in Modern Vietnam* (Boston: Houghton Mifflin, 1976); and Huynh Kim Khanh, *Vietnamese Communism, 1925–1945* (Ithaca: Cornell University Press, 1982). These can be supplemented by Gareth Porter, ed., *Vietnam: The Definitive Documentation of Human Decisions*, 2 vols. (Stanfordville, N.Y.: E. M. Coleman Enterprises, 1979), also available in an abridged, single-volume edition titled *Vietnam: A History in Documents* (New York: New American Library, 1981). For the Philippines, the best brief introduction is by Peter Stanley in James C. Thomson, Jr. et al., *Sentimental Imperialists: The American Experience in East Asia* (New York: Harper and Row, 1981), chs. 8 and 19; but see also Daniel B. Schirmer and Stephen R. Shalom, eds., *The Philippines Reader: A History of Colonialism, Neocolonialism, Dictatorship, and Resistance* (Boston: South End Press, 1987).

4. For the rise of what might be called "radical statism" in China between the late nineteenth and early twentieth centuries, see Jane L. Price, *Cadres, Commanders, and Commissars: The Training of the Chinese Communist Leadership, 1920–1945* (Boulder, Colo.: Westview, 1976), chs. 1–2; Maurice Meisner, *Li Ta-chao and the Origins of Chinese Marxism* (Cambridge: Harvard University Press, 1967); Lee Feigon, *Chen Duxiu: Founder of the Chinese Communist Party* (Princeton: Princeton University Press, 1983); Richard C. Kagan, "Ch'en Tu-hsiu's Unfinished Autobiography," *China Quarterly* (April–June 1972), no. 50, pp. 301–14; and Stuart Schram, "Mao Tse-tung's Thought to 1949," in *Cambridge History of China*, 13:789–818.

5. On these developments in Vietnam, see David G. Marr, *Vietnamese Anticolonialism, 1885–1925* (Berkeley: University of California Press, 1971); Marr, *Vietnamese Tradition on Trial, 1920–1945* (Berkeley: University of California Press, 1981); and Khanh, *Vietnamese Communism.*

6. CCP membership did not exceed one thousand for its first several years. Between 1925 and spring of 1927 it grew to 57,000. Its ranks were thinned by reverses in the late 1920s and early 1930s, but swelled again during the Sino-Japanese War. By 1945 it counted 1.2 million members.

7. The Indochinese Communist Party was submerged in the Vietminh from 1941 until the fall of 1945, when it was nominally disbanded. It was formally revived and renamed the Vietnamese Workers' Party in 1951 to allow room for the development of separate Cambodian and Laotian Communist parties. As late as 1946 the party could claim no more than 20,000 members (though they were to increase to 700,000 by 1950).

8. Recent studies of peasant politics have given rise to two major interpretive

approaches. The account here follows the "political economy" approach with its emphasis on the importance of revolutionary leaders overcoming peasant caution and working out mutually advantageous relations. See Samuel Popkin, *The Rational Peasant: The Political Economy of Rural Society in Vietnam* (Berkeley: University of California Press, 1979); and Joel Migdal, *Peasants, Politics, and Revolution* (Princeton: Princeton University Press, 1974). The alternative, "moral economy" approach deserves serious attention. It argues that peasant longing for community eroded by commercialized agriculture provides the fundamental impulse for revolution. See James C. Scott, *The Moral Economy of the Peasant: Rebellion and Subsistence in Southeast Asia* (New Haven: Yale University Press, 1976); and Eric R. Wolf, *Peasant Wars of the Twentieth Century* (New York: Harper and Row, 1969). For a critical introduction to these competing points of view, see Jonathan Lieberson, *Peasant Values and Rural Development: An Unresolved Controversy* (New York: Population Council, 1981); Charles F. Keyes, et al., "Peasant Strategies in Asian Societies: Moral and Rational Economic Approaches—A Symposium," *Journal of Asian Studies* (August 1983), 52:753–868; and Ian Brown, "Rural Distress in Southeast Asia During the World Depression of the Early 1930s: A Preliminary Reexamination," *Journal of Asian Studies*, (November 1986), 45:995–1025.

9. For an overview, see Benjamin Schwartz, *Chinese Communism and the Rise of Mao* (Cambridge: Harvard University Press, 1951). For a general discussion of peasant politics in China, see Frederic Wakeman, Jr., "Rebellion and Revolution: The Study of Popular Movements in Chinese History," *Journal of Asian Studies* (February 1977), 36:201–37, now somewhat overtaken by new studies; and G. William Skinner, "Chinese Peasants and the Closed Community: An Open and Shut Case," *Comparative Studies in Society and History* (July 1971), 13:270–81.

Particularly important local studies are Elizabeth J. Perry, *Rebels and Revolutionaries in North China, 1845–1945* (Stanford: Stanford University Press, 1980); Yung-fa Chen, *Making Revolution: The Communist Movement in Eastern and Central China, 1937–1945* (Berkeley: University of California Press, 1986); Steven I. Levine, *Anvil of Victory: The Communist Revolution in Manchuria* (New York: Columbia University Press, 1987); Donald G. Gillin, "'Peasant Nationalism' in the History of Chinese Communism," *Journal of Asian Studies* (February 1964), 23:269–89; and Carl E. Dorris, "Peasant Mobilization in North China and the Origins of Yenan Communism," *China Quarterly* (December 1976), no. 68, pp. 697–719.

10. For an overview, see John T. McAlister, Jr., *Viet Nam: The Origins of Revolution* (New York: Knopf, 1969). For peasant politics in Vietnam, see Scott, *Moral Economy of the Peasant*, and Popkin, *Rational Peasant*, Pham Cao Duong, *Vietnamese Peasants under French Domination, 1861–1945* Lanham, Md.: University Press of America, 1985); Jeffrey Race, *War Comes to Long An: Revolutionary Conflict in a Vietnamese Province* (Berkeley: University of California Press, 1972); and James W. Trullinger, Jr., *Village at War: An Account of Revolution in Vietnam* (New York: Longman, 1980).

11. Charles Tilly, *From Mobilization to Revolution* (Reading, Mass.: Addison–Wesley, 1978), pp. 190–92.

12. This wartime designation was short for "Hukbalahap," itself an abbreviation for "Hukbo ng Bayan Laban sa Hapon."

13. The postwar Huks operated under the abbreviation HMB, short for "Hukbong Mapagpalaya ng Bayan."

14. The precise role of the party is a matter of some dispute. Compare Benedict J. Kerkvliet's classic *The Huk Rebellion: A Study of Peasant Revolt in the Philippines* (Berkeley: University of California Press, 1977) against the responses to it by William J. Pomeroy in "The Philippine Peasantry and the Huk Revolt," *Journal of*

Peasant Studies (July 1978), 5:497–517, and by Jim Richardson in "The Huk Rebellion," *Journal of Contemporary Asia* (1978), vol. 8, no. 2, pp. 231–37.

15. The unraveling of the Huk leadership is described from the perspective of the influential non-Communist Luis Taruc in *He Who Rides the Tiger: The Story of an Asian Guerilla Leader* (New York: Praeger, 1967).

16. Stephen R. Shalom, *The United States and the Philippines: A Study in Neocolonialism* (Philadelphia: Institute for the Study of Human Issues, 1981), pp. 68–93; and D. Michael Shafer, *Deadly Paradigms: The Failure of U.S. Counterinsurgency Policy* (Princeton: Princeton University Press, 1988), ch. 8. Magsaysay's election to the presidency in 1953 carried the promise of long-term stability in the Philippines. His death in an airplane crash in 1957 cut down those hopes.

17. It remains an open question whether the Huk defeat marks the end of a revolutionary attempt (or even an unsuccessful rebellion, as Kerkvliet describes it), or whether it was merely the first stage in a struggle now being continued by the New People's Army.

18. There is today a consensus among China scholars on the existence of this tension in domestic affairs, though they differ on the precise labels to apply. See Maurice Meisner, *Mao's China and After: A History of The People's Republic*, 2nd ed. (New York: Free Press, 1986); Lowell Dittmer, *China's Continuous Revolution: The Post-Liberation Epoch, 1949–1981* (Berkeley: University of California Press, 1987); and Carl Riskin, *China's Political Economy: The Quest for Development since 1949* (New York: Oxford University Press, 1987). The origins of this consensus can be found in Stuart Schram's *Mao Tse-tung* (Hammondsworth, U.K.: Penguin, 1966), ch. 10, with its stress on Mao's special and debilitating "military romanticism" (p. 293) derived from his pre-1949 experience.

19. See the accounts in John Gittings, *The World and China, 1922–1972* (New York: Harper and Row, 1974), pp. 181–84; Jürgen Domes, *P'eng Te-huai* (Stanford: Stanford University Press, 1985), pp. 59–61; Carsun Chang, *The Third Force in China* (New York: Bookman, 1952), pp. 285–89; Chow Ching-wen, *Ten Years of Storm* trans. and ed. by Lai Ming (New York: Holt, Rinehart and Winston, 1960), pp. 116–17; Peng Dehuai zixu bianjizu, *Peng Dehuai zixu* (Beijing: Renmin, 1981), p. 257; Peng Dehuai zhuanji bianxiezu, comp., *Peng Dehuai junshi wenxuan* (Beijing: Zhongyang wenxian, 1988), pp. 320–21; and Chai Chengwen and Zhao Yongtian, *KangMei yuanChao jishi* (Beijing: Zhonggong dangshi ziliao, 1987), pp. 55–59.

20. Kuo-kang Shao, "Chou En-lai's Diplomatic Approach to Non-aligned States in Asia: 1953–1960," *China Quarterly* (June 1979), no. 78, pp. 324–38.

21. Allen S. Whiting, "Quemoy 1958: Mao's Miscalculations," *China Quarterly* (June 1975), no. 62, pp. 263–70. It is no longer clear that Mao expected tangible support from Nikita Khrushchev. Frictions in the Sino-Soviet relationship had already formed before the 1958 crisis. The cautious Soviet response may merely have added to the already accumulating mistrust between Beijing and Moscow.

22. Stein Tønnesson, *The Outbreak of War in Indochina, 1946* (Oslo: International Peace Research Institute, 1984), makes clear Ho's forbearance in the face of a provocative forward policy pursued by French colonial authorities and, as a result, his public vulnerability to nationalist attacks.

23. This shift in policy can be followed in Porter, ed., *Vietnam: The Definitive Documentation of Human Decisions*, 1:634–37, 665–66, 669–71, 684–85, 692, 702–703, 2:23–34, 37–41, 44–46, 52–56, 59–70.

24. For references to the literature, see chapter 14, "Breakthrough to the East: Perspectives on Soviet Asian Policy in the 1950s," by Steven I. Levine.

25. See Yano Toru, "Who Set the Stage for the Cold War in Southeast Asia?" and Tanigawa Yoshihiko, "The Cominform and Southeast Asia," in Yōnosuke

Nagai and Akira Iriye, eds., *The Origins of the Cold War in Asia* (New York: Columbia University Press, 1977), esp. pp. 333–36 and 362–77.

26. See Robert A. Scalapino and Chong Sik Lee, *Communism in Korea* (Berkeley: University of California Press, 1972); Dae-Sook Suh, *Kim Il Song: The North Korean Leader* (New York: Columbia University Press, 1988).

27. On this point, see chapter 14.

2

A House Divided: The United States, the Department of State, and China

❂

NANCY BERNKOPF TUCKER
Georgetown University

T he recent burst of historical revisionism transforming evaluations of the Eisenhower administration has made clear that
Eisenhower was not a dolt, Dulles was neither all-powerful nor
thoroughly benighted, and American policy toward China partook of
a far richer blend of views than the surface manifestations suggest. In
examining the record, the State Department emerges as a less mono-
lithic force, facing more severe opposition to some of its policies, and
not as one-dimensional as heretofore portrayed. Of course, the United
States and China did remain enemies throughout the decade, and a
careful reading of new evidence will not change the fundamental
verities. Nonetheless the process can alter assessments of the decade's
potential and the abilities and vision of the nation's leaders.

Consensus existed among the administration's foreign policy-making constituencies — State and other Cabinet departments, Congress,
the military, intelligence agencies, and the White House — that China
had fallen to evil rulers who tyrannized the Chinese people and
threatened peace and stability in Asia. Beyond this they agreed that
the Nationalist regime on Taiwan had to be preserved as a bastion of
freedom and a symbol of American credibility in world affairs. The
United States had interceded in June 1950 to save the Kuomintang
from the Communists and from itself, incurring a responsibility that
could not be abandoned lightly.

On the specifics of these broad assumptions less unity prevailed.

How should the State Department and other agencies deal with the Communist regime? Would the United States be better protected by a policy of unalloyed hostility or through efforts to build bridges of economic exchange? What was the nature and durability of the Sino-Soviet relationship? Should the Taiwan Straits crises be considered episodes of Chinese Communist aggression or were Beijing's aims something other than the takeover of Jinmen and Mazu (Quemoy and Matsu)? How much support for and confidence in Chiang Kai-shek could Americans safely entertain? What likelihood was there that Chiang could regain a mainland following? Should Washington strain relations with its allies on behalf of the Kuomintang?

For some in the State Department the answers to these questions could not have been clearer. They comfortably joined the ranks of early pro-Nationalists such as Walter Judd. Although they worked for the United States government, they assiduously served the interests of Chiang Kai-shek as well. Such individuals, in fact, occupied the key Chinese affairs posts in the Department. Both ambassadors of the decade, Karl Rankin and Everett Drumright, Assistant Secretary for Far Eastern Affairs Walter S. Robertson, and Director of the Office of Chinese Affairs Walter P. McConaughy all staunchly championed the Nationalists.

But, however one-sided this would seem to have rendered the decision-makers, appearance belied reality. Dulles consciously placed people in visible China positions who suited the Republican Right. This protected administration foreign policy generally from the attacks of Dean Acheson's "primitives," whose knives remained sharp after years of attacking Dulles' predecessor. Determined to avoid Acheson's fate, Dulles erected a defensive facade. Of course, such staffing choices circumscribed the Secretary's freedom in conducting Sino-American relations, but, given the nature of his inner circle of trusted advisers (and in light of Dulles' own views on China), flexibility was not foreclosed.

Rankin and Drumright argued that Washington had no choice but to support Free China against Soviet Chinese puppets. Rankin attributed criticisms of the Nationalist regime to American xenophobia overlaid with leftist and even pro-Communist sympathies.[1] To colleagues at the Office of Chinese Affairs he frequently asserted that Chiang displayed the intelligence, honesty, patriotism, cooperativeness and tenacious anticommunism that were most wanted from America's allies.[2] Moreover his government—civilian and military—included Western-trained and pro-American officials, who were generally scarce in Asia.[3] Disparaging such people undermined official American policy.[4] Rankin condemned the idea, which gained currency during the 1950s, that the United States could recognize two Chinas, seeing it as a British plot to weaken commitment to Washington's moral obligations in order to solve Britain's problems.[5] Not only did he oppose China's admission to the UN, he advocated expulsion of the Soviet Union and other Communist nations.[6] In his memoirs the ambassador admitted having written alarmist cables from his post in Taibei to assist those in Washington who shared his views on China policy.[7] Indeed, State Department and White House observers believed that Rankin "seemed to agree with the position of the President [Chiang Kai-shek] no matter what it happened to be."[8] Further, to Robertson, Rankin scoffed at the possibility that Mao Zedong, who was "not a suckling babe," could be "weaned away from evil" by their being "nice to him."[9]

Everett F. Drumright, who followed Rankin as ambassador in March 1958, had served in a succession of China posts, beginning at Hankou in 1931, and was much more a specialist than Rankin. Nevertheless he shared his predecessor's enthusiasm for Chiang's cause and similarly became a pleader for the Generalissimo in Washington.[10] Politically conservative, he satisfied the requirements of the China bloc, which had to approve his nomination in Congress, and was more than acceptable to America's cantankerous ally in Taibei. Indeed in the 1958 Taiwan Straits crisis he would advocate explicit support for the defense of Jinmen and favor giving authority to the Nationalists to attack mainland artillery batteries.[11]

Walter S. Robertson's appointment as Assistant Secretary similarly served to protect Dulles' flanks from harrassment by Republican conservatives. The suggestion had come from Walter Judd, leading light of the China bloc, a group that Dulles wanted very much to win over, and reflected the courtly Virginia banker's enthusiasm for Chiang and his utter contempt for and hostility toward the Communist Chinese.[12] To the Nationalist ambassador, V. K. Wellington Koo, Robertson described the Chinese Communists as "gangsters."[13] This enmity on occasion blurred his vision. Although he had served as an economic adviser to the State Department, he unrealistically projected that American economic pressure could force Communist China to disintegrate from within. Moreover, because Mao Zedong headed a "malevolent" regime, Robertson concluded that his factories could not possibly produce 5 million tons of steel.[14] Indeed, any government that enslaved the hapless Chinese could neither prosper nor survive. "The fanatical Marxists of Peiping come no closer to representing the will and aspirations of the Chinese people," he observed in 1959, "than William Z. Foster comes to representing the will and aspirations of the American people."[15] Robertson did have first hand experience in China gained from eighteen months as chargé d'affaires ad interim between the ambassadorships of Patrick Hurley and Leighton Stuart and as U.S. commissioner at the Peiping Executive Headquarters.[16] Nevertheless his appointment surprised some of his colleagues whose assessments of Nationalist China were far less flattering.[17] But his sense of loyalty to the administration and especially to Dulles leavened Robertson's views. Although the Secretary found him annoying at times, Robertson served him wholeheartedly. British embassy observer Rob Scott, who had reason to remark upon his "obstinacy and blindness" (among other things Robertson shared the pro-Chiang antipathy for Great Britain), added that "it is impossible to doubt that he is a man of honour and integrity."[18]

Walter McConaughy had also served in China and Hong Kong. In those earlier days, as consul general in Shanghai, he had favored American efforts to cultivate a Titoist China, warning against extensive American aid to Chiang's bankrupt regime and about the risks of an angry Taiwan irredentism. He candidly reported that the great majority of local American businessmen and missionaries believed the best way to exploit Sino-Soviet frictions was to recognize and trade with the Chinese.[19] Chinese intervention in the Korean War, however, triggered a reassessment for McConaughy. A December 1953 denunciation of Mao Zedong, although designed to please his audience, reflected his private disillusionment with a tyrant who had "contemptuously rejected opportunities for friendship and normal trade relations" with the United States. McConaughy asserted that the United States must work to slow the growth of China's warmaking capabilities through "a policy of pressure and diplomatic isolation."[20]

At the other end of the spectrum Dulles did not surround himself with exponents of reconciliation with China. Both out of conviction and to avoid political vulnerability he did not find such people congenial. Probably his most outspokenly liberal subordinate, Charlton Ogburn, always operated on the periphery. Considered by many a brilliant firebrand, Ogburn frequently offered the Secretary and others unconventional advice, whether he spoke on China or Southeast Asia, which just as often they ignored.[21] He tried repeatedly while on the Policy Planning Staff to convince his superiors to reexamine their China strategy. He argued that American policy as set forth by NSC 148 called for contradictory approaches: the stabilization of East Asia along with the subversion of Communist China. Suggesting that Washington had to distinguish between alternatives, he generally advocated efforts to improve relations with the Chinese. Ogburn favored recognition of the Chinese Communist government and acquiescence in its entry into the United States. He called for the encouragement of broader Chinese contacts with the free world, including increased trade with Japan and Southeast Asia. The United States should refuse to support Nationalist Chinese attacks on the mainland because external pressure, he asserted, would not undermine Beijing, but would force a closer alignment with Moscow. Moreover, the United States could not count upon its allies in the contest. Rather, should Washington insist upon following a belligerent policy, it would find itself without adequate support or resources.[22]

Ogburn's analysis of the Nationalists predictably tended to be critical. Even were the Communist Chinese to be ousted, he doubted that mainlanders would tolerate Chiang Kai-shek's return. He declared that the Kuomintang would become an embarrassment to the United States. America should expend resources for Burma, Thailand, or Indochina instead of on Formosan defense.[23] Ogburn articulated his views repeatedly, but invariably raised the ire of more conservative members of the State Department's upper echelon, including Mc-Conaughy and Robertson, who made clear that the Department would continue pressures to force the disintegration of the Peking regime.[24]

John Foster Dulles did not, however, consider any of these individuals close advisors. Robertson, for instance, "was not given any real role" in the disposition of either the Geneva or Warsaw talks with the Chinese. According to U. Alexis Johnson, who served as U.S. representative at the ambassadorial meetings, "Dulles evidently felt that Robertson's deep hatred of the Chinese communists would taint his views."[25] Neither Robertson nor the others functioned as part of the Secretary's inner circle, whose insights stimulated his thoughts and facilitated his final decision-making. When Dulles sought opinions other than his own or Eisenhower's, he looked to a small group that would challenge his conclusions without hesitation.

Surprisingly these intimates proved relatively moderate on China policy.[26] Robert Bowie, named Director of the Policy Planning Staff based on the recommendation of Eisenhower's man at State, Walter Bedell Smith, who had been impressed by Bowie's service in occupied Germany, debated American foreign policy with the Secretary on countless, informal occasions, pitting his Harvard Law faculty mind against Dulles'. Generally ranged on the side of flexibility, he opposed a commitment by Washington to defend Jinmen and Mazu and favored a peaceful evacuation with American assistance. Under such circumstances, he argued, Canada, Australia, and New Zealand could be persuaded to pledge their protection to Taiwan. Bowie forcefully contradicted Joint Chiefs of Staff Chairman Arthur Radford's advice, during the Straits crisis, that tactical nuclear weapons could be used to eliminate military targets in China without great loss of life. On the contrary, Bowie demonstrated, using CIA figures, that the death toll would near 14 million even if purely military installations were targeted.[27] Bowie also ranged far beyond public administration policy and provoked congressional browbeating during his 1956 confirmation hearings by advocating Communist China's admission into the United Nations, though he expected a change in Chinese behaviour to warrant it.[28] He considered efforts to continue isolating China ultimately fruitless and the consequences of losing that struggle "formidable" in terms of American prestige and the preservation of a free Asia. Thus he believed that American policy toward China should change before it "use[s] up our means, impair[s] our influence, and ultimately weaken[s] the forces opposed to Communist China."[29]

Herman Phleger, a distinguished lawyer from California, became the Department's legal adviser. His friendship with Dulles, which dated from 1945, made him a particularly close confidant whose views carried weight on issues far beyond the legal arena. Phleger shared the Secretary's combative style, facile mind, and pragmatism. Proving a cautious advocate of American interests, he warned against angry responses to Chinese provocations such as the detention of American military personnel, even when by strictly legal standards Washington might have the right to take strong retaliatory actions.[30]

Livingston Merchant, Assistant Secretary for European Affairs, consistently emphasized the importance of America's European allies, which, he insisted, had to take priority over the less critical Chinese Nationalists.[31] In this way he reflected Dulles' own Atlantic tilt and tended to raise the objections the Secretary himself felt regarding too deep an American commitment to Chiang. Merchant's view of the Taiwan regime grew out of his service in Nanjing during the years of Nationalist decline on the mainland and subsequent duty as Assistant Secretary for Far Eastern Affairs. He had been dispatched to Asia in 1949 to assess the possibility of cultivating an independent Taiwan, but had advised Acheson that the situation there was hopeless— neither the independence movement nor Chiang Kai-shek warranted American support.[32] During those same years he had come to know and admire Dulles, who sought his advice on drafting of the Japanese Peace Treaty.[33] In his post as European Assistant Secretary he continued to work closely with Dulles and also became a trusted aide to the President.[34]

Included in the inner circle was Douglas MacArthur II, who managed close working associations with both Eisenhower and Dulles. MacArthur's wartime service in Europe as General Eisenhower's expert on France and subsequent role in the formation of NATO impressed Ike so much that he chose MacArthur in 1951 as international affairs adviser to the Supreme Command in Europe. His experience as one of the general's "brain trusters" facilitated the assignment as counselor and senior staff officer for the State Department on the NSC in 1953. Although clearly Eisenhower's man, his working relationship with Dulles grew strong as well. MacArthur shared the overwhelmingly European focus of the upper echelon bureaucracy and worried about deepening entanglements with the Kuomintang. Instead, he advocated delay of mutual security arrangements as long as possible. Similarly he warned against a Dulles proposal to respond to an assault on Jinmen and Mazu with a generalized effort to wipe out POL dumps or communications on the mainland. This would be disproportionate, might bring in the Soviets, and would alienate U.S. allies.[35]

If MacArthur successfully turned his association with the President into a close relationship with Dulles as well—indeed, he, Merchant, and Bowie made such a accomplished team that they jokingly rapsodied about their government service as the work of MacMerBo Inc.— others were less able to do so.[36] Bedell Smith and Henry Cabot Lodge remained strictly the President's men. Smith lost his post as director of the CIA when the Secretary of State's brother inherited the intelligence agency mantle, but Eisenhower installed him as Dulles' Undersecretary at State, where frictions between the two finally led to Smith's resignation.[37] More troublesome for the Secretary and more involved with China was Henry Cabot Lodge, who, having obtained the position of UN ambassador with Cabinet rank, bypassed the Department of State whenever mood or issue suited him.[38] On China matters Lodge remained determined to take a hard-line against Chinese Communist admission and sought to champion Nationalist positions even when they did not accord entirely with State Department perspectives on what would serve American interests.[39] Although Lodge challenged Dulles and sometimes pushed policies that the President approached with less certainty, it would appear that Eisenhower found this constraint on his Secretary of State useful and the politically connected Lodge necessary in the administration.

Dulles' views regarding China, culled from experience present and past, from advice of his subordinates, and from current events, reflected a generalist's perspective shared with his inner circle at the Department and with the President. Dulles emphasized Europe and an Atlantic focus, discounting the significance of developments in Asia. He sought not to harm relations with Europe in the interests of Asians, even allies, although he could arrogantly assume he knew best how to protect Europe economically and politically in Asia. This rendered him slow to understand the dynamics of decolonization and third world nationalism.[40] But at the same time his assumptions resulted in his China policies being considerably less zealous than his rhetoric suggested. Dulles opposed the Chinese Communists and supported the Nationalists, but he did not see China as particularly important to American interests or security.

The Secretary fundamentally disliked both sides in the Chinese civil war—a fact that modified his approach. He saw Chiang Kai-shek as the only feasible alternative to communism in China and, therefore, as a leader demanding American favor. However, the Secretary distrusted Chiang, considering him deceitful, devious, and dangerously self-interested.[41] At a National Security Council meeting in the autumn of 1954, Dulles declared that if the people of Formosa were able to vote on their future, they would choose to be independent rather than be governed by Chiang.[42] But Dulles found Chinese Communist fanaticism, reminiscent of Hitler's, "an acute and imminent threat" that rendered efforts to change or replace Chiang too risky.[43] At the Geneva Conference in 1954, he demonstrated his hostility to the Chinese Communists by insulting Zhou Enlai and squandering an opportunity to initiate an informal exchange on neutral territory.[44]

Nevertheless, the Secretary viewed the Communist Chinese in a far more reasonable light than his words or actions suggested. At his confirmation hearings Dulles observed that if the Chinese Communists pursued an independent Communist course, renouncing allegiance to Moscow, it might be in the interests of the United States to recognize them. He wanted to use the prospect of talks with the United States as inducement and so resisted the initiation of Sino-American meetings at Geneva.[45] On the other hand, once the talks had begun, Dulles took considerable personal interest in them and urged his negotiator, Alexis Johnson, to do everything he could to keep the sessions going.[46]

Ultimately Dulles hoped to follow a two China policy, recognizing the existence of both governments. Primarily designed to preserve the Nationalists on Taiwan, it meant that, despite American rhetoric, the United States had accepted the survival of the Communist regime and would deal with it.[47] Moreover Dulles saw this as a solution to the United Nations dilemma. As early as June 1953 he told India's Prime Minister, Jawaharlal Nehru, that if India could be substituted for China in the Security Council both Taibei and Beijing might be given places in the General Assembly.[48]

Dulles, then, confronted the need to make China policy with certain fundamental assets and liabilities in place. He had able advisors who possessed reasonably open minds regarding China but who did not have a wealth of knowledge about the Chinese. He also had several appointees chosen to protect him from the China Lobby/China Bloc who tended to weight policy making in pro-Nationalist directions. Finally, Dulles favored a substitute for communism in China, though he disliked the alternative, Chiang Kai-shek, who restlessly waited to challenge Mao Zedong's hold on the mainland. But Dulles recognized early that neither Mao nor Chiang would be ousted and that he would be forced to deal the China cards much the way he had received the deck from the Truman administration.

PRIVILEGED SANCTUARY

The unleashing of Chiang Kai-shek, announced in Eisenhower's inaugural address, illustrates the complexity of China policy in the 1950s. On the surface the decision to free Chiang from the constraints of the U.S. Seventh Fleet, which had been patroling between Taiwan and the mainland since June 1950, appeared to be a hardline, pro-Nationalist policy. The Rankins, Robertsons, et al. celebrated the turn toward a saner Asian policy.[49] Washington seemed to be proposing that the U.S. provide the Nationalist Chinese a privileged sanctuary. Chiang could attack the mainland and not fear retaliation. Whereas Harry Truman had sought to prevent either assault by China on the island of Taiwan or a Kuomintang effort to invade the mainland, all of which risked creating a dangerous distraction from the Korean War theater, the Eisenhower administration declared its unwillingness to protect the Communists from Free Chinese efforts to return to power.[50]

Unfettering Chiang carried with it the suggestion that Washington sympathized with and supported the Nationalist goal of returning to the mainland. From the first moment of exile on the island of Taiwan, Chiang and his followers had asserted the temporary nature of their retreat. Equally, from the beginning, Nationalist leaders sought to secure pledges of American assistance in accomplishing their mission.[51] Clearly, having been forced to flee superior Chinese Communist forces, they could return only with the provision of U.S. training, equipment, and logistical support.

The unleashing of Chiang, therefore, symbolized a commitment to the welfare of the Nationalist's government. Its entire raison d'être— that is, its rule over the Chinese people, all 400 million and not merely the 10 million on Taiwan—depended upon United States sponsorship of a massively expensive and tremendously difficult military exercise on the mainland of Asia and probable utilization of American forces as well. The Truman administration, given its disillusionment with Chiang Kai-shek, had perceived the risks as far exceeding the questionable benefits. But Eisenhower and Dulles had attacked Truman policy for its weakness and thereby laid a foundation for a different approach.

Whatever the expectations, Eisenhower and Dulles never had the slightest intention of supporting a Nationalist assault on the mainland. In fact, shortly after the President's State of the Union address freed Chiang from constraints, Dulles convinced Eisenhower to suspend deliveries of jet aircraft until the United States could elicit a pledge from the Generalissimo that he would not use them to initiate large-scale operations against the Communists. The roll-back Republicans were withholding planes that the Truman people had been willing to provide.[52]

Return to the mainland, of course, meant more than just a landing and warfare, however difficult; it presumed that Nationalist rule would supplant Communist Chinese control in Beijing. Dulles, Eisenhower, and all of the administration favored such a turn of events. But reality intervened to moderate a policy that to some Washington allies smacked of narrow-mindedness and irresponsibility. Aware that Beijing had stabilized its control and cognizant as well of the unpopularity of the Nationalists, the administration did not elect to try to reestablish Kuomintang authority on the mainland.[53]

Karl Rankin, defending the most pro-Kuomintang (KMT) position, asserted that the *idea* of returning to the mainland could not be jettisoned without serious harm to Nationalist morale and, therefore, to the government's survival. He did not rule out the possibility that a disciplined, efficient, properly armed KMT might invade and destabilize the Communists, although he conceded that the chances were small. Instead, he argued on countless occasions that the concept had to be sustained, even at considerable cost in supplies and training, to prevent Nationalist collapse, secure official cooperation, and keep future options open for Washington. The ambassador may have gone further. At the same time as Dulles and others were trying to convince Chiang to give up fantasies of returning to the mainland, Rankin confided to the Generalissimo that he "hoped and believed that there was today in the United States a growing understanding that China could not remain permanently divided, and that since we certainly did not want it united under communism, it must be united in freedom."[54] It does not appear surprising that Washington had little success in convincing Chiang Kai-shek that United States aid would never support an attack on the mainland when the ambassador was whispering in his ear that he should not give up hope.

Washington officials, more concerned with the nation's global commitments, proved less comfortable with Chiang's rhetoric and less willing to contemplate greatly increased support for the Kuomintang than Rankin. The Taibei embassy was too committed to an Asia-centered view of the world and a Chiang-centered view of China. It might well be desirable to strengthen Nationalist forces, but the resources required had already been pledged to other programs. The present policy of building a modest military establishment, China desk officers contended, would suffice for raids on the mainland or Communist shipping.[55] Indeed, H. M. Holland had observed just the previous spring that "Perhaps the most difficult job facing Formosa policy makers today in connection with developing aid programs is to convince Chinese officials that the U.S. cannot be pressured or cajoled into giving more aid than is considered compatible with U.S. security interests."[56]

THE MUTUAL DEFENSE TREATY

Although responsible in large part for "unleashing" Chiang, John Foster Dulles, having rejected explicit support for an invasion,[57] feared that the Generalissimo might not accept his decision. The United States, he knew, could be manipulated into a war by the Nationalists unless they were carefully circumscribed. Dulles insisted that the Mutual Defense Treaty, which was concluded in the autumn of 1954[58] and tied American power to Chiang's fortunes, act as a vehicle of restraint. The treaty compelled Chiang to disavow major attacks on the mainland without prior American approval, which would not, in reality, be forthcoming. The treaty would therefore strengthen the Kuomintang, but without exposing Washington to heightened risk since it prevented Chiang from flexing his new muscles.[59]

Emergence of the Mutual Defense Treaty as a mechanism to control Chiang did not come easily. The early debates over a defense pact ranged Chiang sympathizers and "Asia firsters" against those primarily concerned with Washington's global, Europe-centered responsibilities. Walter Robertson naturally supported Taibei's appeals for an agreement.[60] Whereas others objected that the convening of a conference at Geneva to resolve the conflicts in Korea and Indochina made the winter and spring of 1954 an inopportune time for even exploring the idea of a treaty, Robertson insisted that one should be negotiated before Geneva. The conference, he asserted, constituted a serious blow to Kuomintang morale, and announcement of a pact would provide much needed reassurance.[61] Chiang had to be told in concrete terms that Taiwan's interests would not be abandoned in order to resolve other issues. Without this type of bolstering the future of Nationalist control on the island would be jeopardized.[62]

Reflecting constant tension between European and China desks, other sectors of the Department insisted that Washington's relations with its allies ought to take precedence over Taibei's needs. America's China policy had not been popular in Europe and parts of Asia for a considerable period.[63] Allied observers lamented resources wasted on an unattractive and fundamentally lost cause—resources badly needed elsewhere in the world. Moreover they feared that Washington could become enmeshed in a war over inconsequential islands off the coast of China. In the State Department, the European and United Nations bureaus and, to a lesser degree, the Policy Planning Staff argued that Washington's allies would see precipitous negotiation of a defense pact as a gratuitous demonstration of U.S. inflexibility. Merchant forcefully contended to the Secretary and Robertson that the allies would consider it a purposeful undermining of the Geneva process. Moreover, Moscow could take advantage of the situation to cultivate dissension.[64] The Near East and South Asian Office, in addition, raised the specter of a disgruntled India being driven closer to the Communist Chinese by a mutual defense treaty between Washington and Taibei.[65]

Dulles, whose own orientation directed him along a European axis, approached the matter cautiously, attuned to allied concerns. In February 1954 he authorized the NSC Planning Board to examine the defense treaty question, but decided to postpone his own decision on it until after he returned from the Tenth Inter-American Conference at Caracas.[66] At the end of March, he rejected a Robertson–Far East Bureau recommendation to proceed. There was not enough time before Geneva, he contended, given the necessity of extensive discussions with Congress.[67] Clearly Dulles was not eager to negotiate a pact, preferring to maintain his freedom of action, but he felt constrained to keep the prospects open because of the continuing pressures from the Judds and Knowlands.

Debate on the issue continued through the summer. The Far Eastern Bureau, under Robertson's unflagging leadership, raised the matter again in August. This time Department Counselor Douglas MacArthur objected. Nothing had changed since March and April, he contended, and the decision not to proceed at that time retained considerable validity. John Jernegan of the Near East and South Asia Desk also persisted in emphasizing the negative impact on India of such a treaty.[68] Even though Robertson had dismissed

India's reaction as of no real importance, the India officers pressed their concerns.[69]

Robertson's determination finally began to make a difference during the long Washington summer. Director of the Policy Planning Staff Robert Bowie relented, dropping his opposition to an agreement. In light of the inauguration of a Southeast Asian pact, he agreed that a firmer commitment to Taiwan would be a good idea. Nevertheless he continued to emphasize his concern that the offshore islands be explicitly excluded from any U.S. guarantee.[70] European Affairs also withdrew its objections at this time with the caveat that America's allies in the new Southeast Asia Treaty Organization must get prior warning of the treaty. Livingston Merchant further emphasized Bowie's point that the treaty had to avoid giving the impression that the United States would assist the Nationalist regime in expanding its control over territories not already in Kuomintang hands.[71] Nonetheless Dulles still hesitated, recognizing a degree of inevitability to the process, although he, like Bowie and Merchant, was fundamentally uncomfortable about any commitment to the offshore islands.[72]

Robertson returned to the fray in October, and finally circumstances shifted the Department balance firmly in his favor, although not for reasons that he welcomed. In September crisis developed in the Jinmen-Mazu area when the Communists initiated shelling of the offshore islands. At least in part a response to SEATO and rumors of a Taiwan–U.S. accord, the confrontation so alarmed Washington that it gave impetus to what the Communists had hoped to prevent. Dulles sought to avoid war by taking a resolution to the United Nations Security Council calling for a cease-fire in the Taiwan Straits. To do this without provoking Nationalist Chinese intransigence or domestic political problems, he hid American initiative behind New Zealand action and concluded that he had to accept the pact Chiang had long sought.[73] Both MacArthur and Edwin W. Martin, Deputy Director of the Office of Chinese Affairs, agreed that the likelihood of Taibei accepting the New Zealand move would be heightened by offering a treaty.[74] Robertson also emphasized that progress on the SEATO agreement made lack of protection for the Nationalists even more apparent and anomalous.[75]

Ultimately, of course, Washington and Taibei signed a mutual defense treaty, although for some misgivings remained. American Ambassador Charles Bohlen cabled from Moscow that a treaty was not necessary in order to deter the Soviet Union. Indeed, the Soviets could use it to exploit American frictions with its allies and heighten the discomfort of neutralist Asian nations.[76] Although Chairman of the Joint Chiefs of Staff Arthur Radford had originally favored a pact, the

JCS, summing up military opinion in the autumn of 1954 contended that the status quo in United States–Nationalist cooperation better suited the needs of defending Formosa than a fixed commitment treaty.[77] Indeed, the military had moved so far in the opposite direction regarding the agreement that no one informed the JCS that the President had authorized the treaty until late October 1954.[78] Secretary Dulles, Bowie, and others in the State Department, however, had come to believe that uncertainty regarding the offshore islands made a less effective deterrent than American guarantees supporting Taiwan.[79] Further, the China desk worried about the possibility of military engagement without congressional sanction. The Department might, in that case, be attacked for not having sought the concurrence of congressional law-makers.[80]

By October, then, Dulles had concluded that the United States needed the treaty. He was ultimately persuaded not by Rankin, Robertson, and the pro-Nationalist contingent, but rather by those who saw a treaty as a mechanism for insuring Washington's control over Chiang. Taiwan could not raid the mainland as it had during the Korean conflict and enjoy special protection from the United States. A mutual defense treaty would give Chiang security but could be used to eliminate the destabilizing threat Taiwan posed to China.[81] Dulles secured the President's agreement as well, convincing him that the blow to Nationalist morale of ruling out recovery of the mainland "would not be fatal . . . because the true defense of Formosa really depended on the United States rather than on Nationalist forces."[82] Although Dulles generally considered Kuomintang stability critical, he did not like Nationalist efforts to corner him and force more aid than he was prepared to give.

CRISIS BEDEVILS THE STRAITS

The Taiwan Straits crisis of 1954–55 not only helped to bring the Mutual Defense Treaty to fruition, but also compelled policy-makers to examine carefully the degree of America's commitment to Nationalist China. Three of the four Joint Chiefs of Staff advocated an immediate pledge by the United States to defend the offshore islands even if this meant the eventual use of nuclear weapons. JSC Chairman Radford, Chief of Naval Operations Admiral Robert B. Carney, and Air Force Chief of Staff General Nathan F. Twining believed that the Communists meant to attack Taiwan and that U.S. determination to prevent an invasion had to be made explicit.[83] Acting Secretary of State Smith strongly objected, and Dulles dismissed this confrontational approach as unacceptable, given its possibly disastrous outcome in a third world war.[84]

Since military leaders could not assure him that islands such as Jinmen, with their proximity to the mainland, could be defended, Dulles sought an alternative to war or abandonment of the Nationalist cause. His plan, as mentioned above, rested upon United Nations supervision of a cease-fire in the Taiwan Straits. But the idea proved unpopular with the Chinese—both Nationalists and Communist— and evoked protests within the administration as well. Secretary of Defense Charles Wilson and Mutual Security Director Harold Stassen feared that the New Zealand initiative might open debate over the entire issue of Chinese membership in the UN.[85] Ultimately Dulles carried the debate, but Operation Oracle did not resolve the crisis. In the winter of 1955 violence in the Straits continued.

Director of the Policy Planning Staff Bowie thereupon declared that the time had come for disengagement. The United States, he insisted, had little to gain—and much to lose in the support and affection of its allies—by adamantly remaining entangled in the Jinmen-Mazu imbroglio. Washington courted disaster, for the Soviets urged an international conference to resolve the issue that would require Communist Chinese representation. Moreover Washington seemed to be contributing to the emasculation of the United Nations. Far better, Bowie maintained, to plan a protected evacuation demonstrating America's determination not to invite useless conflicts. "In short," Bowie concluded, "a program of obtaining the free world's support for our policy toward Formosa in exchange for abandoning the offshore islands would seem to me clearly to serve the U.S. security interest."[86]

Dulles and Eisenhower, in contrast, concluded that if peaceful efforts failed, the United States might well have to use atomic weapons in defense of the islands. Although they agreed privately with Secretary Wilson's feeling that the loss of the offshore islands would ultimately make little difference, they emphasized that, in the short term, preservation of the islands was critical for Nationalist morale and American prestige.[87] In his radio broadcast of March 8, 1955, Dulles talked about atomic bombs as interchangeable with conventional weapons, and even in the confidential deliberations of the National Security Council he suggested that an atomic attack was possible.[88] But although the New Zealand resolution did not resolve the crisis, neither did the United States ultimately resort to a nuclear attack. Instead, however reluctantly, Americans began to meet with the Chinese in Geneva to discuss release of Americans being held in China, and, as a result, the first Taiwan crisis passed.

But confrontation in the Straits did not end in 1955; the State Department found itself engaged in another crisis in 1958. As a result suspicion grew that Chiang perhaps intentionally refused to do enough to help himself, thus necessitating American support, and that he might even have provoked the Communist shelling.[89] The President concluded that this explained the excess of forces Chiang had placed on the offshore islands by 1958.[90] The United States would have no choice, he complained, but to rescue one third of the Generalissimo's army. In August Dulles wrote Robertson and Undersecretary Christian Herter:

> I do not feel that we have a case which is altogether defensible. It is one thing to contend that the CHICOMS should keep their hands off the present territorial and political status of Taiwan, the Penghus, Quemoy, and Matsu, and not attempt to change this by violence. . . . It is another thing to contend that they should be quiescent while this area is used by the CHINATS as an active base for attempting to foment civil strife.[91]

Dulles had come to believe that the Chinese Communists wanted to concentrate on internal development and that therefore a negotiated settlement ought not be too difficult to reach if only the Nationalists could be manipulated.[92] Robertson and Rankin, of course, fended off criticism, insisting that the Nationalists would protect the islands without assistance[93] and had only fortified them in response to United States urging.[94]

The Secretary's view of the crisis differed sharply from that of the Far Eastern Bureau. His desire to take the situation to the United Nations did not obtain the Bureau's support, and the China desk, sharing Undersecretary Herter's reservations, viewed the suggestion of using a third country to intercede as a demonstration of weakness the United States could ill afford.[95] Deputy Assistant Secretary for the Far East James Graham Parsons further argued that, contrary to Dulles' assumptions, the offshore islands were not a significant base for continuing operations against the mainland. By contemplating resumption of negotiations with China on the issue, moreover, the United States risked renewed Chinese pressure for a meeting at the foreign ministers level or even a summit.[96]

Ultimately Dulles' skepticism about Chiang did not lessen his commitment to preserving Taiwan and the offshore islands for the free world. He accepted the view that the loss of Jinmen would so dishearten the Nationalists that Taiwan would fall and that other countries in the area would inevitably follow. When the Department's Intelligence and Research staff suggested that Asian reactions would, in fact, be mixed and that negative responses could be minimized if a turnover came through negotiations, Dulles was unmoved.[97] Gerard Smith, Director of the Policy Planning Staff since 1957, maintained that Kuomintang abandonment of the offshore islands would strengthen a two China policy by eliminating a site where the Communist Chinese could create a crisis whenever they wished. But Dulles, though partial to a two Chinas solution, would not countenance total evacuation of Jinmen and Mazu under existing circumstances.[98] He had briefly flirted with the idea of demilitarizing the islands, but had run into opposition from much of his State Department staff[99] and the Navy. Chief of Naval Operations Arleigh Burke described the Secretary's proposal as an effort to sweep the problem under the rug. "All Communists are tricky," he complained. "So they might accept and later by 'peaceful means' seize the islands and we would have no recourse except blast the hell out of the China mainland and that we couldn't do because of 'public opinion.' "[100]

Dulles had also made efforts to urge reduction of garrison forces on the offshore islands in order to render their loss less crucial to Kuomintang survival. But his attempts proved fruitless during his autumn 1958 visit to Taiwan.[101] An earlier mission, it is worth noting, may have contributed to Dulles' failure and Chiang's obduracy. In 1955 Eisenhower and Dulles tried to convince the Generalissimo to deescalate tensions in the Taiwan Straits by treating Jinmen as a listening post rather than as an integral base. Hoping to avoid China Lobby criticism and desirous of using an emissary the Nationalist leader might listen to, the President sent Walter Robertson along with Arthur Radford to convince Chiang. Robertson's fundamental opposition to loss of the offshore islands and commitment to Chiang's recovery of the mainland, however, meant that he was hardly likely to sell the President's line with any degree of conviction.[102] The mixed message that Chiang received could only have strengthened his conviction that holding on to the islands was necessary to keep America entangled in the Nationalist cause. Although fearful of what Undersecretary Christian Herter termed Chiang's "almost pathological" preoccupation with the islands, Dulles never proved willing to use the weight of American financial and military assistance to force compliance.[103]

POLICY OPTIONS

The Nationalists, however reprehensible, were at least opponents of the Communists who had captured Beijing and had to be preserved as an example of free Chinese. This would be true even if, as some at the Department speculated, a rift developed between the Soviets and the Chinese Communists. Ogburn, frustrated by his conservative superiors, complained that "we do not even admit for planning purposes that the possibility of a split exists," but, in fact, he was not alone in taking Chinese unhappiness with the Russians more seriously.[104]

As early as May 1953, America's ambassador to India, George V. Allen, whose previous service in Eastern Europe had made him something of an expert on Titoism, told a television audience that Mao's China was no satellite on the Eastern Europe model where Soviet leaders "could break a cabinet by telephone calls in a minute."[105] C. H. Peake of the Far Eastern Bureau argued in July 1953 that "the Korean conflict has enabled the Chinese Communists to discover the limits to which the Soviets are able or willing to supply them with military and industrial goods."[106] During the first Taiwan Straits crisis the American ambassador to the Soviet Union reported that Moscow did not intend to become involved directly in a situation having no connection with its own vital national interests. Bohlen contended that he found it "increasingly obvious that the Soviet Government does not have controlling influence over Chinese actions and even [its] degree of influence is problematical."[107] Dulles' position ran closer to these assessments than to his own rhetoric. For public consumption he often described the Chinese as tools of Moscow, but at a top secret briefing he gave to Eisenhower, Churchill, and Bidault at their 1953 Bermuda summit meeting, he suggested the possibility of a rift in the wake of Stalin's death.[108]

The question of whether economic pressure on China would strengthen its attachment to Moscow or would increase strains in the uncomfortable Sino-Soviet alliance accordingly received considerable attention.[109] Robertson and McConaughy believed that any relaxation of trade controls would release the Soviets from burdensome obligations to the Chinese and would, therefore, tend to take an antagonistic factor out of Sino-Soviet relations. Thus, in the spring of 1953 Robertson argued against recommendations by the Office of the Assistant Secretary for Economic Affairs favoring reductions in trade controls against China. On the contrary, the Far Eastern Bureau advocated efforts by the National Security Council Planning Board to devise ways of reinforcing the control structure.[110] As A. Guy Hope, a desk officer, observed, policy toward China ought to be harsher than toward the Soviet Union, even though enthusiasm—in public and governmental arenas—for such a policy had declined significantly.[111] Although not proposing an "economic Hiroshima," he advocated scaring the Chinese into making extreme demands on the Soviet Union.[112]

A hard-line met the needs of European experts less well. Those focusing on developments in Europe recognized that the United States would be increasingly less able to force its allies to observe trade restrictions that were, or appeared to be, impairing economic recovery. Treasury Secretary George Humphrey and Secretary of Commerce Sinclair Weeks had reached the point of believing that relaxation could not be avoided. Although Secretary of Defense Wilson and Admiral Radford agreed with Dulles' views, his determination to preserve stringent controls despite allied objections and British defection ran against the inclinations of the President.[113] Ultimately, under continued pressure from Europe and Japan, the administration had to abandon its uncompromising stance.

Political ostracism fared little better than had efforts at economic isolation. Washington's desire to extricate Americans from imprisonment and house arrest in China along with appeals from U.S. allies led to negotiations with the Red Chinese at Geneva and Warsaw. The decision to relent and enter into such conversations was made reluctantly. Rankin repeatedly cautioned Washington that the mere fact of regular meetings made the Nationalists anxious and that this alone rendered the process questionable. Chiang and others feared American compromises at Taiwan's expense, and Rankin obviously worried that their reservations might be justified. Moreover, the ambassador insisted, "to the great majority [in Asia] these talks represent no less than *de facto* recognition of Red China and proof positive of American determination to reach a general accommodation with the communists at almost any cost."[114]

On the other hand, Ambassador U. Alexis Johnson, American representative at the talks, clearly hoped that negotiations could produce substantive progress in Sino-American relations. Johnson found his Chinese counterpart, Wang Bingnan, tough but not unreasonable. He argued that progress demanded compromise by Washington on the key issue of prisoner releases. Realistically China would not and could not (because of legal logistics) release all Americans at the same moment. But Robertson emphatically rejected Johnson's moderate stance, demanding that we "not give up our main trading points in return for half a loaf or less."[115] Moreover, State Department officials in Washington lacked Johnson's appreciation for Wang and his negotiating tactics and urged Johnson not to "show a great measure of tolerance" without "assured advance."[116]

The Secretary's opinion changed during the course of the contacts. To begin with, he accepted the unavoidability of talks. Enthusiasm in Congress and favorable public opinion polls, along with the urgings of European allies and the overwhelmingly positive response at Bandung to Zhou Enlai's suggestion of talks, led him to conclude that negotiations must be undertaken gracefully.[117] Moreover, he was resolved not to give the Soviets any opportunity to insist upon an international conference that would accord Beijing too much prestige. Nevertheless, he approached them with a determination that nothing of significance would be risked. He paid careful attention to Johnson's cabled reports and often participated in drafting his representative's orders. By the summer of 1955, he demonstrated more flexibility, observing to Johnson that "once the American civilians are out of China, then we may be compelled to alter our policy toward visitors to the Chinese mainland because [the] principal reason for deterring those visitors will have ceased." Johnson, he suggested, might want to "intimate it to them in a very cautious way without of course any promises" that travel might be possible and that the information that would then come out of China "may lead to a different judgment" about the country.[118]

Neither as worried as Rankin nor as hopeful as Johnson, Dulles wanted the talks to continue but had few expectations that they would produce results. So long as the two countries were talking, there appeared to be less likelihood of violence, and so Dulles urged Johnson not to let negotiations break off.[119] He relented on the idea of allowing journalists to travel to China, but only after his initial refusal had provoked heated outcries from the American press and after Chinese interest in the exchange had cooled. He sent Johnson to Thailand in December 1957 and did not replace him with a representative of ambassadorial rank, an action that so chilled the atmosphere that the Chinese suspended further meetings. But in 1958, after the second Taiwan Straits crisis had erupted, having concluded that the Nationalists had provoked it, he tried to use the talks to rectify problems and resolve tensions.

CONCLUSION

The State Department, although playing a central role throughout the period under review, just as certainly was neither as unified nor as determined as often portrayed. Dulles sought to follow a hard line designed to force Communist Chinese collapse or, at least, accommodation on American terms. He deplored Communist control of the mainland and despised the Chinese leaders who had enslaved their people. But his policy was never as inflexible as his rhetoric suggested. In fact, although less often noted, the Secretary committed himself to circumscribing Chiang Kai-shek's activities and continuing talks with China. Dulles proved to be suspicious and wary of the Red Chinese, but barely less so of the Nationalists, and Department policy tended to reflect that dilemma. Its successes in keeping China out of the United Nations and economically isolated were clearly temporary. Trade controls had begun to disintegrate even before an armistice in Korea ended the fighting between China and the West. The Department itself entered into a long-term diplomatic, if unofficial, exchange with Beijing that weakened psychological efforts to make China a pariah. America's hard-line prevented significant progress towards normalization, but did not cut off all contacts; it reflected fear of communism in China, but not, except in a few cases, enthusiasm for the Nationalist alternative.

Dulles followed a policy that sought to deflect the strident demands of the right-wing Republicans who championed Chiang Kai-shek and who viewed with suspicion the far too middle-of-the-road Republican Dwight Eisenhower. Learning from the example of his unfortunate predecessors — Marshall and Acheson — Dulles festooned his State Department with appointees whose conservative, pro-Nationalist credentials could not be questioned. They protected him from attack and left him free to deal as he saw fit with more vital European issues. Even on China policy, they were not the men who provided Dulles the guidance he ultimately followed. Instead, the Secretary benefited from the insights of intimate advisors whose more moderate views helped him devise a two Chinas policy and in the end avoid war with the People's Republic. Perhaps the most flexible and cautious of these confidantes was the President, whose own vision of China, although not based on great knowledge or experience, pragmatically imagined a day when there would be diplomatic relations between Washington and Beijing and China would again sit in the United Nations.[120] And since Dulles ultimately did not make foreign policy alone but rather worked closely with this President who made the final decisions himself, it proved to be the more moderate side of the Dulles equation that mattered. These men, who all wanted to see Communist power subdued and its hold reversed, nevertheless resisted the temptation of great power holders to change reality and learned to deal with it instead.

NOTES

1. Karl Lott Rankin, *China Assignment* (Seattle: University of Washington Press, 1964), pp. 216–18.

2. Rankin to Perkins (CA), June 23, 1952, Karl Rankin Papers, box 18, f: Chiang

Kai-shek, Seeley Mudd Manuscript Library, Princeton University (hereafter cited as Mudd).

3. 793.00/9–450, Rankin to Rusk, General Records of the U.S. Dept. of State, Record Group 59, box 4196, National Archives, Washington, D.C. (hereafter NA). After the anti-American riot of 1957, Eisenhower's special assistant James P. Richards reported to Dulles that Rankin shrugged it off. This was despite the fact that the government made no efforts to stop it, that it had been preceded by a bitter press campaign in the state-controlled media, and that reports linked Chiang Ching-kuo's Youth Corps with inciting it. Memo from Richards, October 9, 1957, U.S. Dept. of State, *Foreign Relations of the United States, 1955–1957*, vol. 3: *China* (Washington, D.C.: GPO, 1987), pp. 625–26 (hereafter cited as *FRUS*).

4. Rankin to McConaughy, February 27, 1957, Rankin Papers, box 32, f: China, Republic of, Mudd.

5. Desp. 610, June 6, 1955, Rankin Papers, box 14, f: Bangkok Conference, Mudd.

6. Rankin, *China Assignment*, p. 185.

7. *Ibid.*, p. vii.

8. Special Assistant to President Eisenhower James P. Richards wrote this following the 1957 anti-American riots in Taibei. *FRUS, 1955–57*, 3:625.

9. Rankin to Roberston, April 6, 1959, box 36, f: China, People's Republic of, Rankin Papers, Mudd.

10. E. J. Kahn, Jr., *The China Hands* (New York: Viking, 1972), pp. 38, 277–78. During the war Drumright had been a critic of John Stewart Service's reporting from Yenan. Gary May, *China Scapegoat* (Prospect Heights, Ill.: Waveland Press, 1979), p. 118.

11. Bennett C. Rushkoff, "Eisenhower, Dulles and the Quemoy-Matsu Crisis, 1954–1955," *Political Science Quarterly* (Fall 1981), 96:467–68; Morton H. Halperin, "The 1958 Taiwan Straits Crisis: A Documented History," RM-4900-ISA, December 1966, Rand Corporation, pp. 146 and 201.

12. Townsend Hoopes, *The Devil and John Foster Dulles* (Boston: Little, Brown, 1973), p. 146. Senator William Knowland reportedly observed that "if we had paid attention to the reports [from China] of Walter Robertson, we wouldn't be in the mess we are today." Norman A. Graebner, "Eisenhower and Communism: The Public Record of the 1950s," in Richard A. Melanson and David Mayers, ed, *Re-evaluating Eisenhower*, (Chicago: University of Illinois, 1987), p. 69. A prominent Democrat, Robertson was an active "Democrat for Eisenhower" in 1952. *Current Biography Yearbook, 1953* (New York: Wilson, 1954), p. 535.

13. Memcon, June 23, 1955, *FRUS, 1955–57*, vol. 2: *China* (Washington, D.C.: GPO, 1986), p. 612; Rankin, *China Assignment*, pp. 162–63; Philip Sprouse to Walter McConaughy, January 31, 1953, Records of the Office of Chinese Affairs (hereafter cited as CA Records), box 38, f: 050 Prominent Persons RG 59, NA.

14. *FRUS, 1952–54*, vol. 14: *China and Japan* (Washington, D.C.: GPO, 1985), part 1, pp. 399, n. 4; Hoopes, *The Devil and Dulles*, p. 147.

15. Graebner, "Eisenhower and Communism," p. 83.

16. Robertson to Philip C. Jessup, October 8, 1949, box 25, f: Communism-China-Correspondence, Christopher Emmet Papers, Hoover Institution on War, Revolution, and Peace, Stanford University (hereafter cited as Hoover); and 611.93/3–2053, box 2861, RG 59, NA.

17. 793.00/3-2753, Ringwalt to Walter McConaughy, box 4204, RG 59, NA. His *New York Times* obituary noted that he was perceived as more rigid in his anticommunism than Dulles. January 20, 1970, p. 40.

18. F0371/110222 (FC10345/12), M. G. L. Joy to W. D. Allen, November 30, 1954, British Foreign Office Records, Public Records Office, Kew, Great Britain, (hereafter cited as PRO). In 1960 Robertson turned down Marvin Liebman's invitation

to write a paper on "The Red China Lobby in U.S. Foreign Policy" because, he insisted, such people have had no influence on foreign policy-making under John Foster Dulles. Robertson to Liebman, February 5, 1960, box 23, f: RC Lobby, Marvin Liebman Associates Papers, Hoover. Hoopes, *The Devil and Dulles*, p. 147; U. Alexis Johnson, *The Right Hand of Power* (Englewood Cliffs, N.J.: Prentice-Hall, 1984), p. 157. Regarding Robertson's views of the British, see H. W. Brands, Jr., *Cold Warriors: Eisenhower's Generation and American Foreign Policy* (New York: Columbia University Press, 1988), p. 83.

19. 793.02/1-550, McConaughy, Shanghai, *FRUS, 1950*, vol. 6: *East Asia and the Pacific* (Washington, D.C.: GPO, 1976), pp. 264–69; and 793.02/1-650, no. 98, *ibid.*, p. 268, n. 9.

20. David Allan Mayers, *Cracking the Monolith* (Baton Rouge: Louisiana State University Press, 1986), p. 95. Walter McConaughy, "China in the Shadow of Communism," speech to the Richmond Public Forum, December 7, 1953, CA Records, box 38, f: 060 McConaughy, RG 59, NA.

21. Interview with Ambassador Edwin W. Martin, June 18, 1988, Washington, D.C.

22. Ogburn to Robertson and Johnson, memo, April 17, 1953, CA Records, 306.1, RG 59, NA.

23. 611.93/10-3053, *FRUS, 1952–54*, vol. 14, part 1, pp. 257–59.

24. *FRUS, 1952–54*, vol. 14, part 1, pp. 397–99.

25. Johnson, p. 247. According to Roderic O'Connor, there were times that "Walter annoyed [Dulles] terribly." Hoopes, *The Devil and Dulles*, p. 147.

26. There has been debate on whether Dulles listened to subordinates at all. According to Richard Immerman, his kitchen cabinet consisted of Robert Bowie, Douglas MacArthur II, Herman Phleger, John Hanes, William Macomber, Livingston Merchant, Robert Murphy, and Roderic O'Connor. "Eisenhower and Dulles: Who Made the Decisions?" *Political Psychology* (Autumn 1979), p. 32. Douglas MacArthur II provided a shorter list in his Oral History, which excluded O'Connor explicitly and made no mention of Hanes, Macomber, or Murphy. The Association for Diplomatic Studies Collection, Georgetown University, Washington, D.C. (hereafter cited as ADSC). U. Alexis Johnson, commenting on the same topic, maintained in his memoirs that "he had an obvious confidence, even arrogance, in the power of his own reasoning that made him impatient with advice from subordinates. . . . Dulles listened only until he heard what he wanted to hear." Johnson, *Right Hand*, p. 153.

27. *Political Profiles: The Eisenhower Years* (New York: Facts on File, 1980), p. 57.

28. Hoopes, *The Devil and Dulles*, p. 147; Barry Rubin, *Secrets of State* (New York: Oxford, 1985), p. 279, n. 11; Memcon, March 28, 1955, *FRUS, 1955–57*, vol. 2:411. Bowie's views got support on the PPS from Robert McClintock, who went even further in advocating entry into the UN and recognition for the PRC. Memo, February 8, 1957, *FRUS, 1955–57*, vol. 3:470–73; and paper, December 31, 1957, *ibid.*, pp. 660–73.

29. Bowie to Dulles, memo June 19, 1957, *FRUS, 1955–57*, 3:545–49.

30. Bowie, memo November 26, 1954, *FRUS, 1952–54*, vol. 14, part 1, pp. 950–51; Hoopes, *The Devil and Dulles*, p. 147.

31. 793.5/2-2654, Merchant to Secretary, memo box 4219, RG 59, NA.

32. 893.50, Recovery/5-449, no. 141, Merchant, Taibei, *FRUS, 1949*, vol. 9: *The Far East: China* (Washington, D.C.: GPO, 1975), pp. 324–26; 894A.00/5-2449, Merchant to Butterworth, memo, *ibid.*, pp. 337–41.

33. Livingston Merchant Oral History, p. 1, John Foster Dulles Oral History Project, Mudd.

34. *New York Times*, May 17, 1976, p. 32.

35. 793.5/3-2054, MacArthur to Harold N. Waddell, memo FE Bureau, sent to Dulles, *FRUS, 1952–54*, vol. 14, part 1, p. 552; Memcon, March 28, 1955, *FRUS, 1955–57*, vol. 2:413–14; Douglas MacArthur II Oral History, ADSC.

36.   Whose memory's so far arrears

        As fails to call back from the years

        Those stirring days when, 'gainst the foe

        Stood ranged the phalanx, MacMerBo.

        Control of arms, aid for the Indian

        Think twice of Matsu, hear out the Russian.

        No cause so lost, no hope so slight

        MacMerBo ne'er eschewed the fight.

Poem written by member of the Tokyo embassy staff for Bob Bowie and sent by Ambassador MacArthur to Livie Merchant, January 22, 1959, Livingston Merchant Papers, box 5, f: MacArthur, Douglas II, 1959, Mudd.

37. *Time*, August 18, 1961, p. 19; *U.S. News & World Report*, October 10, 1952, pp. 47–49, January 16, 1953, p. 49, and July 31, 1953, pp. 47–49; *Current Biography, 1953*, pp. 579–82. Smith's humorless, austere demeanor and sharp tongue contributed to his reputation as a hard-working master of details and reduced the likelihood of rapid assimilation into the foreign service ranks around him. Whereas Dulles always deferred to the President and addressed him with the utmost politeness, Smith, a fellow military man and long-time associate, would offer guidance to Ike briskly and frankly. He frequently served as Acting Secretary, given Dulles' continual travels abroad, and provided the President with a ready and trusted access to the Department.

38. Robert Murphy, early on in his own problems with Lodge over Korean issues at the UN, recalled continuing tensions between Lodge and Dulles. Robert Murphy Oral History, Mudd; *Political Profiles: The Eisenhower Years*, p. 447.

39. Rubin, *Secrets of State*, p. 279, n. 2.; 310.2/6-1153, Secretary of State to Lodge, June 19, 1953, *FRUS, 1952–54*, vol. 3:679–80; 310.2/3-3054, Dulles to Lodge, April 10, 1954, *ibid.*, pp. 728–29.

40. MacArthur Oral History, ADSC.

41. For a detailed discussion of Dulles' relationship with the Nationalists, see my "John Foster Dulles and the Taiwan Roots of the 'Two Chinas' Policy," in Richard H. Immerman, ed., *John Foster Dulles and the Diplomacy of the Cold War: A Centennial Reappraisal* (Princeton: Princeton University Press, forthcoming).

42. 216th mtg., NSC, October 6, 1954, *FRUS, 1952–54*, vol. 14. pt. 1, p. 700.

43. Stephen E. Ambrose, *Eisenhower: The President* (New York: Simon & Schuster, 1984), p. 240.

44. Wang Bingnan in his memoirs has denied that this celebrated event ever took place, but, in conversation with me, U. Alexis Johnson confirmed that he witnessed the entire incident. Wang Bingnan, "Nine Years of Sino–U.S. Talks in Retrospect," *China Report*, August 7, 1985.

45. Mayers, *Cracking the Monolith*, p. 118; extract from James Hagerty diary, June 3, 1954, *FRUS, 1952–54*, vol. 14, part 1, p. 442.

46. Johnson, *Right Hand*, p. 239.

47. Harriet Schwar, "To the Brink of a Two-China Policy: Dulles and the Mutual Defense Treaty with the Republic of China," paper presented at the Annual Convention of the Society for Historians of American Foreign Relations, June 1985.

48. William P. Snyder, "Dean Rusk to John Foster Dulles, May–June 1953: The Office, the First 100 Days, and Red China," *Diplomatic History* (Winter 1983), p. 86.

49. They did, however, deplore the terminology, which they considered insulting to the head of a government.

50. Discussions regarding the lifting of the ban against Nationalist attacks on

the mainland occurring during the Truman years, but the conclusion was reached that large-scale activity would continue to be barred. 793.00/10–852, H. M. Holland (CA) to Martin (CA), memo box 4202, RG 59, NA; 793.00/10-2052, Memcon, Acheson with McConaughy, *ibid.* Raids did occur, however. See 793.00/1–2853, Memcon, F. S. Tomlinson (Counselor, GB Emb) with Allison (Asst Sec), box 4203, RG 59, NA; Ambrose, *Eisenhower*, p. 47. NSC 166/1 of November 6, 1953, explicitly called for U.S. support for aid to the ROC to increase "the effectiveness of its armed forces for . . . raids against the Communist mainland, and for such offensive operations as may be in the United States interest." This document was superceded by NSC 5429/5 on December 22, 1954, wherein the support for such operations was intentionally omitted. Herter to Gordon Gray, memo, January 1, 1959, Dwight D. Eisenhower Papers, NSC Series, box 6, f: Chronological File, January 1959 (1), Dwight D. Eisenhower Library, Abilene, Kansas (hereafter cited as DDE).

51. Chiang argued that neither was the project as difficult as some supposed, nor would it lead to war with the Soviets. See 793.00/6-954, desp. 690, Rankin, box 4208, RG 59, NA: desp. 320, Rankin, November 30, 1953, Rankin Papers, Box 20, f: Chiang Ching-kuo, Mudd.

52. 139th mtg. NSC, April 8, 1953, *FRUS, 1952–54*, vol. 14, part 1, p. 181; 794A.4-1653, no. 848, Dulles to Rankin, *ibid.*, p. 191. The requisite guarantee was given on April 23, 1953. 794A.4-2353, no. 1118, Jones, Taibei, *ibid.*, p. 193.

53. Eisenhower Oral History, pp. 20–21, Mudd.

54. Rankin, *China Assignment*, p. 311.

55. Holland to McConaughy and Martin, memo, September 17, 1953, CA Records, 306.11, RG 59, NA. Desk officers Stryker, Hodge, and Martin a year later continued to contrast Nationalist desires with the U.S. willingness to provide more modest aid. "Formosa: Policy and Problems," briefing paper, November 24, 1954, box 4210, RG 59, NA. In 1957 Rankin would argue that "such a return in [sic] inevitable, particularly since Taiwan has no historical or other significant basis for a prolonged independent existence." Despatch 382, March 5, 1957, Rankin Papers, box 32, f: China, People's Republic of, Mudd; "The Missing Ingredient in United States Policy Toward China," Taibei embassy paper, March 28, 1957, *ibid.*; and again in 1963 in letter to Averell Harriman, Assistant Secretary of State for Far Eastern Affairs, February 22, 1963, Rankin Papers, box 41, f: Chiang Kai-shek, Mudd. The summer 1953 despatch reflected the views of Rankin and his counselor Howard P. Jones but glossed over the dissent of political officers Rinden and Hooper.

56. 793.5-MSP/5-1453, Jenkins to McConaughy, drafted by Holland, box 4222, RG 59, NA.

57. He did so repeatedly. See, for example, Dulles to Ike, memo May 16, 1956, White House Office Files, Office of the Staff Sec. Subj. Series, State Dept. Subseries, box 1, f: State Dept. 1956 (April–June) (3), DDE. At the 214th meeting of the NSC, on September 12, 1954, Dulles wondered whether Chiang himself still believed that he could reconquer the mainland. *FRUS, 1952–54*, vol. 14, part 1, p. 614. Charles Bohlen, who in November 1952 at a CIA briefing called Dulles' desire to see Chiang unleashed senseless because he could not significantly threaten the mainland, would later call it a "cardinal error" of U.S. foreign policy. Charles Bohlen, *Witness to History, 1929–1969* (New York: Norton, 1973), pp. 309–10.

58. For a detailed discussion of the treaty's development, see Su Ge, "A Horrible Dilemma—The Making of the U.S.–Taiwan Mutual Defense Treaty: 1948–1955," ms.

59. 611.93/10-754, JFD to Robertson, memo *FRUS, 1952–54*, vol. 14, part 1, p. 709. Small-scale harrassment activities were not precluded. See 229th mtg., NSC, memo of discussion, December 21, 1954, *FRUS, 1952–54*, vol. 14, part 1, p. 1045. Dulles did not publicly attack the idea of reconquest until September 30, 1958, at

a news conference. See also my "Dulles and the Taiwan Roots of the 'Two Chinas' Policy."

60. The Nationalists submitted a draft treaty in October 1953, desp. 690, RG59, NA.

61. *FRUS, 1952–54*, vol. 14, part 1, pp. 367–68, 370.

62. The Nationalists insisted that the conference would accomplish nothing. See ROC to U.S. Govt., memo, April 7, 1954, appended to desp. 594, Rankin, April 14, 1954, box 3, f: Geneva Conference, China Post Files, RG 84, Washington National Records Center, Suitland, Maryland.

63. The British, for example, had warned against unleashing Chiang. See 186, R. Makins, Washington, January 28, 1953, FO371/105196 (FC1018/5))PRO; "The 'Liberation' of the Chinese Mainland," November 11, 1953, FO371/105198 (FC1018/123g) PRO.

64. 793.5/2-2654, Merchant to Secretary, memo, box 4219, RG 59, NA; 793.5/2-2754, Wainhouse (UNA), memo RG 59, NA: 793.5/3-2054, Bowie to Robertson, box 4219, RG 59, NA. Dulles was, at times, cynical about Allied sensitivities. See Memcon, March 28, 1955, *FRUS, 1955–57*, vol. 2:414, for comment by the Secretary and Undersecretary Herbert Hoover, Jr., about allied willingness to support Washington whenever it took a strong position.

65. 793.5/3-1854, Kennedy (SOA) to Jernegan (NEA), box 4219, RG 59, NA; 793.5/3-2054, Byroade to Robertson, *ibid.*

66. 793.5/3-1554, Robertson to Merchant, memo, *FRUS, 1952–54*, vol. 14, part 1, p. 370, n. 7; McConaughy, memo for the file, February 27, 1954, *FRUS, 1952–54*, vol. 14, part 1, p. 369; 793.5/3-2054, Smith to Robertson, memo, box 4219, RG 59, NA.

67. *FRUS, 1952–54*, vol. 14, part 1, pp. 399–401 and 555.

68. *Ibid.*, p. 552; 793.5/3-2054, Jernegan to Robertson, August 24, 1954, box 4219, RG 59, NA.

69. 793.5/3–2054, *FRUS, 1952–54*, vol. 14, part 1, p. 400.

70. *Ibid.*, pp. 399–401, 552–53.

71. 793.5/3-2054, Merchant to Robertson, memo, August 30, 1954, *ibid.*, p. 553.

72. 793.5/3-2054, no. 132, Smith to Taibei, August 1954, box 4219, RG 59, NA.

73. 793.00/10-754, Robertson to Secretary, memo, box 4209 and 4220, RG 59, NA, and *FRUS, 1952–54*, vol. 14, part 1, pp. 706–7.

74. 793.00/10-2454, Memcon, box 4209, RG 59, NA.

75. 793.5/8-2554, Robertson to Secretary, memo, drafted by Martin, box 4219, RG 59, NA.

76. 793.00/10-954, no. 522, Bohlen, Moscow, *FRUS, 1952–54*, vol. 14, part 1, pp. 720–21.

77. *Ibid.*, p. 369; and JCS 1966/91, p. 754, n. 3.

78. 221st mtg., NSC, memo of discussion, November 2, 1954, *FRUS, 1952–54*, vol. 14, part 1, p. 832. Similarly, Dulles' proposal to take the crisis in the Straits to the UN engendered military consternation in part, at least, because members of the Joint Chiefs felt they had not had sufficient time to evaluate the Secretary of State's idea. Thomas D. White, Acting Chief of Staff of the Air Force to JCS Chairman, memo, October 29, 1954, Records of the Joint Chiefs of Staff, RG 218, Chairman's Files, Admiral Arthur N. Radford, box 7, 091 China 1953–57, f: October–December 1954, NA; Radford to SecDef, memo, October 29, 1954, *ibid.*

79. 611.93/3-1953, Memcon, *FRUS, 1952–54*, vol. 14, part 1, p. 158; Bowie to Robertson, memo, March 22, 1954, noted in *ibid.*, p. 400, n. 5; Memcon, May 19, 1954, *ibid.*, pp. 422–25; 793.5/3-2054, Robertson, memo September 1, 1954, *ibid.*, p. 555; 214th mtg. NSC, memo of discussion, September 12, 1954, *ibid.*, p. 614.

80. 793.5/8-2554, Robertson, memo drafted by Martin, box 4219, RG 59, NA.

81. 611.93/10-1454, MacArthur to Robertson and Bowie, memo, *FRUS, 1952–54*, vol. 14, part 1, p. 757.

82. 221st mtg., NSC, memo of discussion, November 2, 1954, *FRUS, 1952–54*, vol. 14, part 1, p. 834.

83. SM-792-54, memo for the Sec Def (Draft-Navy, Marine Corps–Air Force View), September 7, 1954, Radford Files, box 7: 091 China, f: September 1954, RG 218, NA; Radford to SecDef, September 11, 1954, *ibid.*

84. Hoopes, *The Devil and Dulles*, p. 265.

85. 216th mtg., NSC, memo of discussion, October 6, 1954, *FRUS, 1952–54*, vol. 14, part 1, p. 695.

86. Bowie to Secretary, memo, February 7, 1955, *FRUS 1955–57*, vol. 2:238–40.

87. Eisenhower was furious that the Secretary did not realize how embarrassing his public remarks were to the Secretary of State and the President. Robert Ferrell, ed., *The Eisenhower Diaries* (New York: Norton, 1981), p. 296.

88. Memcon, Pres–Sec, March 6, 1955, *FRUS, 1955–57*, vol. 2:336–37; 240th mtg., NSC, memo of discussion, March 10, 1955, *ibid.*, p. 347; memo for the record, March 11, 1955, Eisenhower Papers, Whitman File, International Series, box 9, f: Formosa, visit to CINCPAC (1955) (1), DDE. See also Gordon H. Chang, "To the Nuclear Brink: Eisenhower, Dulles, and the Quemoy-Matsu Crisis," *International Security* (Spring 1988), 12:96–123.

89. Herter believed this. See Halperin, 'The 1958 Taiwan Straits Crisis," p. 84n., and p. 203, regarding Burke, Quarles, and Twining; JCS to Adm. Felt, JCS 9447931, September 12, 1958, CCS 381 Formosa (11-8-48) sec. 39, RG 218, NA.

90. Eisenhower Oral History, p. 22, Mudd; *New York Times*, August 28, 1958, p. 1. Responsibility for the build-up of forces on the islands was not all Chiang's. After the failure of the Radford-Robertson mission to persuade the Generalissimo to downgrade the islands, American policymakers did little. Indeed, there is reason to believe that Admirals Radford and Felix Stump, CINCPAC, encouraged the effort. Tang Tsou, "The Quemoy Imbroglio: Chiang Kai-shek and the United States," *Western Political Quarterly* (1959), 12:1080.

91. Halperin, "The 1958 Taiwan Straits Crisis," p. 102.

92. Memcon, September 3, 1958, Eisenhower Papers, Whitman File, International Series, box 10, f: Formosa (1958) 2, DDE.

93. Halperin, "The 1958 Taiwan Straits Crisis," p. 91.

94. Rankin to Robertson, March 13, 1955, Rankin Papers, box 26, f: China, Republic of, Mudd.

95. Halperin, "The 1958 Taiwan Straits Crisis," pp. 105–6, 184, 250, 269–70.

96. *Ibid.*, p. 106.

97. The position paper encapsulating the Dulles view received approval also from the JCS, the Defense Department and finally the President on September 4. *Ibid.*, pp. 273–75.

98. *Ibid.*, p. 504.

99. Including Robertson, Assistant Secretary James Graham Parsons, Marshall Green, and Deputy Director of the Office of Chinese Affairs Lutkins. *Ibid.*, pp. 411–12.

100. Op-OO memo 000416-58, September 7, 1958, Burke to Twining, memo, CCS 381 Formosa (11-8-48) sec. 38A, RG 218, NA.

101. Halperin, "The 1958 Taiwan Straits Crisis," p. 529.

102. Eisenhower to Dulles, memo, April 5, 1955, Eisenhower Papers, Whitman File, Dulles-Herter Series, box 4, f: Dulles, April 1955 (2) and in Eisenhower diary, box 10, f: April 1955 (2), DDE; Memcon with President, April 4, 1955, *ibid.*, International Series, box 9, f: Conferences on Formosa, DDE; Eisenhower to Dulles, April 26, 1955, *ibid.*, Eisenhower diary, box 10, f: April 1955 (1); 251010Z Robert-

son, Formosa, April 25, 1955, *ibid.*, International Series, box 9, f: Formosa (c) 1952–57 (4), DDE; memo for the record, April 29, 1955, Rankin Papers, box 26, f: Chiang Kai-shek, Mudd.

103. *New York Times*, September 30, 1958, p. 5.

104. 793.00/5-2653, Ogburn to Robertson and Johnson, memo, box 4204, RG 59, NA, also in *FRUS, 1952–54*, vol. 3: *United Nations Affairs*, (Washington, D.C.: GPO, 1979), p. 640.

105. Interview on CBS-TV "Man of the Week," CA Records, box 39, RG 59, NA; Josiah Bennett, Taibei, to McConaughy, May 25, 1953, and Allen to McConaughy, July 16, 1953, *ibid.*, box 38, f: 112.1 W. P. McConaughy, RG 59, NA.

106. Memo, July 13, 1953, CA Records, box 39, RG 59, NA.

107. *FRUS, 1955–57*, vol. 2:147–48.

108. 4th Tripartite Heads of Government Meeting, Bermuda, memo December 7, 1953, *FRUS, 1952–54*, vol. 3:711.

109. For a more detailed discussion of trade policy, see my "Cold War Contacts: America and China, 1952–56," in Harry Harding and Yuan Ming, eds., *Sino-American Relations, 1945–1955: A Collaborative Reassessment of a Troubled Time* (Beijing: Peking University Press, 1988) and the essay by Qing Simei in this volume.

110. Robertson to the Secretary, memo, June 2, 1953, *FRUS, 1952–54*, vol. 14, pt. 1, p. 202.

111. 460.509/8-852, Hope to McConaughy, memo, *FRUS 1952–54*, vol. 1: *General: Economic and Political Matters* (Washington, D.C.: GPO, 1983), part 2, pp. 866–68.

112. 793.001/8-2752, Hope to McConaughy, memo box 4212, RG 59, NA.

113. 460.6031/6-754, Weeks to Cutler, *FRUS, 1952–54*, vol. 1, part 2, p. 1181; 169th mtg., NSC, memo of discussion, November 5, 1953, *ibid.*, pp. 268, 270–71; 202nd mtg., NSC, memo of discussion, June 17, 1954, *ibid.*, pp. 1201–2.

114. Rankin, *China Assignment*, p. 254; Rankin to McConaughy, August 3, 1956, Rankin Papers, box 29, f: China, Republic of, Mudd.

115. *FRUS, 1955–57*, vol. 3:38, n. 1; *ibid.*, 2:31.

116. *Ibid.*, 3:31, n. 2.

117. Kenneth Young, *Negotiating with the Chinese Communists: The United States Experience, 1953–1967* (New York: McGraw-Hill, 1968), p. 45; George Gallup, *The Gallup Poll: Public Opinion, 1935–71* (New York: Random House, 1972), p. 1329 (May 1, 1955). Less delight was, of course, expressed by the China Lobby; Senator Knowland, for one, called this "another Munich." Walter Robertson to Marvin Liebman, May 25, 1955, Christopher Emmet Papers, box 22, f: Committee of One Million—Correspondence, Hoover; Frederick McKee to Dulles, April 16, 1955, William Knowland Papers, box 274, f: McKee, 1953–55, Bancroft Manuscript Library, University of California, Berkeley, Calif.

118. *FRUS, 1955–57*, vol. 3:41, n. 6.

119. Johnson, *The Right Hand of Power*, p. 251.

120. 271st mtg., NSC, memo of discussion, December 23, 1955, Ike Papers, Whitman File, NSC Series, DDE; Mayers, *Cracking the Monolith*, pp. 110–11; Ambrose, *Eisenhower* pp. 99–100; Roscoe Drummond and Gaston Coblentz, *Duel at the Brink* (Garden City, N.Y.: Doubleday, 1960), pp. 28–29; Memcon, Eisenhower with Nehru, December 19, 1956, Ike Papers, Whitman File, Ike diary, box 20, f: December 1956, DDE.

3

The Best Defense Is a Good Offense: The Evolution of American Strategy in East Asia, 1953–1960

✦

MARC S. GALLICCHIO
Villanova University

S hortly after becoming president in 1953, Dwight D. Eisenhower announced that he would be appointing four new officers to the Joint Chiefs of Staff (JCS). For the post of Chairman of the JCS, Eisenhower chose Admiral Arthur Radford. The Admiral's appreciation of the need to cut defense costs and his views on basic national security policy and nuclear deterrence were compatible with what would come to be called the "New Look" of the Eisenhower administration. According to Defense Secretary Charles Wilson, a former head of General Motors, "Radford's plans were as sharp and clear as the lines of a new Cadillac. You could draw up a budget on them and you would know precisely where you were going."[1] In choosing Radford to head the JSC, Eisenhower also satisfied the Republican Right by naming an "Asia First" admiral as the President's chief military adviser. This other side of Radford's strategic outlook would prove to be a source of embarrassment to the President.

Radford took seriously the Republican pledge to roll back the bamboo curtain, and he showed less compunction about using nuclear weapons than did Eisenhower. In a little over a year, the admiral recommended using atomic weapons in Asia no less than three times.[2] As this record suggests, Radford had difficulty reconciling the essentially defensive nature of the New Look with his own vigorous anticommunism. Indeed, in retrospect the Admiral seems almost the living embodiment of the conflicting impulses of the Eisenhower administration's policies as they applied to Asia. By imposing the budgetary restraints of the New Look, Radford carried out the wishes of the President. His calls for aggressive action in Asia, however, more nearly reflected the views of the JCS and their field commanders than those of the Commander in Chief.

Enough has been written about the influence of budget politics on military policy in the Eisenhower administration to make it clear that the Joint Chiefs rarely lost sight of the bureaucratic implications of their recommendations.[3] Nevertheless, parochialism alone does not adequately explain many of the developments in American military policy in Asia during these years. A genuine tension existed between the cold war assumptions of the Eisenhower administration and the budgetary implications of the New Look. These internal contradictions were, perhaps, most visible when applied to conditions in Asia.

Despite the Republican Party's criticisms of the Truman administration's policy of containment, the New Look remained reactive in nature and European in orientation. Given the Eisenhower administration's own perception of the international setting, the New Look's reliance on nuclear deterrence was more consistent with American aims in Europe than in Asia. In Europe, the two superpowers had established static defensive lines after more than five years of maneuvering and alliance-building.

In Asia, however, the President and the JCS agreed that they faced conditions that were far more threatening. Unless the expansionist tendencies of the Peoples' Republic of China were thwarted, the United States might lose the entire region to the Communist bloc. Precisely how the United States might meet this challenge remained a matter of conjecture. The New Look provided only the broadest of outlines for the implementation of military policy, and, as Eisenhower occasionally acknowledged, it left important questions unanswered. To fill this void, the JCS and their subordinates in Asia began to develop their own solutions to the Asian dilemma. Influenced by shifts in the regional balance of power, the hazards of alliance politics, and new developments in weaponry, as well as by Washington budget battles, American commanders in Asia improvised an offensive-minded and provocative military policy to regain the initiative in Asia.

In the months following the Korean armistice, American strategic planners confronted an imposing challenge in East Asia. Like its predecessor, the Eisenhower administration considered Japan, Okinawa, and the Philippines vital to American security. As a result of the war, South Korea and Taiwan had been added to the U.S. defensive perimeter. Early in the Eisenhower administration, officials also added Indonesia to the list of areas to be defended.[4] Indochina's position remained somewhat ambiguous, but the American stake in preserving the French regime had clearly grown during the war.

Despite the marked nuclear superiority of the United States in the early 1950s, America's obligations continued to excede its capabilities. In the event of a global war, American war plans called for a strategic defensive in the Far East. After a brief period of offensive naval action against Russian ports and airfields, a portion of American forces would be withdrawn for deployment in Europe, the Mediterranean, and the Persian Gulf. The remaining units would be engaged in defending the offshore line from Japan through the Kra Isthmus. The JCS did not think that Thailand, Indochina, or Korea could be held against the combined weight of the PRC and Soviet Union.[5]

The decision to exclude the Republic of Korea from the areas to be defended was the most controversial aspect of this plan. Early versions of the Joint Outline Emergency Plan highlighted the anomolous position of Korea in American strategic thinking. These plans called for an orderly withdrawal of American forces from the peninsula within three months of the outbreak of war. The Army's Commander in Chief in the Far East (CINCFE) criticized this "desertion of an ally" and predicted that it would lead to the defection of all twenty divisions in the ROK army. To remedy the situation, he recommended reducing the number of American troops in Korea to a point where their loss could be militarily acceptable. In the event of war these forces would fight alongside ROK troops until they were driven off the peninsula, thus enabling the United States to make use of the surviving Korean units.[6] In either case, however, American officials expected Korea to be overrun.

America's allies on the Asian rim faced a more immediate threat, however, from internal subversion or from an over-the-border attack from a neighbor other than the Soviet Union. In the case of Korea, the National Security Council rejected the JCS's recommendation to meet any combined PRC and North Korean attack with a nuclear assault on Manchuria. Instead, the NSC approved a plan that confined American attacks to North Korea. The Eisenhower administration expected to use nuclear weapons to defend Korea, but every effort would be made to prevent the conflict from widening into a more generalized war.[7]

Policy and planning papers before the Dienbienphu crisis in 1954 emphasized the strategic importance of Indochina to the security of all Southeast Asia. As in the case of Korea, a Chinese Communist attack on Indochina would trigger American intervention. The real threat to Indochina, however, came from indigenous forces. Unlike a Chinese invasion, a Vietminh drive toward victory was not likely to present the United States with a clear-cut case for intervention. Nevertheless, at least one JCS study called for the introduction of U.S. forces if the French withdrew from the field.[8]

When the siege of Dienbienphu came to a head in the spring of 1954, Eisenhower, as is well known, declined to employ American forces to relieve the beleaguered garrison. Although he gave serious consideration to Americanizing the war even after Dienbienphu fell, the President ultimately decided to concentrate on saving whatever remained in French hands after the Geneva Conference. Eisenhower had sound political reasons for rejecting direct action, and they may have been overriding by themselves, but there were also serious military reasons for arguing against intervention.[9]

The siege at Dienbienphu highlighted a glaring weakness of the administration's reliance on nuclear deterrence. Although the Army's planning staff at first recommended the use of nuclear weapons to lift the siege, the Army's Chief of Staff, Matthew Ridgway, and his chief planner, General James Gavin, rejected the proposal out of hand. Eisenhower likewise vetoed a similar recommendation from Radford.[10]

As this episode demonstrates, the New Look did not contemplate the use of nuclear force in a situation that fell short of direct aggression. There was more support, however, for the use of conventional force. The crisis at Dienbienphu seemed tailor-made for the swift application of conventional force the Navy claimed as its forte. The carrier-based aircraft of the Seventh Fleet had been brought within range of the target area by entering the Tonkin Gulf, but Navy officials were reluctant to undertake such a mission without first striking at the PRC's land-based aircraft on Hainan island.[11]

Eisenhower had no desire to risk starting another conflict with China so soon after the Korean War. After he decided Dienbienphu was beyond saving, Eisenhower did, however, give serious consideration to supporting French ground units with American air and naval forces. Once again it was Ridgway who opposed intervention. He argued that air and sea power alone would not suffice. Eventually a minimum of seven divisions would be required to prop up the French. The Vietminh simply did not present the type of force that was vulnerable to air power. Moreover, the introduction of land-based air power in Indochina would necessitate building and improving port and landing facilities and require even more troops to protect the bases. Ridgway believed that intervention in Indochina would be a huge undertaking that would seriously weaken American defenses in

Europe and elsewhere in Asia.[12] Eisenhower agreed, and the United States waited unenthusiastically for the outcome of the Geneva Conference.

Ridgway previously had expressed concern over the "very dangerous deployment in the Far East." By April 1954, the NSC had approved plans to withdraw four divisions from Korea, leaving two on the peninsula. Of the four divisions withdrawn, one was assigned to Japan and another to Hawaii, while the remaining two returned to the continental United States.[13] Ridgway wanted to move even more troops back to the states but he appears to have accepted the recommendation of Lieutenant General John Hull, CINCFE, that the United States would "have to remain strong in the Far East for some time."[14]

Given the Army's essentially European orientation, it is not surprising that Ridgway sought to reduce its commitment in East Asia. It is probably more significant to note that following the Korean War naval strategy was also in a state of flux.

In the years before the Korean conflict, the Navy, under the leadership of Admiral Forrest Sherman, had gradually developed an offensive strategy, the centerpiece of which was the carrier task group. As part of the Navy's maritime strategy, war plans called for aircraft carrier task forces to destroy the Soviet Union's Pacific naval and air power at their source through strikes against Soviet bases and airfields. Although the fate of the free world would not be decided in the Pacific, this theater received considerable attention from Navy officers who saw it as the one area of operations where naval forces could strike directly at the enemy.[15]

By 1953, however, Navy planners were beginning to question the fleet's ability to carry out the offensive part of its mission. Several factors accounted for this changed outlook. Although the peacetime compliment of carriers stationed in the Pacific never sank to pre–Korean War levels, four of the seven there in 1953 were earmarked for deployment elsewhere within a month of the outbreak of war. Moreover, American carriers now faced a much greater threat in the form of improved Soviet air and sea forces in Asia. Russian land-based aircraft made it hazardous for U.S. ships to close in on Soviet bases, which in turn increased the likelihood that enemy submarines would be able to surge into the Pacific to attack allied shipping. In the opening weeks of a war American carrier-based planes would be preoccupied in defending the offshore island chain and the Sea Lines of Communication (SLOCs) from the combined attacks of Chinese and Russian aircraft. Significantly, a lengthy Navy planning document on force levels listed only this defensive role as the primary mission of American carriers in the Pacific.[16]

A second factor in the Navy's reevaluation of its strategy involved the emergence of the PRC as a perceived threat in the Pacific. Before 1949 American planning had been sharply focused on Soviet power in Northeast Asia. In the years that followed the Navy assumed responsibility for defending Taiwan and assisting in the defense of Indochina. Sizing up this situation, the Secretary of the Navy warned that current naval forces were not adequate to meet all of the service's commitments simultaneously. Notably deficient were "forces in the Pacific to meet and counter any future communist aggression against Formosa, Indochina, or Southeast Asia."[17] Marine deployments also reflected these increased demands on American forces. In early 1954, the JCS approved the Chief of Naval Operations's recommendation to move the First Marine Division from Korea to Hawaii so as to better position the force for possible action in Southeast Asia.[18]

The redeployment of Army and Marine forces and the subtle shifts in naval strategy revealed a military establishment that was off balance and back on its heels. Faced with manpower reductions and an expanding threat, American military leaders momentarily sought to draw back and concentrate their forces on the defense of Japan and the Sea Lines of Communication in the Western Pacific.

In the wake of these strategic developments in East Asia, and especially after the fall of Dienbienphu, the Eisenhower administration made collective action the centerpiece of its East Asian policy. Under this concept, America's Asian allies would provide the necessary ground forces for their own defense. The U.S. contribution was to be limited to air and naval support and small advisory missions.

Military Assistance Advisory Groups did not originate with the Eisenhower administration, but the New Look's reliance on indigenous forces made the MAAGs an increasingly important feature of American military policy in Asia. During the mid-1950s advisory groups appeared in Laos, South Vietnam, and Thailand. Existing missions in Korea, Japan, the Philippines, and Taiwan were continued or enlarged during the same period. At the end of the decade the United States had also begun to advance military assistance to Indonesia. Describing the MAAGs, Ridgway told a congressional subcommittee that he "did not know of any place where an individual member of the Army [gave] a greater yield to the nation than those people."[19]

The increased attention given to the role of military missions also led to a growing realization of the complex nature of the military adviser's job. The Armed Forces Policy Council examined the possibility of creating a special training program for MAAG officers, and a sample curriculum for a four-week program was proposed. The MAAG school never materialized, however, and officers continued to be assigned to country teams on an individual basis.[20] Although the proposed program would have better prepared advisers for their administrative duties, it seems doubtful that a four-week crash course could have equipped Americans for the problems they would face in many of the host countries. As Ronald Spector has shown, language remained the single greatest obstacle officers in Vietnam faced on a daily basis. Moreover, on taking up their posts, military advisers usually entered a world of intrigue and infighting that made Pentagon politics seem tame by comparison. "In this area we are dealing with men rather than governments," concluded one report. "The Chiefs of state are little more than glorified headmen who hold and exercise their power . . . through personal leadership, conspiracy, and skilled maneuvering."[21] "Bangkok, was loaded with Generals," recalled Admiral Harry Felt; "there were more Admirals than they had ships."[22] On Taiwan, Chiang Kai-shek continued his wartime practice of diverting supplies to favored units. "Nepotism, dishonesty, inter-clique jealousy . . . and constant questioning of loyalty to individual personalities" undermined efforts to modernize the Nationalist Chinese Navy.[23] Faced with these conditions, American officers often fell back on the expediency of relying on personal relationships with their military counterparts.

Historians need to learn more about the activities of the MAAGs before they can create an accurate picture of American regional military policy in the 1950s. But the MAAGs also had a broader impact on American–East Asian relations that extended beyond the realm of military affairs. Circumstances varied from country to country, but American officers were influential in determining the active and reserve force levels that the United States would support. In countries such as Korea, where 21 percent of the eligible males served in the armed forces, decisions of this kind were likely to have important implications for the economic and social organization of the host country.

Although military advisers faced a multitude of problems in carrying out their various missions, the most serious obstacle they had to overcome derived from a basic flaw in American strategy. Despite the imminent danger facing most of the countries in the region, U.S. planning continued to treat Southeast Asia as a minor theater. Moreover, within the region, planning continued to focus on the threat of an over-the-border invasion. During the Eisenhower years, Army officers in Vietnam organized and trained regular ground units to fight a Korean-style war. In 1960, after more than $2 billion in aid, the JCS concluded that South Vietnamese forces were inadequately trained and urged immediate action to improve the army's counterinsurgency capabilities. The Defense Department's analysts later concluded that "with regard to the overall effectiveness of U.S. aid, it seems to have had, unfortunately, all the depth the term 'mirror image' implies."[24]

In an effort to compensate for American weaknesses, military advisers also attempted to integrate local forces into a larger regional defense plan. Robert Futrell has noted that "as the United States prepared the Vietnamese to combat subversion and repel invasion as well, it seemed unable to decide which was the greater threat. The objectives for national and regional defenses—even the distinction between the two—were vague, confused, and at times conflicting."[25] The South Vietnamese naval officers who engaged in American sponsored antisubmarine exercises no doubt reached a similar conclusion.[26]

Although these efforts to promote some means of collective defense in the region appear misguided, it must be understood that American officials labored with the knowledge that the one nation capable of shoring up the anti-Communist position in Asia would remain on the sidelines for years to come. Time and again, American strategists emphasized the importance of a revitalized Japanese economy and military establishment to the defense of East Asia.[27]

Resistance to Japan's assuming the lead in the region came from internal and external sources, neither of which lessened greatly during the 1950s. American plans to augment the Self-Defense Forces proceded slowly in part because of regional fears of a resurgent Japanese militarism. Australia's and New Zealand's protests over the loan of a large training submarine to the Coastal Defense Forces torpedoed CINCFE's more ambitious proposal for a force of four light carriers and three light anti-aircraft cruisers.[28] Protests from other allies were more categorical. Writing directly to Eisenhower, Korea's Syngman Rhee strenuously denounced American plans for rearming Japan. Vigorous opposition to Japanese rearmament obviously served Korean national interests by strengthening, although reluctantly, U.S. reliance on Korea. "In the Far East," members of the Joint Strategic Survey Committee observed, "Korea must be looked on as our 'force' in the Far East while no significant increase in support of U.S. objectives can be expected, we will be required to maintain Korean armed forces in sufficient strength to deter another communist attack against them."[29] American efforts to soothe Korean fears and gain Rhee's cooperation made little progress throughout the decade.

American military planners placed such importance on Japanese rearmament that it seems almost certain that the United States would have found some way to overcome Korean resistance, had it not been for domestic Japanese opposition to the defense buildup. The JCS derived its goals for Japanese force levels in the 1950s from the requirements of a Joint Outline Emergency War Plan tentatively approved by the Japanese Joint Staff Council in 1955. The plan called for Japanese forces to assume a strictly defensive role in the event of general war. The Coastal Defense Force, with U.S. naval units, would repel amphibious assaults, conduct antisubmarine warfare in Japanese waters, and otherwise contain surface attacks against shipping lanes. Ground forces were assigned the task of defending against an invasion and maintaining internal security. Japanese air forces would participate in combined operations with U.S. units in defense of Japan.[30] Based on this list of tasks, the JCS called for a Japanese ground force of 348,000 soldiers and the development of a small, but modern navy.

Despite American projections, the Japanese government authorized funding for only 180,000 ground troops, a level they hoped to reach by 1958 and hold constant through 1961. Moreover, the Japanese Defense Agency hinted that once the Self-Defense Force had reached the 180,000 mark, American ground troops could be withdrawn from the home islands. American officials considered this line of reasoning to be completely unrealistic. Japan served as an enormous logistical base area for American ground, air, and naval forces in the Pacific. In addition to housing storage facilities for the Seventh Fleet's massive oil reserves, Japanese bases provided logistical support for the indigenous forces of America's allies throughout Asia. Given these circumstances, the JCS could not allow Japan's understrength units to substitute for American troops any time soon.[31]

In their numerous discussions, Japanese officials consistently countered JCS efforts to prod Tokyo into accepting the higher ceiling by warning that increases in the defense force would endanger Japan's economic recovery and be politically unpopular. As Henry Brands had pointed out, the Eisenhower administration's concern for Japan's economic health weakened the JCS's ability to press for rearmament.[32] But the Chiefs' exertions were further undermined when the United States announced it would be withdrawing the First Cavalry division from Japan without first giving CINCFE time to prepare the Japanese government for the move. In the wake of this announcement, American officials found it all but impossible to convince Tokyo of the need for building up its own forces.[33]

During the latter 1950s, the introduction of new weaponry and the requirements of air defense were a special problem in American-Japanese relations. American planners were greatly concerned by the superiority of combined Chinese–North Korean–Soviet air power in Northeast Asia. To meet this threat, the JCS supported the CINCFE and the Commander of the Far Eastern Air Force in their requests for an improved air defense system comprising new jet aircraft and Nike anti-aircraft missiles.

The new missiles and the conversion to jet aircraft necessitated the purchase of additional Japanese farmland for launch sites and extended runways. Each new intrusion into Japan's private domain was met with protests, strikes, and rallies while pickets blocked access to the designated areas by survey teams. Frustrated, American officials complained at the Japanese government's unwillingness to make a positive declaration in support of the program. Instead, Tokyo issued lukewarm statements explaining that the runway extensions were legal according to the provisions of the security treaty. When Prime Minister Hatoyama Ichiro finally stated that the conversion project was in Japanese interests, it was coupled with an announcement that as many as three bases would have to be dropped from the proposed list.[34] In the period before renegotiation of the security treaty, the problem of runway extensions kept the controversial issue of American bases before the public.

Tokyo's inability to reach the levels set by the JCS's defense plan doomed any hope of Japan's taking the lead in a larger regional defense program. Without Japanese support, the JCS seemed uncertain about how they would shore up allied defenses in Asia while simultaneously withdrawing American troops from Korea. In a revealing session of the NSC, Eisenhower admitted that America's allies were not likely to view the U.S. nuclear deterrent as a satisfactory substitute for ground troops. "There [is] nothing as important as a soldier walking the street to people who are in the jeopardy that these people are in," conceded Eisenhower. The President agreed with Secretary of State John Foster Dulles' defense of the New Look, calling it sound in principle, but he pointedly asked the Secretary to tell him "when he had had his first success in educating people to putting their faith in our retaliatory power."[35]

The creation of SEATO amid much fanfare did little to change the underlying reality described by Eisenhower. The JCS's reluctance to become tied down in the region and their relegation of Southeast Asia to a minor position within a subordinate theater were all too obvious to America's Asian partners. Moreover, even American officials stationed in the Pacific viewed SEATO as a feeble attempt to compensate for what they perceived as two stinging defeats in Korea and Indochina.[36]

To bolster allied morale, Eisenhower discussed leaving a regimental combat team in Thailand or the Philippines as a symbol of the American commitment. American commanders in Asia supported measures of this type, but they also wanted to back such gestures with a show of force. One proposal, floated by General Hull and the head of the MAAG on Taiwan, was to use a portion of Chinese Nationalist forces as a strategic reserve that could be moved throughout Asia as needed.[37] General E. E. Partridge, Commander of the Far Eastern Air Force, developed a scheme to impress world opinion by luring Communist air craft into a fight over Japan. He proposed sending American planes up to the three-mile limit outside Shanghai in the hope that Chinese or Soviet planes would attempt a similar feat. At that point the enemy planes would be "maneuvered into violating international law," making them fair game for American pilots. General Nathan Twining, Air Force Chief of Staff, shelved Partridge's "show of force" proposals, explaining that "the tide of opinion within our government is strongly against provocative action by the U.S. in Asia. Even the most elementary defensive measures on our part are sometimes labelled evidence of a plan to initiate preventive war."[38]

Covert operations offered another means of countering Communist moves in the region. In 1953, as Laos seemed threatened and French fortunes in Vietnam sank, planners recommended increasing the American presence in Thailand through the development of a MAAG. These plans also called for the training of counterguerilla and paramilitary forces to operate beyond the Thai border. One of the French military's shortcomings, the Americans believed, was that they lacked the ability to conduct counterguerilla activities in Vietminh territory.[39] The United States, on the other hand, already had significant experience in this field.

Months after the conclusion of the Korean armistice, Chinese Nationalist forces, with the concurrence of Admiral Felix Stump, Commander in Chief, Pacific (CINCPAC), continued to raid the mainland. In March 1954, Stump proposed stepping up the tempo and increasing the size of Nationalist raids. The Admiral hoped to mount company- or batallion-size raids twice a month, and one division-size operation every quarter. Continuation of these raids would keep PRC forces off balance and force the Communists to disperse their troops. Moreover, Stump believed the attacks were necessary to maintain the "offensive spirit" of Nationalist forces and "wrest [the] military and psychological initiative from [the] ChiComs."[40] Stump's proposal won approval from Chief of Naval Operations Admiral Robert Carney, and, when Defense Secretary Wilson questioned the propriety of conducting raids after the armistice, Admiral Radford came to the defense of the plan.[41]

Significantly, many of the Nationalists' attacks on the mainland were launched from the offshore island groups of Jinmen and Mazu.

As early as June 1953, Stump requested permission to include the defense of the islands in the Seventh Fleet's area of responsibility. The Chiefs denied CINCPAC's request, but asked him to prepare a draft plan for the islands's defense. Completed in early 1954, Stump's plan called for air raids against mainland airbases and troop concentrations. The Admiral also expected to use atomic weapons early in the plan.[42] Thus, the JCS and the Pacific Command had already given some thought to the importance of the islands and their possible defense when the first offshore island crisis began with the shelling of Jinmen on September 3.

The JCS, with the exception of Ridgway, argued for defending the islands even to the point of attacking the mainland if an invasion seemed imminent. The Chiefs, minus Ridgway, believed that possession of the islands enabled the Nationalists to detect a pre-invasion buildup by the Communists. The islands were also vital to Nationalist morale in that they kept alive the hope of returning to the mainland. Most important of all, a strong defense of the islands would restore faith in American commitments throughout the region. Admiral Carney put it bluntly: "There appears to be a growing recognition that at some point, and at the risk of seriously enlarging the crisis, we must give substantial evidence of our determination to oppose Communism with something more than words and dollars. We need a victory."[43]

As in the Dienbienphu crisis, Ridgway's maverick position put him at odds with the JCS, but this time he also alienated the President. Although Ridgway eventually assented to the idea of sending atomic-capable Honest John rockets to Taiwan, he refused to close ranks with the Chiefs. Testifying before Congress, the general stated that the New Look had so weakened the Army that it could not defend Taiwan.[44] Despite the distraction created by this public attack on the New Look, Eisenhower maintained control over policy throughout the crisis.

It is not necessary to recount the full story of the first straits crisis here. It is sufficient to note that a pattern quickly emerged in the relations between the JCS and Eisenhower. The Chiefs consistently recommended strong measures to thwart an invasion and the President just as consistently rejected them. Eisenhower conceded that the islands were important to Nationalist morale, and he eventually took a more bellicose public stand, but he was thoroughly frustrated by what he perceived as the Chiefs' inability to understand his policy of reducing tensions in the straits.[45]

For their part, the Chiefs, likewise were disenchanted by the administration's unwillingness to challenge the Communists. In particular the JCS disapproved of the wording of the Chinese-American Mutual Defense Treaty. Reviewing a draft of the treaty, the Chiefs objected to phrasing that indicated that the treaty applied only to Taiwan and the Pescadores and those territories that were "required for their defense." This language, the JCS suggested, would "invite attack" upon Jinmen and Mazu since they were not required for the defense of the larger islands.[46] Through an apparently unintentional error, however, the original wording remained in the final version of the draft. Subsequently, the head of the MAAG on Taiwan sought to include the offshore islands in the treaty, and the Joint Intelligence Committee (JIC) warned that the Mutual Security Treaty and various statements by American officials "have given the Chinese Communists reason to believe that the U.S. would not intervene over the offshore islands."[47] The JIC also predicted that if the United States succeeded in pressuring Chiang to evacuate the less defensible Dazhens it would diminish American prestige in the region. This view was seconded by Admiral Carney, who considered the Formosa Resolution nothing more than a cover for the retreat from the Dazhens.[48]

Inasmuch as the crisis ended with the Nationalists still in possession of Jinmen and Mazu and with the United States having averted a fight with the PRC, Eisenhower could consider himself vindicated. The JCS, however, appear to have taken a different view of the situation. The President had succeeded, in the narrow sense, but at what cost? The security treaty was demoralizing, especially given the exchange of diplomatic notes that restrained Nationalist military activities. Moreover, Eisenhower's decision to press Chiang for the withdrawal of some of his forces from the islands had, according to the American ambassador, left the Generalissimo "visibly shaken."[49]

If the Chiefs viewed the resolution of the crisis as something short of a triumph, they were also forced to admit that their recommendations could stand some improvement. Stump described Jinmen as a "tough nut to crack," but he and the JCS recognized that atomic weapons would be needed to defend the island from an all-out attack. Although the Chiefs could not agree on the Soviet Union's response in such a case, they all predicted that the political damage to the United States would be enormous.[50] The problem seemed obvious. An alternative to either surrender or nuclear war had to be found.

Given the available evidence, it is impossible to determine the extent to which budgetary politics shaped the development of limited war doctrine in the mid-1950s. Clearly, Dienbienphu and the offshore island crisis provided the Army with ammunition to use against the administration's New Look. The Army's development of the Pentomic Division with its compliment of tactical nuclear weapons was almost certainly designed to secure a larger share of the budget and preserve a role for the service in modern warfare. But emphasis on interservice rivalry may obscure more important disagreements that existed within the Army itself.

In particular, it would seem that some distinction must be made between Ridgway's categorical opposition to intervention in Asia and the position represented by General James Gavin. As chief of planning during the Dienbienphu episode, Gavin supported Ridgway's stand against intervention. But whereas Ridgway opposed intervention on the grounds that the United States did not have enough troops, Gavin opposed involvement on the grounds that the United States did not have enough of the right *kind* of troops.[51] Like Ridgway, Gavin was critical of the Eisenhower budgets, but he also believed that the Army could fight and win the kinds of limited conflicts that were taking place in Asia. Gavin's answer to the problem was the development of "tactical nuclear missiles, sky cavalry, and increased assault airlift."[52]

Although the Army continued to clamor for more money to the end of the Eisenhower presidency, it also took steps to prepare itself for limited warfare using existing resources. Under the direction of General Maxwell Taylor, Ridgway's successor as Chief of Staff, the Army activated a special forces unit on Okinawa in 1957. Soon afterward, they were sent to Nha Trang in South Vietnam, where they began training Vietnamese Ranger units for combat behind enemy lines.[53] The Army also began an intensive program to develop and incorporate transport and assault helicopters, Gavin's "sky cavalry," into existing units to increase their mobility and firepower. By 1960 the Army had twelve helicopter battalions.[54]

The Navy also became a leading advocate of limited war preparation. According to Franz Schurman, the Navy's enthusiasm for limited warfare began about the time of Admiral Radford's retirement as Chief of the JCS in October 1957. His replacement, Air Force General Nathan Twining, was seen as unsympathetic to naval interests, and therefore the Navy, like the Army before it, broke ranks with the administration.[55] Once again it is difficult to gauge the influence of bureaucratic self-interest behind this change in doctrine. It does seem, however, that Schurman has exaggerated the importance of the Navy's budget anxieties during this period.

To begin with, the Navy was on record as predicting that as the Soviet Union improved its nuclear capability, and the credibility of the American deterrent diminished, the United States would have to improve its conventional forces. By 1955, as this moment drew near, Admiral Arleigh Burke began to reemphasize the Navy's conventional role. Ironically, the Navy's efforts to secure its share of the budget by developing a nuclear capability had left it less prepared for the mission it was now most likely to undertake. Studies indicated that long-range carrier-based atomic bombers were crowding tactical aircraft off the decks, leaving the carriers less able to operate in hostile waters.[56] Less glamorous vessels had also been neglected in the post–Korean War period. The evacuation of the Dazhens revealed that the Navy was deficient in destroyers and that assault craft and transport ships were approaching bloc obsolescence. In addition to calling for more funds to replenish its aging fleet, the Navy adopted new methods for conducting "brush fire wars." Like the Army, the Marine Corps also adopted the helicopter. Launched from specially converted carriers, these new units gave the Navy increased mobility for conventional war.[57]

The Air Force, which had long been dominated by the big bomber advocates, also appears to have experienced its share of factionalism in the mid-1950s. Towards the end of the decade, however, the Air Force began to give more attention to the problem of troop transport. During this period the Tactical Air Corps (TAC) also took steps to ready itself for intervention in Asia. Promised a larger share of the budget in 1957, TAC also made several administrative changes to increase its flexibility in the Pacific. In 1957 the boundary between the Far Eastern Command and CINCPAC was dissolved, and the Pacific Mobile Strike Force was readied for emergency deployment to Southeast Asia.[58]

The administration's performance during Dienbienphu and in the Taiwan Straits had convinced most military officers, especially those stationed in Asia, of the inadequacy of the New Look. By 1958, even John Foster Dulles questioned the wisdom of administration policy.[59] The erruption of a second crisis in the Taiwan Straits in 1958, provided the advocates of a flexible response with additional evidence with which to build their case.

Several developments distinguished the second crisis from its predecessor. First, in contrast to the earlier episode, Eisenhower announced early into the 1958 crisis that he considered Jinmen and Mazu to be important to the defense of Taiwan. Shortly after the first crisis had subsided, Chiang had reinforced the islands over the objections of the American adviser on Taiwan.[60] Loss of the islands now would deal a crushing blow to America's troublesome ally. Second, the United States had recently positioned nuclear-capable Matador missiles on Taiwan. Although the Matadors were not established on Taiwan until 1957, the decision to place the Intermediate Range Ballistic Missiles (IRBM) on the island was part of a basing plan drawn up by the Air Force in early 1956. The main objective at the time was simply to place the missiles within range of the Sino-Soviet bloc.

Other bases included those in England, Germany, Libya, Korea, and Japan. There were, however, secondary reasons for placing the Matadors on Taiwan. American officials hoped that the rotation of a squadron of the missiles through Taiwan would help prepare the Japanese for the eventual placement of IRBMs in the home islands. Admiral Stump also supported introducing the missiles into Taiwan because he believed it would boost Nationalist morale and involve the United States more closely in the defense of the island.[61] Although American officials spoke of the missiles in strictly defensive terms, it is clear that the Matadors, with their ability to reach most of Fujian province, raised the stakes of the contest in the Straits.

The third development was, perhaps, the most significant. In the period following the first crisis, the United States had reequipped the Nationalist Air Force with improved F-86 Sabre Jets. During the battle, the United States also began arming Nationalist planes with new Sidewinder air-to-air missiles. The most intensive fighting took place between September 18 and October 10, when Nationalist pilots downed twenty Chinese MiGs and damaged at least six more, while losing only one plane. According to an authority on the PRC Air Force, the outcome was "a clear-cut Nationalist triumph."[62]

The modernization of the Nationalist Air Force gave the Republic of China a vast superiority in air power and enabled its pilots to fly almost unopposed over PRC air space for years to come. In this sense, the transfer of the Sabre Jets and Sidewinders can be seen as a provocative escalation in the struggle over the straits.[63] There is evidence to suggest, however, that Eisenhower's intention was strictly defensive. During the first crisis a presidential aide had reported that the offshore islands were defensible providing the Nationalists did not face the massed power of the Communist Chinese Air Force.[64] Eisenhower probably reasoned that by modernizing the Nationalist Air Force, he minimized the chances of a successful Communist attack on the offshore islands, thereby reducing the need for direct American intervention.

Eisenhower, no doubt, viewed the conclusion of the crisis with a sense of relief. The advocates of flexible response, especially within the Navy, reacted somewhat differently. It would be difficult to exaggerate the Navy's sense of exhilaration following the 1958 crisis. "The Generalissimo's Air Force just whipped the hell out the Red Chinese," recalled Admiral Felt.[65] But Navy officers also emphasized the deterrent value of the more than 140 ships, including seven carriers, that had been committed to the support of Taiwan. Describing the crisis, the CINCPAC annual report boasted that "this was an outstanding case in which sea power was effectively used as a deterrent to aggression, and emphasized the need for adequate mobile naval and marine forces to counter limited aggression and to prevent the further spread of communist military advance."[66]

The second offshore island crisis not only affirmed the Navy's faith in flexible response, it also appears to have convinced observers of the need for even more demonstrations of U.S. power in the region. The Nationalist Air Force's victory did more than display the effectiveness of the latest U.S. technology. The second offshore crisis revealed the widening gap between the Soviet Union and its Chinese ally. American estimates of Communist Chinese air power had been calculated on the assumption of continued Russian support for the PRC's program. The dismal performance of Communist planes in the crisis indicated that these estimates and the overall assessment of the Sino-Soviet alliance might have to be revised.[67] The evidence, although slight at this time, seems to suggest that after 1958 American officials developed a split perception of the Chinese Communist threat. In the minds of these officials, the PRC still remained a revolutionary and wildly unpredictable force in Asia. At the same time, however, there appears to have been a growing sense that China was the most vulnerable it had been since the Korean War.

In the period after the second offshore island crisis, the JCS and their subordinates in the Pacific seemed almost eager for a test of strength on the periphery of China. Assessing the overall situation in East Asia in the summer of 1959, the JCS advocated a "long-range policy for support of some form of military activities by certain nations against Communist China, North Korea, and North Vietnam. These actions, which include reconnaisance in force, nuisance raids, probes, limited objective attacks and actions to rectify boundaries would be carried out without overt U.S. support."[68] The American response to the Laotion crisis that same year suggests that the JCS regarded these recommendations as more than just talking points.

During the summer and fall of 1959, CINCPAC and the JCS developed plans for possible intervention in support of the ailing Royal Laotion government. OPLAN 32(L)-59, as the plan was designated, immediately became the source of controversy within the JCS. As devised by CINCPAC, the plan called for the deployment of Marine units to hold the Vientiane and Seno airbases and the city of Vientiane. The plan also called for the preparation of an Army brigade task force comprised of two battle groups in the event they were needed to relieve the Marines. The overall concept of the plan was to hold the key areas of Laos with U.S. forces so that Laotian troops would be free to concentrate on the Pathet Lao, but an unseemly debate quickly developed over the use of Marines instead of Army forces in the initial operation.[69] Citing a 1958 Defense Department directive that defined the missions of each service, the Army Chief of Staff argued that the Marines were usurping the Army's role in Laos. The Navy countered that Army forces in the Pacific were not immediately available for the operation. Not to be left out, the Air Force weighed in with a recommendation that the expeditionary force be augmented with tactical air units from the Pacific Command.[70]

The dispute was eventually settled by permitting CINCPAC to continue planning for the use of Marine units until such time as Army forces were better prepared for emergency airlift into Laos. In early 1960, the JCS approved the stationing of an Army airborne battle group of two thousand men on Okinawa. The Army wasted little time in making the deployment. Although he was informed that the troops would be billeted in dilapidated housing abandoned by the Air Force and that no space was available for dependents, General Lyman Lemnitzer, the Army Chief of Staff, decided that conditions in Southeast Asia necessitated stationing troops on Okinawa for the normal three-year tour of duty.[71] In positioning this new airborne unit on Okinawa, the Army took a small but significant step toward intervention in Southeast Asia.

In December 1960, as the Laotian "crisis" worsened, Admiral Harry Felt, CINCPAC, called for American unilateral intervention to save the American-backed government of Phoumi Nosavan. Felt advised Washington that "the Reds are bluffing as they were in the Taiwan Strait affair and will back down if fired upon."[72] The President, as he had during the Diebienphu crisis, spoke of the need to prevent a Communist takeover, but ultimately decided against action. The Laotian "crisis" temporarily subsided only to flare up again the following year as the Kennedy administration took office.

Once again Eisenhower had decided "not to go to war." Events in Southeast Asia had come full circle, or so it seemed. In reality, important changes had taken place. In contrast to the earlier Indochinese crisis, the JCS, and in particular the Army Chief of Staff, showed a greater willingness to intervene. The difference between the two crises is important for what it reveals about the emerging consensus within the armed services.

When they first began to apply the New Look to Asia, the JCS and their field commanders confronted a host of obstacles. The specter of Chinese expansionism and the revolutionary conditions in Southeast Asia strained American capabilities and compelled a shift in strategic emphasis. The internal weaknesses of America's allies and the persistence of regional animosities impeded efforts to build a collective defense system for Asia. Some of these deficiencies could be offset by the integration of new weaponry into the region, but as the protests in Japan demonstrated, these new systems could be a mixed blessing. No easy solution to these problems emerged in the 1950s, but the JCS and their field commanders believed that without a consistently firm and assertive policy, the United States would fail to produce the "climate of victory" that the administration had declared as one of its goals when it entered office.[73]

We do not know how successful the JCS were in getting the President to accept their proposals for covert operations, but the available record does show that during periods of crisis the Chiefs failed to prod Eisenhower into bolder action. It is important, however, not to make too much of Eisenhower's skill as a crisis manager. A balanced assessment of the administration's Asian policy must take into account the less dramatic but equally important developments that occurred while the President attended to other business. The omnipresent military advisers, military aid missions, alliances, and mutual security treaties and Matadors on Taiwan, B-52s on Guam, and Honest Johns and Nikes in Korea, Okinawa, and Japan expanded and further militarized the American commitment in Asia. Given the momentum created by this buildup, it does not seem surprising that American field commanders sought to apply greater pressure against the Communist bloc. Nor does it seem surprising that what historians have praised as Eisenhower's skillful leadership looked to American commanders in Asia like a refusal to accept the logic of his own policies.

ACKNOWLEDGMENTS

Research for this essay was made possible through the generous support of the Navy Historical Center in the form of a Vice-Admiral Edwin B. Hooper postgraduate award. I also wish to thank J. Britt McCarley, Edward J. Marolda, and Michael A. Palmer for their assistance in preparing this paper.

NOTES

1. Edgar Kemler, "The Asia First Admiral," *Nation* (July 1954), 179:3, 47.

2. Stephen B. Ambrose, *Eisenhower*, vol. 2: *The President* (New York: Simon and Schuster, 1984), p. 213; Kemler, "Asia Admiral," p. 45; Leslie H. Gelb with Richard K. Betts, *The Irony of Vietnam: The System Worked* (Washington, D.C.: Brookings Institution, 1979), p. 57.

3. Franz Schurman, *The Logic of World Power* (New York: Pantheon, 1974); Richard Aliano, *American Defense Policy from Eisenhower to Kennedy: The Politics of Changing Military Requirements, 1957–1961* (Athens: Ohio University Press, 1975); Douglas Kinnard, *President Eisenhower and Strategy Management: A Study in Defense Politics* (Lexington: University Press of Kentucky, 1977); John L. Gaddis, *Strategies of Containment: A Critical Appraisal of Postwar American National Security Policy* (New York: Oxford University Press, 1982). For a study that deemphasizes the importance of economic considerations in Eisenhower's policy-making, see Richard Challener, "The National Security Policy from Truman to Eisenhower: Did the 'Hidden Hand' Leadership Make a Difference?" in Norman Graebner, ed., *The National Security in Theory and Practice, 1945–1960*, pp. 39–75 (New York: Oxford University Press, 1986).

4. Robert J. Watson, *History of the Joints Chiefs of Staff*, vol. 5: *The JCS and National Policy, 1953–1954* (Washington, D.C.: GPO, 1986).

5. Reexamination of U.S. Programs for National Security, NCS 141, January 19, 1953, reel 1, Documents of the NSC, First Supplement, University Publications of America (UPA); Brief of Far East Command Emergency War Plan, February 8, 1954, box 295, and Strategic Concept for Global War, September 7, 1955, box 314, both in OP-30S/OP-60s, Subject and Serial Files, series xvi, Records of the Strategic Plans Division, Operational Archives, Naval Historical Center, Washington, D.C. (hereafter cited as OP-30S, SPD, OA, NHC).

6. CINCFE to JCS, April 27, 1954, CCS USSR (3-2-46), sec. 73, RG 218 (Records of the JCS), Geographic File, 1957, Modern Military Reference Branch, National Archives, Washington, D.C. (hereafter cited as MMRB, NA).

7. Watson, *JCS and National Security*, pp. 228–29.

8. Review of U.S. Policy toward Southeast Asia, JSPC 958/141, December 21, 1953, CCS 092 Asia (6-25-48), sec. 52, RG 218, MMRB, NA: Ronald Spector, *Advice and Support: The Early Years, 1941–1960*, in The United States in Vietnam series, p. 209 (Washington, D.C.: GPO, 1983).

9. *Ibid.*, pp. 208–9; George C. Herring, *America's Longest War: The United States in Vietnam, 1950–1975*, 2nd ed. (New York: John Wiley 1986), pp. 35–37.; George C. Herring and Richard Immerman, "Eisenhower, Dulles, and Dienbienphu: 'The Day We Didn't Go to War' Revisited," *Journal of American History* (September 1984), pp. 343–63.

10. Spector, *Advice and Support*, pp. 200–3; Herring, *America's Longest War*, p. 32; Gelb with Betts, *Irony of Vietnam*, pp. 56–57.

11. The Navy did send reconnaissance flights over North Vietnam, and the American carriers steamed within a hundred miles of Hainan. Edwin B. Hooper et al., *The United States Navy and the Vietnam Conflict*, vol. 1: *The Setting of the Stage to 1959* (Washington, D.C. GPO, 1976), pp. 252–53; Herbert Malloy Mason, Jr., *The United States Air Force: A Turbulent History* (New York: Mason/Charter, 1976), p. 233.

12. Army Position on NSC 1074-A, ND, doc. 31, *Pentagon Papers*, Senator Gravel edition (Boston: Beacon Press, 1971), pp. 471–72; Spector, *Advice and Support*, pp. 208–9.

13. Memo for the Record, October 19, 1953, box 28, Official Correspondence, Matthew B. Ridgway Papers, Military History Institute, Carlisle, Penn. (hereafter cited as MHI); Watson, *JCS and National Security*, pp. 231–32.

14. Notes on talk with General Hull, October 28, 1953, box 28, Official Correspondence, Ridgway Papers, MHI.

15. Michael A. Palmer, *Origins of the Maritime Strategy: American Naval Strategy in the First Postwar Decade* (Washington, D.C.: G.P.O., 1988), 21–32.

16. *Ibid.*, pp. 82–83; Study of Attack Carrier Force Levels, October 13, 1953, A-4, box 286, 1953, OP-30S, SPD, OA, NHC.

17. SecNav to SecDef, January 21, 1953, A-16-1, 1953, 00 (Chief of Navy Operations Correspondence), OA, NHC.

18. Redeployment of U.S. Forces from the Far East, memo, July 8, 1954, A-16-1, box 229, OP-30S, SPD, OA, NHC.

19. Army Chief of Staff's Testimony before Congress, Department of the Army Appropriations for 1955, Hearings before the Subcommittee of the Committee on Appropriations, House of Rep., 83rd Cong., 2nd sess., Ridgway Papers, MHI.

20. MAAG Personnel School, memo, October 9, 1957, CCS 352 (4-9-57); SecDef, Tour of Duty MAAG Chiefs, memo, December 7, 1959, CCS 9143/5791, Japan, RG 218, MMRB, NA.

21. JSSC et al. to Chairman JCS, memo, March 22, 1956, CJCS 381 Military Strategy and Posture, RG 218, Chairman's Files (Radford), MMRB, NA.

22. Admiral Harry Felt, U.S. Naval Institute Oral History (copy in OA, NHC), p. 445.

23. Memo to CNO, OPPlan nos. 41–52, April 14, 1953, A-4-3, box 280, OP-30S, OA, NHC.

24. *U.S.–Vietnam Relations,* 1945–1967 (Washington, D.C.: G.P.O., 1971) iv, A.4, pp. 1.1–4.1, 24.

25. Robert F. Futrell, *The United States Air Force in Southeast Asia: The Advisory Years to 1965* (Washington, D.C.: G.P.O., 1981), p. 40.

26. Edward J. Marolda and Oscar P. Fitzgerald, *The United States Navy and the Vietnam Conflict,* vol. 2: *From Military Assistance to Combat, 1959–1965* (Washington, D.C. G.P.O., 1986), p. 336.

27. Basic National Security Policy, NSC 162/2, October 30, 1953, *U.S.–Vietnam Relations,* bk. 9, V. B. 3, pp. 171–200; Watson, *JCS and National Security,* pp. 229–51, 275.

28. MDAP Support for Japanese Submarine Construction, memo, July 27, 1954, box 307, and Commander VavFE to CINCFE, September 30, 1953, EF-37, box 289, both in OP-30S, SPD, OA, NHC.

29. JSSC et al. to CJCS (Radford), March 22, 1956, CJCS 381 Military Strategy and Posture, RG 218, Chairman's Files (Radford), MMRB, NA; Henry William Brands, Jr., "The United States and the Reemergence of Independent Japan," *Pacific Affairs* (Fall 1986), 59:3, 391.

30. CINCFE to JCS, January 10, 1955, CCS 092 Japan (12-12-50), sec. 19, 218, MMRB, NA; Director Strategic Plans to DCNO, June 27, 1955, EF-37 Japan, box 326, 1955, OP-30S, SPD, OA, NHC. See also Martin Weinstein, *Japan's Postwar Defense Policy, 1947–1968* (New York: Columbia University, Press, 1971).

31. CINCFE to JCS, JSDF Levels, March 19, 1955, CCS 092 Japan (12-12-50), sec. 20, and CINCFE to General Taylor, August 29, 1955, CCS 092 Japan (12-12-50), sec. 21, both in RG 218 Geographic File, MMRB, NA. In 1960 the JCS estimated that eighty mobile tankers would be needed to replace facilities in Japan. Review of Overseas Military Bases, April 1960, NSC minutes of mtgs., with Special Advisory Reports, reel 3, UPA.

32. Brands, "Reemergence of Japan," p. 396.

33. CINCFE to JCS, January 18, 1957, CCS 092 Japan (12-12-50), sec. 22, RG 218, Geographic File, MMRB, NA.

34. CINCFE to Taylor, August 19 and 27, 1955, CCS 092 Japan (12-12-50), sec. 21, RG 218, Geographic File, MMRB, NA; George Packard, *Protest in Tokyo: The Security Crisis of 1960* (Westport, Conn.: Greenwood Press, 1978), pp. 35–41.

35. 206th mtg., NSC, memo of discussion, July 30, 1954, Declassified Documents Reference System, NSC, 002165, 1986 (hereafter cited as DDRS).

36. On SEATO, see Radford to SecDef, February 11, 1955, 092.2 SEATO, RG 218, Chairman's Files (Radford), MMRB, NA; U.S.–Vietnam Relations, iv, A.4, p. 11; Radford to SecDef, Preparations of DOD on Geneva Conference, U.S.–Vietnam

Relations, bk. 9, v. B. 3., pp. 266–70; interview with General Hull, July 23, 1954, J. E. Hull Papers, MHI.

37. Hull also wanted Taiwan included in SEATO, *ibid.* Hull to CINCPAC, January 14, 1954, CCS 381, Formosa (11-8-48), sec. 13; William Chase, Chief, MAAG Taipei, to DeptAr, February 7, 1953, CCS 381 Formosa (11-8-48), sec. 10, RG 218, MMRB, NA.

38. E. E. Partridge to Twining, ca. February 1955, and Twining to Partridge, February 23, 1955, box 81, Chief of Staff Files, Nathan F. Twining Papers, Library of Congress, Washington, D.C. (hereafter cited as NFT Papers).

39. U.S. Psychological Strategy, July 2, 1953, reel 2, minutes of NSC mtgs. with Special Advisory Reports.

40. Carney to JCS, forwarding CINCPAC Plan, March 31, 1954, OP-30S, SPD, OA, NA.

41. *Ibid.;* Wilson to Robert Cutler, October 5, 1954, and Radford to Wilson, October 10, 1954, DDRS, DOD, 001836-37, 1986.

42. CNO to JCS, June 29, 1953, CNO to JCS, July 30, 1953, and CNO to JCS, September 21, 1953, EF-16 China, box 289, 1953, OP-30S, SPD, OA, NHC; U.S. Policy Regarding Offshore Islands, September 6, 1954, CJCS 091 China, RG 218, Chairman's Files (Radford), MMRB, NA.

43. Navy comments on U.S. Policy Regarding Offshore Islands, September 6, 1954, Air Force comment, September 6, 1954, and Chairman JCS comment, September 11, 1954, CJCS 091 China September 1954, RG 218, Chairman's Files (Radford) MMRB, NA. Also CINCPAC to CNO, October 10, 1954, CCS 381 Formosa (11-8-48), sec. 15, RG 218, Geographic File, MMRB, NA.

44. Ambrose, *Eisenhower*, 2:234.

45. Leonard Gordon, "United States Opposition to Use of Force in the Taiwan Strait, 1954," *Journal of American History* (December 1985), 72:3, 641. Robert A. Divine, *Eisenhower and the Cold War* (New York: Oxford University Press, 1981), pp. 60–61.

46. Memo for SecDef, December 1, 1954, CCS 381 Formosa (11-8-48), sec. 16, RG 218, Geographic File, MMRB, NA.

47. JIC, Intelligence Estimate of Situation in Tachen Islands," *ibid.;* Chief of MAAG, Taipei, January 10, 1955, CJCS 091 China RG 218, Chairman's Files (Radford), MMRB, NA; Watson, *JCS and National Security*, p. 264.

48. Ambrose, *Eisenhower*, 2:232.

49. Rankin to Dulles, April 22, 1955, CJCS 091 China (April–December 1955), RG 218, Chairman's Files (Radford), MMRB, NA.

50. CINCPAC to CNO, October 10, 1954, CCS Formosa (11-8-48), sec. 15, RG 218, Geographic File, MMRB, NA; Director Strategic Plans (Navy) to CNO, March 19, 1955, A-16-1, OP-30S, SPD, OA, NHC; Joint Intelligence Group to Radford, March 16, 1955, CJCS 091 China (February–March 1955), Chairman's Files (Radford), MMRB, NA.

51. Lt. Gen. James M. Gavin, *War and Peace in the Space Age* (New York: Harper, 1958), pp. 127–28. Spector also indicates that there were some disagreements within the Army staff. Spector, *Advice and Support*, pp. 200–1. The Army's reorganization is described in Russell F. Weigley, *History of the United States Army*, enl. ed. (Bloomington: Indiana University Press, 1984), p. 538.

52. Gavin, *War and Peace.*

53. Larry E. Cable, *Conflict and Myths: The Development of American Counterinsurgency Doctrine and the Vietnam War* (New York: New York University Press, 1986), pp. 143–48.

54. Allan R. Millet and Peter Maslowski, *For the Common Defense: A Military History of the United States of America* (New York: Free Press, 1984), pp. 528–30.

55. Schurman, *Logic of World Power*, pp. 291–92.

56. DCNO (Air) to CNO, October 26, 1955, A-16-3, 00 Files, Chief of Naval Operations, and Commander 7th Fleet, Report of Operations, July 1, 1956–June 30, 1957, Command File, both in OA, NHC; Edward J. Marolda, "The Influence of Burke's Boys on Limited War," *U.S. Naval Institute Proceedings* (August 1981), 107:8, 36–42; Challener, "Policy from Truman to Eisenhower," p. 65.

57. Millet and Maslowski, *Common Defense*, p. 529; Report of Operations, U.S. 7th Fleet, July 1, 1954–June 30, 1955, Command File, OA, NHC.

58. Futrell, *Air Force in Southeast Asia*, p. 45; Samuel P. Huntington, *The Common Defense: Strategic Programs in National Defense* (New York: Columbia University Press, 1961), pp. 352–53.

59. Challener, "Policy from Truman to Eisenhower," p. 65.

60. MAAG (Formosa) to CINCPAC, June 17, 1955, and MAAG (Formosa) to CINCPAC, September 18, 1955, both in CCS 381 Formosa (11-8-48), sec. 29, RG 218, MMRB, NA; Chalmers Roberts, "Caught in a Trap of Our Own Making," *Reporter*, October 2, 1958, pp. 11–13.

61. Twining to Secretary of the Air Force, March 28, 1956, box 92, Chief of Staff, 1957, NFT Papers; CINCFE to JCS, May 29, 1956, and memo for Chairman, JCS, March 20, 1957, both in CCS 381 Far East (11-28-50), sec. 29, 30, RG 218, MMRB, NA. The negotiations for basing the missiles can be followed in *Foreign Relations of the United States, 1955–1957*, vol. 3: *China* (Washington, D.C. GPR, 1986), esp. pp. 283–84, 356–57, 406–7.

62. Richard Bueschel, *Communist Chinese Air Power* (New York: Praeger, 1968), p. 54; Hooper et al., *U.S. Navy and the Vietnam Conflict*, pp. 358–59; Radford to Asst. SecDef, September 2, 1955, CCS 381 Formosa (11-8-48), sec. 29, RF 218, Geographic File, MMRB, NA.

63. Bueschel, *Chinese Air Power*, p. 56.

64. Ambrose, *Eisenhower*, 2:237.

65. Admiral Harry Felt Oral History, p. 390.

66. CINCPAC Annual Report, July 27, 1959, Command File, OA, NHC.

67. Asher Lee, "Red China's Air Power," *Military Review* (August 1963), 43:8, 80-85; David Allan Mayers, *Cracking the Monolith: U.S. Policy Against the Sino-Soviet Alliance* (Baton Rouge: Louisiana State University Press, 1986), p. 155.

68. Memo for Depy. Asst. SecDef, July 14, 1959, *U.S.–Vietnam Relations*, bk. 10, pp. 1211-36. See also Jaya Krishna Beral, *The Pentagon Papers and the Making of U.S. Foreign Policy: A Case Study of Vietnam, 1960–1968* (New Delhi: Radiant Publishers, 1978); Marolda and Fitzgerald, *U.S. Navy and the Vietnam Conflict*, p. 96.

69. CINCPAC to CINCUNC, OPLAN-32 (L)-59, May 21, 1959, CCS 3146 CINC-PAC-CINCUNC, RG 218, Central File, MMRB, NA; Marolda, *U.S. Navy and the Vietnam Conflict*, pp. 26–38; Spector, *Advice and Support*, p. 359.

70. Director of Operations to Sec, JCS, July 27, 1959, and Air Force comment, August 24, 1959, both in CCS 3146 CINCPAC-CINCUNC (May 21, 1959), RG 218, Central File, MMRB, NA; Spector, *Advice and Support*, p. 359.

71. JCS 2147/188, February 12, 1960, memo for Twining, February 10, 1960, Memo from Army Chief of Staff, February 9, 1960, and memo for SecDef, February 12, 1960, all in CCS 9147/3410, Ryuku Islands (Okinawa), September 5, 1959, RG 218, Central File, MMRB, NA.

72. Marolda and Fitzgerald, *U.S. Navy and the Vietnam Conflict*, p. 54.

73. U.S. Psychological Strategy with respect to the Peoples of Southeast Asia, July 2, 1953, reel 2, minutes of mtgs. of NSC with Special Advisory Reports, UPA; William B. Pickett, "The Eisenhower Solarium Notes," *Society for Historians of American Foreign Relations Newsletter* (June 1985), pp. 1–10.

4

Eisenhower and Sino-American Confrontation

☯

WALDO HEINRICHS
Temple University

The declared foreign policy of the Eisenhower administration is not in doubt. The premise was a long, worldwide struggle with the Communist powers. It was taken for granted that Moscow and its minions—most importantly Red China—sought the destruction of the United States and the free world. The United States was determined to defend, by war and nuclear war if necessary, the Western Hemisphere, the NATO zone, the Western Pacific offshore island chain, and South Korea, where U.S. troops remained. It was also determined to honor commitments to a growing list of associated and client states around the rim of Eurasia, even if these commitments might eventuate in war.

The United States could not fight everywhere and anywhere, however. Even one more Korea was too much. The health of the American economy and support of the American public must be sustained. Accordingly, by Eisenhower doctrine, the United States would respond to Communist aggression by means, including nuclear, and at places of its own choosing. Conventional attack by a Communist satellite nation could incur massive retaliation against the center, the Soviet Union. The threat of using nuclear weapons and the means of delivering them offered the best hope, it was held, for deterring Communist expansion at an affordable cost. The United States would build up its strategic weapons—in the Air Force and carrier component of the Navy—and reduce its personnel, especially in the Army.

This way the nation could sustain a prolonged cold war. Stabilizing confrontation ultimately offered the prospect of change in the Communist world, which would lead to settlement and peace.

The United States did not expect to carry on alone. Allies were no less important in the Eisenhower theory of policy than in the Truman. They formed the cold war lines, controled strategic locations, and provided bases and the bulk of conventional forces. America's free world alliances provided the sanction for use of force. Therefore, while little was expected of diplomacy with the enemy, much was required of diplomacy among friends.

The dilemmas and dangers of this scheme were apparent even at the time. In 1953, when Eisenhower was considering use of atomic weapons to end the Korean War, he worried about Soviet retaliatory strikes against Japanese cities. As the decade passed, the stakes vastly increased. Thermonuclear weapons arrived, as well as Soviet and American intercontinental bombers, then intermediate range and intercontinental ballistic missiles. Nuclear war would now be heartland to heartland and world-devastating. Uniting allies to confront anything but an absolute challenge would be difficult. Yet, in Eisenhower's view, the free world position was in danger of being nibbled to death by subversion and marginal encroachments. Unqualified objectives, burgeoning commitments, and limited means, short of nuclear, meant inherent contradiction in Eisenhower policy.

But it seemed to work, if only because Dwight David Eisenhower was President. At least, so the prevailing view contends. The picture of a passive, bumbling President is gone. Historians now see him as forceful, intelligent, shrewd, subtle, cautious, flexible, and realistic. There was beauty in his ambiguity, control in his indirection. The farther we get from the Eisenhower years, the better they look: he kept the peace; the country flourished; the free world remained secure.

East Asia is an attractive sector of the cold war for testing the Eisenhower virtues. It offers an opportunity for best-case analysis. Middle East policy was tangled and obscure. Summitry came to a dismal end, arms limitation never got going, and an open-ended, escalating race continued in strategic arms. In East Asia, on the other hand, the United States did not (but almost did) go to war. There, confrontation was clear-cut, stable, and policy was a showcase of consistency, firmness, and restraint. Or so it seems.[1]

A mong the crises that defined the East Asian confrontation the most lethal was the first, reaching an armistice in the Korean War. It was explosive because American troops were immediately involved and the public and leaders had reached a stage of impassioned frustration over the war. Taken in isolation, the armistice negotiations seem brisk and businesslike. Twenty-one months after the talks began, progress occurred on the most difficult issue, prisoners of war, and in ten weeks the two sides had a solution. Chinese Foreign Minister Zhou Enlai accepted an exchange of sick and wounded March 28, 1953, and two days later relaxed Communist insistence on an all-for-all exchange. On April 6 the two sides met to make arrangements for exchange of sick and wounded; on April 20 the exchange began, and on May 3 it was complete. Meanwhile plenary sessions resumed at Panmunjom on April 26. The real issue was provision for political asylum for prisoners who did not wish to return to their native lands. On May 7 the Peoples Republic of China (PRC) and North Korea adopted a key provision of the United Nations General Assembly resolution of December 1952 by accepting a neutral nations repatriation commission. They no longer insisted on moving prisoners out of Korea to the custodial nation. The United States accepted the commission idea but sought to exclude Communist personnel from South Korea, to allow release of Korean nonrepatriates without neutral custody, and to limit the custodial period. On May 26 the United States backed off on release of nonrepatriates, on June 4 the other side implicitly accepted a time limit, and on June 8 the delegates at Panmunjom signed. Concessions were mutual and reciprocal, but by far the most important of them, allowing asylum, came from the PRC–North Korean side.[2]

The paths to settlement were by no means as straightforward as these formalities suggest, however, and Washington was not pulling all the strings. The most important factor in the settlement surely was the Chinese concession of March 30 on exchange of prisoners. The stand against forced repatriation had been central to American policy since 1951, and it could hardly be less so for Eisenhower. It is true that the breakthrough began with an American suggestion for exchange of sick and wounded, but this, in turn, was based on the belief that the idea would soon be laid before the UN General Assembly and that the United States could scarcely lose by supporting it. China and the Soviet Union must have understood from American tough talk such as "unleashing" of Chiang Kai-shek that the new administration was likely to intensify and extend the war if it failed to get a settlement before too long and that its patience was not inexhaustible. Nevertheless, it is hard to imagine the Zhou initiative occurring without the death of Stalin and new Soviet interest in a relaxation of cold war tensions.

As Edward Keefer shows, the Eisenhower administration really had no conception of how to end the war except by expanding it—and it "thrashed about" for months on how to expand it. In these deliberations within the National Security Council (NSC), the President, in his curious way, exercised a restraining influence. He made sure his advisers understood that he was prepared to use atomic weapons in certain circumstances, but he never concurred in any specific recommendation as to their use. On the contrary, when the military advised that Korea did not offer adequate nuclear targets, he suggested use of these weapons at Kaesong and against deeply entrenched positions along the Korean front. When the military talked of the atomic bombing of Chinese bases, he worried about Soviet retaliation. And once the Panmunjom negotiations resumed, he bluntly overrode the suggestion of John Foster Dulles that the UN improve its position by striking for the "waist" of Korea. These presidential negatives made it clear to all at the NSC that he would stay on the diplomatic track. Knowing what probably would occur if diplomacy failed, officials were the more inspired to look for satisfactory formulas.[3]

An old hand in managing alliances, Eisenhower nevertheless fumbled his way in dealing with South Korea. President Syngman Rhee, as the United Nations Command and the State Department were aware, posed a serious problem. Deputy Assistant Secretary of State U. Alexis Johnson put it bluntly: Rhee wanted to get to the Yalu with American help or get a security pact.[4] To appease Rhee, the United Nations Command (UNC) was allowed on May 13 to propose that Korean nonrepatriates be released as soon as an armistice came into effect. This, as Undersecretary of State Walter Bedell Smith later admitted, was a mistake.[5] It overturned the principle of neutral custodianship upon which compromise depended. The United States was perceived as upping its demands, while the other side conceded—a backward step, as the Communist side said, and America's allies soon learned of it.

Distrustful of the Eisenhower administration to begin with, Britain and the NATO partners were furious. As the NSC considered military alternatives May 13, the President asked about the effect on Europe of a broadening of the war. NATO might fall apart, he was told, but could be rebuilt if general war were avoided. "We desperately need . . . to maintain these outposts of national defense," said Eisenhower, "and we do not wish our allies to desert us." Relations with Britain, he admitted, had come to the lowest point since World War II. They were, Smith warned Eisenhower May 18, "deteriorating daily," especially on the point of Korean nonrepatriates and insistence on unanimity of the members of the custodial commission.[6] At this point the United States accepted the turning over of all prisoners to the neutral commission and a vote by majority on that commission. Furthermore, it accepted disposition of nonrepatriates by the United Nations without time limit as an alternative to disposition by a peace conference with time limit. With the American position now approximating the United Nations General Assembly resolution, the Panmunjom negotiations moved on to successful conclusion.

Accompanying these concessions and what the United States considered its final offer of May 23 were warnings to China by way of India and to the Soviet Union.[7] Failure of settlement would result in stronger exertion and might extend the area of conflict. The precise nature of this warning is in question. Certainly the United States wished to convey the possibility of nuclear attack, which was indeed an alternative under active consideration in case the negotiations failed. But the warnings on record (as distinct from recollections) were not explicitly nuclear, and Eisenhower had not decided that this would be his alternative in case of diplomatic failure. In fact, he had expressed anxiety about it. Furthermore, nuclear attack, according to the plan, would be accompanied by a ground offensive in Korea, which would require several months to prepare. Accordingly, the nuclear option must be considered hypothetical at this stage, and the warning very serious but deliberately ambiguous. It was designed to give a final shove to a movement already underway rather than to turn the other side around.

Eisenhower and his advisers had still not fully reckoned with President Rhee. On June 18 he released 25,000 of the 35,000 Korean prisoners who rejected repatriation. The armistice now depended on whether the PRC and North Korea would tolerate this defiant repudiation of a key provision of the signed agreement. The Americans were not without responsibility for the crisis. They had themselves put forward this alternative to appease Rhee. The UNC had located prisoners rejecting repatriation in camps on the mainland mostly under Korean guard, while those seeking it were kept on offshore islands.

To pacify Rhee, the Eisenhower administration finally accepted what it had so far rejected, a mutual defense treaty with Korea. Dulles feared that such a bilateral arrangement would detract from the United Nations character of the Korean action and that it would provide an American guarantee of South Korean control of the North when Rhee did not possess it.[8] With the whole settlement in doubt, however, Eisenhower concluded that Rhee's price would have to be paid, and therefore he reluctantly accepted a more explicit Asian mainland commitment than he wished or expected.

The Eisenhower administration did not bungle the peace. It succeeded. It demonstrated realism, caution, sense of strategic priorities, and at times skill. It was not especially perceptive, nor always in control of events. Like other nations, Eisenhower's America reacted at critical times to pressures from elsewhere; it depended on others; it paid a price. To secure an armistice, it raised the stakes of confrontation and expanded commitments and the parameters of confrontation beyond Truman's.

I n 1954 Indochina, as John Foster Dulles said at the time, was "fraught with anxiety and danger."[9] Korea and Indochina were both serious crises but for opposite reasons. Korea was a closed-end crisis with fixed circumstances and few variables: a circumscribed, established battle front, allies, a UN sanction, and a narrow agenda for negotiation. Indochina was a large, novel, indeterminate sector of the cold war. At risk, in the American mind, was not just Indochina but all of Southeast Asia. The challenge was not cross-frontier aggression but the more obscure and morally ambiguous condition of externally supported national revolution. Here the United States had no alliance system in place. On the other hand, in Indochina American troops were not yet in the fight. The flag had not been thrown forward. American public feeling had not become engaged. In Korea the danger lay in crossing lines, transcending the narrow limits of the conflict; in Indochina it lay in drawing lines.

The Indochina crisis of 1954 came in three stages, which can conveniently be labeled the Dienbienphu, Indochina, and Southeast Asia stages. The first of these began with the Vietminh investment of the French battalions in that remote Tonkin valley in December 1953 and became acute on March 13, 1954, when the Vietminh attacked. While discussion among Eisenhower policy-makers turned on the larger question of defense of Southeast Asia, the practical question of this period, especially after the visit to Washington of General Paul Ely, was American assistance in sustaining that embattled outpost. The Dienbienphu phase ended April 4, 1954, when the President laid down conditions for intervention that ultimately proved impossible to fulfill. This was a formative stage in which the conceptual and practical difficulties of the Eisenhower foreign policy scheme were painfully evident.

One problem was identifying the enemy. Was it the Vietminh or the PRC? Eisenhower and his advisers assumed the latter; China, to Eisenhower, was the "head of the snake." The PRC had supplied artillery, trucks, and communications equipment for the siege of Dienbienphu. Yet the fighters were Vietminh, and they incurred huge casualties. In intelligence estimates the Chinese role, if anything, dwindled during the crisis: fewer Chinese personnel than suspected were among the besiegers. Five Chinese divisions lay close to Indochina, but PRC armies lay well back from the frontier; the nearest jet airfields were at Canton.[10]

The international facts of life were there to see. Powerful indigenous revolutionary forces were at work in Vietnam. Since they were succeeding, China had little to do but maintain its existing flow of supplies. With Geneva in the wings, it had every interest in avoiding overt intervention and maintaining a low profile.

Into the gap between American preconception and international reality crept wishful thinking, comforting but inaccurate historical analogies, and oversimplifying imagery. "Falling dominoes" and its companion image "chain reaction" are a case in point. The domino image had a powerful hold on Eisenhower, perhaps because it derived from painful personal experience. Historians easily forget that his selection for the Operations Division at Washington in December 1941, opening his way to high command, came as a result of his East Asian experience. He had served four and one-half years as chief of staff to the military adviser of the Philippines government, General Douglas MacArthur. His job in the OPD was to rush reinforcements to the region, and he watched helplessly as Japanese forces, staged from, among other bases, Indochina, cascaded triumphantly southward through Malaya and the Philippines to the Dutch East Indies and almost to Australia.[11] Rippling catastrophe in that particular setting was easy for him to imagine. Successive Japanese assaults in 1941–42 strengthened the idea of a sequence of revolutions directed from afar in 1954. Giap could be seen as a modern Yamashita.

The idea of Chinese Communist imperial expansion in Southeast Asia was the regnant image of Eisenhower's approach to the Indochina crisis. Reinforcing it was the lesson of appeasement in the 1930s, the failure, as Eisenhower put it to Winston Churchill, "to halt Hirohito, Hitler, and Mussolini by not acting in unity and in time."[12] This central notion affected the way he looked at all elements of the problem, not least the French aspects.

France wanted American material aid but shunned formal partnership in Indochina. French and American military staffs and technicians worked closely together, but covertly. The French finally sought an American air strike at Dienbienphu, but almost as a parallel and separate war not as a joint enterprise. France saw no point in fighting for Indochina without ultimate control and found it impossible to conceive of sharing a colony with another power. Regarding Indochina's ultimate disposition, it was determined not to tie itself to the United States and hoped that Geneva would, if necessary, provide an honorable or at least practical way out.

Eisenhower was slow to accept these realities. He was no Francophile. France, in his view, was a declining power, lacking effective leadership, blind to the fact that the Soviet Union, not Germany, was its enemy now. The French, he had said during the war in Europe, were causing him more trouble than anything but the weather. Their policies in Indochina seemed totally benighted. Their Vietnamese troops lacked the will to fight because France failed to promise complete independence. Such a promise now, he believed (the example of the Philippines undoubtedly in mind), would permit France to remain as protector for twenty-five years and to retain bases thereafter. When the United States made such an offer to the Puerto Ricans, he wrote, they "ran for [the] cover" of American protection. What France needed, he told the NSC, was a "good Buddhist leader to whip some real fervor" into the Vietnamese. Someone pointed out, to everyone's merriment, that unhappily Buddha was a pacifist.[13]

Nevertheless France seemed indispensable. It was the centerpiece of NATO. It was close to a vote on the European Defense Community, a project Eisenhower had pressed as NATO commander. And it was currently the front line of defense against communism in Asia. Therefore, he met every practicable French request for assistance through March 1954. Somehow, he believed, the French must be brought to their senses. "This means frank talk" with them, he wrote Churchill, which is what the latter himself had prescribed for such occasions. Eisenhower pointed to *Their Finest Hour:* had the British voiced their misgivings about French strategy and dispositions at the start of war in 1939, Churchill's history read, the debacle of 1940 might have been avoided.[14] The idea that frank talk would move the French in this excruciating moment of their history was sheer illusion.

United Action, the idea of a broader coalition to defend Indochina, was no less chimerical. Dulles described the purpose of the coalition as deterrence, but it was more than that. It was coercive, designed, as Eisenhower explained to Churchill, to force the Chinese to cease materiel support to the Vietminh and accept "discreet disengagement" from Indochina. The key to any such coalition was Britain, but Churchill and Anthony Eden, with Geneva in view, had no desire whatsoever for confrontation with the PRC. For every possible reason—personal, Parliamentary, strategic, historic, economic—British policy was firmly set on the diplomatic track, as Eden and Sir Roger Makins tried again and again to convey to the Americans. Dulles and Eisenhower stressed that Britain, with twenty-two battalions fighting Communist insurgency in Malaya, had an equal stake in Indochina.[15] However, whereas Americans looked upon Malaya as the left flank of a northward-facing common defense, London regarded it as the eastern extremity of British power. No amount of American blandishment could warm the British to intervention in this form at this time. To borrow the words of Lord Curzon on a similar occasion in a bygone era, the feet of the Prime Minister were "positively glacial."

What the United States might have done in various circumstances to prevent a Communist victory in Indochina is hard to tell. It seems clear that in the unlikely event of Chinese air intervention over Indochina, the President would have retaliated after securing authority from Congress. It also seems clear that, as George Herring and Richard Immerman have shown, Eisenhower at this stage had not excluded an air strike at Dienbienphu. Dulles' memorandum of his conversation with the President March 24 suggests that Eisenhower did not rule out a "single strike if it was almost certain to produce decisive results," even though his political conditions for intervention had not been met. Admiral Arthur Radford, chairman of the JCS, warned the same day that the United States must be ready to act "promptly and in force possibly to a frantic and belated request by the French for intervention."[16] He was authorized to go ahead with joint planning for the operation that came to be designated VAUTOUR. On April 6, after France had called for a strike, Eisenhower criticized Radford, not for the plan, but for promising a foreign government to do his best to win acceptance of it. Only later did he find the idea "astonishing."[17] On several occasions in the following days, Eisenhower mentioned the possibility of intervention in the battle, though in varying and obscure ways. Meanwhile, without a decision for intervention, planes from U.S. carriers in the Gulf of Tonkin were conducting reconnaissance of South China airfields, which flights of course served as a display of strength.

If the possibility of a strike was very much on his mind, so were the risks and preconditions. Eisenhower was a Grant and not a Sherman; he liked to operate on a broad front at low risk. He could not imagine why the French had sent troops to Dienbienphu in the first place. His every instinct would recoil at the idea of launching a battle group deep into hostile territory without a secure line of communication. To reporters he mentioned Anzio as an appropriate analogue, disappointing and costly as that precarious lodgment in Italy was. More likely he had in mind Arnheim, Stalingrad, or Bataan. Considering the proximity of French and Vietminh forces, only yards apart, he may also have remembered the casualties suffered, in spite of extravagant precautions, by American soldiers from bombing by their own planes during the breakout phase of the battle of Normandy. He undoubtedly worried about General Matthew Ridgway's warning that aerial attack was bound to lead to ground involvement. He had once described Ridgway as "one of the finest soldiers" World War II had produced.[18] Eisenhower was horrified by the idea of another land war in Asia: "Indochina would absorb our troops by divisions." The United States must protect its mobile reserves: "outpost forces should not be drawn from the central 'keep.' "[19] Fighting a colonial war, fighting a war without a broad coalition including Britain, fighting any war without authority from Congress, went entirely against the grain of Eisenhower's beliefs, experience, and professional values.

The President had to consider the possibility that intervention would lead to war with China, which in turn would escalate to general war. Here, however, the state of the arms race may have been more encouraging to intervention than a restraint, for Washington still believed in the spring of 1954 that it had several years' lead, if not in thermonuclear weapons, then in the means of delivering them. Some officials felt that the Southeast Asia question should be definitively resolved while there was time.[20]

Powerful influences restrained Eisenhower. Yet at this stage a more powerful, even mesmerizing one pushed him ahead. This was the idea of drawing the line against the spread of communism in Southeast Asia. On March 29 word arrived that the second and what appeared to be final Vietminh assault on Dienbienphu had begun. Eisenhower now had to decide whether to intervene or not because a French request was bound to arrive soon. He had to balance the costs and risks and determine the conditions that would make intervention possible. Domino imagery still cast its spell, but certain realities began to sink in. First, all four service chiefs opposed, though in varying degrees, American air intervention under present conditions; Radford, in favor, was a solitary military voice. Second, the French gave every evidence of looking to Geneva to rescue them from an impossible situation in Indochina. Third, the British reiterated that they were unprepared to consider any form of "active military participation" in Indochina and suggested that partition was the least undesirable solution.[21] Fourth, leaders of Congress, briefed on plans for an air strike, withheld support for use of American sea and air power until the administration gained commitments from allies, especially Britain. Eisenhower and Dulles had hoped to use congressional support to encourage British and French participation in United Action. Now all elements needed persuasion. On Sunday evening, April 4, when the President returned to the White House from Camp David, he met with his principal advisers and decided that collective action including Britain and France and a French guarantee to remain in Indochina and promise independence were indispensable conditions for any American intervention. Immediately thereafter the French request arrived and was promptly turned down as impossible without fulfillment of certain conditions.

Eisenhower had postponed a decision on military intervention, but he had not decided against it, even implicitly. Nor had he ruled out the possibility of unilateral intervention in certain dire cases. Rather, he had ceased to explore the possibilities and had set down the conditions for intervention. It has been tempting to see behind these conditions a clever mind seeking to avoid intervention, drawing impossible conditions that placed the onus of losing Indochina elsewhere. The evidence suggests, to the contrary, that Eisenhower believed it was essential to build a front and if necessary fight and that he tried hard to make intervention practicable.

The President was, to be sure, elusive. At the NSC meeting of April 6 he spoke both ways about Indochina, insisting on the possibility of a Southeast Asia defense "even if Indochina should be lost," but also placing Indochina in the front rank as the first domino. When Treasury Secretary George Humphrey worried about overextension of forces, Eisenhower responded "with great warmth" that "in certain areas at least we cannot afford to let Moscow gain another bit of territory." United Action must go forward with "the greatest urgency." With a regional grouping for the defense of Indochina the battle would be "two-thirds won."[22]

The second phase of the crisis lasted from April 4 to April 29 and consisted of a powerful campaign by Dulles to bring the British and French around to the American way of thinking. Dulles was too clever by half if he was laying a smokescreen to cover retreat. He recalled the Stimson-Simon misunderstanding over stopping Japanese aggression in 1932, but insisted that "if we put our case to them [the British] strongly they may come along this time."[23] He put it so strongly that he came near a replay of the earlier affair. He managed to move Churchill and Eden part way toward United Action in discussions at London April 13. Eden approved the idea of an informal working group in Washington, including the British ambassador, to discuss means. When Eden later reneged, Dulles was furious, according to some accounts pounding the table with his fist. Dulles-Eden conversations at the end of April in Geneva marked a low point in the alliance. Dulles put it mildly when he said he intended to use "extreme bluntness." At one point he lost his temper and "stalked out of the house without a word." A British diplomat wrote of "the almost pathological rage and gloom of Foster Dulles."[24] Can there be doubt that he was absolutely serious about securing British support for collective defense of Indochina?

The Secretary of State's campaign to stiffen the French was no charade either. American diplomats pressed the French time and again to grant the Associated States of Indochina the right to withdraw from the French Union. They appear to have found some satisfactory formula, for Dulles informed Premier Joseph Laniel on April 24 that this precondition "seemed to have been substantially met and should present no difficulty."[25] The other precondition he named was that the United Kingdom join in. At the same time, the American demand to share in the training of Vietnamese troops seemed negotiable: the French agreed on April 8 to accept twenty-five to fifty American officers. The United States gave every evidence of wanting to assist the French, airlifting French troops to Indochina, for example, and sending a mission to study the feasibility of a B-29 raid on Dienbienphu. The evidence presented by John Prados is slim, but one cannot rule out the possibility that Dulles offered two atomic bombs.[26] The conditions for American intervention remained the same: British and congressional concurrence and French agreement to stay the course and not withdraw under the cover of a Geneva agreement. The United States gave every evidence of wanting and seeking fulfillment of these conditions.

The Indochina phase of the crisis ended at an NSC meeting on April 29 because these conditions were not fulfilled. The British remained opposed. The French, despairing in the last days of Dienbienphu, sliding toward a negotiated exit at Geneva, begged for an air strike. Americans feared that the fall of Dienbienphu would lead to a collapse of French resistance everywhere in Indochina before any intervention could be mounted—and every sort of intervention posed problems, technical as well as political. At Geneva Dulles became impressed with the possibility of Chinese intervention if the Americans went in. Eisenhower, at the NSC meeting of April 29, agreed. Unilateral intervention, he said, was impossible. Before squandering American armed forces and prestige in an attempt "to police the entire world," he would have to consider preemptive war against the Soviet Union. In that connection, the April 29 meeting received a sobering briefing on the BISON, a new Soviet bomber comparable to the B-52. The same day, at his news conference, the President spoke of steering between the unobtainable and the unacceptable. He said he was seeking a "practical way of getting along" in the region and alluded to Germany and Berlin as examples. Partition was now tolerable to the United States.[27]

The NSC did not rule out intervention—planning and consultation continued—but the April 29 meeting was the decisive turning point. Franco-American negotiations became more formalistic and thickety, aimed more at shifting blame than achieving common action. American policy took two directions: on the one hand, loss limitation at Geneva, where Bedell Smith concluded on July 23 that "we got more than I expected," and on the other, construction of a collective defense organization at Manila.[28] Ultimately the line was drawn at the seventeenth parallel rather than the frontier of China.

Eisenhower deserves credit for negative results—he did not follow the path to war all the way and he did not lose Indochina—yet it is difficult to find constructive value in his Indochina policy. It was shaped by illusion. It contradicted the differing requirements of allies and failed to address the military circumstances. It engendered much of the difficulty and danger the United States encountered. It severely strained relations with the principal allies. It undercut the promising emergence of East-West diplomacy. And it entangled the United States beyond the zone of its vital interest.

The offshore islands crises of 1954–55 and 1958 (really one crisis with an intermission for buildups) superficially resembled the Korean armistice crisis in the sharply defined and bounded issues at stake, but it was in reality, at least so far as American policy was concerned, a replay of the Indochina crisis—only now for the first time the PRC itself was on the other side of the drawn line.

The inner offshore islands (as distinct from the greater chain of Japan-Taiwan-Philippines) related to the mainland of China like Martha's Vineyard to Newport and San Clemente to San Diego. They were useful to Taiwan and the United States for radar surveillance, passing agents onto the mainland, interdiction of coastal shipping, and detection of and protection against invasion of Taiwan itself. The United States encouraged Chiang Kai-shek to garrison the islands. They also provided whatever substance existed in the Chinese Nationalist claim to represent more than Taiwan and sally ports to keep alive the hope of some day recovering the whole. On the PRC side, Taiwan's control of the offshore islands severely hampered Fujian province and national reconstruction and development. They, no less than Taiwan, were unredeemed national territory. They posed a threat to the legitimacy of the PRC and, given hard-line Eisenhower policies, a menace to PRC national security. After the Korean War and Geneva, the PRC determined to go as far as possible in recovering them. It could not state limited objectives, however, without undermining its claim to Taiwan, and therefore on both sides the offshore crisis had all-or-nothing proportions.

The shelling of Jinmen in September 1954 came as an unwelcome surprise to an American presidency quite tired of crisis. At the NSC that indefatiguable cold warrior Harold Stassen as well as Nixon and Radford argued the importance of the islands, Secretary of Defense Charles Wilson their unimportance. Secretary Dulles was remarkably cautious and hesitant. It was a "horrible dilemma." An "over-whelming case" could be made either for necessary resistance to Communist probing or the danger of war with China in which America stood alone and condemned. He suggested defining the case as an incipient aggression and taking it to the UN Security Council, a suggestion greeted with relief by the President.

This prompt shunting of the crisis onto the diplomatic track reflected U.S. reluctance to become engaged. Dulles looked hopefully to British cooperation on this basis and perhaps even "the beginning of our coming together on the Far East." Eisenhower spoke of the need to engage the American public and world support, to secure congressional authorization, and to avoid pinning down American forces. "Quemoy is not our ship," he warned. He referred to his mail: people were saying "what to we care what happens to those yellow people out there?"[29]

Nevertheless, the Eisenhower administration's tendency toward confrontation with the PRC persisted. The President warned that use of force in defense of the islands meant war with China and that meant general war; the Soviet Union was now the "head of the snake." Just how cautionary this sort of talk was depended on the importance Eisenhower attached to the offshore islands. They were not really important, he said, "except psychologically." That was an important exception explored by Dulles. If the Chinese Communists were probing for weakness, and perhaps the Indochina settlement had encouraged this, then a retreat from the offshore islands would have "disastrous consequences in Korea, Japan, Formosa, and the Philippines." So the whole question turned on how a retreat was perceived, especially in Taibei. Hoping to bury the problem at the UN, while "keeping them guessing partly because we're guessing ourselves," as Dulles put it to Eden, the NSC decided not to decide whether to hold the offshore islands.[30]

In the following months the United States slid down this slope of uncertainty and apprehension into defense of Jinmen and Mazu. As in Korea, it had resisted a mutual defense treaty; as in Korea, it conceded one. On January 18, 1955, after heavy air attack, PRC troops captured Yijiang in the Dazhens, two hundred miles north of Taiwan. The Dazhens, so remote that they required a separate carrier group, were impractical to defend.[31] Dulles urged their evacuation, but Taibei resisted. On January 19 Dulles recommended American assistance in evacuating them. The inducement to Taibei would be help in holding Jinmen and possibly Mazu. Eisenhower agreed. Possible use of force in either case meant for Eisenhower congressional authorization.

The NSC was not easily convinced the following day. Humphrey and Wilson, the voices of restraint, vigorously resisted the idea of fighting China over these "darn" little islands. The President and Dulles rebutted. The problem was the "psychological consequences of abandoning these islands," in terms of the morale of soldiers defending them as well as those on Taiwan, but also in terms of American prestige in Asia. Jinmen and Mazu to Eisenhower qualified as "outposts for the defense of Formosa." This was a test of American defenses. The question was whether U.S. naval and air power could sustain the armies of its Asian allies. He now authorized logistical support of Jinmen and Mazu.[32]

Public declaration was a different matter. Dulles believed it was time to end the fuzziness of policy. The congressional resolution authorizing use of force must make "crystal clear" American commitment to the defense of these islands. The British were sturdy allies in a crisis, Eisenhower said, and he hoped for their support at this juncture. He received it, but for Taiwan not Jinmen. Now Dulles changed his mind. Rather than "nail the flag to the mast," he sought ambiguity.[33] The congressional resolution authorized defense of positions related to the defense of Taiwan. Chiang would be given a secret commitment with the threat of denial if he disclosed it. The Generalissimo insisted on public disclosure; the British opposed it. Finally Chiang conceded. Under cover of a large concentration of American air and sea power, with elaborate restrictions on retaliation, the evacuation of the Dazhens was successfully completed on February 24. Reflecting on the difficulty of dealing with Chiang, Eisenhower said it was wrong to assume that Orientals thought logically, "as we do."[34]

The crisis then entered its most acute phase. PRC preparations opposite Jinmen intensified. Dulles returned from a visit to Asia believing Chinese Communist aims to be more "virulent" than he suspected. He likened the situation to Europe in the 1930s. The President now accepted that in face of an attack on Jinmen atomic weapons would have to be used.[35]

Once the United States was locked into the defense of the offshore islands, it became cautious. Pending European defense treaties (substituting for the European Defense Community) must not be jeopardized by belligerency in East Asia. On March 11 Dulles urged avoidance of intervention if possible, or at least use only of conventional weapons, for the next forty to sixty days. The military was optimistic about a conventional defense unless the PRC air force intervened. On April 5 Eisenhower urged a cautioning of Chiang. The Chinese leader must understand that outposts are outposts, not main bastions, and that he had no American commitment to "fill out" the defense of Jinmen and Mazu. In fact, he should remove excess personnel. Now the President doubted that retention or loss of the islands was critical to Taiwan. He was reminded of the British defense of Malta in World War II, a "temporizing" holding action.[36] On April 20 at Bandung Zhou brought the crisis to a close with a speech shunning war and calling for talks.

B y April 1955 the pattern of PRC–U.S. confrontation had been established for the remainder of the Eisenhower administration and indeed the next seventeen years. The grooves of policy were deeply cut. Talks at Geneva made no substantial progress. The Eisenhower administration not only tolerated a doubling of Chinese Nationalist forces on Jinmen but added atomic missiles to the well-stocked arsenals of Taiwan. The offshore crisis of 1958 was short because the fundamentals of the confrontation were understood on both sides. The American policy of isolating Communist China economically and politically was firmly in place.

The great offshore chain (Japan-Taiwan-Philippines) was central to Eisenhower's concept of Pacific defense, as it had been (with modifications) to that of his predecessor. Inherent in that concept was a tendency for the line to wash ashore, as it had in 1950. Eisenhower himself allowed that Malaya, for example, was included. While the line was not unnatural for defense, it was sterile and dangerous as the principal way of defining American relations with East Asia. This, however, is what it came to be during the Korean War, and this is what it remained, greatly reinforced, under Eisenhower. The obsessive defensiveness and militarization of relations in East Asia of his administration, as represented in the Korean, Indochina, and Taiwan Straits cases examined here, was undoubtedly due in part to preoccupation with Europe and a tendency to be indifferent to Asia except in crisis. Indifference encouraged illusion, and illusions about East Asia generated their own persisting, self-inflicted wounds.

NOTES

1. On the Eisenhower presidency and foreign policy, see Dwight D. Eisenhower, *The White House Years*, 2 vols. (New York: Doubleday, 1963); Stephen E. Ambrose, *Eisenhower*, vol. 2, *The President* (New York: Simon and Schuster, 1984); Fred I. Greenstein, *The Hidden-Hand Presidency: Eisenhower as Leader* (New York: Basic Books, 1982); Robert J. McMahon, "Eisenhower and Third World Nationalism: A Critique of the Revisionists," *Political Science Quarterly* (1986, No. 3), 101:453–73.

2. On the Korean armistice crisis, see Burton I. Kaufman, *The Korean War: Challenges in Crisis, Credibility and Command* (Philadelphia: Temple University Press, 1986), chs. 9, 10; Edward C. Keefer, "Dwight D. Eisenhower and the End of the Korean War," *Diplomatic History* (Summer 1986), 10:267–89; Walter G. Hermes, *Truce Tent and Fighting Front* (Washington, D.C.: GPO, 1966).

3. Minutes of NSC mtgs. (hereafter cited as NSC minutes), February 11, March 31, April 8, May 6, May 13, May 20, 1953, U.S. Dept of State, *Foreign Relations of the United States, 1952–1954*, vol. 15: *Korea* (hereafter cited as *FRUS 1952–54*) (Washington, D.C.: GPO, 1984), pp. 769–70, 826–27, 892–95, 975–78, 1012–17, 1064–68; Keefer, "Eisenhower and the End of the Korean War," p. 268.

4. State Dept.-NSC mtg., minutes, May 18, 1953, *ibid.*, pp. 1038–44.

5. Smith memo, May 19, 1953, *ibid.*, pp. 1052–56.

6. NSC minutes, May 13, 1953, *ibid.*, pp. 1012–17; Smith to Eisenhower (hereafter cited as DDE), May 18, 1953, *ibid.*, p. 1046.

7. Dulles-Nehru conversations, memos, May 21 and 22, 1953, *ibid.*, pp. 1068–69, 1071; Bohlen to Dept. of State (hereafter cited as DOS), May 28, 1953, *ibid.*, pp. 1109–11.

8. DOS-NSC mtg. memo, May 18, 1941, *ibid.*, pp. 1038–44.

9. Bipartisan legislative mtg, January 5, 1954, Diaries of Dwight D. Eisenhower, 1953–1961, Ann Whitman file (cited as DDE Diaries), University Publications of America edition. On the Indochina crisis of 1954, see John Prados, *The Sky Would Fall; Operation Vulture: The U.S. Bombing Mission in Indochina, 1954* (New York: Dial Press, 1983); George C. Herring and Richard H. Immerman, "Eisenhower, Dulles, and Dienbienphu: 'The Day We Didn't Go To War' Revisited," *Journal of American History* (September 1984), 71:343–63; James Cable, *The Geneva Conference on Indochina* (London: Macmillan, 1986); Robert F. Randle, *Geneva, 1954: The Settlement of the Indochinese War* (Princeton: Princeton University Press, 1969).

10. NSC mtg, April 6, 1954, *FRUS, 1952–54*, vol. 13: *Indochina* (Washington, D.C.: GPO, 1979), pp. 1250–53.

11. Alfred D. Chandler Jr., ed., *The Papers of Dwight D. Eisenhower: The War Years*, 5 vols. (Baltimore: Johns Hopkins University Press, 1970), vol. 1, ch. 1.

12. DDE to Churchill, April 4, 1954, *FRUS, 1952–54*, 13:1240.

13. NSC mtgs, January 8, February 4, April 1, April 6, 1954, *ibid.*, pp. 948–50, 1013, 1201, 1250–63; DDE to Gen. Alfred Gruenther, April 26, 1954, DDE Diaries; Bipartisan Legislative mtg, January 5, 1954, *ibid.*; DDE to Churchill, July 22, 1954, *ibid.*

14. DDE to Churchill, April 4, 1954, *FRUS, 1952–54*, 13:1240.

15. *Ibid.*; Drumright memo, April 2, 1954, *ibid.*, pp. 1214–17; Aldrich to DOS, April 6, 1954, *ibid.*, pp. 1249–50.

16. DDE-Dulles conversation, memo, March 24, 1954, *ibid.*, p. 1150; Radford to DDE, March 24, 1954, *ibid.*, pp. 1158–59.

17. DDE-Dulles phone conversation, memo, April 5, 1954, *ibid.*, pp. 1241–42; DDE to Gruenther, April 26, 1954, DDE Diaries.

18. Joseph Patrick Hobbs, *Dear General; Eisenhower's Wartime Letters to Marshall* (Baltimore: Johns Hopkins University Press, 1971), p. 223.

19. Bipartisan Legislative mtg., January 5, 1954, DDE Diaries; NSC mtg., January 8, 1954, *FRUS, 1952–54*, 13:948.

20. NSC mtg., April 6, 1954, *ibid.* p. 1255.

21. Drumright memo, April 2, 1954, *ibid.*, p. 1216.

22. NSC mtg., April 6, 1954, *ibid.*, pp. 1250–63.

23. *Ibid.*, p. 1256.

24. Geneva to DOS, April 26, 1954, *The Pentagon Papers, The Senator Gravel Edition; The Defense Department History of United States Decisionmaking in Vietnam*, 5 vols. (Boston: Beacon Press, 1971), 1:479; Cable, *Geneva*, ch. 4.

25. Dulles to DOS, April 24, 1954, *FRUS, 1952–54*, 13:1294–95.

26. Prados, *Sky Would Fall*, pp. 114, 153–56.

27. Geneva to DOS, April 29, 1954, *Pentagon Papers*, 1:482; NSC mtg., April 29, 1954, *FRUS, 1952–54*, 13:1440; Prados, *Sky Would Fall*, p. 171; Ambrose, *President*, p. 183.

28. DDE phone conversation with Smith, memo, July 23, 1954, DDE Diaries.

29. NSC mtg., September 12, 1954, *FRUS, 1952–54*, vol. 14: *China* (Washington, D.C.: GPO, 1979), pp. 613–23.

30. Dulles-Eden conversation, memo, September 17, 1954, *ibid.*, 650–51.

31. Dulles-Yeh conversation, January 19, 1955, *FRUS, 1955–57*, vol. 2: *China* (Washington, D.C.: GPO, 1986), pp. 38–41.

32. NSC mtg., January 20, 1955, *ibid.*, pp. 69–82; White House conversation, memo, January 19, 1955, *ibid.*, pp. 41–43.

33. NSC mtg., January 21, 1955, *ibid.*, pp. 90–96.

34. NSC mtg., February 17, 1955, *ibid.*, p. 285.

35. Dulles-DDE conversations, memos, March 6 and 11, 1955, *ibid.*, pp. 336–37, 353–55; Cabinet mtg., memo, March 11, 1955, *ibid.*, p. 353.

36. Andrew Goodpaster memo, March 15, 1955, *ibid.*, p. 366–67; DDE to Dulles, April 5, 1955, *ibid.*, pp. 445–50; Dulles-DDE conversation, memo, April 17, 1955, *ibid.*, p. 491.

5

Eisenhower's Foreign Economic Policy with Respect to East Asia

BURTON I. KAUFMAN
Virginia Polytechnic Institute and State University

I n terms of the development of United States foreign economic policy, the administration of Dwight D. Eisenhower (1953–1961) was critical. Eisenhower was the first Chief Executive to concern himself intimately with the economic development of third world nations. Moreover, the thirty-fourth President moved his administration from a program based on the concept of "trade not aid," in which he sought to promote economic development in third world nations through a combination of liberalized world trade and private foreign investment, to one predicated on the principle of "trade and aid," in which he attempted to assist these countries through a mix of freer trade and economic aid (mainly in the form of "soft loans," or loans on terms more favorable than ordinary commercial loans). Although Eisenhower was generally unsuccessful in bringing about third world economic development, he established the basic framework for the subsequent foreign economic programs of Presidents John F. Kennedy and Lyndon Baines Johnson.[1]

One area of the world that greatly troubled Eisenhower, particularly during his first term as President, was East Asia. This vast region of the Far Pacific was one, of course, that many Old Guard Republicans believed had been ignored by Eisenhower's Democratic predecessors, with the results that China had been "lost" to the Communists and the danger had grown of Communist expansion elsewhere. The President could hardly have disregarded these plaintive pleas within his own party to halt the Communist menace in Asia, even had he been so inclined. But because he held many of the same beliefs about the Communist danger, he was not prone to ignore the call for a more forceful application of the containment policy in Asia. Besides, his first priority as President was to end the war in Korea, which had been languishing for nearly three years when he took office in 1953.

Eisenhower was also greatly disturbed by the deteriorating position of the French in their war against the Vietminh in Indochina, and his administration had an almost schizophrenic view of the PRC, which, too, affected his policy with respect to East Asia. On the one hand, the White House regarded the Chinese Communists as little more than puppets of their Moscow masters; on the other, it recognized serious differences within the Sino-Soviet alliance. In either case, however, the President's policy was predicated on the application of diplomatic, military, and economic pressure on the Chinese, either to cause additional strain within the Communist alliance or merely to limit further Communist aggression.[2]

Like much of the rest of his foreign economic policy, Eisenhower's economic program for East Asia was predicated on his perception of the Communist menace in the region. Because the threat there seemed particularly acute when he entered the White House,[3] it received his highest priority. As the program evolved over the next two years, it consisted of three essential elements.

First was maintaining the economic embargo that had been imposed on the PRC following that country's entry into the Korean War in December 1950. Not only did the United States prohibit the export of all American goods, strategic *and nonstrategic*, to China; it also forbade American ships to call at Chinese ports. Under a selective embargo resolution adopted by the United Nations in May of 1951, other Western powers, most notably England, also maintained controls on certain strategic goods to China, such as arms, ammunition, and other implements of war.[4]

England's export controls, however, did not apply to nonstrategic trade. Also, while its commerce with China was generally regulated more tightly than with other Communist nations, London was already applying considerable pressure on the United States to support a loosening of the selective embargo as part of its process of normalizing relations with the PRC, protecting its interests in Hong Kong from Chinese retaliation, and taking advantage of China's vast economic potential. In fact, England favored a general relaxation of restrictions on all East-West trade, limiting controls to a narrow list of strategic items and placing trade with China on the same basis as that with other Soviet bloc nations.[5]

Eisenhower was not unsympathetic to the British position. He too favored a loosening of controls on commerce with Communist-controlled countries as part of his larger policy of widening the channels of trade throughout the world. As some of his later remarks about the impossibility of maintaining a complete embargo against the PRC suggest, the president even included Communist China among the countries with whom he thought trade restrictions should eventually be relaxed.[6]

In the early spring of 1954, however, Eisenhower felt the British proposals went too far, too fast. Not only did they define their list of proscribed items too narrowly, he believed, but Congress and the American public would not tolerate such an expansion in East-West trade as London proposed. Certainly they would oppose any immediate resumption of commerce with the PRC, a nation with which the United States had just ended hostilities in Korea. To to do as the British asked, he thus told Prime Minister Winston Churchill in 1954, would be "to go beyond what is immediately safe or in the common interest of the free world." Accordingly, the United States agreed in 1954 to soften its restrictions on trade with most Soviet bloc nations, but not with the PRC.[7]

A second component of Eisenhower's economic program for East Asia was to assist in the economic development of the region through the establishment of a special Asian foreign aid package. Although the President took office committed to replacing economic aid with liberalized trade and private foreign investment, others within his administration, especially Harold Stassen, maintained that only an expanded program of public capital could prevent Asia from falling to the Communists. As early as 1950, Stassen, who directed the Foreign Operations Administration (FOA), which Eisenhower had established in 1953 to administer foreign aid, had proposed a "Marshall Plan for Asia."[8] In the wake of the French debacle in Indochina in 1954, he once more advocated a massive infusion of economic assistance to the region administered on a programmatic (or economically integrated) basis. Addressing a meeting of members of the Colombo Plan (an organization of Asian members of the British Commonwealth), Stassen proposed in October the establishment of a regional economic organization to run the program, much as the Organization for European Economic Cooperation (OEEC) had run the Marshall Plan.[9]

Although Stassen offered no specific figures, he left the impression that the American contribution to the program would be in the billions of dollars, an amount totally unacceptable to an administration committed to cutting back on federal spending and only just beginning to reconsider its foreign economic policy of "trade not aid."[10]

Nevertheless, President Eisenhower had also concluded that the United States would have to develop a new economic program for Asia or lose it to the Communists. In December, therefore, he agreed to recommend to Congress the establishment of a special Asian fund, the size of which he would determine later. Although the President assured members of his administration that it would be nothing along the lines intended by Stassen and some Asian leaders, the fact that Eisenhower had even decided to ask Congress for the fund underscored the importance he attached to Asia's economic development and his new willingness to employ public capital in order to prevent further Communist expansion.[11]

The final—and, in many ways, the most important—element of Eisenhower's foreign economic program for East Asia, however, was the liberalization of world trade in goods from Japan and the expansion of Japanese interests in Southeast Asia. Indeed, Japan was vital to all of Eisenhower's plans for the area. In terms of geography alone, it posed the region's major threat to the Soviet Union and the PRC.[12] But because Japan had the area's only significant industrialized economy and skilled labor force, it would also have to assume the major responsibility for East Asia's economic development. Conversely, Japan's economic—and political—security depended on expanding its own commerce, which meant developing new sources of raw materials for its factories and new markets for its industrial production. Absent the PRC, Southeast Asia (Indochina, Indonesia, Malaya, Taiwan) and the Western industrial powers offered the only realistic prospects for achieving these aims.

Both Secretary of State John Foster Dulles and President Eisenhower made clear how vital they considered Japan's economic security to be to the United States' own military security. Believing that Japan was "the key to the future political complexion" of much of the Far East, the President and the Secretary of State supported the organization of something resembling the Greater East-Asian Co-Prosperity Sphere, which Japan had sought to establish before World War II. Emphasizing the importance of an economically strong Japan tied closely to the West, the President was also convinced that the policies the United States adopted regarding Japanese trade "might well dictate whether these areas remain within the free world or fall within the Communist orbit."[13]

By the end of Eisenhower's second year in office, then, the administration had responded to what it perceived as a critical situation in East Asia by designing a foreign economic policy intended to keep Communist China economically isolated, promote the region's economic growth along integrated lines, and tie that growth to Japan's own economic development. By this time, too, Eisenhower had begun to move from an economic program based on the principle of "trade not aid" to one predicated on the concept of trade *and* aid, including the establishment of a special economic fund for Asia.

In most respects, however, Eisenhower's economic program for East Asia was a failure. In the first place, the administration proved unsuccessful in maintaining its embargo on commerce with Communist China. Notwithstanding American opposition, England and other allies of the United States loosened their restrictions on the China trade, placing it on the same footing as commerce with other Communist bloc nations and limiting it to a narrow list of strategic items. Second, the special fund for Asia was abolished within a year after it was formed without being replaced by a similar institution. Finally, while Japan experienced sustained economic growth during the 1950s, it did so by relying primarily on military procurement and other assistance from the United States rather than by assuming the role of regional economic leader and tapping the markets of the West, as Eisenhower had intended. Ironically, the technology and industry that Japan was still able to develop in the 1950s as a result of American procurement put the country in the position in the 1960s to compete successfully in the very markets that had discriminated against it a decade earlier.

To a considerable extent, Eisenhower was responsible for the failure of his own policy. In at least one important sense—having to do with the economic embargo imposed on the PRC—the President had a better understanding of world economic and political realities than his own Secretary of State, John Foster Dulles. More than Dulles, he recognized the importance of the China market to Japan. He also concurred in the argument of America's other allies that trade restrictions applied to China should be limited to the most essential strategic goods. Had he been more forceful in advocating this policy, a compromise might have been reached with these allies and trading partners. But even though other persons within his administration agreed with him, the President failed to back them when the issue of the trade embargo came under White House review. As a result, proponents of strict controls prevailed, causing England to break ranks with the United States and forcing Japan to look increasingly to markets outside of China, including those in the United States and Western Europe.

Eisenhower's failure to press for a relaxation of the embargo against China appears to have been part of a larger change in the administration's priorities during his second term. This is not to say, of course, that Eisenhower lost all interest in economic issues affecting East

Asia. Certainly his concern for Japan's economic development remained strong. His administration also continued to make the case for increased economic aid for the area, particularly in support of regional schemes of economic integration. As in other areas of the world, the President was greatly disturbed by what his administration viewed as a "Soviet [or Sino-Soviet] economic offensive" in which Moscow (and, to a much lesser extent, Peking) courted third world nations with official state visits and lavish promises of economic assistance.[14]

Far more than in Asia, however, the Eisenhower administration worried about the Soviet economic challenge in the Mideast, coincident as it was with a rising tide of Arab nationalism and anti-Western sentiment, which raised the specter of Communist domination of the region. So, too, Latin America became an area of increasing concern to the White House, especially following the 1958 riot in Venezuela during a visit there by Vice President Richard Nixon. One result of this incident was new administration support for a program of regional economic development in Latin America. The enthusiasm for Fidel Castro that followed his successful revolution in Cuba in 1959 only heightened the urgency the administration attached to this proposal. Finally, toward the end of Eisenhower's presidency, the administration had to pay increasing attention to a nagging balance-of-payments problem that would become even more serious after Eisenhower left office.[15]

All of these developments after 1956 distracted Eisenhower from the problems and issues that had so concerned him earlier. Questions of trade and aid for East Asia did not receive the attention they had before because they did not seem as crucial. The President's annual skirmishes with Congress over foreign aid and his ongoing struggle with protectionist forces on Capitol Hill may also have caused him to narrow his list of legislative priorities and to lessen his will to fight for his entire foreign economic program. Without doubt he became increasingly frustrated with Congress and, indeed, with the entire legislative process.[16]

Eisenhower's diminished interest in economic issues affecting East Asia was clearly evident in the lengthy—and sometimes heated—debate within the administration following England's decision in 1956 to lift its trade embargo against Communist China. Actually, the British had been pressing the United States since 1954 for a further relaxation of all controls on East-West trade. After the Geneva Summit Conference of 1955, the United States responded by joining England and France in offering to remove barriers to Soviet trade, travel, and cultural exchange. But the following January, while visiting

Washington, Prime Minister Anthony Eden asked Eisenhower for a gradual lifting of controls on trade with the PRC. The British position remained that, ultimately, the same control list should apply to China as applied to other Communist countries. Although the President made no promises, he directed the Council on Foreign Economic Policy (CFEP), which he had organized in 1953 to coordinate foreign economic policy, to review a list of items for decontrol that Eden had left with him.[17]

Eisenhower was concerned about the domestic political consequences of easing the trade embargo. In fact, over the next eight months opposition to a further relaxation of East-West trade became so great that the administration was forced to retreat from its efforts to expand the channels of commerce with Soviet bloc countries.[18] Nevertheless, Eisenhower believed that modifying the restrictions on trade with China was both right and necessary. With Japan's economic welfare so crucial to his own plans for East Asia, he recognized China's importance for Japanese trade. He was also under intense pressure from Tokyo to lift the restrictions on Sino-Japanese commerce, which Japan had accepted in 1952 in order to assure congressional approval of the 1951 San Francisco Peace Treaty. Japanese businessmen and politicians continued to view China in much the same way they had since before World War II—as potentially the richest market for Japanese goods. Because Eisenhower shared a similar view, he was certain that any "effort to dam up permanently the natural currents of trade, particularly between such areas as Japan and the neighboring Asian mainland, [would] be defeated."[19]

Others in the administration agreed with him. Even Treasury Secretary George Humphrey, a strident anti-Communist—and, along with Secretary of State Dulles, one of the two most powerful members of the Cabinet—believed that treating China differently from the Soviet Union was "seeking to lock the barn door after the horse was gone."[20] But the leading advocate of lifting controls was Clarence Randall, the chairman of the Council on Foreign Economic Policy (CFEP). A longtime proponent of free trade, Randall maintained that restrictions on trade with any Communist country, including the PRC, should be limited to a narrow list of strategic goods. Like Eisenhower, he also understood the importance of the China market to Japan. As early as 1953, while an assistant to the President, he took issue with State Department officials opposed to permitting Sino-Japanese trade. "I suspect that is not logical but emotional," he remarked."[21]

Opposition to relaxing the embargo, however, was also strong. On Capitol Hill, it centered on Senator John McClellan of Arkansas, who, as chairman of the Senate's Permanent Investigations Subcommittee, had already forced the administration to delay its plans for expanding East-West trade. At the State Department, it included Secretary Dulles, whose obsessive anticommunism overrode his usual broad-mindedness and tactical flexibility on most foreign economic issues. But Dulles remained in the background.[22] Instead, he left it to Assistant Secretary of the State Walter Robertson—who had been recommended for the position because of his strong support for Chinese Nationalist leader, Chiang Kai-shek, and his belief in the absolute evil of the PRC—to lead the State Department's opposition.[23]

The issue of relaxing controls came to a head in the fall of 1956. Already committed to ending the China differential (that is, the restrictions applied to China but not to other Communist countries), England sought a meeting with the United States before the end of the year in a final effort to iron out differences between the two countries. By this time, the CFEP, led by Chairman Randall, was also preparing to recommend a relaxation of the trade embargo. In October Randall called a meeting of his Council to review the matter.[24]

Immediately he ran into problems from Robertson at the State Department, who remained opposed to any relaxation of the embargo. Randall appealed over Robertson's head to Undersecretary of State Herbert Hoover, Jr., who officially represented the State Department on the CFEP but who did not get along well with its chairman and rarely attended any of its meetings. What followed were months of quibbling and backstabbing among Randall, Hoover, and Robertson, which left Randall frustrated and angry and the China differential intact.[25]

Hoover persuaded Randall to delay a decision on the differential until after the new Congress was elected and consulted—or, in other words, until early 1955. When the CFEP finally met in February to discuss the matter, the State Department agreed to a document by which the United States would retain the differential but conduct negotiations with the British about lifting controls on 207 items proscribed to the PRC but not the Soviet Union.[26]

Even then, Robertson and Admiral Arthur W. Radford, Chairman of the Joint Chiefs of Staff and another opponent of easing restrictions, insisted on keeping so many items on the proscribed list that in May, it was rejected by England, France, and eight other nations during negotiations with the United States in Paris. In fact, as Randall later commented, the Paris meeting was a "complete defeat" for the Americans. Following the meeting, London announced that it would disregard the multilateral agreement on trade with China and, instead, establish its own policy.[27]

What role had Eisenhower played while the issue of the China differential was being debated in Washington? Apparently a very small one. There is no question that the President wanted to ease trade restrictions with China. Several of those who talked with him privately indicated just how strongly he felt on this question. At one point, he even considered offering the Chinese some technologically unsophisticated weapons. But although Randall never complained about the President, there is no evidence that Eisenhower ever gave him the personal and public support he needed. To the contrary, when Randall met with Eisenhower in March, the President told him that while he supported liberalizing trade with the PRC, there were still a number of matters that first had to be "talked out," such as congressional reaction to the news that the United States would be discussing a modification of the China differential.[28]

Nor does the President appear to have been much involved in the discussions that followed. Even after Randall reported to the White House in May that the Paris meeting was going to break up if the American delegation was not given more flexibility in negotiating with its trading partners, Eisenhower failed to intervene on Randall's behalf. Indeed, when Randall attempted a few months later to reconsider American policy, he found "little sentiment for any liberalization of this trade." Modification of the China differential, in other words, had become a moot issue for the President, not because he opposed it, but because he was unwilling to make the effort needed to bring it about. As a result, the United States remained committed to a policy the President did not really believe in and which, in any case, was being ignored by its own allies. For those who, like Eisenhower, wanted to reopen trade with China, the administration's policy was bankrupt.[29]

The second component of Eisenhower's foreign economic policy, which also proved disappointing to those promoting it, was the formation of a special Asian fund to aid in the region's economic development. The brief history of the fund can be easily recounted. After the President decided in 1954 to establish a fund, he instructed the NSC to make recommendations concerning its size and functions. In January 1955, the NSC recommended that the President ask Congress for an appropriation of $205 million; this figure, of course, represented the administration's intention to keep the fund small and was the one (rounded to $200 million) Eisenhower proposed to Congress in his annual message on foreign aid. In forwarding this recommendation, the President remarked that while economic development in Asia ultimately rested with the Asians themselves, the United States had "the capacity, the desire, the concern to take the lead in friendly help for free Asia."[30] Unfortunately for the administration, Congress had become restive over the whole foreign aid program, which it accused of gross waste and inefficiency and which, it claimed, the United States could not afford. As a result, it chopped the President's recommendation in half, appropriating $100 million rather than $200 million for the fund.[31]

Angered by the House and Senate action, Eisenhower came back to Congress the next year with a request for the $100 million it had failed to appropriate a year earlier. Significantly, he also asked for a special $100 million fund for the Middle East and Africa, whose friendship, he said, the United States also needed. In asking for these funds, the President was clearly concerned by the Soviet economic offensive, particularly in the Mideast. It "was idle to suppose," he said, that the Soviet Union had "any friendly interest in the countries that she proposes to help." Moscow's purpose was to damage the United States' relationship with these countries and then to use its "economic penetration to accomplish political domination."[32] By this time, however, Congress was in open revolt against the administration's foreign aid requests, and, despite White House appeals to the contrary, it cut $1 billion from the $4.67 billion Eisenhower had recommended. As part of its cuts, Congress refused to include the President's newly requested funds for the Middle East and Africa, and it eliminated the Asian Economic Development Fund established just a year earlier.[33]

In this way, the House and Senate killed the second pillar of Eisenhower's economic program for East Asia. Although the President lashed out at Congress for the cuts it had made, he never attempted to reestablish the Asian fund or anything resembling it. This was particularly odd because in his last years in office, his administration attached increased importance to regional schemes, like the Asian fund, to foster economic growth. Disorders in Iraq, Jordan, and Lebanon in the summer of 1958 and fear of Soviet economic penetration of the Western Hemisphere as part of the Soviet economic offensive increased the tendency within the White House to perceive the problem of economic development as a regional one. As a result, Eisenhower proposed more area-wide schemes for the Middle East, including the establishment of an Arab development institution. He also promoted a regional program for Latin America known as "Operation Pan America," central to which was the establishment of an Inter-American Development Bank.[34] But the President made no similar effort for Asia, despite the fact that a special interagency committee, which Randall had formed in 1957, made a number of proposals to bring about greater regional unity,[35] and Randall himself promoted a meeting of Asian nations to discuss the same question.[36] Developments in the Mideast and Latin America apparently made the economic situation in these regions seem more critical to the President than in Asia.

Even had Congress fully approved Eisenhower's request for the Asian fund, it is questionable how much it could have accomplished. In the first place, plans for the fund were far too optimistic. In instructions for preparing the 1956 aid requests, the FOA had outlined the rationale for the new agency. It would contribute to the planning and carrying out of a sound and comprehensive long-range plan for economic development, the FOA remarked. "[I]t would be aimed at dealing constructively with the economic problems that threaten the political, social and economic stability [of Asia] and which are creating the kind of conditions which lend themselves to successful political and economic aggression and subversion on the part of the Communists."[37] Given the complexity of the problems in Asia, at the very least, these were extremely ambitious objectives for an agency fully funded at $200 million, when compared, for example, to those in Europe after World War II. As Randall's predecessor on the CFEP, Joseph Dodge, pointed out in 1954, when the administration was still debating whether to create a special Asian fund, unlike Europe, "the Far East [was] a problem of creating a pattern of life that [had] not existed in the past."[38]

Beyond the economic barriers to regional economic integration, however, there were also major political obstacles. One especially— fear that Japan would dominate any regional economic scheme—also contributed to Washington's failure to achieve the final element of Eisenhower's economic program for East Asia—an expanded Japanese trade with Southeast Asia and the Western industrial powers. In purely economic terms, the concept of a regional commerce dominated by Japan and excluding the PRC was flawed. As already indicated, that part of the world simply lacked the financial resources to be a major trading partner with Japan or any other nation. Although figures are sketchy, they suggest that per capita annual income for all the countries of East Asia in 1955 was under $100 compared to about $220 for Japan. There was also very little industry and a desperate shortage of capital. Long-term capital was almost nonexistent, and the foreign exchange needed to make purchases abroad was extremely limited. Even FOA Director Stassen had serious doubts about the region's prospects for economic development. Returning from a trip to South and Southeast Asia in early 1955, he concluded that the odds were "at least even" that the United States could accomplish its economic (and political) objectives in that part of the world. But he also pointed out that "success [was] by no means certain" and that it would "be a long term struggle" before real economic growth could take place.[39]

At least as great as these economic obstacles to Japanese trade in East Asia, however, were political factors. With memories of World War II still fresh in their minds, the countries of the region were reluctant to establish commercial ties with their former captors.[40] Moreover, they feared that their own interests would be dwarfed by an economically resurgent Japan supported by the United States. In May 1955 thirteen of the smaller countries of East and Southeast Asia met at an Asian economic conference in Simla, India, in order to discuss how to use the $200 million that Eisenhower had proposed for the Asian fund. There, they expressed some of these concerns, pointing out that the Japanese economy towered over the rest of East Asia and that the United States' plans for the region rested on Japan's playing the major role in its economic development.

Accordingly, the Simla meeting rejected the idea of establishing a regional organization to plan the use of American aid. Instead, financial experts at the meeting issued a statement in which they noted that "in the present stage of economic development of the Asian region" there would be no advantage in having a regional organization. The meeting also rejected a proposal for establishing a permanent secretariat as part of some existing body, such as the Colombo Plan Consultative Committee, to deal with the regional use of aid funds. As for the moneys authorized for the Asian fund, the conferees recommended merely that the funds be split among the recipient countries.[41]

Even after the Simla Conference, people like Clarence Randall continued to espouse the necessity of economic regionalism in Asia. So did the Japanese. In July 1957, a senior Japanese official, sent to Washington to make arrangements for a state visit by Prime Minister Nobusuke Kishi, met with Randall. He talked abut the necessity for the economic integration of Southeast Asia in terms, the CFEP Chairman remarked, that sounded very much like his own. Pointing out that neither Japan nor the United States was "well liked in the area," the Japanese visitor raised the possibility of a joint Japanese-American venture in Burma or Thailand "to prove [Washington and Tokyo's] good intentions." But nothing came of this scheme, and the White House abstained from offering any proposals of its own. The thrust of its efforts on behalf of regional integration had clearly shifted to Latin America and the Middle East.[42]

Attempts by the White House to liberalize world trade in Japanese commerce also were largely unsuccessful. Fear of Japanese competition was prevalent throughout much of Western Europe and in the United States, particularly among textile interests already losing markets to cheaper Japanese imports and alleging unfair business practices. These complaints were not unjustified, for while the Japanese had the advantage of cheaper labor costs, Japan had also permitted the textile industry—and other industries—to form cartels in order to develop markets abroad and restrict competition at home.[43]

Responding to the threat from Japan, the nations of Western Europe, along with members of the British Commonwealth, discriminated against Japan imports and refused to acccord Japan the full privileges of membership in the international trading community. More specifically, they blocked Japan's membership in the General Agreement on Tariffs and Trade (GATT), the international forum responsible for liberalizing world trade. Even in the United States protectionist sentiment mounted against Japan. For example, the women's blouse industry sought to apply restrictions on imports of Japanese blouses, despite the fact that Japan had already restricted its exports of blouses and a few other items to the United States in order to assuage protectionist sentiment.[44]

As part of its effort to buttress Japan's economy and to strengthen its ties to the West, the White House sought to remove these barriers to Japanese imports. Beginning in the spring of 1954, President Eisenhower conducted an extensive campaign on behalf of Japan. In public speeches, in meetings with legislative officials, and in talks with British diplomats, the President stressed the need to open more markets to Japanese commerce, including negotiating a multilateral trade agreement with Tokyo. In July, he instructed Secretary of State Dulles to "turn the heat on" the British. At the same time, he spoke out against protectionists at home, commenting repeatedly on the importance to the security of the United States of a close economic and political relationship with the Japanese. Finally, he urged that country's admission into GATT, remarking that it was "of absolutely vital importance" that Japan be "a full trading partner in the free world."[45]

As a result of a year-long diplomatic effort by the United States, America's trading partners, meeting in Geneva from February to June 1955, did agree to admit Japan into GATT and to make tariff concessions on items that accounted for about 40 percent of Japan's export trade in 1953.[46] In the United States, the administration was also able to beat back most attempts by protectionists to place quotas on Japanese imports. The Trade Agreements Act of 1955, which contained a list of trade concessions to be offered Japan in the forthcoming Geneva negotiations, was widely regarded as a great political victory for the administration.[47]

These were Pyrrhic victories, however, rather than significant departures from past trading practices. Although Japan was admitted into GATT, fourteen of its thirty-three contracting parties, including a number of European and British Commonwealth countries, refused to apply the GATT in their relations with the new member. While this was permitted under an escape clause provision allowing member nations to protect themselves against unfair and unusual competition,[48] the United States joined Japan in complaining about the lingering discrimination against that country. In October, the American delegation to the tenth session of GATT informed the other delegations that it was "matter of serious concern to the United States" that so many members continued to deny to Japan its normal privileges under GATT. At the same gathering, the Japanese warned that nondiscrimination was essential if Japan was not to establish trade ties with Communist countries. They also threatened to retaliate against countries utilizing the escape clause by raising their own tariffs. But the delegates agreed only to take up the problem at intersessional meetings and at the next annual session of GATT. Not until the mid-1960s did Japan establish formal GATT relations with all the major contracting parties.[49]

As for the Trade Agreements Act of 1955, approval of the measure represented considerably less than the "victory" President Eisenhower claimed. Although the legislation gave the President the authority to reduce tariffs by 5 percent each year for the next three years, it contained a number of protectionist features broadening the conditions under which American industry could seek relief from foreign imports. With respect to Japan, the measure prohibited any further tariff cuts on Japanese products receiving reductions of 15 percent or more at the Geneva negotiations. The White House had sought additional concessions for the Japanese, but Congress had turned the administration down.[50]

The administration was thus unsuccessful in its efforts to free the flow of international commerce or to align the Japanese economy more closely to the West, just as it had failed to isolate Communist China economically or to encourage the economic development of non-Communist Asia through a program of regional economic integration. As a result, Japan was forced to become more competitive with its trading rivals and to rely heavily on military orders from the United States—which expanded rapidly in the 1950s and 1960s during America's military buildup in Southeast Asia—for its own economic growth.[51]

The technology and industry that Japan was still able to develop because of American procurement and its own determined efforts to be competitive put the country in a position by the late 1960s to do business successfully in the very markets that had discriminated against it a decade earlier. In this odd way, the failure of Eisenhower's efforts to establish a community of nations in East Asia, tied together by a common interest in their economic development and aided by the United States, had consequences even more apparent in the 1980s than they were twenty or thirty years ago.[52]

NOTES

1. Burton I. Kaufman, *Trade and Aid: Eisenhower's Foreign Economic Policy* (Baltimore: Johns Hopkins University Press, 1982).

2. For a provocative essay on this divided view of the PRC, see David Mayers, "Eisenhower and Communism: Later Findings," in Richard A. Melanson and David Mayers, eds., *Reevaluating Eisenhower: American Foreign Policy in the 1950s,* pp. 88–119 (Urbana: University of Illinois Press, 1987). This should be contrasted, however, with Norman A. Graebner, "Eisenhower and Communism: The Public Record of the 1950s," in *ibid.,* pp. 67–87.

3. On this point, see, for example, Telephone Log, Eisenhower to Secretary Humphrey, December 20, 1954, box 7, DDE Diary Series, Papers of Dwight D. Eisenhower, Dwight D. Eisenhower Library, Abilene, Kansas.

4. Eisenhower to J. Bracken Lee, December 30, 1953, White House Central File, OF 116-B, Eisenhower Papers; U.S. Cong. Sen., Committee on Government Operations, *East-West Trade,* 84th Cong., 2d sess., 1956, S. Rept. 2621, pp. 3–8; Kaufman, *Trade and Aid,* p. 60.

5. Churchill to Eisenhower, March 24, 1954, DDE Diary Series, box 6, Eisenhower Papers.

6. Conversation with Bernard Baruch, March 28, 1956, DDE Diary Series, box 10, *ibid.*

7. Eisenhower to Churchill, March ?, 1954, DDE Diary Series, box 6, *ibid.*

8. U.S. Dept. of State, "Special Report on American Opinion Prepared by the Division of Public Studies, January 15, 1951," *Foreign Relations of the United States, 1951, v. 1, National Security Affairs: Foreign Economic Policy* (Washington, D.C.: GPO, 1979), p. 272 (hereafter cited as *FRUS*).

9. *New York Times,* October 8 and 9, 1954; *Business Week,* October 16, 1954, pp. 25–26.

10. John Foster Dulles to Pres, memo, October 28, 1954, box 38, Administration File, Eisenhower Papers; Joseph M. Dodge to Pres, memo, December 15, 1954, Dodge Series, Correspondence Subseries, box 1, Council on Foreign Economic Policy, Office of the Chairman, Records, Dwight D. Eisenhower Library, Abilene, Kansas.

11. *Public Papers of the Presidents of the United States: Dwight D. Eisenhower, 1954* (Washington, D.C.: GPO, 1960), p. 1088; Bipartisan Leadership mtg., December 14, 1954, box 1, Legislative Meeting Series, Eisenhower Papers; Marquis Childs, "Humphrey Vetoes Large Asian Aid," *Washington Post and Times Herald.*

12. On this point, see also *FRUS, 1951,* 7:993–1001.

13. Eisenhower to Secretary of State, memo, June 1, 1954, box 1, Papers of Gabriel Hauge, Dwight D. Eisenhower Library, Abilene, Kansas; Minutes of Cabinet mtg., August 18, 1954, box 3, Cabinet Series, Eisenhower Papers.

14. Kaufman *Trade and Aid,* pp. 58–60, 63–68.

15. *Ibid.*, pp. 63, 153–66, 176–79, and 199–200.

16. See, for example, *ibid.*, pp. 109–10, 113–14, and 140–41.

17. Joseph Dodge to Admiral W. S. DeLany, February 13 and March 2, 1956, Dodge Series, Correspondence Subseries, box 1, Council on Foreign Economic Policy, Office of the Chairman, Records.

18. Kaufman, *Trade and Aid*, pp. 62–63.

19. Conversation with Bernard Baruch, March 28, 1956, and diary entry, March 30, 1956, box 8, DDE Diary Series, Eisenhower Papers.

20. Phone calls, April 19, 1956, DDE Diary Series, box 8, Eisenhower Papers.

21. Clarence Randall, Journals, 1953–61, November 20, 1953, box 1, Dwight D. Eisenhower Library, Abilene, Kansas (hereafter cited as Randall Journals).

22. This was typical of Dulles who preferred to deal with the more purely political problems of international relations. On this point, see Kaufman, *Trade and Aid*, p. 30.

23. C. D. Jackson Papers, Dwight D. Eisenhower Library, Abilene, Kansas; Townsend Hoopes, *The Devil and John Foster Dulles* (Boston: 1973), pp. 146–47.

24. September 25 and October 12, 1956, box 3, Randall Journals.

25. October 3, *ibid.*

26. October 16 and 17, 1956, November 14, 1956, and February 7 and 26, 1957, boxes 3 and 4, *ibid.*; Jack Beal to C. D. Jackson, April 12, 1957, box 91, Jackson Papers.

27. April 26, 1957, May 15, 22, and 29, 1957, and June 6, 1957, box 4, Randall Journals.

28. March 6, 1957, and April 10, 1957, *ibid.*

29. August 19 and 21, 1957, *ibid.*

30. *Public Papers of the Presidents of the United States: Dwight D. Eisenhower, 1955* (Washington, D.C., 1959), pp. 303–4.

31. *Congressional Quarterly Almanac* (1955), 11:235–39; see also U.S. Cong., Senate Committee on Appropriations, *Mutual Security Appropriations Bill*, 1956, 84th Cong., 1st sess., 155, S. Rept. 1033, pp. 1–13.

32. Eisenhower to Lewis Douglas, January 20, 1956, attached to Ann Whitman to Joseph M. Dodge, January 21, 1956, Dodge Series, Correspondence Subseries, box 1, Council on Foreign Economic Policy, Office of the Chairman, Records; see also Bipartisan Legislative Leaders mtg., December 13, 1956, box 1, Legislative Meeting Series, Eisenhower Papers.

33. *Congressional Quarterly Almanac* (1956), 12:418, 427–28.

34. Kaufman, *Trade and Aid*, pp. 159–76.

35. Randall to James Smith, Jr., and Dempster McIntosh, January 8, 1959, and Paul Cullen to Mr. Randall, memo, May 23 and December 16, 1958, box 7, Council on Foreign Economic Policy, Policy Papers Series.

36. On the importance Randall attached to holding this meeting, see January 7 and 17, February 6 and 13, March 29, and April 17 and 26, 1957, box 4, Randall Journals.

37. Memo for Mr. Hensel, February 8, 1955; Memo for Mr. Nolting et al., February 8, 1955; and "Programming $205 Million AEP Fund in FY 1956 Budget," February 22, 1955, Dodge Series, Subject Subseries, box 2, Council on Foreign Economic Policy, Office of the Chairman, Records.

38. In fairness to the historical record, it should be pointed out that Dodge was a fiscal conservative who generally opposed the use of public capital for development purposes. Joseph Dodge to Pres, memo, April 28, 1955, and attachment, Dodge Series, Correspondence Subseries, box 1, Council on Foreign Economic Policy, Office of the Chairman, Records.

39. Memorandum to President, March 14, 1955, box 38, Administration Series,

Eisenhower Papers; Walt Rostow to C. D. Jackson, December 27, 1954, box 75, C. D. Jackson Papers, Dwight D. Eisenhower Library, Abilene, Kansas.

40. Takafusa Nakamura, *The Postwar Japanese Economy: Its Development and Structure* (Tokyo, 1981), pp. 53–66.

41. "Aid to Asia—Meeting with Mr. Stassen on 1–3 1955," attached to O. J. McDiarmid, March 21, 1955, box 5, Dodge Series, council on Foreign Economic Policy, Office of the Chairman, Records; *New York Times,* May 14 and 15, 1955; *Washington Post,* May 13, 1955. See also Lalita Prasad Singh, *The Politics of Economic Cooperation in Asia: A Study of Asian International Organizations* (Columbia: University of Missouri Press, 1966), pp. 9–11.

42. July 1, 1957, box 4, Randall Journals. See also Eisenhower to Robert R. Mullen, June 8, 1959, box 27, DDE Diary Series, Eisenhower Papers. Significantly Eisenhower rejected Mullen's proposal to make Japan "the chosen instrument" of American development assistance, remarking that he was now encouraging greater European participation and more use of private foreign capital in Asian economic development.

43. Nakamura, *The Postwar Japanese Economy,* pp. 47–48.

44. Cabinet mtg., December 17, 1954, box 7, Cabinet Series, Eisenhower Papers; "Contracting Parties to GATT Conclude Ninth Session," *Department of State Bulletin,* December 19, 1955, 33:167; June 23, 1954, box 1, Randall Journals.

45. Memo to Secretary of State, June 1, 1954, box 1, Gabriel Hauge Papers, Dwight D. Eisenhower Library, Abilene, Kansas; June 23, 1954, box 1, Randall Journals; Pres. to the Secretary of State, phone call June 12, 1954, box 7, DDE Diary Series, Eisenhower Papers; Cabinet mtg., minutes August 18, 1954, box 3, Cabinet Series, *ibid.*

46. U.S. Dept. of State, *General Agreement on Tariffs and Trade: Analysis of Protocol (Including Schedules) for Accession of Japan; Analysis of Renegotiations of Certain Tariff Concessions, Negotiated in Geneva, Switzerland, February–June, 1955,* Commercial Policy Series, no. 150 (Washington, D.C.: GPO, 1955).

47. *Business Week,* June 19, 1954, pp. 146 and 148; Kaufman, *Trade and Aid,* pp. 41–43.

48. "Agreement Reached on Japan's Participation in GATT: U.S. Renegotiates Agreements with Benelux Countries and Canada," *Department of State Bulletin,* June 27, 1955, 32:1951–54; *New York Times,* November 4, 1955.

49. *Department of State Bulletin,* November 21, 1955, 33:860–61; *ibid.* December 19, 1955, p. 1067; *New York Times,* October 29 and November 7 and 21, 1955; May 24, 1955, box 3, Randall Journals.

50. *Business Week,* May 14, 1955, p. 32; June 8, 1955, box 3, Randall Journals. See also Kaufman, *Trade and Aid,* pp. 41–43.

51. For an extended discussion of Japan's dependency on American military procurement in the 1950s, see especially William S. Borden, *The Pacific Alliance: United States Foreign Economic Policy and Japanese Trade Recovery, 1947–1955* (Madison: University of Wisconsin Press, 1984), pp. 213–19; Michael Schaller, *The American Occupation of Japan: The Origins of the Cold War in Asia* (New York: Oxford University Press, 1985), pp. 295–97.

52. *Ibid.,* pp. 297–98.

6

The Eisenhower Administration and Changes in Western Embargo Policy Against China, 1954–1958

❧

QING SIMEI

People's University, Beijing

After the Korean War, particularly after the MacArthur hearings in 1951, the Truman administration took an uncompromising position with respect to future relations with the Chinese Communists. In the economic field, a first step was the establishment of separate machinery, the China Committee (CHINCOM), within the framework of the Consultative Group Coordinating Committee (CO-COM), in September 1952. CHINCOM set up a much broader export control list for China and North Korea than for the Soviet Union, and this list came to be known as the "China differential." A second step was a U.S.–Japan bilateral agreement, also in September 1952, which required that Japan maintain export controls toward China at a level even higher than the CHINCOM levels.

The Western embargo policy against China underwent significant changes in the Eisenhower era. From 1954 to 1958, step by step, the Eisenhower administration accepted decisions by the allies to ease curbs on their trade with China. In 1954, the United States agreed to release Japan from the U.S.–Japan bilateral agreement on China trade control. In 1958, the United States agreed to elimination of the China differential. Also in 1958, the United States made exceptions, for the first time since the Korean War, to its legal restrictions, under the Wartime Trading with the Enemy Act, for Canadian subsidiaries of American firms that accepted orders from China.

121

This chapter will discuss how these important changes occurred from 1954 to 1958 and why the changes in Western embargo policy against China did not lead to the final breakdown of barriers to U.S. trade with China.

I

Within the Eisenhower administration, there were two opposing approaches to the Western embargo policy toward Chinese Communists. Eisenhower advocated a relaxation of the curbs on Western trade with China, but most of his Cabinet members insisted that the West should impose a stricter embargo policy on China than on the Soviet Union.

Eisenhower's ideas on the relaxation of Western embargo policy were an integrated part of his conception of American national security, a conception that was, in some respects, different from that of the Truman administration. In the heat of the Korean War, emphasis on national security policy was heavily directed towards building up the military strength of the United States and its allies at a rapid rate, "to a state of readiness on a specified D-day on the premise that at such time the West should be ready to meet the greatest threat of aggression by the Soviets." It was assumed that the United States had no choice but to build up Western military defenses around the Russian and Chinese land mass, whatever the cost financially to the United States.[1]

Eisenhower, however, stressed the necessity of preserving in the United States a sound, strong economy. He feared that further continuance of a high rate of federal spending in excess of federal income, at a time of heavy taxation, would weaken and eventually destroy the economy. For him, there were two threats to American national security: the external threat posed by the Soviets and the Sino-Soviet alliance and the internal threat posed by the magnitude of federal spending. This concept of national security maintained that the United States could not obtain security if it continued draining its economy. To reduce the drain on the U.S. economy of continuing grants-in-aid to its allies, Eisenhower dropped emphasis on getting ready for a global war by some specified D-date. Instead, he emphasized an ability to mobilize rapidly in Western countries before a "floating D-day," which encouraged the allies to develop "a self-supporting economy," capable of providing their own military strength with limited U.S. aid. Eisenhower argued that American donation diplomacy must end: "If at the end of seven years after WWII, and 33 billion dollars of foreign aid, the central problem is as far from solution as it is today, I think something has been wrong in our thinking." He thus strongly urged finding "a substitute for the purely temporary business of bolstering the free nations through annual handouts." The substitute, in Eisenhower's view, was mainly a liberalization of world trade, including a reduction of the U.S. tariff on its allies' products and reestablishment of East-West trade, as well as a "foreign aid program" to meet the most urgent financial needs of U.S. allies. In this way, he said, the United States could get "more security with fewer dollars." Within the new concept of American national security, the President thought the multilateral China trade control was to the detriment of the West, economically and politically.[2]

Eisenhower asserted that the maintenance of China trade controls had been damaging the economies of certain U.S. allies, particularly the Japanese and Western Europeans, limiting their capacity to provide forces and facilities for the common defense. The United States would have to either expand vastly its own military effort, or put many more U.S. dollars into these allies' economies. In Japan's case, Eisenhower maintained that the solution of Japanese economic problems should lie, in part at least, in trade between Japan and China. The alternative, he feared, would be endless subsidization of the Japanese economy by the American taxpayer. He insisted that "many of the nations in the free world have to trade with Communists, if they are to survive economically, and therefore the items in the strategic list should be held to an absolute minimum."[3]

Politically, Eisenhower considered a relaxation of Western embargo policy against China an effective instrument for dealing with the external threat posed by the Soviet Union and Sino-Soviet alliance. For Eisenhower, a weakening of the Sino-Soviet alliance would change the structure of the balance of power in favor of the United States. He was not convinced that the vital interests of the United States were served best by a hostile policy against the PRC. He argued at his first Cabinet meeting in 1953 that all an embargo policy—a naval blockade of China—could do was to drive the Chinese over to the Soviet Union, and "they have got to stay there." He maintained Americans could never split the Soviet bloc unless they gave something to the Communists in the bloc "in the way of inducement to come out from under that umbrella." "You just can not preach abstraction to a man who has to turn for his daily living in some other direction." But how could Americans keep those Communists interested in them? Eisenhower argued that "if you trade with them, you have got something pulling their interest your way." Therefore, he warned his Cabinet members, "The last thing you can do is to begin to do things that force all these Communists to depend on Moscow for the rest of their lives."[4]

It is clear that the President regarded a relaxation of Western embargo policy against Chinese Communists as a useful instrument to strengthen the allies' economies and to split the Sino-Soviet alliance. However, most members of the cabinet did not believe that a relaxation of China trade controls could split the Sino-Soviet alliance. On the contrary, they maintained, only with maximum pressure, with a much stricter trade control imposed on China than on the Soviet Union, might the alliance be split in the long run. The relaxation of China trade control, according to Walter Robertson, Assistant Secretary of State for Far Eastern Affairs, might even further solidify the Sino-Soviet alliance: relaxation would help "strengthen the Chinese Communists' negotiation position with respect to the USSR." The Chinese Communists could thus "obtain more concessions from the Soviet Union" and better their relations with the Soviets. "Only by keeping Communist China under the feasible maximum of pressures," only by "refraining from coming forward with those things the Soviets cannot or will not supply," Robertson asserted, could the United States "best contribute to a realization of the Chinese Communists' part of what actually is entailed in the Soviet embrace."[5]

A stricter trade control imposed on China than on the Soviet Union could not prevent China from getting the Western goods in the Soviet market. The Council on Foreign Economic Policy argued, however, that the transportation fees from the Soviet market to China in either Eastern European vessels or the Trans-Siberian Railroad would represent an annual loss to China of roughly $200 million, which otherwise would be "sufficient to enable China to increase its imports of capital goods by as much as 50%." With this loss to its industrialization, the CIA was convinced that China would have to turn to the Soviet Union for more help, thus becoming a heavier burden. The Naval Intelligence Agency told the Cabinet that strained relations had already begun to emerge between the Soviets and the Chinese "due to differences arising directly from foreign trade difficulties." No wonder most members of the Cabinet concluded that the China differential "would appear to be the best means" of generating a rupture in the Sino-Soviet front.[6]

For most members of the Cabinet, even the policy of maximum pressures on the PRC seemed unlikely to bring about a rupture of the Sino-Soviet alliance in the foreseeable future. For them, the potential difficulties of the Sino-Soviet connection "will stem primarily from the internal workings of partnership and only secondarily from the nature of external pressures." And the internal workings of partnership, according to Secretary Dulles, "might take 100 years to assert themselves." Dulles was worried about "the question of gains for Communist China in the intermediate period"; "There would be no profit for the non-Communist world," he claimed, "if difference emerged between the Soviet Union and Communist China after our vital interests have already been impaired." Before the final collapse of this alliance, the United States had to rebuild the structure of the balance of power in the Far East in its favor. For Dulles and the Pentagon, this required reduction of the "growth and power and prestige" of the Chinese Communists. The control of trade with China became, in their eyes, a powerful instrument to reach this objective. The China differential could, as Dulles saw it, give Chinese "the sense of ostracism—being treated as different, and not morally the equal of other countries." "I believe," Dulles asserted, "the sense of ostracism is the greatest pressure we can bring to bear" on China. Although the China trade control would retard the economic progress of China, Dulles said, "the psychological factors were perhaps more important than the commercial ones."[7]

The China differential could also, as the Office of Chinese Affairs and the Pentagon stressed, hold up the morale of the governments and peoples in the offshore island chains. The governments and peoples of this region, in the words of the American Embassy in Taiwan, were "fence-sitters, who watch carefully the firmness or softness of American policy toward Communist China." "Their greatest fear," the JCS claimed, "is the possibility of a change in U.S. policy which indicates a lack of resolution" in resisting the PRC. Hence any slight hint of U.S. accommodation with the PRC, not to mention a formal relaxation of Western embargo policy, the JCS warned, would gravely undermine anti-Communist morale and strength throughout the critical area, particularly in Taiwan.[8]

In short, within the administration, there was an agreement (excepting Robert Bowie's State Department Policy Planning Staff) that a stricter Western embargo policy against China should be maintained, both as an effective means to split the Sino-Soviet alliance in the long run and before the final rupture, as a psychological instrument to leave the Chinese Communists feeling isolated and to hold the insular position of the PRC.

It is obvious that President Eisenhower's approach to the China trade control was different from that of his Cabinet. With his team style of leadership, he did not impose his own ideas upon the Cabinet. He agreed to some of Cabinet members' arguments, compromised with them on others, and formally approved all NSC decisions on this issue. But this did not mean that he gave up all his approaches. And he was prepared to ease curbs on the Western trade with China when he had opportunities. Such opportunities arose when the major allies of the United States strongly urged removal of the restrictions on their trade with the People's Republic of China.

II

As the Korean War came to an end in 1953, the allies' pressures upon the United States to reduce the embargo's coverage became intense. Most of the U.S. allies had been dragging through a recession, and evidence began to appear that the West's embargo policy was becoming increasingly costly to the cooperating nations. Furthermore, Marshall Plan aid was terminated in 1953, and the sanctions incorporated in this program for forcing compliance with the U.S. embargo policy ended with it. All this led to negotiations in late 1953 and early 1954 among the United States and fourteen other nations, resulting in considerable relaxation of restrictions previously imposed on shipments of strategic goods to the Soviet Union. However, this relaxation, the U.S. representatives in the COCOM insisted, should not apply to China. But Japan and Great Britain particularly were not satisfied with this insistence and began to press for relaxation on their trade with the Chinese Communists.

Japan's prewar trade with Asiatic countries accounted for 65 percent of its total trade volume, over half of which was represented by trade with China. However, because of the international embargo policy toward the PRC, Japan was obliged to purchase iron ore, coking coal, salt, and other essential raw materials in the U.S. and South American markets, via the Panama Canal and the Pacific Ocean. Japan was also obliged to export manufactured products to nondollar areas, since the high cost of importing raw materials made it almost impossible to bring the price of Japanese manufactured products down to a competitive dollar market level. The new Japanese trade pattern thus caused essential difficulties in balancing Japan's dollar account. Indeed, the Korean War was the chief source of the fragile stability for the Japanese economy. And with the close of the Korean War fear began to arise in Japan that a slump in Japan's economy might well follow. The end of the Korean War would oblige the Japanese to seek alternative outlets for the goods that went to bolster the U.S. war efforts. Hence the idea that "Japan must trade with Communist China—it is inevitable" was affirmed by such figures as Hisaakira Kano, spokesman for Japan's most powerful industrial group. In the industrial circles in Japan, as a Japanese newspaper described in 1953, "the call for China trade is desperate, the demand for China trade contains a sort of hysteria."[9]

But the Japanese government was reluctant to facilitate the expansion of Japanese trade with the PRC despite pressures from the business community. And the business community's demand for relaxation of China trade control thus spilled over into the 1953 election campaign and was intensified by the formation of a suprapartisan "Dietman's League for the Promotion of Sino-Japanese Trade," which became the largest organization in the Diet, with its over 300 members, consisting of 70-odd conservative liberals, 40-odd progressives, and all members of the left-wing Socialist Party, to press for the reopening of the China trade.[10]

When the new Hatoyama Cabinet was set up, it immediately took the lead in encouraging China trade. Beyond purely economic consideration, enlarged trade with mainland China was desired by the new Cabinet as an essential stepping stone toward a politically independent Japan. As Foreign Minister Shigemitsu Mamoru argued, broader relations with China on the part of West were inevitable, and Japan was particularly well qualified to act as a "bridge." In the process of mediating between the United States and China, Japan could reassert its independence and leadership in Asia. The Hatoyama Cabinet thus began to push hard for elimination of the bilateral U.S.–Japanese agreement.[11]

In Washington, State Department officials were very suspicious of the political roots of the demand, maintaining that the Japanese plan of serving as a go-between would be detrimental to U.S. national interests in Asia. However, they were also deeply concerned with the economic situation in Japan. Secretary Dulles urged opening more American domestic markets for Japanese goods. He called for the support of all agencies in the Cabinet to overcome the resistance to Japanese goods in the U.S. He maintained that the interests of individual industries in the United States, which would be hurt by the importation of Japanese goods, "must be weighed against the overall national interests."[12]

The Commerce Department, however, was not enthusiastic about opening more domestic markets to Japanese products. Assistant Secretary of Commerce Lothair Teetor argued that some domestic industries had already been hurt badly by the limited import of Japanese goods. In the cotton textile industry, for instance, because of the competition from Japanese and other low wage countries, "total employment has declined nearly 40% since 1947."[13]

Secretary Dulles had to admit: "There is little future for Japanese products in the U.S." Thus, he urged opening more markets in Southeast Asia for Japanese goods. "If we could salvage a substantial part of Southeast Asia there would be the possibility of developing Japanese trade with that area." However, Dulles said, this plan could not be realized in a short time, since "the Japanese had left bad memories in Southeast Asia and would not be welcomed back easily."[14]

While the Cabinet was deciding, the Japanese economy continued deteriorating. In March 1954, the American Embassy in Tokyo warned that "a serious economic crisis may develop as early as this summer as a result of the continuing deterioration in Japan's foreign exchange position."[15] At this point, Eisenhower strongly advised his Cabinet to give concessions to the Japanese. In August 1954, he commented at a Cabinet meeting:

> It is an absolute fallacy to say that there should be *no* East-West trade. Instead, some Japanese trade with her Communist neighbors should be encouraged and would set up influences behind the iron curtain [that] would hurt Russia rather than help the Soviets because it would turn Peiping away from Moscow and create a friction between the Communist countries.[16]

The Cabinet accepted the President's proposal. In August 1954, the National Security Council agreed to release Japan gradually from its obligation "to maintain export controls at a higher level than the CHINCOM levels."[17]

While the Japanese were pressing for relaxing the bilateral U.S.–Japanese agreement on China trade controls, the British demanded abolition of the China differential. Since 1953, the economic situation in Britain had worsened. The previous sizable balance-of-payments surplus disappeared, and dollar reserves dropped by $900,000,000 to the low level of over $2 billion in 1954. In 1955, the Governor of the Bank of England warned that the dollar reserves were only just above the danger mark. Balance-of-payments difficulties arose primarily from the failure of exports to match the massive increase in importation. The British were thus deeply disturbed when the report came that the U.S. Congress would further tighten the import policy, requiring the President to accept tariff commission escape clause recommendations except when national security was involved. This meant that it would be impossible in the future for the President of the United States to reject duty increase recommendations on important U.K. manufactured products, since most such products had little national security significance. The American ambassador in Britain warned that such an action from U.S. Congress would hit a wide range of U.K. exports to the United States and "change the whole direction of British commercial policy."[18]

"All eyes are now turned to Peking," a French newspaper reported in London at that time. British trade with China was only a very small proportion of British world trade. But the British business community regarded this trade as "a very valuable contribution" to the United Kingdom economy. In addition, there was widespread concern for Hong Kong, which depended on China for its main supplies of food. Finally, the British business community's desire to enter Chinese market also came to be motivated by anxieties lest Britain be left behind in the race for China's market. As the Federation of British Industries said, the opportunities in China, "if neglected by the United Kingdom, will be seized by our competitors." And the competition in China among the Western countries was so acute that "British, West German, French, Japanese . . . feel triumph when they manage to conclude a contract with Communist China," a West German reporter declared; "and they feel jealous and worried, if somebody else manages to do the same."[19] The business community's pressure for relaxation of China trade control showed keenly at Westminster.

In the parliamentary debates, both Conservatives and Labourites complained that "we have lost very heavily from these embargoes at a time when our economic situation is not bright" and "when our export trade is vital to the existence of this country." They asserted that the China market would surely "help to maintain the not too certain chances of full employment in this country." As a Labourite peer claimed in the House of Lords, the British government should "knock off quickly these artificial restrictions and allow our merchants and traders to get busy. China is a great market, and we cannot afford to neglect it in the future." A resolute anti-Communist Conservative at Westminster also claimed that the British China policy "must be that of Whitehall and not Washington."[20]

The British Conservative government, in fact, considered relaxation of China trade control an integrated part of British national policy of accommodation with the PRC. A hostile policy against China might raise the nightmare possibility of Western involvement in a land war with China and of Soviet moves in Europe and the Middle East to take advantage of such involvement. Indeed, Churchill declared that nothing could be more foolish than for Western armies to be swallowed up in the vastness of China. Therefore, the British government considered stability in the Far East best suited to its interests. And a stable settlement with the PRC, to the Conservative leadership, was not one imposed and maintained by armed forces or by an encirclement of the PRC, but by a reasonable arrangement in which dissatisfaction on both sides would be reduced to a minimum, no matter how much the Conservatives disliked the ideology of the Chinese Communists. Moreover, the Conservative leadership accepted the argument of the Labour leadership that a hostile policy against China would leave China with Russia as its only friend. Prime Minister Eden argued that with a policy of accommodation, particularly a relaxation of China trade controls, the West might drive a wedge into the Sino-Soviet alliance.[21] Although the Conservatives, unlike the Labour leadership, were willing to keep in step with the United States in relaxing the Western embargo policy against China, they had to consider the possibility that if the British economic situation was deteriorating while strategic trade controls still existed, the opposition party could threaten the government. The British government thus resolutely pushed the Eisenhower administration to abolish the China differential.

While British pressures to relax China trade controls were building up in 1954 and 1955, within the Eisenhower administration, no agreement could be reached on whether the United States should take actions to force the British to maintain the China differential. U.S. military and diplomatic representatives in Europe were unanimous in their opinion that the United States had to make concessions to the British and "approve a sizable reduction in the Differential if the multilateral controls are to be preserved." Joe Walstrom, Director of the Office of Security Trade Controls, U.S. Mission to NATO, told Washington that the pressures from the business community in Great Britain and other European countries were so strong that these governments simply did not know how to explain to their own parliaments and exporters why the China differential must be kept.[22]

However, in Washington, the Pentagon demanded that the United States bring as much pressure as possible to bear upon the British to keep the China differential. "From a strictly military point of view," the JCS asserted, "any relaxation of the China differential would cause the gravest probability that the Pacific offshore island chain will fall under Communist domination" and the United States would suffer "a complete loss of the balance of power in favor of Communists."[23]

The Commerce Department also asked to maintain the China differential. Commerce officials were deeply concerned with the impact of relaxation on the American business community. They complained that in the past, while the United States maintained a complete embargo, "other countries permit their businessmen to conduct trade within certain limits" with China, and this difference had already caused grave troubles for certain U.S industries. The American Brush Manufacturers Association, for instance, bitterly complained that, with high quality and cheap China hog bristles, British brushes were easily "underselling the American brush market." "We are now living under the specter of economic ruin," it remarked. The Commerce Department thus joined the Pentagon in calling for continued pressure upon the British.[24]

But the State Department's position was that "to ask a country to apply the China Differential was a political decision," and Secretary of State Dulles said he was "not prepared to ask the allies for such a decision." Dulles said the Western European countries were much more dependent upon foreign trade than was the United States, so "our allies' budget problems are even more acute than ours and are no longer being relieved by such U.S. liberality as to put $30 billion of economic aid into Europe during the six years 1946–1951." Therefore, Dulles argued that "perhaps some minor adjustments are inevitable" on the issue of the China differential "in order to maintain the essentials."[25]

While the Cabinet members' opinions remained divided on how to react to the British demands, President Eisenhower pushed ahead to ease curbs on British trade with China. In December 1956, the President suggested discussing the China differential with the British Prime Minister at the forthcoming Eisenhower-Eden talks (January 31–February 1, 1956). The U.S. position paper prepared by the Council on Foreign Economic Policy (CFEP) recommended that Eisenhower advise Eden that "the Free world should at this time strengthen rather than soften the multilateral export controls against Communist China." At the Eisenhower-Eden talks, the President showed openly that he was not in agreement with his Cabinet. Secretary Dulles advised Eden, "it would be very important to avoid any indication that there has been a change in policy." And the President remarked: "Surely we cannot say that we made a flat decision in 1952 that cannot be altered in any detail." While Deputy Undersecretary of State Herbert Prochnow told Eden that the net gain in relaxing the differential "would be greater for the Chinese Communists," the President immediately objected: "We are trying hard to help IndoChina, Burma, and other countries in Southeast Asia," and a relaxation of trade "might help them economically if they are able to sell to Communists various raw materials." For the CFEP, the United States could "acquiesce only in a *minimum* adjustment whereby *19 items* would be dropped from the multilateral China embargo list." But the President told Eden that the nineteen items, which his Cabinet had approved for decontrol, were certainly not sufficient to negotiate with the British government; and he suggested that the British government offer a list of items for decontrol. In the Eisenhower-Eden communiqué, instead of calling for a maintenance of the China trade controls, it was announced that "the restrictions on trade with Communist China are to be reviewed in the light of changing conditions" by both governments.[26]

At the President's request, the CFEP began to examine a list of items submitted by the British for decontrol and to review the China differential. But the CFEP members were so divided that no agreement could be reached. Although the State Department was a little more willing than other departments to give British some minor concessions, the reluctant willingness was blocked from time to time by the Defense and the Commerce Departments. As a matter of fact, some officials of the State Department were sympathetic with the views of the Pentagon. Walter Robertson complained that he was "shocked" at Eden's position on China trade controls; he thought it "a position without principle as illustrated by Eden's remark that 'nobody was ever hurt by trading and making a few dollars.'" For almost all of 1956, the CFEP members could not decide, and with the presidential election coming closer, they stopped trying.[27]

In December 1956, right after the election, the Economic Defense Advisory Committee (EDAC) suggested to the CFEP that the United States should exert strong pressures to tighten multilateral trade control against China. Clarence Randall, Chairman of the CFEP, was deeply disturbed because "the President has made it quite clear to me, and to members of the National Security Council, that he believes that controls over trade with the Communist countries should be somewhat liberalized rather than tightened." Randall decided to follow Eisenhower's instruction and to provide for "a substantial reduction" in the CHINCOM list—that is, to retain a "meaningful" but much smaller China differential.[28]

In February 1957, the NSC approved the new Western embargo policy toward China proposed by the CFEP.[29] For the first time since it was established in the Korean War, the China differential was eased. However, the action still fell far short of the desires and intentions of the British, Japanese, French, and others, who demanded the complete abolition of the China differential.

On May 15, 1957, British Foreign Minister Selwyn Lloyd stated that the British would "have to gain greater freedom in respect to China trade and do so quickly because of the Parliamentary situation." Lloyd told Dulles that, in Britain, "there has been rising criticism of the United States in areas where there was unemployment, which was ascribed rightly or wrongly, to the United States' refusal to let them trade with China." Dulles urged that Eisenhower advise British Prime Minister Harold Macmillan not to eliminate the differential. But Eisenhower indicated that he agreed with the British position: "Basically, the Chinese Communists and the Soviets should be treated alike in this matter."[30] Nonetheless, he followed Dulles' advice and sent a letter to Macmillan on May 16 protesting the proposed British move. In his reply to Eisenhower, Macmillan argued: "The commercial interests of our two countries are not at all alike. We live by exports—and by exports alone. So I feel that we cannot any longer maintain the existing differential between Russia and Chinese trade and we shall be making a statement to this effect in Parliament tomorrow."[31] In a private letter to Macmillan, Eisenhower admitted:

> As an individual I agree with you that there is very little of profit in the matter either for your country or for any other. . . .
> We understand your predicament . . . [but] we may be compelled, in the final result, to differ sharply in our official positions.[32]

On May 29, 1957, the British government declared in the Parliament that it had decided to abolish the differential controls on strategic exports to China. The Defense Department and the JCS became so furious at this announcement that they urged the President to punish the British. The Defense Department insisted, "limited sanctions, carefully selected for maximum effect with minimum disruption to mutual security program and political relations, are justified and would result in net security advantage."[33] However, the President decided to firmly support the British decision on abolition of the China differential. He held a news conference and declared:

> Now there is a very great division of opinion in America . . . about the value of trade with Communists.
> . . . There is one school of thought that thinks any trade with the Communist countries is bound to be to their benefit; whereas there is another school of thought that thinks that . . . trade in itself is the greatest weapon in the hands of a diplomat, and if skillfully used, it can be used as a very great instrument of governmental policy.

He explained that those who wanted to abolish the China differential claimed that it was foolish to say the Chinese could not have something and then ship it to the Russians who then passed it on to the Chinese. Those who wanted to retain the differential argued that the communists would have to use their transportation space to get the goods from the Soviet Union to China—and that cost the communists money. The president also explained that the Japanese needed to trade with China, especially when the United States and other nations flirted with protectionist measures to exclude Japanese textiles and light machinery. But, he noted, some people feared that if Japan traded with China, Japan would be "communized." After outlining the opposing positions, the president tilted toward elimination: "frankly, I am personally of the school that believes that trade, in the long run, cannot be stopped . . . I don't see as much advantage in maintaining the differential as some people do. . . ."[34] British Prime Minister Macmillan wrote with relief that "largely due to the President's influence, this Chinese affair which had caused me much concern, was not elevated by the American government or press into a great issue."[35]

The American and British experts began to talk over revision of the embargo list, and the talk was followed by five months of negotiation in Paris within a fifteen-nation Consultative Group. In June 1958, the Consultative Group declared that the West would drastically reduce the COCOM and the CHINCOM lists of strategic items and merge the two lists into one. In other words, henceforth it would be all right with the United States for any of its allies to sell China everything it sold to the Soviet Union. The China differential was formally abolished.

I n 1957 and 1958, the Canadians were also pushing the Eisenhower administration to relax the China trade controls.

In June 1957, the Progressive Conservative Party regained power in Canada for the first time since the Great Depression. This party was in a vulnerable position because it failed to win a majority in the House of Commons. The party was anxious to call a new election in the next spring, which might give it a working majority. And before the new election the party was eager to enhance its popular appeal by making certain changes in U.S.–Canadian economic relations. Progress along this line would be very popular with the Canadians. There had been considerable criticism in Canada of U.S. dominance in Canadian industry and high U.S. tariffs on Canadian products. The Canadian government was particularly concerned with the problem of unemployment, which was expected to be more serious than usual in the coming winter. Increasing unemployment would surely kill the Progressive Conservative Party's chances in the next election, since it was closely associated with the Depression.[36]

In early 1958, when a recession hit the Canadian economy, Chinese trading agents made an inquiry to the American Ford Motor Company's subsidiary in Canada about buying one thousand automobiles or trucks. Inhibited by the Trading with the Enemy Act, which was applied not only to American corporations but to subsidiaries in foreign countries as well, the Ford of Canada refused to fill the order from the PRC. Since this order coincided with layoffs in the Canadian automobile industry, the firm's refusal greatly offended the Canadian government. It was considered an example of American extraterritorial interference. Gordon Churchill, Minister of Trade, and James Moir, president of the Royal Bank of Canada—the biggest and most conservative financial institution in Canada, were striving to have the order filled and to expand Canadian trade with China. Prime Minister John Diefenbaker regarded loud proclamation as the only way of gaining attention south of the border. He thought the policy of the former Liberal government of speaking softly and privately to Washington was bankrupt. Diefenbaker insisted that Canada must not be treated as an extension of the U.S. market. Donald Fleming, Minister of Finance, announced that it was Canada's intention that "Canadian law and Canadian law alone is to prevail over persons or corporations carrying business in Canada."[37]

In Washington, the State Department did not want to offer any concessions to the Canadians. Dulles warned the Canadian government that the Chinese Communists dangled an order before the Canadians only to damage the ordinarily excellent relations between the United States and its northern neighbor. He said he seriously doubted if the Red Chinese could ever pay. He complained that the whole matter "was picked up and used in Canada quite a little bit politically as indicating the U.S. was attempting to give extraterritorial effect to its policies to the damage of Canadian economy because . . . presumably it would have improved Canadian economy and reduced unemployment if such an order could have been accepted."[38]

However, President Eisenhower agreed to make an appropriate concession. He informed Diefenbaker in July 1958 that the United States would make exceptions to its legal restrictions under the Wartime Trading with the Enemy Act for Canadian subsidiaries of American firms that received orders from the People's Republic of China.[39]

In 1958, the Eisenhower administration finally accepted the allies' decision to relax substantially the multilateral China trade control system. In the middle of 1958, the changes in Western embargo policy against China were so significant that the prospects for increased trade between China and the West, as the *New York Times* commented, "take on their rosiest hue since the onset of the Cold War ten years ago." The *Los Angeles Times* was even more optimistic: "It can now be expected that the Eisenhower administration . . . decided to accept as inevitable the gradual breakdown of all barriers to free world trade with Communist China."[40] Eisenhower, however, decided to continue American controls, largely because of the domestic situation.

III

Immediately after the announcement in the Eisenhower-Eden communiqué of February 1956 that restrictions on trade with China were to be reviewed, opposition had emerged in the press and in Congress. A nationwide poll indicated that 61 percent of the American people "disapproved of changing U.S. policy to permit Americans to trade with Communist China." In Congress, Senator John McClellan (D-Arkansas) led the attack with support from Republican minority leader William Knowland, who together threatened to block aid to allies who traded with the PRC. Eisenhower had to bow to congressional pressures, especially after Dulles warned that the Mutual Security Act was endangered. The President decided to temporize until after the November election.[41]

In June 1957, after Eisenhower had determined it was politically safe to agree to the abolition of the China differential, he asked the CFEP to study the possibility of eliminating restrictions on direct American trade with the PRC. The CFEP report argued for continuation of the U.S. embargo. The report contended that the economic benefits to resumed trade between China and the United States would be insignificant. The American exports to China after the relaxation would probably only range between $40 million and $70 million annually. Therefore, the comparatively low level of trade after the relaxation "would have no major impact on the American economy in terms of the balance of payments, providing employment, or supplying needed raw materials." Strategically, the authors of the report maintained that the impact of relaxation of Sino–U.S. trade upon the Sino-Soviet alliance would be also insignificant. Since China's gains from trading with the United States after the relaxation would be modest, they thus would not "materially affect China's dependence on the Soviet Union." The Pentagon's representatives on the Committee repeated their concerns about the psychological effect of a policy shift on Taiwan and the offshore countries. They feared defections that would pose "an important additional burden" on U.S. efforts to defend the region. Finally, the report concluded that ending the U.S. bilateral embargo would have a disastrous effect on Congress, where the administration's foreign aid programs would be jeopardized.[42]

In 1957 and 1958, Eisenhower's Reciprocal Trade and Mutual Security bills, two of the cornerstones in Eisenhower's conception of national security, were in trouble in Congress. In 1958, he wanted a five-year rather than a one-year Reciprocal Trade Act. He also wanted a substantial increase in funds for mutual security. Any cuts the Congress might make in the Mutual Security Bill, Eisenhower feared, would have a "most serious" effect on American national interest. However, the situation in Congress was not favorable for the passage of the Reciprocal Trade Act or for the Mutual Security Bill. In order to win the support of Republican congressmen, Eisenhower turned to Knowland, Walter Judd, and other influential Republicans for help. Most of them belonged to the Republican Right and were staunch supporters of Chiang Kai-shek. To win their support, the President had little choice but to abandon his efforts to open direct trade between the United States and the People's Republic.[43]

If, on the one hand, Eisenhower had to face strong domestic opposition to the relaxation of U.S. bilateral China trade control, then, on the other hand, he did not have strong and unified support from the American business community for relaxation. Pressures for relaxation did exist among certain parts of the American business community in 1950s, particularly on the West Coast, where the competition from Japanese shipping and export firms had a serious adverse effect on shipping and export interests. This business community thus felt that "formal resumption of trade with Communist China would help to alleviate the situation." But at the same time, strong opposition to the relaxation of China trade control also came from other sectors of the American business community. For instance, some warned that "the domestic tung oil industry would be bankrupted by dumping of vast quantities of Chinese tung oil on our market for a prolonged period of time," although it was admitted that such imports could benefit certain "tung oil consuming interests, the brokers, and the importers." Hence, compared with the allies' business communities' voices demanding relaxation of the embargo policy, the U.S. business community's was much weaker. From time to time, Eisenhower instructed the Commerce Department to investigate the business community's attitudes toward the resumption of East-West trade and China trade, and from time to time, the Commerce Department reported that "there has been increasing interest within the U.S. export-business community in the possibility of trade with Communist China."

However, reports added, "the interest evinced does not constitute a significant pressure on the U.S. government to lift the embargo."[44]

Clearly public opinion and political pressures from the Republic Right limited Eisenhower's freedom of action in relaxing the U.S. bilateral China embargo. Eisenhower commented:

> Our trouble was that our domestic political situation compelled us to adopt an absolutely rigid policy respecting our trade with Communist China and the Soviet Union. . . . Hadn't the history of the world down to this time proved that if you try to dam up international trade, the dam ultimately bursts and the flood overwhelms you?[45]

IV

By early 1957, the Chinese government was aware that President Eisenhower and some of his advisers wanted to relax the China embargo, while John Foster Dulles, Walter Robertson and the Pentagon advocated retaining it. In the analysis of the *Renmin Ribao* (People's Daily), Eisenhower, under the pressures of British and other Western countries and of Democrats on Capitol Hill as well as some influential businessmen, was forced to adopt a more realistic approach to the China embargo. In other words, Eisenhower's new approach was interpreted in terms of the President's response to domestic and international pressures, rather than in terms of the President's new conception of American national security and his strategy of splitting the Sino-Soviet alliance with the weapon of trade.[46]

Suspicious of the Eisenhower administration's total strategy in the Far East, the Chinese government was cautious in sending encouraging signals to Eisenhower. By the time of the collapse of the China differential, the Eisenhower administration had sent missiles into Taiwan, and atomic weapons into South Korea, organized SEATO, and violated the Geneva agreement on Indochina. All these moves made the Chinese government conclude that the Eisenhower administration wanted to continue its essentially hostile policy against the People's Republic of China.[47]

Moreover, by 1957, the Chinese economy had already been more closely tied to that of socialist countries due to the Western embargo policy against China. Mao Zedong claimed in early 1957; "Who helped us to design and equip so many important factories in the past few years? Did the United States help us? Did Great Britain help us? No. None of them has done that for us." Therefore, Mao argued, "Our basic interest now lies in our unity with the Soviet Union, with the other socialist countries." As for the Western countries, Mao maintained, "We should co-exist with the West, do some business with them." However, he warned, "Let us not cherish any impractical vision of their help for our industrialization."[48]

Finally, an encouraging gesture to President Eisenhower was considered useless in changing any U.S. attitudes toward China. According to Premier Zhou Enlai, India's Prime Minister Nehru always sent friendly gestures to Eisenhower, but never got anything he wanted from the United States. Zhou said, "This is an important lesson for us." And the memory of Dulles' insult at the Geneva Conference was surely fresh when Zhou maintained, "The Americans always want the other side to make concessions, but they themselves never want to make any concessions. Only when both sides go forward, can they shake hands with each other. But the United States even refused to go forward when we held out our hands."[49]

In the 1950s, if the Chinese were neither fully aware of nor enthusiastic about the policy of inducement, they were certainly aware of the policy of punishment and proudly defied it. After one hundred years of humiliation from foreign powers, the Chinese were determined to demonstrate to the whole world that the policy of high pressures, the policy of punishment, could no longer work on the awakening land of an independent China.

Thus, from 1954 to 1958, Eisenhower's conception of U.S. national security, together with the allies' strong pressures and partial support from the State Department, brought about the relaxation of the Western embargo policy against China; but the political pressures of the Republican Right on Capitol Hill, the opposition of the Cabinet, and the divided opinions in the American business community finally resulted in the failure of the administration to break down the barriers to U.S. direct trade with China.

NOTES

1. John Foster Dulles Papers, White House Memoranda Series, box 8, Dwight D. Eisenhower Library (hereafter cited as DDE).

2. Dwight Eisenhower Diary, entry for July 2, 1953, Dwight D. Eisenhower Papers, Ann Whitman File, Dwight Eisenhower Diary Series, box 9, DDE; Eisenhower to John Foster Dulles, memo, September 8, 1953, Eisenhower Papers, Whitman File, International Series, box 33, DDE; Speech of Winthrop W. Aldrich, November 19, 1952, Dept. of Commerce Decimal File, R640, U.S. National Archives (hereafter cited as NA); Eisenhower to Dulles, September 20, 1953, and June 20, 1953, Eisenhower Papers, Whitman File, Dulles-Herter Series, box 1, DDE.

3. Robert J. Donovan, *Eisenhower: The Inside Story* (New York: Harper, 1956),

p. 132. Memo of conversation, April 18, 1956, Eisenhower Papers, Whitman File, Eisenhower Diary Series, box 14, DDE.

4. Cabinet mtgs., minutes, December 15, 1954, microfilm, Michigan State University Library (hereafter cited as MSU); Cabinet mtgs., minutes, January 12, 1956; 205th mtg., NSC, memo of discussion, April 8, 1954, Papers of White House Office, Office of the Special Assistant for National Security Affairs, NSC Series, box 5, DDE.

The Office of Chinese Affairs and the Bureau of Far Eastern Affairs of the State Department were very upset by the President's approach to China trade controls. See 411.9331/11-2253, A. Guy Hope to Mr. Drumright, memo, December 1, 1953, Dept. of State Decimal File, RG 59, NA; 793.00/8-1853, American Embassy in Taipei to Dept. of State, Foreign Service desp., August 18, 1953, *ibid.;* 793.00/12-1354, Briefing Paper of FE, "Communist China—Policy and Problems," December 19, 1954, *ibid.*

5. 611.93/1-754, conversation re U.S. Policy toward China, memo, January 7, 1954, *ibid.;* 611.93/3-1254, Robertson to Burton H. Young, March 22, 1954, *ibid.*

6. Sinclair Weeks and Harold Stassen to Joseph M. Dodge, Chairman, CFEP, memo, January 21, 1955, Records of the CFEP, Policy Papers Series, box 1, DDE; CIA to Joseph Dodge, memo February 10, 1955, Records of the CFEP, Policy Papers Series, box 1, DDE; CIA to the CFEP, memo, Policy Papers Series, box 1, DDE; Dept. of State to Dept. of Defense, memo, August 30, 1953, Papers of Office of Secretary of Defense, RG 330, CD 388, 1953, NA.

7. 793.00/12-1354, Briefing Paper of the Bureau of Far Eastern Affairs, December 1954, Dept. of State Decimal File, RG 59, NA; Memo of conversation, Eden Talks, Washington, D.C., January 20–February 1, 1956, Eisenhower Papers, Whitman File, International Series, box 20, DDE; 218th mtg., NSC, memo of discussion, December 10, 1954; Eisenhower Papers, Whitman File, NSC Series, DDE; memo of conversation with John Foster Dulles, August 7, 1956, C. D. Jackson Papers, box 56, DDE.

8. 793.00/8-1853, American embassy in Taipei to the State Dept., August 19, 1953, Dept. of State Decimal File, RG 59, NA; JCS to Sec Def, memo December 12, 1955, JCS Chairman's File, Admiral Radford, 1953–1957, 091 China (1956), NA.

9. 493.949/1-6353, American embassy in Taipei to the State Dept., Foreign Service desp., June 3, 1953, Dept. of State Decimal File, RG 59, NA.

10. "Japan's Desire for Trade with China, Businessmen's Resentment at U.S. Policy," *Manchester Guardian*, April 24, 1953.

11. 611.93/6-954, Walter P. McConaughy to Mr. Drumright, memo, June 9, 1954, Dept. of State Decimal File, RG 59, NA; State Dept. Position Paper on Foreign Minister Shigemitsu Visit, August 23, 1955, Eisenhower Papers, Whitman File, International Series, box 18, DDE.

12. Memo of discussion, March 31, 1953, Papers of John Foster Dulles, White House Memo Series, box 8, DDE.

13. Lothair Teetor to Sinclair Weeks, memo, July 9, 1954, Dept. of Commerce, Office of the Secretary of Commerce Central File, 1950–1955, R640, NA.

14. U.K.–U.S. mtg., minutes, July 2, 1954, Eisenhower Papers, Whitman File, International Series, box 18, DDE.

15. 493.949/7-353, American embassy in Taipei to State Dept., Foreign Service desp., March 4, 1954, Dept. of State Decimal File, RG 59, NA.

16. Cabinet mtgs., minutes, August 6, 1954, microfilm, MSU.

17. NSC Progress Report on U.S. Policy on Economic Defense by the Secretary of State and the Director, Foreign Operations Administration, August 30, 1954, Papers of White House Office, Office of the Special Assistant for National Security Affairs, NSC Series, box 5, DDE.

18. Office of Intelligence Research, Dept. of State, "The United Kingdom: Eco-

nomic Position and Outlook," Intelligence Report, no. 7158, February 1, 1956, Diplomatic Branch, NA. American Ambassador in London to Secretary of State, telegram, no. 3995, March 12, 1955, Dulles Papers, General Correspondence and Memo Series, box 2, DDE.

19. "The Race for the Chinese Market," *Le Monde*, March 30, 1955; "America Misled about British Trade with China," *Daily Telegraph*, July 24, 1953, London; "The Business Road to Peking," *Director* (February 1954), London; "The Competition for China Trade," *Frankfurter Algemeine*, July 22, 1954.

20. House of Lords Hansard, April 28, 1953, columns 24–50; "Trade with China," *Birmingham Post*, November 21, 1953; "British Traders Eager to Re-Enter 'Great Eastern Markets,' " *Le Monde*, April 24, 1953.

21. U.K.–U.S. mtgs., minutes, Churchill-Eden Visit, July 2, 1954, Eisenhower Papers, Whitman File, International Series, box 18, DDE.

22. U.S. officials in Europe and Clarence Randall, Chairman, Council on Foreign Economic Policy, minutes of discussions, September 1956, Records of the CFEP, Policy Papers Series, box 2, DDE; Joe D. Walstrom to Clarence Randall, memo, September 1956, Records of the CFEP, Randall Series, box 2, DDE.

23. Arthur Radford, Chairman, JCS to General Twining re U.K. Proposals for Relaxation of Trade Controls with Communist China, June 24, 1955, Records of the JCS, RG 218, Chairman's File, Admiral Radford, 091 China (1956), NA.

24. Sinclair Weeks to John Foster Dulles, memo, August 12, 1955, Office of the Secretary of Commerce, Central Files, 1950–1955, R640, NA; 411.935/3-1154, American Brush Manufacturers Association to John Foster Dulles, May 11, 1954, Dept. of State Decimal File, RG 59, NA; NSC 5429/3, November 19, 1954, Papers of White House Office, Office of the Special Assistant for National Security Affairs, NSC Series, box 6, DDE; U.S.–U.K. mtgs., minutes, Eden Visit, February 1, 1956, Eisenhower Papers, Whitman Files, International Series, box 20, DDE.

25. 091.31, W. B. Thorp, Director, Office of Foreign Economic Defense Affairs, to the Asst. Sec Def, memo March 25, 1953, Dept. of State Decimal File, RG 59, NA; Dulles to Eisenhower, memo, September 6, 1953, Eisenhower Papers, Whitman File, International Series, box 10, DDE; Cabinet mtg., minutes, January 20, 1956, microfilm, MSU.

26. Briefing Paper for Council on Foreign Economic Policy, April 3, 1956, Records of the CFEP, Policy Papers Series, box 1, DDE; Eisenhower-Eden Talks, minutes, February 1, 1956, Eisenhower Papers, Whitman File, International Series, box 20, DDE; *New York Times*, February 3, 1956.

27. Joseph M. Dodge to Andrew Goodpaster, Memo, April 4, 1956, Records of the CFEP, Policy Papers Series, box 10, DDE; memo of conversation, February 3, 1956, Papers of C. D. Jackson, box 56, DDE.

28. Clarence B. Randall to Admiral W. S. Delany, Chairman, Economic Defense Advisory Committee, memo, January 4, 1957, Records of the CFEP, Policy Papers Series, box 9, DDE.

29. NSC 5704/2, February 14, 1957, Records of White House Office, Office of Special Assistant for National Security Affairs, NSC Series, box 20, DDE.

30. Eisenhower and Dulles, memo of conversation, May 16, 1957, Dulles Papers, White House Memo Series, box 5, DDE.

31. Harold Macmillan, *Riding the Storm* (London: Macmillan, 1971), pp. 317–18.

32. Eisenhower to Macmillan, May 24, 1957, Eisenhower Papers, Whitman File, Eisenhower Diary Series, box 24, DDE.

33. Office of the Asst. Sec Def to the Chairman of the EDAC, memo, June 20, 1957, Records of the CFEP, Policy Papers Series, box 9, DDE.

34. Transcript of President's news conference of June 5, 1957, Records of the CFEP, Policy Papers Series, box 8, DDE.

35. Macmillan, *Riding the Storm*, pp. 402–3.

36. Office of Intelligence Research, Dept. of State, "Canada: Economic Position and Outlook," Intelligence Report, no. 9238, September 12, 1957, Diplomatic Branch, NA.

37. *New York Times*, February 6, 1958; *Times*, April 9, 1958; Diefenbaker to Dulles, April 20, 1958, Dulles Papers, General Correspondence and Memo Series, box 6, DDE; *Times*, May 2, 1958.

38. Dulles to Eisenhower, memo, April 30, 1958, Dulles Papers, White House Memo Series, box 6, DDE.

39. Eisenhower-Diefenbaker mtgs., minutes, July 2, 1958, Eisenhower Papers, Whitman File, International Series, box 8, DDE.

40. *New York Times*, July 28, 1958; *Los Angeles Times*, July 31, 1958.

41. Herbert V. Prochnow to Joseph M. Dodge, memo re American Opinion on Trade with China, March 9, 1956, Records of the CFEP, Policy Papers Series, box 8, DDE.

A number of newspapers, such as the *New York Herald Tribune*, the *Christian Science Monitor*, and the *Detroit Free Press*, were sympathetic to the President's decision of reviewing the China trade controls. See, for instance, "Trade with Red China: It's a Choice of Two Risks," *Detroit Free Press*, February 3, 1956.

U.S. Senate, Report re East-West Trade, 84th Cong., 20th sess., p. 3; Eisenhower, Dulles, and Herbert Hoover, Jr., Memo of discussion April 19, 1956, Dulles Papers, General Correspondence and Memo Series, box 4, DDE; Dodge to Eisenhower, memo March 29, 1956, Records of the CFEP, Dodge Series, box 3, DDE.

42. Walter Williams, Chairman, CFEP Committee to Study All Aspects of Policy on United States Trade with Communist China, to Clarence B. Randall, Chairman, Council on Foreign Economic Policy, memo, August 13, 1957, Records of the CFEP, Randall Series, box 2, DDE; C. Edward Galbreath to Clarence Randall, memo, August 5, 1960, *ibid.*, box 4, DDE.

43. Walter Williams to Clarence Randall, memo August 13, 1957, *ibid.*, box 2; DDE; memo of conversation, July 7, 1958; Eisenhower Papers, Whitman File, Diary Series, box 35, DDE; Eisenhower to Ezra Taft Benson, March 20, 1958, *ibid.*, box 62, DDE; Eisenhower to Swede, July 22, 1957, *ibid.*, box 25, DDE.

44. *Los Angeles Times*, November 18, 1952; American Tung Oil Association to the Secretary of Commerce, June 24, 1953, Office of the Secretary of Commerce, Central Files, 1950–1955; Eisenhower to Sinclair Weeks, December 1, 1954, Office of the Secretary of Commerce, Central Files, 1950–1955; Walter Williams, Chairman, CFEP Committee to Study All Aspects of Policy on United States Trade with Communist China, to Clarence B. Randall, Chairman, CFEP, memo, August 13, 1957, Records of the CFEP, Randall Series, box 2, DDE.

45. NSC mtgs., minutes, December 22, 1955, Eisenhower Papers, Whitman File, NSC Series, DDE.

46. *Remin Ribao* (People's Daily), April 20, 1957; June 15, 1957.

47. *Ibid.*, February 9, 1957; March 2, 1957; April 30, 1957.

48. *Selected Works of Mao Zedong* (Beijing: People's Press, 1964), 5:92.

49. *Remin Ribao*, January 30, 1957.

7

The Search for a *Modus Vivendi:* Anglo-American Relations and China Policy in the Eisenhower Era

🕲

ROSEMARY FOOT
University of Sussex

I n the period immediately following the Korean armistice, there seemed to be a genuine possibility that Britain and America could reduce the differences between them over their respective policies toward the People's Republic of China (PRC). In late 1953 and in 1954, the Eisenhower administration placed its relationship with Chiang Kai-shek on a new footing, putting the emphasis on U.S. assistance with defense against, rather than support for, attacks upon the mainland. President Eisenhower and his Secretary of State, John Foster Dulles, also intimated to the British and other Atlantic allies that more far-reaching adjustments in America's policy toward China might shortly be forthcoming, policies that suggested U.S. acceptance of a "two Chinas" formula.[1] British ministers, for their part, hoped to provide content to these policies in the form of less restrictive trading policies with the PRC, representation for Beijing in the United Nations, a cessation of hostilities in the Taiwan Straits area, and the return of the Chinese coastal islands to the control of the mainland.

At the close of Eisenhower's term of office in 1961, however, British and American hopes of a meeting of minds on China policy were shown to have been unrealistic, falling victim at one level to diametrically opposed notions of how best to deal with the existence of Chinese Communist power in Asia. Whereas Britain sought to accommodate that power by integrating the Chinese government into the international system of states and affording that country some role in sustaining an Asian regional order, the United States sought publicly to erode and deny the existence of that power in the belief that any acknowledgement of it would tip the balance further toward a dynamic and disruptive regime, intent on undermining regional stability. Only when the Chinese had been taught to "behave" would due acknowledgement be given.[2] This divergence of approach, with its echoes of 1930s policies toward Japan when British pragmatism came up against an American preference for legal and moral embargoes, must have been familiar on both sides of the Atlantic.[3]

More specific domestic and international factors also contributed to the divergence in British and American China policies. Britain's opposition Labour Party and the new Commonwealth states (especially India) pulled Conservative prime ministers in the direction of a more conciliatory approach, whereas the familiar band of Chiang's congressional supporters, certain powerful administration officials, and anti-Communist allies in Asia moved Eisenhower in the opposite direction. Britain, having been reduced to a power of only middle rank, was in the process of casting off its international obligations, unlike the United States, whose hegemonic role required constant attention to the maintenance of world order. Eisenhower and Dulles were well aware that any easing of international tension could backfire if it undermined the unity of the anti-Communist bloc and the set of policies the United States had been developing since the start of the cold war.

Neither British nor American officials dwelt long on the underlying reasons for their differing approaches to the PRC, but these conflicting conceptions conditioned responses toward situations of both crisis and noncrisis—for example, toward the offshore islands in 1954–55 and 1958; over the question of UN representation for the PRC, and regarding the scope and purpose of the Sino-American ambassadorial talks.

The issue of PRC representation in the United Nations after the Korean War quickly caused strain in Anglo-American relations. The armistice in July 1953 had encouraged London to press Washington at the first opportunity for a change in the "moratorium" resolution, a policy that had dictated the approach of the two allies (and therefore the organization) to the issue since 1951. British ministers questioned whether recognition could be delayed much longer and argued that the phrasing of the moratorium resolution should be altered to reflect a possible future change in policy. Frustration with this policy was at its height in Britain in mid-1955, not only because Eden, as the new British Prime Minister, was much less willing than Churchill had been to defer to the Americans, but also because he believed that continued postponement of the question was unrealistic. Selwyn Lloyd put it more plainly in a telegram to Washington that year, complaining that it was becoming "more and more difficult [for the British government] to defend" the policy and that it was "only a sense of comradeship, not real agreement" that kept London and Washington together at the United Nations. On a visit to Washington in January 1956 Lloyd reminded Dulles that "the question was not an easy one for the United Kingdom. It 'weakened the alliance a bit' on the British side. British acceptance of the moratorium idea was widely considered 'not reasonable' in the U.K."[4] Later in the year, Eden went so far as to recommend the overturning of the moratorium agreement after the 1956 UN session. He was only dissuaded from this policy by strong representations against it from the Foreign Office and from the Foreign Secretary. When, in 1958, the PRC had removed the last of its troops from North Korea, the British government, among other Atlantic allies, argued even more energetically for PRC representation, given that the reasons for denying it the UN seat had now been purged.[5]

Nevertheless, for the rest of Eisenhower's term of office, until 1961, when Britain at last voted for the PRC to assume the seat, Britain stayed in step with its most important ally. London had remained susceptible to a variety of American pressures, including the threat of a violent and incalculable reaction in Congress, and in 1956, to the realization that the administration would never yield in an election year, especially since both Republican and Democratic party platforms contained statements rejecting UN recognition for the PRC. Eisenhower also invested his prestige in the policy, informing the British that he too shared the strong feelings against seating Beijing "in the present circumstances" and that he and certain members of Congress believed that it would be necessary to withdraw from the organization altogether and remove its headquarters from New York if Chiang's government were unseated. If it came therefore, to an "ugly choice of a break with the United States or trouble in Parliament," the Minister of State, Anthony Nutting, spoke for many in the Foreign Office when he said he would infinitely prefer the latter, since the "consequences of a break with the United States would be immeasurably greater." Sir Roger Makins, the British ambassador in Washington, who was "notoriously solicitous for the preservation of good Anglo-American relations," staunchly supported him in this view. And in London, C. T. Crowe of the Foreign Office bluntly argued that there was no "direct U.K. interest which would justify the harm which we would do to our relations with the Americans, and possibly also with the old Commonwealth [who were likely to side with the U.S. administration on the issue] if we withdraw our support now"— a statement that demonstrated Britain's diminished freedom of policy maneuver in the postwar world.[6]

From the Eisenhower administration's perspective, U.S. support for PRC representation was too dangerous a policy to contemplate. In November 1953, Dulles had witnessed the impact that "loose remarks" about this issue could have in Taiwan, and similar rumors in 1954 caused Senator Knowland to threaten to quit his job as senator in order to lead the fight to take the United States out of the United Nations.[7] There was also the question of America's unwillingness to contribute further to the prestige of the PRC, especially in the aftermath of French losses in Indochina and China's participation in the 1954 Geneva Conference on Korea and Indochina. As Dulles told Lloyd in January 1956, the United States "must avoid enhancement of the power position of the Chinese Communist regime . . . . The question of gains for Communist China in the intermediate period was one of great gravity for the U.S." and should be for Britain, too, Dulles said, given U.K. interest in the future of Australia, New Zealand, Malaya, and Singapore.[8]

Grudgingly, Britain acquiesced in the policy during the 1950s, convinced that there must be a middle course and taking comfort from the knowledge that the moratorium procedure allowed London to raise the issue each year. The hope was that something positive would happen in Sino-American relations that would make movement on the U.S. side possible.

B ritish governments in the 1950s tried in various ways to improve the political climate between China and the United States. At the Geneva Conference in 1954, the British Foreign Secretary, Anthony Eden,—the co-chair of the conference—kept in as close contact as possible with Foreign Minister Zhou Enlai, a decision which resulted in a marked improvement in Sino-British relations. Eden's objectives, however, were far more extensive than this, but were pursued at the cost of a bitter clash between himself and Dulles over U.S. proposals concerning China and Southeast Asia. In Berlin in February, the Eisenhower administration had argued against the PRC being named one of the convenors of the five-power conference at Geneva and subsequently claimed that China had only been invited "to account before the bar of world opinion." Dulles also sought, prior to the conference discussion on Indochina, to establish a defensive alliance in South East Asia in order to deter the PRC from open intervention in support of Ho Chi Minh's forces. Eden, on the other hand, argued against a move that he believed would jeopardize any chance Geneva had of succeeding and, instead, put forward the notion of establishing a Locarno-type arrangement for Southeast Asia, implying that the Chinese would be invited in as one of the guarantors of the future peace of the area. China's leaders were interested in the notion, but the American reaction was wholly negative, not perhaps as Eden believed because Dulles equated the idea with British appeasement policies of the 1930s, but more because the proposal in Dulles' view would amount to expressing "moral approval of a Communist success."[9] London and Washington thus found themselves to be working at crosspurposes during the conference, the former seeking to bolster China's regional position, the latter attempting to prevent any augmentation of that country's prestige. Moreover, the clash between Eden and Dulles badly soured relations between them, further diminishing any possibility of a sympathetic consideration of each country's China policy.[10] Britain therefore had to be content at this stage with facilitating direct negotiations between Beijing and Washington outside the main body of the conference on the single issue of trying to secure the release of nationals detained in each adversary's country.

The U.S. agreement to sit down with the Chinese, with however restricted an agenda, provided a moment of quiet triumph for the British. In the initial stages, the British ambassador to Beijing acted as intermediary between the two sides, but was reluctant to continue in this role in what certain U.S. officials, such as Drumright (Deputy Assistant Secretary of State for Far Eastern Affairs), McConaughy (Director, Office of Chinese Affairs) and Dulles believed was part of a scheme to secure direct negotiations. Nevertheless, Dulles eventually agreed to direct talks, perhaps not so much as a result of pressure from the British, but because James Hagerty, the President's press secretary, and the Undersecretary of State, Walter Bedell Smith, both argued that the humanitarian aspects of the issue would outweigh the probable domestic criticism that negotiations implied movement toward recognition of the PRC.[11] It is likely that the United States, having agreed to direct negotiations in 1954, found it difficult to refuse to formalize the process at the ambassadorial level in August

1955. The British felt entitled to derive some satisfaction from their role in the process.

The talks that started in 1955, still concerning the issue of the detained citizens, precipitated new tensions in the Anglo-American relationship. The U.S. draft statement agreeing to the discussions had said that the United States was willing to go ahead with such contacts provided the subject matter was restricted to the fate of American citizens in China and to other issues that would not infringe on third party rights. London pressed successfully to have this last part of the statement modified to read that such talks would include "practical matters now at issue" between the two countries.[12] Nevertheless, despite the limited nature of this victory over phrasing, Britain quickly came under criticism from Walter Robertson, the Assistant Secretary of State for Far Eastern Affairs, who pointed out to Dulles in July that it was "difficult to think of any additional topics which might be fruitful and do not either directly involve the rights and essential interests of the Chinese Nationalists or else open a Pandora's box."[13] At San Francisco on June 20, Dulles had raised the hopes of Harold Macmillan, the new Foreign Secretary, about the future of America's China policy by suggesting that the United States might be willing to do something about attacks on fishing vessels and might attempt more generally to ease the situation in the Taiwan Straits; but when Macmillan suggested that these points could form later stages of the negotiations, Robertson accused Britain of having a particular "axe to grind" on these topics. In Robertson's view, the United States should not be influenced by Macmillan's argument that Washington's formula was "too restrictive." He was clear from the outset that the only thing the United States should agree to discuss in addition to the matter of U.S. civilians in China was the "renunciation of force by the Chinese Communists in the entire area of the Taiwan Strait," in the expectation that it was "highly unlikely" in his view that Beijing would agree either to the release of all Americans or to a renunciation of force. "Such being the case," he said, "we would have good grounds for refusing to discuss other topics until these are set-tled." Subsequent instructions from Dulles to the U.S. ambassador at the talks, U. Alexis Johnson, confirmed that the latter should first discuss the repatriation of civilians, then the cases of Americans listed as missing in Korea, and after that could go on to "emphasize the deep concern of the U.S. in getting assurance that the CPR is prepared to renounce force to achieve its ambitions."[14]

Within a few weeks, the United States and China did devise a formula concerning the repatriation of civilians from the respective countries, but U.K. optimism regarding this was quickly undermined by the U.S. decision to distort the meaning of the agreement reached. On September 10, 1955, the United States and China agreed that both governments would "adopt appropriate measures" so that the civilians could "expeditiously exercise their right to return" home.[15] The U.S. interpreter at the talks has subsequently explained the source of America's delight at the Chinese suggestion of the term "expeditiously," for the word, in addition to meaning quickly, also had "connotations of efficacy and efficient action," whereas the Chinese text proposed the compound *chin-su*, which only implied "utmost speed."[16] The Eisenhower administration used these different interpretations of the term as a weapon with which to berate the Chinese for not releasing all the Americans detained in China immediately, even those cases that were subject to judicial review. But as Makins reported from Washington, the Chinese ambassador at the talks had made it clear to the Americans that the agreement would still mean that an "unspecified number of what the Chinese call 'unfinished cases' would be left in Chinese hands."[17] Furthermore, Makins said, the Americans had accepted "expeditiously" on the private understanding that Washington's publicity about the agreement "would so involve Chinese face" that Beijing would be forced to comply with the meaning the United States had attached to the term. The British chargé d'affaires in Beijing also endorsed the Chinese understanding of the agreement and noted that the British embassy, involved in assisting with its implementation, would be embarrassed by U.S. publicity claiming "Chinese bad faith" when, at the time of the announcement, Washington "seemed to be under no illusions about Chinese intentions."[18]

As the talks continued along their difficult path, it became clear that the Chinese were trying to use those Americans still detained in China as bargaining chips in their attempts to compel the United States to discuss other points at issue between them. Despite Beijing's tactics, British urgings to move on to new items, and similar pressure from the U.S. ambassador at the talks, the administration continued to stall on the basis of Walter Robertson's argument that the first task was to "ensure that promises already made [were] kept." Robertson also advised that if there were to be any new items for discussion, the two sides should start with the prisoners missing from the Korean conflict—a suggestion that led British officials to conclude at the end of 1955 that, beyond the release of the Americans in China, nothing much of substance was going to be negotiated.[19] The talks did grind on until their temporary suspension at the end of 1957, after which, in the autumn of 1958, they were transferred to Warsaw. But as the

British government had predicted, only the one agreement was signed, and the Eisenhower administration remained inflexible until 1959, when the Chinese themselves had become more rigid.[20]

U ndoubtedly, fears about how the issue of negotiations with the Chinese would be treated in 1956, an election year, partly explain the administration's caution. But the undermining of the U.S. position in Southeast Asia after the French defeat at Dienbienphu and the 1954–55 crisis concerning the offshore islands also foreclosed a number of options, and in these circumstances to have raised expectations regarding the possibility of a settlement in the Taiwan area was irresponsible. Though the offshore islands crisis in 1954–55 helped precipitate the negotiations discussed briefly above, it also made compromise with the PRC that much more difficult, since it also prompted a clarification of the boundaries of America's relationship with the Chinese Nationalists in the form of the Mutual Defense Treaty and the Formosa Resolution.

The conflict involving the coastal islands of Jinmen and Mazu roused Britain to energetic attempts to moderate U.S. policy. Both Churchill and Eden believed Eisenhower and Dulles to be on very weak legal grounds, as well as to have a doubtful position politically and strategically in claiming Chiang Kai-shek's right to retain these islands. More importantly, their genuine fear that war between the United States and the PRC could well result led the British to consider risking a serious public breach with the Americans over the issue.

Dulles gave London its initial entrée into the policy debate. At a National Security Council (NSC) meeting on September 9, 1954 (at which Dulles was not present), the Chairman of the Joint Chiefs of Staff, (JCS) Admiral Radford, outlined the majority view of the Chiefs concerning America's most appropriate response to an attack on the islands. The JCS, except for General Ridgway, believed their retention to be of "great importance" to the United States and that U.S. armed forces should be used to "prevent Communist seizure of these islands." Furthermore, Radford said, "it could be taken as certain that operations by U.S. armed forces would require some action against the mainland"; thus, the U.S. commander in the area should be "permitted to attack such mainland military installations as he deemed necessary."[21]

On Dulles' return from the Manila Conference and from the signing of the Southeast Asia collective defense treaty, he put before the NSC the nature of the "horrible dilemma" facing the United States: either to acquiesce in the Chinese Communist capture of the islands "with disastrous consequences in Korea, Japan, Formosa and the Philippines," or to go to their defense, which could mean war with the PRC and world and domestic condemnation. He therefore recommended that the administration should raise the issue of Beijing's attacks at the UN Security Council with a view to stabilizing the situation and reinforcing the status quo in the area, adding that it would be "important to find out if the U.K. will go along with this plan" and further suggesting that, if it would, it "might mark the beginning of our coming together on the Far East."[22] consequently, the idea was put to Eden in the middle of the month, with the added inducement that "it was in [Dulles'] mind (and he asked you to keep this as close as possible) that this might initiate a general review of the Chinese problem." Dulles was "casting about for some way of starting a peaceful process which might eventually lead to a solution of the problems of the area."[23]

Dulles expanded on the details of his UN plan—code-named "Oracle"—at a meeting with Eden in London on September 17. However, he also took the opportunity to explain the nature of the pressures that were compelling the U.S. administration toward a defense of Jinmen and Mazu, including the loss of morale that would result in Taiwan if the islands, containing some 50,000 of Chiang's troops, were lost, and the dangers to the U.S. global position if, after the recent defeat at Dienbienphu, America showed itself again to be unwilling to fight alongside an ally. This realization that Washington was close to giving a commitment to defend Jinmen sparked Eden's interest in Oracle, but he warned that the PRC might well reject UN intervention given that, technically, it believed itself still to be at war with that body. In that event, direct negotiations between the United States and PRC might be preferable, Eden said, a suggestion that Dulles quickly rejected for domestic reasons.[24]

Oracle thus received tentative U.K. endorsement, subject to certain modification of its terms. With the 1951 UN "aggressor" resolution presumably in mind, London convinced Washington of the need to take action under chapter 6 rather than under chapter 7 of the UN Charter, since the former referred to situations likely to endanger peace, the latter to an actual threat to peace, thus involving the danger that the Security Council might move from the resolution to measures utilizing armed force. Dulles and Eden also agreed that New Zealand, a current member of the Council, would be invited to initiate Council action and that London would sound out Beijing and Moscow in advance of submitting the resolution.[25]

In early October, however, disagreements arose between London and Washington concerning the scope of the proposed UN discussion and over the U.S. decision to go ahead at the same time with the signature of the Mutual Defense Treaty with the Chinese Nationalists. In Eden's view, the U.S. draft minute on the UN resolution, drawn up to clarify Wellington's, London's, and Washington's obligations concerning Oracle and stating that the three would make "every effort to limit the discussion of and action on the New Zealand resolution in the United Nations to the hostilities around Quemoy," was "unduly restrictive." Eden had thought (and had been encouraged so to think by Dulles during the latter's recent London visit) that the three were engaged in taking a "cautious first step" toward a wider settlement. Thus, in the British Foreign Secretary's view, the draft minute not only should indicate that the initial phase of UN action would be limited but also should convey the impression that the three were "looking toward an eventual settlement" in the region. State Department officials, however, notably Walter Robertson, quickly poured cold water on this proposal, suggesting instead wording that demonstrated the incremental U.S. approach to China policy: "Any future action, if any, to be taken in the light of conditions as they may develop in the future."[26]

This debate over the phrasing of the draft minute led Dulles to draw back from the promises implied in his earlier conversations with Eden. Fearing, perhaps, that he was losing control of the direction of the Oracle operation, he stated his position more plainly. He had not meant to imply, he said, that if the Jinmen issue was successfully dealt with, Washington "would move right on from there to a general settlement of the Formosa problem," only that the allies would have "increased the chances of peaceful as opposed to violent change." The administration, he warned, would "be unable to take this first step if it were to be represented as being a first step in a longer-range program, leading perhaps to recognition of Communist China and its admission to the UN." On the other hand, the alternative to not going ahead was, of course, "fraught with perilous possibilities."[27] Not unexpectedly, with the threat of inactivity and a dangerous outcome over their heads, Britain and New Zealand agreed to the U.S. draft and its strict limitation of discussion to the subject of hostilities around Jinmen, with only the minor amendment Eden had suggested, that instead of voting against any attempted change of substance to the resolution (as Dulles had wanted), the three would "make every effort . . . to prevent" any such amendment.[28]

Dulles' chariness on this issue stemmed in large part from his realization that powerful officials such as Radford and Robertson had been brought around to agreeing to Oracle only in the belief (as

Radford had said) that the resolution had as its "ultimate aim the creation of a situation which will lay the groundwork for U.N. acceptance of U.S. or allied assistance to the Nationalist Chinese in holding the offshore islands."[29] Robertson and the U.S. ambassador in Taibei, Karl Rankin, had already used Oracle as a method of persuading Dulles to press ahead with the signature of the defense treaty with Nationalist China, to offset what they saw as an inevitably negative Nationalist reaction to the UN resolution. In these circumstances, Eisenhower and Dulles decided to go ahead with the treaty negotiations in October, provided that Chiang was prepared to assume a defensive posture on Taiwan and that the treaty was truly defensive.[30]

Welcome as this aspect of the treaty was to them, British officials realized that the timing of the negotiations with Chiang and the likely outcome would undermine or destroy completely the chances for Oracle's success.[31] To salvage something from the operation, it was imperative in London's view for the Eisenhower administration to give full publicity to the defensive provisions of the treaty and to curb all attacks from Taiwan. Dulles was reluctant to offer such information at this stage, however, agreeing only to allow the British to make this feature known during private talks in Beijing and Moscow.[32] London next pressed for publication of the exchange of letters between Dulles and the Chinese Nationalist Foreign Minister, Yeh Kung-ch'ao [George Yeh], which made clear that any Nationalist attacks on the mainland would be a "matter of joint agreement" between the two allies. This time, Robertson passed on Washington's refusal, stating that the United States had pledged to Chiang that it would not reveal the contents of the notes without a definite reason for doing so.[33] Oracle was therefore stalled again.

The treaty negotiations, the cementing of SEATO, and fears in Beijing that NEATO was a likely next stage provided the context for intensified Chinese assaults on the offshore islands, notably on the Dazhen group.[34] Air attacks were launched on January 10, and on January 18, four thousand PLA troops overran Yijiangshan, ten miles north of the Dazhens. The Eisenhower administration quickly took an operational decision that the Nationalists should evacuate the Dazhens on the grounds that they were too vulnerable and of insufficient importance strategically to justify a U.S. defense of them.[35] However, in compensation for the expected loss of Nationalist morale that would result from evacuation, the administration moved toward giving Chiang a commitment that "under present circumstances" the United States would assist in the defense of Jinmen and possibly of Mazu too. Dulles suggested this crucial modification in NSC policy toward the islands to President Eisenhower on January 19, Radford indicating that he was in "strong agreement" and that the time had come for the United States to make clear its policy toward Jinmen and Mazu. Eisenhower gave his assent and authorized Dulles to go ahead with his planned consultations on the matter with the British, the Chinese Nationalists, and congressional leaders, the three key spokes in this particular policy wheel.[36]

In discussions with the British ambassador, Dulles revealed U.S. plans to give a provisional guarantee to defend Jinmen, explained that this required a congressional resolution to give full force to the decision, and requested British cooperation in pressing ahead with Oracle. Eden, alarmed at this change in policy, and remembering that Dulles had earlier said that Jinmen could not be defended without the tactical use of atomic weapons, seized on the request involving Oracle and authorized Makins to put it strongly to Dulles that London would agree to go ahead in the UN only if Washington gave up its idea of guaranteeing Jinmen: "If the Americans cannot defer the guarantee," Eden explained, "then once again the whole basis on which we originally agreed to Oracle has been changed and we should have to look at the whole situation very carefully once more."[37]

The President and his chief advisers met further resistance to the plan to defend Jinmen from within the administration. Robert Cutler, Special Assistant for National Security Affairs, believed it could lead to war with the PRC, and the Treasury Secretary, George M. Humphrey, found it hard to justify retention of islands that "were set right down in the middle of a Chinese Communist harbor." The Secretary of Defense, Charles Wilson, also felt it was wrong "to fight a terrible war with Communist China simply in order to hold all these islands." In his view, "we should defend only Formosa and the Pescadores and let the others go." Eisenhower, Dulles, and their other supporters at the NSC responded with arguments that stressed the psychological effect on Chiang and the "free nations of Asia" that loss of these islands would have and discounted as far as possible the likelihood of war with the PRC. The compromise they offered their uneasy colleagues was that the United States would word its intentions toward the islands "so as not to tie ourselves down on them forever."[38]

In the light of this compromise and a report that London was extremely reluctant to see Washington take the proposed step on Jinmen—especially since the administration might be obliged to use atomic weapons, a subject on which the British were "always very sensitive"—Dulles reported to the next NSC meeting that he had come to the view that in the President's message to Congress it would be "best not to nail the flag to the mast by a detailed statement respecting our plans and intentions on evacuating or holding certain of these islands." Only the Chinese Nationalists would be told privately exactly what the administration had in mind. To soothe further anxieties expressed at that meeting, Eisenhower explained that the new U.S. position on the coastal islands meant "no permanent extension of the defense area of Formosa," only that the United States would continue to defend the islands "until some other arrangements could be made to quiet the Formosa area."[39]

Subsequently, Dulles reported to Makins that the United States had agreed to give only a private and not a public commitment to defend Jinmen, at the same time taking the opportunity of warning London that whereas it might be in British minds that the islands should eventually pass into mainland control, the United States could not give such a commitment. His wish was that the islands might diminish in importance some time in the future, which might permit some adjustments in status to be made. Unfortunately, however, Makins' report of that meeting implied that the United States had gone much further in adjusting its views to London's: that it had, in fact, "abandoned the notion of a provisional guarantee" and would make "no additional private or public commitment to the Chinese Nationalists."[40] This error, perhaps borne of Makins' enthusiastic support for the closest of Anglo-American relations, was to cause difficulties between the allies later.

Within a few days, at an off-the-record press briefing, Dulles did indeed give that private undertaking; and in a message approved by Eisenhower, Chiang Kai-shek was informed that "under present circumstances it is the purpose of the President to assist in the defense of Quemoy and Matsu against armed attack if he judges such attack is of a character which shows that it is in fact in aid of and in preparation for an armed attack on Formosa and the Pescadores and dangerous to their defense." The message also included the following crucial sentence: "An attack by the communists at this time on Quemoy or Matsu which seriously threatened their loss would be deemed by the President to be of this character."[41]

In the next few weeks, the British stepped up their attacks on the American policy, a defense commitment that London regarded as "legally untenable and militarily unsound." Not once did they urge a modification in U.S. policy toward Taiwan—and London did indeed make clear its own distinction between the PRC entitlement to the coastal islands and its claims to Taiwan—but reserved their fire for what they saw as the stronger part of their case. On February 9, 1955, the Churchill government confirmed that neither it nor the Commonwealth prime ministers, then meeting in London, would support the

United States over the islands, "which were regarded as part of China."
Furthermore, the breach with the United States was likely soon to be
obvious to all, since the U.K. government was being pressed to define
its attitude toward the area more clearly and "could not continue the
evasion indefinitely."[42] Eisenhower's letter to Churchill on February
10, which revealed that "under existing conditions" he had given the
Chinese Nationalists "certain assurances with respect to the offshore
islands" (the implied importance of which Dulles tried to downgrade
by stating that "the word [assurances] was not used in any technical
sense of an agreement or commitment but merely that present circumstances were somewhat reassuring to them") prompted Churchill
to send Eisenhower the letter that he had been wanting to despatch
for some time. In it, Churchill first requested clarification about the
nature of these "assurances" and then went on to report the British
view that, while the regime on Taiwan should be protected, "a war to
keep the coastal islands for Chiang would not be defensible here." In
no sense were the islands a "just cause for war," he argued.[43]

In a tough response, Eisenhower refuted Churchill's arguments and
resorted to the familiar domino thesis to bolster the U.S. position:
"All of the non-Communist nations of the Western Pacific—particularly Korea, Japan, the Philippines, and, of course, Formosa itself, are
watching nervously to see what we do next." The President also drew
the stock analogy with the 1930s: "further retreat becomes worse than
a Munich because at Munich there were at least promises on the part
of the aggressor to cease expansion and to keep the peace. In this case
the Chinese Communists have promised nothing." His final thrust
was to raise doubts about U.S. willingness to support Britain in the
event of attacks on Malaya or Hong Kong, action that "would surely
not be popular in this country," though he added that if the case were
presented well, no doubt "we would be at your side."[44] Despite the
British Cabinet's concern at the tone of this letter,[45] London still
remained unconvinced by the U.S. argument, and when Dulles and
Eden came together again in late February in Bangkok, they once
more rehearsed their opposing positions.[46]

Against this background of allied opposition, Dulles had returned
from the Thai capital convinced that a serious deterioration in the
military situation in the Taiwan area was imminent, a conclusion
that served to sharpen U.S. thoughts about the crisis still further. On
March 11, the President called a meeting to discuss how to avoid
direct U.S. involvement in the Taiwan area "at a time while the
Western European Treaties were pending"; and how "to limit U.S.
intervention as much as possible if it became necessary to intervene;
and to discuss what action the U.S. would take if [it] had to inter-

vene." The conclusions as summarized by Eisenhower were that the United States should do everything it could to help the Chinese Nationalists defend themselves; that if the United States had to intervene, it would first do so with conventional weapons; but if the intervention did not prove decisive, it might have to use atomic weapons. The key point, however, Eisenhower said, was to "avoid involvement during the next sensitive weeks, because any U.S. direct involvement might critically damage us in Europe."[47]

Eden had already added to the public criticism of U.S. policy during this period in a speech to the House of Commons in which he urged Chinese Nationalist withdrawal from the coastal islands, called on the PRC to give a pledge that it would not take Taiwan by force, and suggested that in this event consideration should be given internationally to the question of Chinese recognition in the United Nations and to the future status of Taiwan. Privately, Eden became even more obstinate about pushing ahead with Oracle, warning Eisenhower and Dulles that introducing the resolution now would not focus "attention on our desire to have a ceasefire" but rather "on the difference between the United States on the one hand and other free nations on the other regarding the coastal islands." Dulles, apparently stung by this, replied: "I rather expected the Soviets to veto the Resolution but I must confess I did not expect that you would," and Eisenhower weighed in with another letter to Churchill in which he derided London for regarding "Communist aggression in Asia as of little significance to the free world future."[48]

At the end of March, however, it was clear that divisions within the administration as well as those between America and its allies were forcing a shift in emphasis within U.S. governing circles. On March 28, Dulles observed (in something of an understatement) that he thought that the United States was drifting in "very dangerous waters without an adequately prepared chart." He wanted to give more thought to the most effective deterrents to war and not so much time to contemplating war itself. Robertson, alarmed by these signals, went straight to the nub of the problem: if the administration was going to change its mind on defending Jinmen and Mazu, "an awful lot of work" would have to be done on Chiang, to whom the United States "had given . . . a commitment to his own certain knowledge."[49]

Nevertheless, despite the agreement with the Chinese Nationalists and Chiang's argument that he had acquiesced in the evacuation of the Dazhens only because of that commitment to the defense of Jinmen and Mazu, the administration did continue to back away from its earlier position. On April 5, Eisenhower and Dulles discussed their predicament at length, concluding that the preferred option was to persuade Chiang that the coastal islands should be regarded as "out-posts, not citadels." While, on the one hand, if the islands were given up it could lead to a collapse of morale on Taiwan and consternation in Thailand, the Philippines, Laos, and Cambodia, on the other hand, a defense of the islands, Eisenhower feared, would divide "our people" and would be repudiated by world opinion. On balance, therefore, Eisenhower now concluded that for the sake of U.S. prestige, it would be much better if the United States "were not even remotely commit-ted to the defense of these islands and if greater force . . . were concen-trated on Formosa and the Pescadores."[50]

Chiang Kai-shek, of course, was the key to the success of this latest plan, and the two negotiators he would most trust (Radford and Robertson) were dispatched to try and persuade him of the proposal's merits. Unfortunately, however, it was also these two who were most enamored of the commitment to Jinmen and Mazu and had been involved in the transmittal of that commitment; thus, not surpris-ingly, they did not pursue the "outposts" idea with any great convic-tion in Taibei.[51] U.S. policy in the area thus began to drift and became limited to the notion of seeking a de facto cease-fire and playing for time, in the hope that tempers would cool and the islands would lose their significance.[52]

The situation had calmed appreciably during this period anyway as a result of Zhou Enlai's offer at the Bandung Conference to have direct talks with the Americans. The British were grateful that Dulles responded favourably to this invitation and gave him credit for what they saw as a brave acceptance speech; but there was not much else on the horizon to provide comfort in this area of American policy. At Geneva in 1955, Eisenhower tried to persuade Eden—Prime Minister at last—of his desire to be quit of the islands, but Eden was not impressed by Dulles' confirmation that the United States would still intervene if the islands were attacked and the Nationalists put up a gallant but unsuccessful resistance. Eden thought it "terrible" that the onset of a world war could depend on how long Chiang's forces could hold out.[53]

Between 1955 and 1958, the Eisenhower administration did little to encourage Chiang to reduce his forces on the islands, and indeed the numbers of troops steadily rose throughout the period. In the Foreign Office view, Chiang had become firmly entrenched, and the United States had become ever more firmly committed and had "al-lowed the moment to pass" when they could have got the Nationalists to quit the coastal islands. Dulles confirmed the correctness of this analysis in October 1957, when he stated to the NSC that "it seemed to him that defense of all of the off-shore islands was now so complete and so integral a part of the defense of Taiwan, that it was not to be compared with the fluid situation of three years ago." Furthermore, "if there were an all-out attack on Quemoy or the Matsus, the United States should not sit to one side and permit the loss of these islands, because their loss would surely result in the loss of Taiwan and the Penghus."[54]

London was not surprised, therefore, when a new outbreak of tension arose over the islands in 1958, given Chiang's continued sorties against the mainland and his steady reinforcement of the coastal islands until they contained 100,000 men, one third of his total army.[55] Yet this time the British were much more reluctant to argue their case, despite the fact that the stakes were higher, with U.S. national prestige publicly "nailed to the mast." On this occasion, the United States quickly made a public commitment to defend the islands, Dulles (with Eisenhower's agreement) arguing on September 4 that not only should the PRC not attempt to take the islands by force, since this violated the principles of world order, but also that the territory had never been under Chinese Communist authority.

The new British Prime Minister, Harold Macmillan, reacted to the news in such a way as to show the continuity of the constraints on U.K. China policy: "if we abandon the Americans . . . it will be a great blow to the friendship and alliance which I have done so much to rebuild and strengthen [after the Suez breach]. If we support them, the repercussions in [the] Far East, India and through the Afro-Asian group in the Middle East may be very dangerous. At home, Parliament and the public will be very critical of any change from our public position three years ago." In an attempt to balance these conflicting elements, the Prime Minister confined himself to repeating Churchill's 1955 view that war over the islands was "not defensible."[56] Students of this period have thus rightly concluded that British advice this time seemed to have been given "for the record" and was "not pursued with vigour." One analyst, Morton Halperin, working with official sources, has concurred and has categorically stated that while the U.K. government was kept informed and its dissent from policy was noted, its "position did not . . . have any specific direct affect on U.S. policy."[57]

Analysis of these policies underlines the restricted nature of British influence on America's China policy and London's essentially junior role in the allied relationship. They also indicate steady British disillusionment that change in U.S. policy would be forthcoming within a reasonable time period. Admittedly, during the first offshore islands crisis in 1954–55, the U.K. government did make its mark at an important stage of policy formation. By marshalling Commonwealth support, Churchill and Eden were able to demonstrate more clearly to Eisenhower and Dulles just how isolated they had become, and by withholding their support for UN cover of American policy, they were able to prevent the United States from making public their private commitment to the defense of the islands—an important gain, given U.S. disinclination to make a public retreat in the face of Communist forward movement.

Yet, even in this area, it cannot be claimed that it was British influence alone that served to modify U.S. policy; in 1954–55, as in 1958, the administration was split and domestic opinion far from united,[58] and this disunity encouraged an uneasy administration to reappraise its policy. During the 1958 crisis, it was apparent that British advice in the area of China policy was even more easily discounted and less readily given, a consequence in part of the serious breach in relations that had occurred over Suez and of Macmillan's replacement of the truculent Eden. There was, then, a recognition in Eisenhower's second term of office that on Asian policy there was unlikely to be a fusion of views, that each would, when necessary and as far as circumstances allowed, go their separate ways. This is indeed what happened in 1956 and in 1957, when London decided that its "chief concern" would be to try to persuade the United States to let it trade on a less restricted basis with the PRC. Even on this question, however, Britain was forced to break with the United States, American criticism of London's policy being tempered only by Macmillan's plea that Britain lived "by exports alone" and by Eisenhower's obvious private sympathy for the trading policy.[59] The "Special Relationship" might have had some remaining force in Europe, but in Asia it had little impact, "except when allies were needed to embellish a basically American initiative."[60]

Though some within the Eisenhower administration came to recognize the merits of the British case with regard to China and that the U.S. refusal to compromise was exhausting its political capital, their time had still not come. The underlying premises of Dulles' speech in San Francisco in June 1957 still dictated U.S. China policy and epitomized the root of the disagreement with London and with those, such as Robert Bowie (Assistant Secretary of State for Policy Planning), who agreed with Britain. U.S. accommodation with the PRC, the Eisenhower administration believed, would add to Beijing's prestige, destroy morale on Taiwan, dispose others in Asia to seek to regularize their relations with Mao's regime, and discourage the PRC from modifying its behavior.[61] London was unable to convince Washington of the value of its integrationist approach and thus had to be content with moderating some policies and facilitating contacts whenever such opportunities arose. Despite some small successes on Britain's part, however—successes that may have "engendered more lasting delusions of grandeur"—the tenacity with which the Eisenhower administration held to its position toward the PRC should not be doubted. As Eisenhower prepared to hand over to his Democratic successor at the end of 1960, the NSC could still reaffirm its earlier decision "not to allow the attitudes and emotions of European countries to influence unduly actions considered essential to attaining or preserving U.S. objectives in the Far East," the key one being the "reduction of growth and power and prestige of China."[62]

NOTES

1. Prime Minister's Office (hereafter cited as PREM) 11/418, December 7, 1953, Public Record Office (hereafter cited as PRO), London; David Allan Mayers, *Cracking the Monolith; U.S. Policy against the Sino-Soviet Alliance* (Baton Rouge: Louisiana State University Press, 1986), pp. 128–29.

2. For an earlier U.S. attempt to make the Chinese "behave," see Michael Hunt, *Ideology and U.S. Foreign Policy* (New Haven: Yale University Press, 1987), p. 71.

3. Christopher Thorne, *The Limits of Foreign Policy: The West, the League and the Far Eastern Crisis of 1931–1933* (London: Macmillan, 1973); Dorothy Borg, *The United States and the Far Eastern Crisis of 1933–1938* (Cambridge: Harvard University Press, 1964).

4. FO 371/115213, August 3, 1955, September 8, 1955, PRO; Memo, January 31, 1956 *Foreign Relations of the United States, 1955–1957*, vol. 3; *China* (hereafter cited as *FRUS*) (Washington D.C.: GPO, 1986), p. 290; David Carlton, *Anthony Eden* (London: Allen & Unwin 1986), p. 300.

5. FO 371/121024, August 9, 1956; Robert Amory to Robert Cutler, memo, March 5, 1958, Declassified Documents Reference System, (hereafter cited as DDRS) (Virginia: Carrollton Press, Doc. No. 7, published 1985).

6. James Cable, *The Geneva Conference of 1954 on IndoChina* (London: Macmillan, 1986), p. 49; FO 371/115213, September 7, 1955; 121022, March 18, 1956; 115213, June 10, 1955; 121023 June 19 and June 6, 1956, PRO; William Roger Louis and Hedley Bull, eds., *The 'Special Relationship: Anglo-American Relations since 1945* (Oxford: Clarendon Press, 1986), esp. ch. 1.

7. Mayers, *Cracking the Monolith*, p. 128; FO 371/109101, Weekly Political Summary, June 26–July 2, 1954, PRO.

8. Memo, January 31, 1956, *FRUS, 1955–57*, 291–92.

9. Cable, *Geneva Conference*, pp. 110–11; Robert Boardman, *Britain and the People's Republic of China, 1949–1974*, (London: Macmillan, 1976), p. 70. Humphrey Trevelyan, *Living with the Communists* (Boston: Gambit, 1971), p. 135.

10. Cable, *Geneva Conference*, esp. ch. 4; George Herring and Richard Immerman, "Eisenhower, Dulles and Dienbienphu: 'The Day We Didn't Go to War' Revisited," *Journal of American History* (September 1984), vol. 71, no. 2.

11. Smith to Department of State, Memo, May 27, 1954, *FRUS, 1952–54*, vol. 14, part 1: *China* (Washington D.C.: GPO, 1985), pp. 434–36; telegram, May 28, 1954, *ibid.*, pp. 436–37; telegram, May 30, 1954, pp. 438–40; Drumright to Sec. of

State, Memo May 31, 1954, *ibid.*, pp. 440–41; extract from diary June 3, 1954, *ibid.*, 442.

12. Telegram, July 11, 1955, *FRUS, 1955–57*, vol. 2: *China* (Washington, D.C.: GPO, 1986), p. 643; FO 371/115008, July 12, 1955, PRO.

13. Robertson to Sec. of State, Memo, July 12, 1955, *FRUS, 1955–57*, 2:648.

14. FO 371/115054, June 20, 1955, PRO; Macmillan to Sec. of State, July 10, 1955, *FRUS, 1955–57*, 2:642; Memo, July 12, 1955, *ibid.*, p. 648; Sec. of State to Johnson, July 29, 1955, *ibid.*, 685–87.

15. Announcement, Sept. 10, 1955, *FRUS, 1955–57*, 3:85.

16. Robert B. Ekvall, *Faithful Echo* (New York: Twayne, 1960), pp. 90–91.

17. FO 371/115010, September 5, 1955, PRO.

18. FO 371/115012, October 25, 1955, PRO.

19. FO 371/115010, September 14, 1955; 115013, Dec. 17, 1955, PRO.

20. J. H. Kalicki, *The Pattern of Sino-american Crises* (London: Cambridge University Press, 1975), pp. 163–67; Kenneth T. Young, *Diplomacy and Power in Washington-Peking Dealings: 1953–1967* (Chicago: University of Chicago Center for Policy Study, 1967), esp. pp. 10–20.

21. NSC mtg., memo, September 9. 1954, *FRUS, 1952–54*, 14:586, 588.

22. NSC mtg., memo, September 12, 1954, *ibid.*, esp. pp. 619–21.

23. FO 371/110231, September 15, 1954, PRO.

24. September 17, 1954, *ibid.;* Merchant to O'Connor, memo, September 19, 1954, *FRUS, 1952–54*, 14:649–51.

25. FO 371/110231, September 28, 1954, PRO.

26. Memo, October 8, 1954, *FRUS, 1952–54*, 14:710–12, incl. n. 1–3.

27. Memo, October 9, 1954, *ibid.*, pp. 716–18.

28. Memo, October 10, 1954, *ibid.*, p. 726.

29. Memo, October 29, 1954, *ibid.*, p. 818.

30. Robertson to Sec. of State, memo, October 7, 1954, *ibid.*, p. 706, Sec. of State to Robertson, memo, 1954, *ibid.*, 708; Sec. of State to Robertson, memo, October 8, 1954, *ibid.*, p. 709.

31. FO 371/110236, October 29, 1954, PRO. Trevelyan, chargé d'affaires in Beijing, for example, argued that the Chinese would never accept the indefinite separation of Taiwan that a treaty of this kind implied; neither was relief from Chiang's raids on the mainland a sufficient inducement for them to accept the permanent loss of Taiwan. He also believed that U.K. association with Oracle would lead the Chinese to regard the British as "irretrievably committed to and participating in, the United States policy on Formosa" and that they would in consequence "give up all hope of our securing a moderation in American Far Eastern policy."

32. Memo, November 5, 1954, *FRUS, 1952–54*, 14:866.

33. Memo, December 7, 1954, *ibid.*, pp. 1002–3. The exchange of notes was not made public until January 14, 1955.

34. Kalicki, *Pattern of Sino-American Crises*, pp. 127–28, 140, 142.

35. Pres. and Sec. of State, tel. con., January 18, 1955, *FRUS, 1955–57*, 2:37; Memo, January 19, 1955, *ibid.*, p. 46; FO 371/115023, January 19, 1955, PRO.

36. Memo, January 19, 1955, *FRUS, 1955–57*, 2:41–43.

37. Memo, *ibid.*, p. 45; FO 371/115023, January 20, 1955, PRO.

38. NSC mtg., memo, January 20, 1955, *FRUS, 1955–57*, 2:69–82.

39. NSC mtg., memo, January 21, *ibid.*, 1955, pp. 91–92.

40. Memo, *ibid.*, pp. 96–98; FO 371/115023, January 21, 1955, PRO.

41. Acting Sec. to Embassy, ROC, telegram, January 31, 1955, *FRUS, 1955–57*, 2:182–83.

42. Memo, February 9, 1955 *ibid.*, p. 245.

43. Eisenhower to Churchill February 10, 1955, *ibid.*, p. 260 and n. 2; Churchill to Eisenhower undated, *ibid.*, p. 270; FO 371/115037, February 16, 1955, PRO.

44. Sec. of State to Embassy, U.K., telegram, Feb 18, 1955, *FRUS, 1955–57*, 2:294–95.

45. Cabinet Conclusions (hereafter cited as CAB) 16(1), 128/28, February 22, 1955, PRO.

46. Sec., of State to Dept., telegram, February 25, 1955, *FRUS, 1955–57*, 2:307–10.

47. Memo, March 11, *ibid.*, pp. 357–59; Richard Betts, *Nuclear Blackmail and Nuclear Balance* (Washington, D.C.: Brookings Institution, 1987), p. 58.

48. Parliamentary Debates, House of Commons, March 8, 1955, vol. 538, Cols. 160–61; Eden to Dulles, message, March 25, 1955, *FRUS, 1955–57*, 2:397; Sec. of State to Embassy, U.K., telegram, March 26, 1955, *ibid.*, p. 404; Carlton, *Anthony Eden*, p. 366.

49. Memo, March 28, 1955, *FRUS, 1955–57*, 2:409–15.

50. Robertson to Sec. of State message, April 25, 1955, *ibid.*, pp. 510–12; Pres. and Sec. of State, memo, April 4, 1955, *ibid.*, p. 444; Pres. to Sec. of State, memo, April 5, 1955, *ibid.*, pp. 445–50.

51. See Robertson's presentation of the "outposts" idea. He replied in the affirmative when Chiang categorized Eisenhower's plan as equivalent to giving up Jinmen and Mazu in exchange for the interdiction of a limited area of the China coast. As Eisenhower later remarked: "As long as our representatives did not feel they could suggest any attractive position between evacuation on the one hand and a 'fight to the death' on the other, there was no possibility of a meeting of minds." Robertson to Sec. of State, message, April 25, 1955, *ibid.*, p. 511; Pres. to Sec. of State, April 26, 1955, *ibid.*, p. 523.

52. FO 371/115049, May 3, 1955, PRO.

53. FO 371/115047, April 26, 1955; 114974, July 17, 1955, PRO.

54. FO 371/120913, May 4 and May 11, 1956, PRO NSC mtg., memo, October 2 1957, *FRUS, 1955–57*, 3:617.

55. Stephen E. Ambrose, *Eisenhower vol. 2: The President, 1952–1969* (London: Allen & Unwin, 1984), p. 482.

56. Harold Macmillan, *Riding the Storm, 1956–59* (London: Macmillan, 1971), pp. 544, 549.

57. Boardman, *Britain and the PRC*, pp. 129–30; DDRS, Doc. no. published 26B (Published 1979), Morton Halperin, *The 1958 Taiwan Straits Crisis: A Documented History*. (Santa Monica, California The Rand Corporation, 1966)

58. Indeed in 1958, mail was running 4–1 against the policy. See Townsend Hoopes, *The Devil and John Foster Dulles* (Boston: Little, Brown, 1973), p. 452; Robert Divine, *Eisenhower and the Cold War* (New York: Oxford University Press, 1981), p. 70.

59. Harold Macmillan, *Tides of Fortune, 1945–55* (London: Macmillan, 1969), p. 630; Macmillan, *Riding the Storm*, p. 318; CAB 10(1), 128/30, February 2 1956, 24(6) March 21, 35(9) May 10, 48(1) July 11, 50(1) July 17, 68(4) October 3, PRO, for examples of discussions of the trade issue in 1956.

60. Louis and Bull, *The 'Special Relationship'*, p. 381.

61. Bowie to Sec. of State, memo, June 19, 1957, *FRUS, 1955–57*, 3:545–49; address by Sec. of State, June 28, 1957, *ibid.*, 558–66.

62. Cable; *Geneva Conference*, p. 143; DDRS, Doc no. 1286, (published 1983), November 10, 1960, "U.S. Policy in the Far East", reaffirming policy conclusions in NSC 5913/1, September 25, 1959.

8

Japan and the Soviet Role in East Asia

Two of the conference participants, Kimura Hiroshi of Hokkaido University and K. O. Sarkisov of the Institute of Oriental Studies, Soviet Academy of Science, wrote on Soviet policy toward East Asia and especially Japan. They indicated the intensity of feeling in their respective countries and the current political sensitivity of the central issue in bilateral Soviet-Japanese relations: the question of the "Northern territories," the islands of Habomai, Shikotan, Kunashiri, and Etorofu. These islands, once part of the Japanese empire, have been held by the Soviet Union since the close of World War II. Japan is determined to regain possession. The Soviets may be willing to surrender them, but so far the price asked, a significant lessening of the ties between Japan and the United States, has been deemed too high by Japanese leaders.

Kimura declared that Soviet-Japanese relations were not good, as evidenced by the failure to sign a peace treaty more than forty years after World War II ended and after more than thirty years of diplomatic relations. He did not believe agreement on a treaty would be reached in the near future.

Perceiving the important link between the "Northern territories" issue and the security treaty between Japan and the United States, Kimura suggested that the United States, specifically John Foster Dulles, deliberately contrived to keep Japan and the Soviet Union apart. He wrote

> . . . Dulles was an architect of what is called the "San Francisco system," and hence of postwar Soviet-Japanese relations. Prior to his appointment as secretary of state in the Eisenhower administration, Dulles organized the San Francisco Peace Treaty Conference in 1951. As a result he helped Japan to become not only an independent nation but also a politico-diplomatic and military-strategic close ally of the United

164

States. At the same time, Dulles was successful in driving the Soviet Union from the Conference, thus driving a wedge between Japan and the U.S.S.R.

After Stalin's death, the Soviet leadership was more conciliatory toward the outside world. Kimura noted that in the mid-1950s, the Soviets withdrew from Austria in the context of the Austrian peace treaty and returned naval bases to both Finland and the People's Republic of China. Nikita Khrushchev was also eager to normalize relations with Japan and, in 1956, he succeeded in restoring diplomatic links between Moscow and Tokyo. But negotiations for a peace treaty, for a formal ending of the state of war that had existed since 1945, faltered because of the territorial issue.

Kimura's analysis of the negotiations denigrated both Soviet tactics and disunity among Japanese leaders. The Soviet Union was unwilling to return all of the disputed islands, but did offer to return the Habomais and Shikotan. Some Japanese were willing to compromise, especially when the Soviets linked acceptance of their offer to a seat for Japan in the United Nations, fishing rights in Soviet waters, and the repatriation of Japanese prisoners of war. Kimura, however, insisted that "the Soviet Union's retention of Japanese war prisoners' was an illegal action to be rectified immediately by the Soviet side in accordance with the Potsdam Proclamation." Similarly, he charged the Soviets with violating an agreement on fishing rights issues reached early in the negotiations. Despite the understanding that the issue would be discussed after the conclusion of the peace treaty, "Moscow announced that additional fishing restrictions would be imposed on Japanese vessels in the North Pacific for the coming season." Kimura contends that the Soviets, recognizing Japan's desperate need for access to additional fishing grounds, were attempting to bludgeon the Japanese into accepting their terms. Only countervailing pressure from the United States prevented Japanese leaders from accepting Soviet conditions.

An agreement to resume diplomatic relations without a peace treaty, postponing resolution of the territorial question, was reached in October 1956. Japan succeeded in regaining the Habomais and Shikotan without surrendering its claim to Kunashiri and Etorofu. Prime Minister Hatoyama Ichiro, "trying to be different from his predecessor, Yoshida [Shigeru], who had pursued Japan's foreign policy by leaning exclusively toward the United States and its West European allies, . . . was eager to promote Japan's relations with the Soviet Union as well." Yoshida and his followers failed to prevent the agreement which, of course, had the approval of the Japanese Socialist Party.

Kimura noted that major newspapers such as the *Asahi Shimbun* and the *Mainichi Shimbun* were critical of the terms Hatoyama accepted.

Citing the work of Donald Hellman, Kimura detailed the domestic political influences on Japan's negotiating posture. He labeled the process the "domestication" of foreign policy and left little doubt as to his disapproval of leaders who allowed personal and factional ambitions to influence their roles in the debate. Kimura also complained that the United States had been unhelpful in the discussion and argued that American pressures forced Shigemitsu Mamoru, Japan's foreign minister, to retain Japan's claim to all of the northern islands. Kimura cited a report that Dulles told Shigemitsu that "If Japan formally recognizes Kunashiri and Etorofu as Soviet territory, the United States would ask Japan to confirm Okinawa to be American territory" and denounced the logic of Dulles' position.

The United States, Kimura contended, was pleased to see the territorial question between Japan and the Soviet Union unresolved. Certainly at no time in the 1950s, was Washington in favor of a Soviet-Japanese rapprochement and Kimura portrayed the American government as pursuing a "wedge strategy" to keep its principal ally in Asia from becoming too cozy with its principal adversary in the Cold War.

In 1960, the Soviets made the connection between the territorial issue and the Japanese-American alliance explicit. When the Japanese abrogated the Japanese-American security treaty, the islands would be returned—and not before. More recently, Kimura reported, Soviet spokesmen have indicated a desire for closer relations with Japan while accepting the special Japanese-American relationship. Nonetheless, at this time, the Soviets are the least popular of the world's peoples with the Japanese public and polls indicate clearly that the lack of friendly feeling derives from the question of the Northern territories.

S arkisov approached East Asia more broadly, but his focus on Japan dovetailed neatly with Kimura's argument. He was sharply critical of the aggressive activity of the United States and shared Kimura's suspicion that Washington was primarily responsible for the failure of Japan and the Soviet Union to conclude a peace treaty in 1955 or 1956. He wrote of a "US bloc strategy," aimed against the Soviet Union and its friends, which included the U.S.-Japan security treaty and SEATO. But he also complained of Japan's uncompromising attitude on the territorial question and its failure to pursue an independent foreign policy.

When he looked closely at the United States, Sarkisov distinguished between Dulles and Eisenhower. Dulles was the evil demon, whose "influence was one of the subjective factors of decisive importance. It is hardly possible to find in postwar American history another example of such tremendous influence on the formulation and determination of foreign policy strategy ... Dulles was not only a supporter but the creator of the methods of diplomacy of force."

Sarkisov's portrait of Eisenhower was far more sympathetic. The president's attitude was evolving in this period, "becoming more constructive instead of tough," and he displayed a willingness to compromise. Eisenhower defined and interpreted "the most important notion of the military industrial complex" and warned of the detrimental effect of the arms race on socioeconomic development. His analysis had proved useful to Soviet political scientists.

It was Dulles who drove the wedge between Japan and the Soviet Union during the 1955–1956 negotiation:

> Dulles resorted to direct pressure and blackmail: he threatened to retain Okinawa if the Japanese government signed the peace treaty on the terms of the Joint Declaration [which would have left Etorofu and Kunashiri in Soviet hands]. ... In the mid-1950s, Dulles' diplomacy precluded the signing of a peace treaty between Japan and the Soviet Union, believing that the "territorial problem" would be a very effective deterrent to the development of [good] Soviet-Japanese relations. History has demonstrated the general correctness of that calculation.

Having denounced Dulles' diplomacy, Sarkisov hinted at the possibility of Soviet culpability in the failure of the negotiators to conclude a peace treaty: "it would be wrong, both essentially and methodologically, to explain all difficulties in the bilateral relationship by Japan's territorial claims and by American influence." He resumed criticism of the "pronounced confrontational nature" of the American approach to Japanese-Soviet relations, repeated his estimate of American success, and then remarked "it would be wrong to put the blame for everything negative and difficult in Soviet-Japanese relations entirely on the American factor."

Sarkisov did not elaborate on the possibility of Soviet errors, but he did detail changes in Soviet policy in Asia after 1953, after Stalin's death. He wrote in particular of economic and technical assistance to Burma and Afghanistan, of efforts to increase trade with India, and of support for the principles expressed by the Afro-Asian nations at the Bandung Conference. He also thought it worth noting the results of the 20th Congress of the Communist Party of the Soviet Union in 1956, especially the commitment to peaceful coexistence with the capitalist world.

Another important issue touched upon by Sarkisov was the Sino-Soviet split. He seemed surprised that despite the fact that "elements of crisis became apparent" in Soviet-Chinese relations in the late 1950s, "despite the signs of the cooling of relations between the two socialist countries," the Eisenhower administration's policy toward China remained "confrontational." Sarkisov perceived evidence of an "ideological approach." But he conceded that "Soviet diplomacy, too, found itself in rather complicated circumstances" as the Chinese-Indian border conflict smoldered. He concluded, with palpable sadness, by referring directly to the deterioration of the Sino-Soviet relationship: "Abnormal and, later, even hostile relations between the two countries were one of the main factors destabilizing the structure of international relations in East Asia. This factor played a role of paramount importance in the strategic calculations of the United States and Japan in the region."

9

From San Francisco to Suez and Beyond: Anglo-Japanese Relations, 1952–1960

ROGER BUCKLEY
International Christian University, Tokyo

I n a recent interview with the Japanese press the British ambassador to Tokyo put forward the claim that both Europe and Japan had failed to adopt active policies towards each other in the 1950s and 1960s.[1] Such remarks invite a critical response from international historians. The argument that Britain and Japan had merely ignored one another in the period from San Francisco to Suez (and beyond) will be countered by an examination of the sources now available to the student. The unwillingness of British spokesmen to recognize the mistakes of the past is not without consequence for those who are instructed to defend the present state of European-Japanese ties. It is convenient for the British government to downplay its share of responsibility for the current impasse with Tokyo by asserting that London was not guilty in the immediate postwar decade.

This chapter attempts to weigh the conventional picture of benign neglect against the evidence of recently released official records and the published findings of earlier authors on postwar relations between Britain and Japan. What follows is lopsided. The Japanese Diplomatic Record Office has yet to open its hoardings for the 1950s. Too many senior figures from that era are too near the center of power today for this to change in the near future. Six later prime ministers who were on the greasy pole in the years after the San Francisco peace settlements remain active over thirty years later. The dawn of open government in Japan will be much later than the advent of open markets.

Reliance on British sources will form the basis for a critique of its diplomacy towards post-treaty Japan. Largely an examination of how Britain failed to create an adequate relationship with a newly emergent Japan, this is a survey of missed opportunities, considerable antagonism, and not a little prejudice. The culprits are easy to identify; more to the point is an analysis of why British officials and their masters made such a mess of a situation that cried out for reconciliation and imagination. It may also reveal some of the tensions frequently sensed but less often openly articulated behind Anglo-American ties in the Pacific, the limits of British power, and the domestic restraints that could all too easily be employed by the Cabinet to justify inaction. It is not a pretty tale.

"Europe first" has been the basis of British foreign policy throughout the postwar period. Neither the Foreign Office nor successive postwar governments ranked Asia as an area of priority in British foreign policy in the years following the defeat of Nazi Germany and Imperial Japan. On a rare number of occasions London was obliged to take events in Asia seriously and commit military forces, but this was invariably done in the expectation that the crisis would be short-lived and within the regular ordering of British national priorities. All other European governments, with the exception of France at the height of the Indochina War, have similarly downplayed their activities in Asia.[2] Britain's largest military effort was in Malaya, not Korea.[3] It was jungle police actions not limited warfare on the inhospitable Korean peninsula that brought Guards battalions to Asia.

Confirmation of the relatively slight interest placed on the region by British postwar cabinets can be seen from remarks drawn from ministerial briefs in the years immediately following the end of the Pacific war. As early as February 1947 the Foreign Office recognized that the writing was on the wall. In a stock-taking memorandum for Secretary Ernest Bevin's use in preparation for the Moscow ministers' conference the message was spelled out clearly. The situation in the Far East (defined grandiosely as the region from India to the Pacific) was depicted as determined by three factors: British ignominy in the recent war, American leadership (then and since), and the tide of nationalism.[4] Under such circumstances there was room for no more than a degree of optimism. Most British attention was clearly to be paid to Southeast Asia, with Singapore as the fulcrum of regional economic and defense groupings. In China the Foreign Office was not displeased to see Washington taking over the West's burden, while

Anglo-American relations in occupied Japan were regarded as encouraging.[5]

After the outbreak of the Korean War, analysis of the American record appeared to change. Bevin told the Cabinet in 1950 that the United States in East Asia have "tended to be a law unto themselves since the end of the [Pacific] war, with results which have been far from happy."[6] This American insistence on going it alone had met failure in China, little success in Korea,[7] and recent disappointment in Japan, where the successes of the past five years were in danger of collapse due to present "lack of direction."[8] The only seeming advantage from the Korean crisis was Bevin's pleasure on being able to announce that "for the first time since the war the United States Administration have shown a desire to consult with us on Far Eastern affairs."[9] Events would cut short this British hope as the Truman-Attlee talks of December 1950 were to demonstrate.[10] Three months later the Foreign Office advised Attlee that a war limited to Korea that could be ended by a negotiated settlement was the way forward since it is "the policy of H.M.G. to restrict their military commitments in the Far East as much they can." Although this was quickly qualified in Attlee's brief by saying the loss of Western power in the region would be "incalculable," it was apparent that London would not be moved from its insistence that it was Europe that ultimately counted. Britain recognized that "in the event of a war with Russia, Europe will be the most vital theatre," despite rhetoric on the dangers of weakness in Asia and the need for "firm resistance to Communist aggression everywhere."[11]

Following the end of the Korean War the British government was even less enamored of the prospect of continuing to station troops on the Korean peninsula. Anthony Eden could write to Walter Monckton in 1956 to ask why it was necessary to continue to keep the remaining 1,600 British troops in Korea.[12] Anglo-Korean relations were hardly cordial in this period thanks to the view in Seoul that Britain was out of sympathy with the rigid Korean-American approach to the cold war.[13] Korean developments remained very much an American responsibility throughout the 1950s, and any British influence in the region was at best marginal.

Three factors conditioned the British government's attitudes towards Japan after 1952. First, the "collective memory" of Whitehall and Westminister with regard to things Japanese was highly uncomplimentary. Recollections stretching back to the 1930s, the war years, the occupation period, and the lengthy negotiations leading up to San Francisco were rarely positive. Small numbers of bureaucrats took in each other's washing and repeated the conventional wisdom to their successors. Attitudes towards Japan's parliamentary democracy were constantly unflattering, fears over textiles equally enduring. Second, despite the reformist claims of the architects of institutional change, the British Foreign Office persisted in doubting the likelihood of serious alteration to the character of Japanese society in either the occupation era or the 1950s.[14] Evidence to support this scepticism was certain to be incorporated in ambassadorial reports and likely to receive appropriate comment when digested in London. And third, the government wished to do what it could to reduce the seemingly incestuous nature of U.S.–Japan ties created by the overwhelmingly strong American role in the Allied occupation. It was expected that a loosening of this nexus would follow from the ratification of the settlements.

In all three cases the past appeared to serve up plentiful examples of Anglo-Japanese disagreement. Evidence of American ambition only compounded the problem. In any Pacific alliance it would be Britain that stood to lose the most. It had no security pact with Tokyo, and, as if to underline its present incapacity, the ANZUS treaty, too, had no room for Britain, not even with observer status. By the late 1950s most of the very considerable fears and doubts of Britain over Japanese behavior had been realized, without there being much evidence that serious attempts were ever made to prevent the Cassandras proving their case. Anxiety and suspicion were hardly the best weapons with which to greet a newly independent Japan. At times this led to almost self-fulfilling prophecies.

the legacy of the past was ever present. It lurked in the minds of ministers (Anthony Eden's son had died with the RAF in Burma), pervaded veterans' associations, and united the workforce and mill owners of Lancashire. It fed on itself because for two decades the British had heard little or nothing pleasant about Japan. It was an amalgam of prewar recollections of sweated labor and dumped cotton shirts, wartime atrocity stories, and the recent suggestion that the Americans had been too soft on occupied Japan because it wanted Tokyo to stand firm against continental opponents. The image was not necessarily false, but it was decidedly one-sided. Nothing then or now can excuse Imperial Japan's war record, and the British government had reason enough for wanting some degree of retribution and recompense. (It might be noted, however, that India and Hong Kong, to take the largest and smallest territorial units under British sway in 1945, thought little of extracting reparations from Japan; nor did they reckon that war trials would contribute much to the future.)[15]

Yet the other side of the story after 1945 was rarely given an adequate airing. Too little positive news was explained to the British public; too much remained unsaid on how Japan had changed and ministers were not necessarily better informed, since the Foreign Office reckoned that it knew best. The past fueled ministerial briefs. The road back to good relations had barely been charted by 1960 and even less was done to start senior-level consultations. A great deal of time and Japanese goodwill was lost, never to be regained.

To start with the Allied occupation of Japan. In many ways British objectives in this exercise were a mismatch of means and ends. At both the beginning of the occupation in 1945 and the belated conclusion of 1950–51 London pressed hard for a significant role that it was unable to gain. The British contributions to Allied control machinery, the military garrisoning of Japan, and the drafting of the peace settlements were never sufficient for the United States to accord it more than a junior status. Ambitions outweighed realities, though close personal ties between the British mission in Tokyo and General MacArthur went some considerable way on occasion to overcome the objective handicaps.[16]

The peace settlements were an additional disappointment. Here the British government avoided its errors of 1945 and came well prepared and determined. But paper plans, lengthy treaty drafts, and Commonwealth consultations never proved sufficient to shift the United States from its national goals. Dulles generally got what he wanted. The British might cosponsor the San Francisco Peace Treaty, but they failed to gain the admission of the People's Republic of China to the proceedings, though temporarily they did shut out Nationalist China. London was not a party to any of the military pacts that the United States created for its allies around the Pacific rim. The San Francisco Peace Conference saw Tokyo ending the occupation years attached even closer to Washington. It was confirmation of the ties established during the occupation. Dulles was certainly correct to assert that there were now only two powers of importance in the Pacific. The status of the United States was self-evident, and Japan would soon demonstrate its "potential."[17]

The Foreign Office probably gained all that a middle power could, given the obvious limitations of resources behind its diplomacy. Yet there is evidence to suggest that members of both major political parties deeply resented parts of the San Francisco settlements (the Tories having been returned to power by the time of ratification of the peace treaty), particularly over the question of which Chinese regime should gain recognition from Japan, the humiliation of exclusion from the ANZUS pact, and the failure to obtain safeguards against the revival of Japanese trade competition, especially in third markets.

In each instance ministers pressed Dulles hard, but he was able to throw up a smokescreen and hold his ground. He maneuvered precisely as the Foreign Office had feared over the issue of Taiwan, first by agreeing to the suggestion that disagreement between friends should leave the Chinese seat vacant at San Francisco, but then by quickly gaining Yoshida's reluctant consent to deal only with Taibei.[18] Equally Anthony Eden turned almost apoplectic when he learned that Britain was not welcome to join ANZUS.[19] His anger at what he correctly assessed to be a major blow to British prestige in the region, as with Attlee's earlier conversations with Dulles over the peace treaty texts, suggests that British prime ministers were yet far from disregarding the Pacific.

Sir Esler Dening, the key British official responsible for Anglo-Japanese relations in the years immediately following San Francisco, acknowledged that "there is a growing feeling of coldness and of an unsympathetic attitude on the part of the United Kingdom towards Japan."[20] Little was to change over the following decade. Indeed memories of the war could not easily recede so long as paperback publications such as Russell Braddon's *Naked Island* and Lord Russell of Liverpool's *Knights of the Bushido* continued to keep the pot boiling.[21]

This unfortunate state of British public opinion paralleled the generally cavalier views of ministers on the subject of Japan during the 1950s. The lack of interest in responding to frequent soundings from the Anglophile Yoshida Shigeru deserves stricture; so too does the prejudicial statement of one junior minister in May 1954 that "Japan is still the greatest long term danger in the Far East."[22] Those that knew better tended unfortunately to keep their heads well below the parapet. Churchill had minuted in April 1953 that "I am in principle in favour of the re-armament of Japan within carefully considered limits and under United States guidance. This might well be the only effective manner of balancing the growing power of Communist China in the next decade,"[23] but attempts to inform the public of the political and strategic advantages of closer ties with a reformed Japan were clearly considered too risky. Ministerial caution over Japanese defense programs has to be seen against a backdrop of more damaging economic developments.

"We judge that their principal concern is with the impact of Japanese commercial competition during the post-Treaty period." Dulles' prediction to General MacArthur following private talks with members of the Far Eastern Commission in November 1950[24] accurately summarizes Anglo-Japanese relations for the 1950s and beyond. Economic differences were at the heart of post–San Francisco relations between Britain and Japan. Indeed, little has changed since those days: the Europeans remain disappointed and baffled by Japan's current successes and resolved to complain until the seemingly intractable trade balances are corrected.

There has long remained an almost set-piece British response to Japanese competition. Opinion in the Foreign Office (and leaders in the *Times*) invariably suggests that open trade is best, while the Board of Trade and its successor, the Ministry of Trade and Industry, speaks of the need to restrict Japanese trade, both to safeguard British industry and to chastise Japan for allegedly unfair practices. Forty years ago it was the cotton textiles industry. Today it is car and electronic manufacturers who wish for market share agreements and controlled trade. As early as 1948 Ernest Bevin met with Harold Wilson, the youthful President of the Board of Trade, to hear Lancashire's demands for an international cartel among Britain, the United States, and Japan on global textile production and sales.[25]

Dulles described the Japanese economy as little more than a basket case, and other Americans made the point that there would be few goods that the United States could possibly purchase from what today might be described as no more than a NIC (newly industrialized country). Indeed, Japan's developmental status was sufficiently problematic for it to attend the Bandung Conference of nonaligned nations in April 1955,[26] where Japan's presence would prove to be a stage on the road to eventual reconciliation between Tokyo and Beijing.[27] The 1950s era, when even the British assembled their cars in Japan for local sale,[28] is now almost impossibly difficult to recall.

Such perceptions, however, of Japanese economic immaturity were not shared by the British government. It had been constantly reminded by the textile, pottery, and ship-building interests from 1947 onwards that Japan was a threat that would require careful watching. The 1950s show considerable evidence that the Cabinet and its advisers were less sympathetic towards Japan's efforts to restore its economy as the decade progressed. No longer would the argument that Japan needed a breathing space in order to prevent the democratic reforms of the occupation from collapsing find much support. If, during the occupation years, the Board of Trade had generally lost out to the Foreign Office in such debates on the threat posed by reviving Japanese competition, the position was now reversed. Considerable time and energy was expended on reviewing the state of the Japanese economy. The popular view of Japan as a source of cheap labor was not entirely off the mark. Less, however, appears to have been reported on what would later be described as the beginnings of the era of government-induced high-speed growth,[29] though British fears of the Japanese phoenix inevitably grew as Japan's reconstruction gathered pace. These anxieties may have been misplaced, but no government was about to ignore them. Lancashire had its share of marginal constituencies with pockets of support for the Liberals to further complicate the usual two party split.

Economic diplomacy forms the bedrock of Anglo-Japanese relations throughout the 1950s. The reluctant British retreat from Asia, encompassed in the postwar era essentially between Indian independence in 1947 and the final British withdrawal from Singapore in 1971, left little room for grand political discussion. Britain's concern was economic; so too was Japan's. Given the pressures on both governments to rebuild their economies after the war, this was hardly surprising, though the extent of the advantages that Britain appeared to possess in this period can easily be overlooked by those who constantly recall the end of the story.[30]

In the 1950s both Britain and Japan feared each other's economic challenge. It is too easy to imagine that Lancashire was correct and to ignore the concerns of Osaka. Both nations could hold out dated impressions of the other. The first questions asked by the BBC, for example, of Lord Selkirk on his return from an official visit to Japan in November 1956 concerned what the Japanese were doing about their population explosion and the extent of plans to encourage emigration.[31] Time and again, though, questioners returned to Japanese economic competition. It was the subject that dominated Anglo-Japanese debate, in part because of its intrinsic merit and also because of the absence of other more pressing political issues. Selkirk went so far as to say that "in the political side there is nothing between us."[32] Yet a broader definition of economic diplomacy and an examination of the British record might lead one to conclude that trading issues were themselves highly political and left Anglo-Japanese relations in a state of considerable disrepair.

The roots of postwar difficulties lie in the occupation period, when Britain felt it had exhibited a rational approach to Japanese reconstruction only to discover that, as the era lengthened, Washington was intent on what British officials felt was the imposition of a preferential series of financial and commercial arrangements for Japan. While it is certainly true that the Foreign Office was eager to avoid any trade restrictions on occupied Japan, it has to be acknowledged that the pressures on ministers grew as the preparations of rival Allied peace treaty drafts commenced. The attitudes of the Foreign Office and the stubbornness of Dulles combined to preclude any specific references to restrictions on Japanese exports in the peace settlements. Yet it was not for want of trying on the part of the Board of

Trade and the industrial associations. The cotton textiles industry, the shipbuilders, pottery manufacturers, and cutlers displayed little enthusiasm in getting on with the job of facing Japanese competition. In that sense Correlli Barnett is correct to speak recently of British industry as "a geriatric of nervous disposition,"[33] though textiles, for example, were given repeated encouragement by the Labour government to put their house in order. Until the 1950s little official sympathy existed for those who deplored Japanese capture of British Asian markets.

As the 1950s progressed, the relative strengths of the British economy came under renewed challenge. Officials had long predicted that all the immediate postwar years would grant Britain was a breathing space before Japanese (and German) competition once again revived. The major difficulty facing a number of British industries with regard to Japan after San Francisco was that insufficient effort was put into employing this valuable interlude to reequip industrial plants and rethink traditional practices.

The Labour government of 1945–1951 failed to persuade the cotton textiles industry to reorganize itself. Bevin, in particular, had no hesitation in producing scathing commentaries on the malaise of Lancashire in revising or repairing its industrial relations. The prosperity of the early postwar years did little to encourage millowners or trade union leaders to alter their behavior. Consequently, when overseas competition began to bite once more, there was little but criticism of cheaper priced products and calls for protectionism. Endless attacks on Japanese copyright infringements, cheap labor, and price-undercutting continued to appear.

The best most sustained pieces of journalism on Lancashire's attitudes were published in the *Financial Times* in the period immediately prior to the San Francisco Peace Conference.[34] Then (and now) this paper produced the lengthiest and most detailed accounts of things Japanese. The paper went to the crux of the matter when it exposed some of the weaknesses of Lancashire's complaints and noted the contradiction between anxiety and Manchester's fat orderbooks. Others too complained. British shipyards experienced a golden period as nations ordered merchantmen to replace sunken or outdated vessels, but this did not prevent the industry from hoping to restrict Japanese tonnage and exclude Japanese participation from shipping conferences.

Japan's perceptions of British industry were also at fault. Tokyo and Osaka saw a larger British threat than appears to have existed and also paid London the compliment of thinking that it would be able to strongly influence Commonwealth and colonial trading patterns. The British government, in reality, could do little about its own territories' behavior[35] and almost nothing when it came to nudging Canberra[36] or Ottawa. Japan seemingly saw the commonwealth and the Sterling Area as "designed to conceal effective British economic control of large parts of the earth. Colonies and Dominions remain indistinguishable still in Japanese eyes, and it is popularly believed that if, say, Australia restricts the entry of Japanese goods, it does so on orders from Whitehall."[37]

British fears and Japanese hopes were equally concentrated on third markets. Home markets were not yet the problem since Japan had relatively few goods to sell and the British were not particularly interested in exporting to Japan. The British ambassador to Tokyo was obliged to note how limited was the number of British companies based in Japan, itself an early indication of what was to prove to be a continuing complaint.[38] It was the Sterling Area that was the center of Japanese interest. Statistics were quoted by the British government in 1956 to suggest that this multilateral trade was worth £300 million,[39] though it was also frequently alleged that Japan ought to have been purchasing more but tended to let its sterling balances run down deliberately.

The Churchill and Eden governments attempted to steer a path between what today might be called "Japan-bashing" and a slight degree of sympathy for the efforts of a Japan under reconstruction and seeking to win its way back to a modicum of prosperity and thereby secure its democratic framework and pro-Western foreign policy alignment. The Japan question reappeared frequently in Cabinet, but British policy remained far from clear. Much was seen to depend on domestic political developments and the most recent trade statistics. It is hard to discern a long-term strategy. It was not until 1962, after almost a decade of intermittent negotiations, that a trade treaty between Japan and Britain could be initialed.[40]

The cabinets of the 1950s preferred to play it safe. It was better to wait on events than to initiate programs that might further antagonize British industry and commerce. Yet Japanese penetration into many formerly British overseas preserves made sense. No one else could provide textiles, for example, at the price that consumers in East Africa and Southeast Asia badly needed. Colonial governors made this point repeatedly to Whitehall and noted that if Japan did not fill the demand, then nobody else could, since Lancashire's products were seen to be too expensive. Such arguments unfortunately made only a limited impression on successive chancellors of the Exchequer and presidents of the Board of Trade.[41] Recognition that Japan had to employ an export strategy to survive cut little ice when domestic industries kept up substantial pressure on the government. What London endeavored to obtain from Tokyo was annual Sterling Area agreements that would permit British territories to import from Japan at a level that avoided the buildup of embarassing sterling surpluses by Japan. It was the policy of the Board of Trade negotiators to press Japan to spend as much sterling as it earned.[42] Friction certainly continued, but the region undoubtedly needed Japanese products, and with its export earnings, Japan was better equipped to purchase British invisibles.[43] Ministers in London, however, were also convinced that British trade faced discrimination from a Japanese bureaucracy equipped with a range of methods, including formidable exchange controls, for leading its manufacturers and financial interests. Such "administrative guidance" would later become a key aspect of European and North American complaints against the failure of Japan to liberalize trade. It was a product of postwar austerity that undoubtedly gave the British government some grounds for complaint in the 1950s.[44]

Lancashire gradually received an increasingly sympathetic hearing from Whitehall and Westminister. But this attention on the Japanese textile "menace" tended to preclude serious attention to the transformation taking place elsewhere within the Japanese economy. It was too easy for the British to remain satisfied with the old slogans and images of prewar days and to ignore the improvements in Japanese labor standards and the ominous reinvestment programs that would kill off rival foreign industrial competition in the next two decades. By 1960 Japanese textiles had had their day and would be replaced in turn by chemicals and heavier industries to propel Japan forward.

There was little prospect of compromise over economic diplomacy. Britain had tried to keep Japan out of GATT before 1955 and wished to be able to invoke safeguard clauses if it was later held that Japan had been suspected of unfair practices. British industry fought unsuccessfully against Japanese entry to GATT but did persuade the cabinet that its fears could not be ignored. It was for this reason that bilateral trade and payments talks dragged on at a decidedly slow pace. Japan was not prepared to give up its own pervasive licensing agreements, and Britain was not about to throw away its safeguards.[45]

"To us, the Far East is distant and relatively unimportant, compared say to Western Europe, the Atlantic, or the Mediterranean," while for the United States "the defence of the Pacific ranks with the defence of the Atlantic, in both cases to be assured by bases and a friendly littoral on the farther shore."[46] Such British thinking persisted throughout the decade. National priorities were apparently rigid, with the Foreign Office hoping from 1952 for detente in Asia and describing Korea as "an area of negligible importance to Britain and the western powers."[47] London and Washington differed over Anglo-American approaches to Japan in the 1950s largely on the relative attention each placed on strategic and economic issues. For the United States the concern was to build up a Pacific relationship that satisfied American defense interests in the region, whereas for Britain the perspective was far narrower and almost exclusively economic. On Japanese-American relations the Foreign Office held its peace, though it frequently felt that Tokyo was being mishandled by American military personnel.[48] Such reservations make it improbable that recent claims of substantial Anglo-American cooperation can be seriously entertained.[49] It was felt safer for the Foreign Office to remain silent and avoid giving offense. Japan, it was acknowledged, was America's "oyster."

In contrast to the generally satisfactory, if low-key, Anglo-American relationship in Tokyo, which was assisted by the sturdy links between Sir Esler Dening and Ambassador John Allison,[50] much went amiss with Britain's narrow and almost frigid attitudes towards Japan. British criticisms of the quality of Japan's leaders and the nature of its parliamentary system were entirely predictable. Yoshida had long been seen as less than energetic, Shigemitsu described as old and out of touch, while Hatoyama was termed "gaga." Even Dening began to despair of ever persuading British ministers to visit Tokyo and start to repair the damage of the past two decades.[51] The quarantining of Japan continued.

Ministers never attempted to disguise the twin pressures that impeded any substantial improvement in Anglo-Japanese relations in the 1950s. Time and again reference was made to Lancashire and POWs. The first official evidence of a slight British thawing came with Selkirk's visit to Japan and British sponsorship of Japan's application to join the United Nations. Yet parliamentary and ministerial soundings were not much to place against the constant cold-shouldering of Japan and the bitterly resented action to invoke article 35 when reluctantly consenting to Japan's accession to GATT and the refusal to consider a response to Japan's request for a commercial treaty.[52] Japan could see nothing but obstacles to gaining a modicum of British friendship. It remains difficult to square the constant British profession of the importance of Japan to the free world with the equally persistent attempts to curtail its commercial livelihood and to reject approaches for a fresh start. The official mind ignored this contradiction, with the result that when, in later years, the boot was on the other foot, and London was obliged to ask for charity, many senior Japanese officials were unsympathetic.

Cabinet papers testify to the impasse over Japan. In institutional terms it is clear that the Foreign Office was no longer the force it had been in guiding British policies towards Japan. The Board of Trade was able to make a greater impression on ministers in the 1950s, and the Cabinet took an increasing interest in the economic debate. What was lacking, however, was a clearer lead from the government and a willingness to accept the unpopularity that this implied. Selkirk was correct to argue that "the Japanese will . . . only respect either strength or real marks of friendship. We cannot produce the first, and I am very doubtful whether public opinion is prepared to consider the second." Until the Cabinet was adventurous enough to shift its ground, there was no prospect of winning over Japan.[53]

The Japanese government's response to the Suez crisis underlined the general state of Anglo-Japanese affairs. Shigemitsu, regarded as more moderate in his criticisms than others within the foreign ministry, advocated a United Nations solution and informed the Diet that Britain and France had unwisely used their veto power in the security council and risked widespread censure.[54] Japan was not prepared to exhibit any sympathy towards Britain; it would again refuse pressing overtures during the Indonesian confrontation with Malaysia and in the more recent Falklands War. In post-1952 crises Japan has rarely been able to see the advantages in following a British line. The inability of Britain to gain its policy objectives was the consequence of both its declining power in East Asia and the increasing antagonism exhibited toward Japan. Pursuit of narrow economic advantages may have uncomfortable political consequences.

British diplomacy towards Japan by the mid-1950s had deteriorated into a largely economic exercise. Events had followed the private prediction of the head of the United Kingdom mission in May 1947 that his successors after the peace treaty would hardly possess "a real Embassy" and instead would be merely in charge of "a reporting centre."[55] The speed with which Gascoigne's fears had been realized accurately reflects the British retreat from the region and the narrowing of horizons within the government and its advisors. The wider public, unfortunately, had even less knowledge of the realities of the exclusive nature of American-Japanese relations and the economic transformation already underway within Japan.

NOTES

1. Sir John Whitehead, interview in *Mainichi Shimbun*, April 19, 1987. Among Japanese scholars interested in the 1940s Hosoya Chihiro and Kibata Yoichi have

written in depth on the early postwar Anglo-Japanese relationship, but little has been published yet on the years following the San Francisco peace treaties.

2. See Roger Buckley, *Europe in the Pacific: The EC and Contemporary Asian-Pacific Relations*, International University of Japan series, the Pacific Basin: International Perspectives, Center for Japan–U.S. Relations (Niigata:IUJ, 1987). Limited British casualties in the Korean war confirm how wary London was of anything more substantial than police actions in Asia during the 1950s.

3. Field Marshall Lord Carver *The Seven Ages of the British Army* (London: Grafton Books 1986), pp. 292–95. Carver terms his final chapter "The Age of Templer" after the architect of the Malayan counterinsurgency campaign. See also A. J. Stockwell, "Insurgency and Decolonialization during the Malayan Emergency," *Journal of Commonwealth and Comparative Politics* (March 1987).

4. F2616/2616/6(FO371/63549) Foreign Office stock-taking memo for Bevin, February 22, 1947.

5. See Roger Buckley, "Working with MacArthur: Sir Alvary Gascoigne, UKLIM and British Policy towards Occupied Japan, 1945–52," in Ian Nish, ed., *Aspects of the Occupation of Japan*, (London:LSE, ICERD, 1986).

6. "Review of the International Situation in Asia in the Light of the Korean Conflict," Bevin memo, August 30, 1950, CP (50) 200.

7. *Ibid.* Britain held what was little more than a watching brief, since the issue was almost entirely between the United States and the Soviet Union as occupying powers.

8. The objection of Bevin was to the drift in American minds over the future Japanese peace treaty and the unwillingness to consult Britain over "a country of more than 80 million people which cannot be ignored in the context of Asia. The treatment of Japan will determine whether in the future she is with us or against us."

9. This, of course, ignored the very considerable cooperation that had occurred over Japan, where Britain gained a more cordial reception than MacArthur for most of the occupation than the value of its political, military, and economic commitments warranted.

10. See Roger Dingman, "Truman, Attlee, and the Korean War Crisis," in Ian Nish, ed., *The East Asian Crisis, 1945–1951* (London: LSE, ICERD, 1982). Aside from discussing the Korean War, recent biographers of Attlee, Bevin, and Eden have disappointingly ignored East Asian events.

11. F1022/8(FO371/92063), Prime Minister's brief for meeting with Signor de Gasperi, March 6, 1951. The FO did point out, however, that retreat in Asia could be counterproductive in that it might require additional forces to hold the line elsewhere.

12. F1193/G(FO371/120856), Eden to Minister of Defense Monckton, June 20, 1956, 'A'. By the end of 1956 all British troops would have left their support base in Japan and the Commonwealth role in Japan would end. It was, in effect, the breaking of the last British link with the occupation.

13. See, for example, FK1911/1(F0371/121103), section on Korea–United Kingdom relations, Korea: Annual Review for 1955, January 31, 1956. Lack of British interest was apparent from Selkirk's short visit to South Korea and his comments on the staffing inadequacies of the British mission.

14. Ironically there were large areas of occupation reform based on British precepts. In some instances SCAP Government Section modified existing Japanese institutions on American lines; in others, such as in the cases of trades unions, the scheme for constitutional monarchy and parliamentary government, it was obliged to reckon with British forms. See Roger Buckley, "The British Model: Institutional Reform in Occupied Japan," *Modern Asian Studies* (April 1982). Those American

observers who would explain the allied occupation in terms of "Wilsonianism" have some difficulties to confront in both the political and economic fields.

15. On the International Military Tribunal for the Far East, it was Justice Pal of India who opposed all sentences. Hong Kong's mood was somewhat less charitable and complicated by trials of conventional war criminals. See Roger Buckley "From Reoccupation to EXPO: Hong Kong–Japanese Relations, 1945–1970," *The Journal of Social Science* [ICU, TOKYO] 28 (1989).

16. See Buckley "Working with MacArthur."

17. Dulles to MacArthur, March 18, 1951, Dulles Papers 1951, box 53, Princeton University.

18. Hosoya Chihiro, "Japan, China, the United States, and the United Kingdom, 1951–2: The Case of the 'Yoshida Letter,'" *International Affairs* (Spring 1984).

19. "We cannot accept this," wrote Eden, F1072/25/9 (F0371/99221), June 26, 1952. He threatened to speak publicly on this "most unsatisfactory" rebuff.

20. FJ1011/1(F0371/110400), Sir Esler Dening, "Japan: Annual Report for 1953."

21. Braddon's attitude was "They'll Get You Yet! Beware those Japs," *Daily Express* November 25, 1955. Russell Braddon's *Naked Island* remained in print thirty years later. His recent account of contemporary developments is entitled *The Other Hundred Years War: Japan's Bid for Supremacy, 1941–2041* (London: Collins, 1983).

22. FJ10345/2 (F0371/110412), A. D. Dodds-Parker, Parliamentary Undersecretary for Foreign Affairs, May 7, 1954. In reality successive British Chiefs of Staff and Cabinets agreed that "controlled rearmament" was essential if Japan was to play its necessary role in Western strategy for defending the Asian-Pacific region. London's private complaint was usually that Japan was moving with disappointing slowness to assume this defense burden.

23. FJ1192/22 (F0371/105391), Churchill's instructions to his Chiefs of Staff, April 21, 1953. Alexander's reply to the Prime Minister termed the Japanese rearmament "acceptable," FJ1192/239 (F0371/105391), May 7, 1953, top secret.

24. J. F. Dulles to MacArthur, November 15, 1950, Dulles Papers box 49, Princeton University. In the same correspondence Dulles had suggested that the United States and Japan ought to gain an agreement to which the other Allies might be permitted some alterations "of form rather than substance." Sir Alvary Gascoigne had made similar predictions privately to the *Times'* correspondent in Japan; the division of British personnel in the Tokyo embassy by 1955 deliberately favoured commercial rather than political officers. See FJ1013/7 (F0371/115222), R. T. D. Ledward, June 8, 1955.

25. F109294/23(F0371/69814), Ernest Bevin, report of his meeting with Harold Wilson and Sir Raymond Streat, August 18, 1948. Esler Dening noted that "there seems to be some tendency, particularly in Lancashire, to cry 'wolf' too soon. Japanese textile production, in spite of greatly increased population, is still far below pre-war levels and we are, in practice, giving Japanese goods something very much like m.f.n. treatment already." Dening, August 17, 1948, *ibid.* See also John Singleton, "Lancashire's Last Stand: Declining Employment in the British Cotton Industry, 1950–70," *Economic History Review* (February 1986).

26. See "Asian-African Conference: Final Communiqué, Bandung, April 18–24, 1955," in Odette Jankowitsch and Karl P. Sauvant, *The Third World Without Superpowers*, (Dobbs Ferry, N.Y.: Oceana Pubications, 1978) 1:lvii–lxvii. The communiqué was signed by State Minister Takasaki Tatsunosuke. By the time of the Belgrade nonaligned summit of 1961 Japan was only represented unofficially by its Socialist party and the Sohyo trades union federation.

27. See discussion of the Takasaki-Liao agreement, November 1962, which followed later from Chou En-Lai's soundings at Bandung, in Chae-Jin Lee, *Japan Faces China* (Baltimore: Johns Hopkins University Press 1976) pp. 31, 46, 47.

28. The car was the Hillman Minx. A very few still survive today on Japan's roads.

29. See Chalmers Johnson, *MITI and the Japanese Miracle* (Stanford: Stanford University Press 1982) for development of this thesis. Opponents are sceptical that industrial policy deserves the degree of notice accorded to it by Johnson. For a review of the debate see Andrea Boltho "Was Japan's industrial policy successful?" *Cambridge Journal of Economics* (1985), 9; 187–201. For the hypothesis that the occupation set the economic direction for later growth see Yuichi Shionoya, "Patterns of Economic Policy in Occupied Japan (1945–50)," in Gordon Daniels, ed., *Europe Interprets Japan* (Tenterden, Kent: Paul Norbury Books, 1984).

30. The reception given Corelli Barnett's *The Audit of War* (London: Macmillan 1986) suggests that the British public is eager now to hear the worst. Barnett has, however, practically nothing to say on Japanese reconstruction other than enthusiasm. His premise that wartime developments set the seal on subsequent British decline is improbable. Barnett's conclusion that "by the time they took the bunting down from the streets after VE-Day and turned from the war to the future, the British in their dreams and illusions and in their flinching from reality had already written the broad scenario for Britain's postwar descent" is pure determinism. A parallel study of the Japanese postwar "miracle" and British failure would be intriguing. His references to the British working class as industrial "coolies" and contempt for those at Trafford Park and on Clydeside who produced Britain's munitions and ships is perverse. Reviewers rightly objected to Barnett's simplistic comparison of British wartime productivity levels with those achieved by Nazi (and Japanese) slave labour.

31. FJ1054/51(F0371/121049), transcript of BBC overseas service broadcast, November 1, 1956. Selkirk termed the population issue "the central problem which the Japanese government have got to face. And if I could solve it for them in two minutes I know they'd be very grateful." Selkirk, Chancellor of the Duchy of Lancaster, was hardly an inspired choice, and perhaps his dispatch was intended to underline what the government thought of Japan.

32. *Ibid.* Selkirk's remarks on Japan's demographic and economic difficulties were widely shared in Britain. See, for example, Guy Wint, *Spotlight on Asia* (Harmondsworth, Penguin, 1955) p. 155. Wint's views mattered since he was also a leader writer for the *Manchester Guardian*. He was generally sympathetic towards Japan and critical of the "ludicrous" side of the American occupation.

33. Barnett, summarizing the wartime Official Subcommittee on Industrial Problems and a Ministerial Subcommittee on Industrial Problems (Export Questions), *Audit of War*, p. 55. Whitehall threw cold water at those who spoke of an easy return to prosperity based on British exports.

34. See Roger Buckley, "Gambling on Japan: The British Press and the San Francisco Peace Settlements, 1950–1952," *Bulletin of the Graduate School of International Relations, International University of Japan* (December 1984), no. 2.

35. On Hong Kong, see Buckley, "From Reoccupation to Expo."

36. See Alan Rix, *Coming to Terms: The Politics of Australia's Trade With Japan, 1945–57* (Sydney: Allen and Unwin 1986).

37. "Anglo-Japanese Motes and Beams," *Economist*, October 20, 1956.

38. Dening was a formidable figure, who, in his day, had clashed with a host of British and Allied officials. There was a touch of Sir Harry Parkes in the way he challenged Japanese bureaucrats and politicians. He is certainly deserving of further study.

39. Selkirk interview, *BBC Radio Home Service*, October 23, 1956. The subject of Sterling Area trade remains another ignored field. Its importance leaves a possible lopsidedness in recent accounts by American students of the period. See, for example, William S. Borden, *The Pacific Alliance: The United States Foreign*

Economic Policy and Japanese Trade Recovery, 1947–1955 (Madison: University of Wisconsin Press, 1984).

40. Sir Hugh Cortazzi, "British Influence in Japan since the End of the Occupation (1952–1984)." I am grateful to Sir Hugh for kindly providing the text of his lecture given at the Nissan Institute, Oxford, January 1985.

41. Cabinet memoranda noted both that "increased imports of Japanese textiles into the colonies have certainly hit Lancashire a serious blow" (C.P. (55) 104, August 13, 1955) and "it was becoming increasingly difficult to persuade the colonies to restrict their imports from Japan. There was a growing demand for cheap Japanese textiles" ("Japan; Trade and Payments Negotiations," CAB 128/29 (1955).

42. "Japan, Trade and Payments Negotiations: Report by the Overseas Negotiations Committee," CAB 129/77 (1955).

43. So, too, did Britain itself. This did not, however, prevent the imposition of import quotas in 1954 on Japanese cotton grey cloth, toys, and pottery products. Japanese fibers and textiles led the national export drive in the 1950s. See Kazushi Ohkawa and Henry Rosovsky, *Japanese Economic Growth* (Stanford: Stanford University Press, 1973) p. 182. On the demise of Lancashire see William Lazonick, "The Cotton Industry," in B. Elbaum and W. Lazonick, eds., *The Decline of the British Economy* (Oxford: Oxford University Press, 1986).

44. The Overseas Negotiations Committee warned in 1955 that the Tokyo government and its bureaucracy had been "reluctant to formulate any general procedure [on liberalization]. They have not made any concessions on passenger fares, insurance business, or tourist allowances. They are apparently discriminating against British banks in Japan." Chalmers Johnson also repeatedly stresses the importance of exchange controls leading to what can now be seen as the heyday of MITI power in the 1950s.

45. Japan and Gatt, statement by the president of the Board of Trade, January 28, 1955, C(55)27. Britain wished to be able to invoke Article 35, if necessary, since "the decision to offer Japan most-favoured-rights would be regarded by Lancashire —and indeed by industry in general—as an important concession to the Japanese. In order to defend this step forward in our commercial relations with Japan, we would have to be in a position to say that we intended to take powers to impose countervailing duties against dumped goods within the same limits as are permitted by Gatt."

46. F10345/10(F0371/99218), R. H. Scott to Sir Gladwyn Jebb, April 18, 1952. Scott was suggesting ploys with which to tackle American audiences eager to confront British diplomats for "un-American activities in that we dare to have a view of our own." What British attention there was on Asia tended to be devoted to Beijing and Singapore. Britain failed to gain any substantial dealings with either the PRC or Japan because it was seen to be in the shadow of the United States.

47. *Ibid.*

48. See, for example, comments such as "one can do nothing but thoroughly agree with Sir E. Dening [that] the U.S. are obstinately inept in dealing with Asian, and particularly Japanese, opinion. The fault probably lies at the top levels at which, possibly by default, the US Armed Services are allowed far too much political authority." FJ10345/2(F0371/121042), R. T. Higgins, January 18, 1956.

49. See Roger Garson, "The Origins of the Cold War in Asia" review article, *Review of International Studies* (1986), vol. 12.

50. Dening permitted Allison to read his draft annual review for 1955, to which the FO minuted "one would like to see Mr Allison's Annual Review, if he makes one." Exchange of low-grade intelligence briefings typified the extent of Anglo-American cooperation over Japan.

51. Dening, the doyen of the diplomatic corps in Tokyo by December 1954, was reduced to practically apologizing to his masters for reminding them of their faults over Japan. Shigemitsu wrote to Eden, whom he had known in prewar London, urging future meetings in vain. See FJ1051/10(F0371/115326), Shigemitsu to Eden, February 11, 1955. Yoshida had visited London in the autumn of 1954 as part of a global tour. His hold on power was by then weak and little was accomplished in Britain or the United States.

52. Australian behavior in part mirrored that of Britain. See Rix, *Coming to Terms*. London was held responsible by Japan for the fact that fourteen nations invoked article 35.

53. Selkirk's suggestion that when the Japanese "get tired of the Americans, they can turn to us rather than to one or other of the countries of the Asian mainland" was absurd. FJ1054/59/F(F0371/121049), Selkirk to Selwyn Lloyd, October 24, 1956. Minister of State Lord Reading appears to have monitored Japanese events closely without necessarily wishing to extend an olive branch. Nor was the Labour party, given its industrial constituency. See Kenneth Younger, "Britain and the Far East," *Dyason Lectures, 1955* (Melbourne: 1955), p. 22.

54. Shigemitsu speech to the Diet, November 16, 1956. Dening charged that this speech was altered in translation by juniors eager to attack their foreign minister.

55. Buckley, *Occupation Diplomacy: Britain, the United States, and Japan, 1945–1952* (Cambridge: Cambridge University Press 1982), p. 123. An example of this work would be the voluminous reports forwarded to London on the Soviet-Japanese peace negotiations. See FJ10388/68 (F0371/121041), British embassy Tokyo to FO, October 31, 1956, and FJ10338/77, December 20, 1956, *ibid*. The British position was that Japan had come out rather well from these negotiations, but London hoped it would not be asked to give its views on the Northern Territories dispute.

10

Alliance in Crisis: The Lucky Dragon Incident and Japanese-American Relations

ROGER DINGMAN
University of Southern California

O n May 19, 1952, John Foster Dulles published an article entitled "A Policy of Boldness" in *Life* magazine. Although written as a campaign document, it proclaimed what became the
essential diplomatic strategy of the Dwight D. Eisenhower administration. National security and world peace could best be preserved,
Dulles argued, through imaginative use of traditional alliance diplomacy and exploitation of strategic opportunities presented by the
atomic revolution. Strong alliances in Europe and Asia in combination with nuclear weapons could contain America's Communist foes
and deter them from launching wars of aggression.[1]

Barely two years after Dulles wrote the *Life* article, his "policy of
boldness" appeared to be a policy in doubt. On March 1, 1954, the
detonation of America's first thermonuclear bomb at Bikini accidentally irradiated twenty-three Japanese tuna fisherman aboard the
Lucky Dragon #5. Shockwaves of concern over this incident reverberated around the world, "driving our Allies," in Dulles's words, "away
from us." To the worried Secretary of State it appeared, for a moment, that the thermonuclear explosion at Bikini might rip apart the
essential elements of American national security policy. Something
had to be done, and done quickly, lest Americans and their friends
across both the Atlantic and the Pacific conclude that alliances and
atomic weapons were not complementary instruments for the preservation of national security and world peace.[2]

The tale that follows traces the Eisenhower administration's search for that something. The story is not a long one; within a year American and Japanese leaders found a solution to problems created by what came to be known as the *Lucky Dragon* incident. It is an account that necessarily focuses on particulars: why the accident occurred; how Japanese and American leaders and ordinary citizens responded to it; and how and why alliance managers first failed, then succeeded in resolving specific problems arising from America's first thermonuclear accident.

But the *Lucky Dragon* story brims with broad significance for the student of American–East Asian relations during the Eisenhower years. The 1954 incident imposed the most serious strain on Japanese-American relations since 1945.[3] It raised troublesome questions about basic assumptions underlying the alliance between Washington and Tokyo. The affair stirred long-sublimated antagonisms and activated new interest groups that reshaped the subsequent course of Japanese-American relations. For all of these reasons, a microscopic examination of the *Lucky Dragon* incident can illuminate the macrocosmic forces that shaped America's East Asian policies throughout, and even beyond, the Eisenhower years.

THE EVENT AND ITS ORIGINS

What occurred on March 1, 1954, can easily be explained. On January 22, 1954, the one hundred ton wooden tuna trawler *Lucky Dragon #5* left the port of Yaizu in Shizuoka Prefecture for the vicinity of Midway. But fishing proved poor there, and on February 11 the ship headed south toward warmer, richer waters around the Marshall Islands. A little more than two weeks later, on March 1, the *Lucky Dragon* was approximately eighty-five miles east-northeast of Bikini atoll.[4]

That put the ship downwind from the site where Americans were preparing to test their first and largest hydrogen bomb. Months earlier, Washington had proclaimed a danger zone around Bikini and Enewetak Islands without indicating when the tests would begin. On the eve of BRAVO shot, patrol planes searched the seas below the projected path of its radioactive cloud to be certain no ships were there. Weather conditions were favorable, and, until a few hours before the test, upper-level wind conditions were stable. Then, at 0645 on the morning of March 1, engineers created a fission reaction that triggered a fusion explosion. It dug a crater approximately a mile wide, pushed a fireball nearly three miles in diameter into the dawn, and released fifteen megatons of energy into the atmosphere.[5]

That amount far exceeded anything scientists had predicted. It forced emergency evacuation of the crew that triggered the test, of weathermen at observation stations nearly two hundred miles away, and of 242 Marshall Islanders previously presumed out of harm's way, to Kwajalein. Most importantly, a sudden change in upper-level wind patterns pushed radioactive debris from the test to the northeast — over the *Lucky Dragon* — rather than in the previously predicted direction.[6]

These unexpected developments produced bizarre happenings aboard the tuna trawler. When a wakeful crewman went up on deck to look astern for one of the buoys that marked the ship's fishing lines, he suddenly saw a great light in the west. He hurried below to tell his shipmates, and within minutes they were debating whether he had seen an atomic blast or not. Seven minutes later, a sound reminiscent of the concussion from B-29 bombs split the crewmen's ears, and two hours after that the sky clouded over with a mist that rained down whitish grey ash. The ship's radioman, Kuboyama Aikichi, pinched and tasted it; he suspected it might be dust from an American atomic bomb explosion. That surmise, plus low fuel stocks and a poor catch, prompted the captain to put the *Lucky Dragon* on a course for home.[7]

Neither Japanese tunamen nor American testers anticipated the strange events of March 1, 1954. But why did more powerful and presumably more prescient policy-makers fail to foresee dangers to the Japanese-American alliance in thermonuclear testing? The past provided a partial answer to that question. America had exploded its first thermonuclear device in November 1952 and reestablished a danger zone around the test site a year later without triggering Japanese protests. That precedent was important, but preoccupation with other seemingly more urgent contemporary concerns blinded President Eisenhower and Prime Minister Yoshida Shigeru to the troubles that lay ahead. Early in 1954, the President worried about Senator Joseph McCarthy's attacks on the U.S. Army, the future of the European Defense Community, and the fate of Indochina. He was too busy to accept Atomic Energy Commission (AEC) Chairman Lewis L. Strauss's invitation to witness one of the tests. Prime Minister Yoshida was so preoccupied with fending off conservative challenges to his leadership that even if he had known the precise date of the test, he might well have said nothing.[8]

Different national self-images also contributed to American and Japanese inability to foresee problems arising from tests at Bikini. Hubris blinded Americans. Driven by the logic of containment and supremely confident of their scientific prowess, virtually none of them questioned the need for H-bomb testing or Washington's ability to do so in a responsible manner. What AEC Chairman Strauss said at the christening of the *U.S.S. Nautilus*, prototype of the nuclear-powered guided-missile submarine, on the very day the *Lucky Dragon* left Yaizu encapsulated Americans' beliefs: Superiority in nuclear technology was essential to preserve the peace.[9]

Weakness kept Japanese leaders from anticipating and preventing the events of March 1. That infirmity was partly intellectual. Prime Minister Yoshida had no scientific adviser to warn him of radiological and biological dangers arising from thermonuclear testing. It was also political and economic. While the Yoshida government could have taken administrative steps to keep tuna trawlers like the *Lucky Dragon* away from the test area, doing so would have provoked the well-organized, politically potent fishing industry. That would have been economically foolish, for it employed a million citizens, helped feed a growing population, and gained export earnings that reduced Japan's balance-of-payments deficit. Preventing tunamen from pursuing their pelagic prey on the high seas would also have been politically suicidal for the Yoshida government. Having acquiesced in externally defined fishing limits in the Sea of Japan and facing tough talks with Moscow over catches in Siberian waters, it simply could not afford to accept limitations on trawling in the Pacific.[10]

Finally, each nation's perception of the other as ally kept it from questioning the wisdom of H-bomb tests. While Washington regarded Tokyo as its most important Pacific partner, senior Eisenhower administration officials could not imagine Japan as a critic of fundamental American national security policies. They did not yet think of Japan in nuclear terms, either as a site for storing or launching atomic weapons or as a voice to be heard in arms control negotiations. Hoping that Japan would become a friendly, democratic, and prosperous ally that would contribute to the stability of the Asia-Pacific area, they concluded a Mutual Security Aid Agreement with Tokyo only a week after the BRAVO test at Bikini. But Japan's deficiencies—its reluctance to rearm, sluggish economic performance, and rising trade deficit—blinded American officials to the possibility that Japan might expose weaknesses in their policies.[11]

The Japanese government hardly seemed likely to do so, given its image of America as patron and protector. From the moment he signed the U.S.–Japan Security Treaty, Yoshida insisted that it would protect and strengthen Japan. Attacks by critics, Right and Left, on the American connection, forced the Prime Minister to argue that history had proven him right. While hopes for dollar loans had proven

false, American military procurements for the Korean War had fueled
a boom in the Japanese economy. The prospective loss of that income
early in 1954 prompted Yoshida to look East for some new form of
assistance. He may even have glimpsed dividends to be gained from
American thermonuclear testing. If it sped the development of new
and more effective weapons of deterrence, his government might not
have to rebuild costly and controversial conventional armed forces.
For all of these reasons, then, Tokyo was loath to question Washington's policies.[12]

Thus neither the Eisenhower administration nor the Yoshida ministry took steps that might have prevented the strange and terrible
events of March 1, 1954. But could the two governments keep the
thermonuclear accident from poisoning their alliance relationship?

DAMAGE CONTROL?

The way in which the world learned what had happened to the
Lucky Dragon made damage control extremely difficult. At first,
victims and perpetrators alike tried to keep the accident secret. The
tunamen said nothing about it in their daily radio reports to Yaizu.
Although some among them suspected irradiation as the source of
their illness, no one proposed calling for help or proceeding to the
nearest island. The sick men naturally wanted to get home as quickly
as possible. One of the most obviously irradiated crewmen had been
a prisoner of war during World War II and did not want to put himself
in American hands again—even for medical treatment. The *Lucky
Dragon*'s young captain, brooding over a poor catch as well as the
strange events of March 1, may well have concluded that it would be
best to say nothing until he could speak to the ship's owner in person.[13]

The Americans responsible for the accident remained silent for
different reasons. The testers did not want to jeopardize other planned
shots in the series. AEC scientists, who had only incomplete data and
imperfect explanations for what had occurred, believed they could
isolate, treat, and keep quiet persons known to have received unexpectedly high doses of radiation. Thus AEC Chairman Strauss, although he knew weathermen and Marshall Islanders had been evacuated and hospitalized, simply told President Eisenhower that the test
might have caused unexpected injuries and advised waiting for further medical reports. The President and the Chairman also decided to
say nothing lest Moscow learn what was going on at the Pacific Islands test site.[14]

But once the *Lucky Dragon*'s crew came ashore at Yaizu on Sunday, March 14, their secret was bound to leak out. One of the men told the ship's owner that they had seen an atomic explosion. Fishing master Misaki took the tunamen to a local hospital, where the physician in charge gave him a letter that would introduce the two most obviously burned men to experts at Tokyo University Hospital. The next afternoon, after they left for the capital, a high school student told a *Yomiuri shimbun* "legman" what he had heard about the crewmen from relatives who had talked with them. The enterprising reporter confirmed the facts and contacted his editor, who in turn tipped off colleagues who went to Tokyo University Hospital. Their report became a "scoop" that *Yomiuri* editors published the next morning. Within twenty-four hours this first tentative account spawned sensational stories in all three national dailies about how the *Lucky Dragon* had been "dusted by the ashes of death." The secret was out.[15]

The differing ways in which the American and Japanese governments responded to this news made matters still worse. In Washington, the AEC immediately asserted its primacy in damage control. Its officials worried about security, science, public health, and relations with allies—in that order. The commission had already issued a brief statement on the test and evacuation of the Marshall Islanders. The fact that Chairman Strauss had flown to the test site to witness the next shot gave President Eisenhower an excuse to dodge reporters' questions. Secretary of State Dulles, preoccupied with Indochina while Dienbienphu was under siege, called the accident "regrettable" and declined further comment until all the facts were known. Yielding to AEC pressure to do "everything possible" to keep foreigners from learning anything about the BRAVO device through chemical analysis of the ashes that had fallen on the *Lucky Dragon*, Dulles ordered Ambassador John M. Allison to get the Japanese government to put the ship under de facto U.S. Navy control.[16]

The AEC then took two more steps to minimize damage from the accident. To prevent panic at home that might disrupt tuna industry profits, administrators persuaded Federal Food and Drug Administration officials to begin monitoring fish imports at Pacific ports. To calm the Japanese, the commission rushed two experts, Dr. John B. Morton of the the Atomic Bomb Casualty Commission and H. Merrill Eisenbud of the AEC Laboratory in New York City, to Tokyo. Morton was to examine the men, while Eisenbud would investigate the irradiation of the ship, its cargo, and other tuna catches. But the two Americans were also supposed to keep the "secret" of the physical and chemical processes that had produced the March 1 explosion from the Japanese. At the same time, they were to seize the opportunity to study the effects of prolonged exposure to high levels of radiation on human beings.[17]

The AEC's protectiveness frustrated initial American efforts to minimize diplomatic fallout from the incident. Ambassador Allison, an old "Japan hand," knew what Japanese etiquette demanded in accidents and immediately sought permission to tell Minister of Foreign Affairs Okazaki Katsuo that Washington would pay damages if Americans were shown to be at fault. Although he peppered his superiors with requests for "promptest . . . action" lest U.S.–Japan relations be seriously harmed, a week passed before he received qualified authority to discuss compensation for the irradiated fishermen.[18]

In the meantime, Eisenhower and Yoshida inadvertently made matters worse. The president admitted that scientists were surprised by the magnitude of the blast and by declining further comment until Chairman Strauss returned to Washington fuelled press speculation about the power of the H-bomb. Yoshida sidestepped responsibility and ordered his foreign minister to seek prompt payment of compensatory damages from Washington. But Okazaki, who had no independent political base and represented a district which included Japan's most important tuna-fishing port, was not the man to put out the flames of this particular controversy.[19]

In the Diet, fishing industry spokesmen demanded reassurance that other ships and catches would not be contaminated and confirmation of compensation for their losses. When reports of unusual radioactivity on two other ships prompted housewives to cut their purchases of fish, wholesale prices plummeted, and Tokyo's famous Tsukiji Central Fish Market closed its doors for the first time since 1935. Under these conditions, fishing industry representatives in the Diet objected to Washington's enlargement of the danger zone around the test site. While that might lessen the chances of future accidents, it would also increase the length of tuna trawlers' journey to prime fishing grounds and add to the cost of their product. Okazaki simply passed on these questions about the necessity and legality of closing large areas of the high seas to Ambassador Allison.[20]

The Foreign Minister also failed to control the words and deeds of physicians and scientists treating the *Lucky Dragon*'s crew. While all but two of the men languished in a prefectural hospital, experts wrangled over responsibility for their treatment. Their quarrel, and the provocatively nationalistic behavior of Dr. Tsuzuki Masao, grew out of developments during the American occupation of Japan. The conquerors had forced changes in the relationship between clinical and research medicine. They had also alienated Dr. Tsuzuki, a radiobiologist and former rear admiral in the Imperial Japanese Navy, by confiscating his original notes on the radiological effects of the bombing of Hiroshima and Nagasaki and publishing them without crediting him. Now Tsuzuki spoke out in a way that angered and alarmed Americans and Japanese alike. He predicted that at least two of the crew would die and insisted that Japanese professionals did not need interference by Americans who had acted "irresponsibly" in conducting the Bikini tests.[21]

By late March, Japanese and American medical and scientific experts had fallen into a catch-22 situation that fanned the flames of controversy still higher. Despite AEC fears about what Dr. Tsuzuki knew, Japanese scientists were not yet aware of the physical and chemical composition of the "ashes of death." Without that information, Tokyo physicians could not properly diagnose and treat the *Lucky Dragon* crew. Yet his instructions and the Atomic Energy Act of 1946 kept the AEC's Eisenbud from giving them the necessary facts. Thus a medical standoff, tinged with latent racism, developed. The tunamen were loath to be examined by American doctors; Japanese physicians insisted upon retaining exclusive responsibility for their care; and Japanese scientists vowed to discover and tell the world just how the American hydrogen bomb worked.[22]

In these circumstances, it was hardly surprising that the Japanese people came to see themselves as nuclear victims. They blamed their supposed protector and ally for poisoning their food, polluting the rain that watered their crops, and threatening their countrymen with disease and death. They lashed out against the Yoshida government for pusillanimous defense of the national interest.

Officials did everything they could to try to dampen the flames of anger sweeping over the public. They established a six-agency vice ministerial committee to coordinate handling of problems related to the *Lucky Dragon*. They agreed upon a division of medical management responsibilities that sent the crewmen to two Tokyo hospitals. They acceded to Ambassador Allison's request to warn the press against inflaming public opinion with speculative stories. They formed an American-Japanese committee to study the incident. In the Diet, the three major ministries concerned presented a united front while Foreign Minister Okazaki refused to condemn the American tests. All of this was done in the hope that time would dampen emotions, make people aware of the value of the American alliance, and bring payment from Washington for the damage done.[23]

But the Eisenhower administration did not act as the Yoshida government hoped it would. By late March, John Foster Dulles realized that AEC-imposed silence about the accident must end. He had little luck, however, in persuading Admiral Strauss that something had to be done to moderate the wave of H-bomb hysteria that was disrupting relations with America's allies. The AEC Chairman retorted that those who wished America did not have the H-bomb had "grossly exaggerated" what had happened on March 1 and then announced successful completion of a second thermonuclear test at Bikini.[24]

Dulles had better luck with the White House, which faced pressures from Capitol Hill and allies to say more about the BRAVO test. California Democrat Chet Holifield, who had witnessed it and then reported from Kwajalein that the evacuated islanders were healthy and happy, changed his tune. He told the President in person that the time had come to "tell the people the facts about . . . atomic-hydrogen weapons." This kind of pressure prodded the White House into action. The next day Chairman Strauss was summoned there twice—first to talk with the President, then to rehearse what the public would be told.[25]

Ironically, what Strauss said at Eisenhower's press conference the next morning made relations between Tokyo and Washington still worse. After explaining why search planes had not seen the *Lucky Dragon* before the test and how unexpected upper-level wind changes pushed debris from the explosion to the point where it rained down on the ship, he downplayed consequences of the accident: none of the evacuated Marshall Islanders had developed radiation-related illnesses; there was no evidence of widespread contamination of tuna; and ocean currents were not carrying radioactivity to Japan or the United States. He then inadvertently raised levels of alarm by revealing that a bomb like that detonated on March 1 could "take out . . . any city—even the entire New York City metropolitan area."[26]

Strauss' performance stirred very different reactions in America and Japan. In the United States it focused popular attention on the need for civil defense. In Japan, it produced newspaper maps with concentric circles indicating the degree of H-bomb destruction to major cities—sketches that stirred popular fears that American "protection" might increase the likelihood of thermonuclear attack. In America, Strauss was perceived as a man who had revealed terrible truths. In Japan, he appeared as one who erroneously disclaimed responsibility for grave damage done. He used maps that mistakenly placed the *Lucky Dragon* within the danger zone. He cast doubt on Tokyo's claims and rubbed already raw racial nerves by pointing out that American physicians had not been allowed to examine the tunamen. Contrary to Dulles' hopes, Strauss made resolution of the incident more difficult rather than more likely.[27]

Nonetheless, diplomats on both sides of the Pacific thought they had correct strategies for bringing the crisis to an early conclusion. Ambassador Allison conceived a three-pronged plan for doing so. First, Washington should coopt Tokyo's alliance managers into the search for a speedy solution to the *Lucky Dragon* affair. Second, the United States should be demonstrably cooperative in treating the victims and monitoring other ships and their catches so as to quiet popular fears. Third, fair final compensation for the accident should be agreed upon as quickly as possible. While this approach made sense, developments on both sides of the Pacific doomed it to failure by early June 1954.[28]

The Japanese diplomats upon whom Allison relied could not deliver the cooperation he sought. When Foreign Minister Okazaki told the Diet that Japan would cooperate with the United States' thermonuclear testing program, the *Asahi* caricatured him as a victim of the Americans, his face and bald pate pockmarked with burns from the "ashes of death." Reactions of that sort made Kasumigaseki officials loath to appear too "soft" in dealing with Washington.[29]

Prime Minister Yoshida found it impolitic to rush into settlement of the *Lucky Dragon* affair. When Allison urged him to correct his ministry's "continued failure" to cooperate, he responded informally by promising to talk with his Cabinet. His formal reply a month later blamed "embarrassing circumstances" for "present irritations" and his inability to comply fully with Washington's desires. Behind those vague words lay hard political realities and a cautious political strategy. Yoshida faced a bribery scandal within his administration and strong Diet opposition to the mutual security agreement and legislation establishing a Defense Agency. Determined to fight on those issues, he preferred to placate rather than control popular feelings about nuclear testing. Thus his minions in the Diet quashed Socialist resolutions calling for an immediate end to the tests and a ban on the use of nuclear weapons. But they succeeded only by introducing a more mildly worded resolution that said essentially the same thing. Its unanimous approval fueled the growth of popular antinuclear sentiment, and by early June, three weeks after beginning their campaign, a citizens' group based in Tokyo's Suginami-ku had collected more than half a million signatures on a petition to ban the H-bomb.[30]

By that time, "cooperation" between medical and scientific experts had become part of the problem rather than a process leading toward its solution. After failing to gain meaningful access to the *Lucky Dragon*'s crew and to examine other allegedly irradiated ships, Dr. Morton and Merrill Eisenbud left Tokyo under a cloud of controversy. When Tokyo decided to send its own research vessel, the *Shunkotsu maru*, to the Bikini area to investigate possible contamination of ocean currents and marine life, Washington raised objections that forced alteration of the ship's planned course. Japan then imposed conditions that kept two AEC scientists from joining the expedition.[31]

These conflicts had complex origins. Japanese physicians' refusal to let American doctors examine all of the *Lucky Dragon*'s crew reflected professional pride, latent racism explained away as the "simple" fishermen's fear of foreigners, and probably embarrassment over their own earlier quarrels over responsibility for treatment. The American experts, thinking more as researchers than as clinicians, were upset that their counsel was not automatically accepted. They were shocked at the bureaucratic antagonisms they encountered, alienated by Dr. Tsuzuki, and angered by an "antiwhite policy" that effectively subordinated American standards to "inferior Japanese medical practices."[32]

The collapse of medical and scientific cooperation prefigured the emergence of sharp differences in negotiations over compensation payments. While both sides looked to cash to end the *Lucky Dragon* affair, their approaches to its use differed considerably. Tokyo wanted repayment for its expenditures on care of the fishermen, a solatium for their families, and recompense to the fishing industry for wasted catches and lost profits. Loath to set a figure until the full measure of harm done could be known, Japanese diplomats also sought payment for indirect damages. Ambassador Allison found that preposterous. He favored making a single, ex gratia, nonprecedent-setting payment. The last provision especially appealed to AEC officials and State Department lawyers, who had nightmares about the setting a precedent for claims for damages from future nuclear tests.[33]

By late May, the compensation negotiations had reached an impasse. Ambassador Allison, relying on the precedents of the Japanese Mariners' Law, had offered to settle all claims for $150,000. Asian Affairs Bureau Chief Nakagawa Toru balked at that and presented an incomplete list of claims that totalled more than $7.5 million. Logical inconsistencies in their respective positions also separated the two sides. While Tokyo demanded both unquantifiable indirect damages and more time to document real harm done, Washington wanted a quick political settlement that had somehow to be substantiated by still unprovided medical data.[34]

Discord over the particulars of a settlement prompted Ambassador Allison to reflect, late in May, on the forces that had shattered his strategy for settling the *Lucky Dragon* affair and their implications for the future of Japanese-American relations. He did not blame the AEC for insisting upon continuation of the tests, and he felt his embassy had done everything humanly possible to reach an accord. But Allison did fault the Japanese. He perceived "severe deficiencies" in Tokyo's security, administrative discipline, emotional stability, and cooperativeness. Japanese doctors, "many of whom were fuzzy-minded leftists, pacifists, and neutralists," had triggered the uproar over the *Lucky Dragon*, but the Yoshida ministry's unwillingness to control "insubordination" in the bureaucracy, the professions, and the media was the real problem. That lack of cooperation raised questions in the ambassador's mind about Tokyo's willingness to be the kind of ally Washington wanted. He foresaw difficulties, in time, over deploying nuclear weapons in Japan, over mutuality of the security treaty, and over its revision. In Allison's view, Washington needed to devise a new defense strategy for Japan that would take account of the "enormous new complications" created by the *Lucky Dragon* incident.[35]

Allison put these thoughts into a dispatch meant to ring alarm bells in Washington, and they did so. Impressed, John Foster Dulles sent it to the White House with a note commending the ambassador's thoughts to the President's attention. Eisenhower read the dispatch and recommended staff study of its suggestions. That must have pleased John Allison. By early June, when he left Tokyo for Washington to help prepare a Yoshida-Eisenhower meeting, he probably hoped that this first American-Japanese summit conference would provide an occasion for amicably settling the *Lucky Dragon* affair.[36]

STALEMATE AND DEATH, JUNE–OCTOBER 1954

It did not. Political turmoil among conservatives over succession to the prime ministry and Socialist disruption of the Diet over legislation implementing rearmament forced Yoshida to postpone his visit to Washington for five months. During that period, alliance managers inched toward settlement of the *Lucky Dragon* affair, only to be thwarted by Japanese politics and death itself.

By the time Ambassador Allison arrived in Washington, officials there were willing to pay a great deal to end the crisis within the alliance. Deputy Undersecretary of State Robert Murphy recommended nearly tripling the proposed compensation in return for Yoshida's providing more effective cooperation and control over his government. The day after Allison's arrival, Secretary of State Dulles agreed that the *Lucky Dragon* incident was "primarily [a] political and not [a] legal" problem that should be resolved by paying Japan between $.5 million and $1 million. Over the next two weeks, Allison met with the President, Vice President, Secretary of State, and the Joint Committee on Atomic Energy (JAEC). When the National Security Council's Operations Coordinating Board considered the problem, it recommended using already appropriated Mutual Security Assistance funds to compensate Japan. Ten days after he returned to Tokyo, Allison was authorized to conclude an executive agreement that would pay Japan up to $1 million to settle the *Lucky Dragon* affair.[37]

What explained Washington's sudden willingness to spend so much to end it? While Allison emphasized the dangers that the incident posed to Japanese-American harmony, other, broader concerns prompted his masters to change their position. Chairman Strauss, reversing himself, agreed to quick compensation even before the AEC could determine the truth of Tokyo's claims. He probably gave way on this "small" matter to strengthen his position on larger issues. Under attack for excessive secrecy and refusal to renew J. Robert Oppenheimer's security clearance, he may have hoped that paying off the Japanese would quiet liberal critics of continued nuclear testing. A shrewd bureaucratic politician, Strauss probably also realized that yielding to diplomats' desires for a quick settlement would salve wounds inflicted by his bitter and successful opposition to a limited moratorium on thermonuclear testing.[38]

The President and his Secretary of State were willing to pay more to end the *Lucky Dragon* affair quickly because they feared its effects on America's alliances generally and on Japanese behavior in particular. European reactions to the incident were especially troublesome. Although Winston Churchill, with Dulles' encouragement, had defended the necessity of H-bomb testing, the House of Commons had called for a ban on nuclear tests. The British Prime Minister was due in Washington late in June, and he could be expected to press for some concession on nuclear matters. Yet Dulles and Eisenhower had abandoned their initial openness to a moratorium on nuclear testing because they feared that taking that first step would enable Moscow to force them down the road toward abolition of all nuclear weapons. Quickly settling the *Lucky Dragon* affair might soften European protests arising from their rejection of a limited test ban.[39]

Dulles and Eisenhower were also concerned about Japan's apparent drift away from alliance toward alignment or, worse still, neutralism. Both men worried lest the northernmost "anchor" of the anti-Communist offshore island chain come unstuck at the very time they were trying to strengthen its southern counterpart by creating the Southeast Asia Treaty Organization. Dulles was shocked when Socialists disrupted Diet proceedings and forced postponement of Yoshida's visit to Washington. Troubled by the shakiness of Japan's economy and its impact on Japan's ability to bear greater responsibility for its own defense, Eisenhower lectured legislators and Cabinet members on the importance of opening American markets to Japan to keep Japanese merchants from becoming dependent on trade with China. The President also spoke out on the importance of keeping the "essential domino" across the Pacific standing at America's side. If $1 million could remove an irritant like the *Lucky Dragon* affair, which spewed frictions into the United States' most important Pacific alliance, then the money would be well spent.[40]

Thus by early July Ambassador Allison had the authority and the cash with which to negotiate a settlement. But Japanese leaders were not ready. Yoshida was angered and embarrassed by the forced postponement of his overseas journey. Determined to name the leader of a united conservative party who would succeed him, he concentrated on domestic politics and let his inner circle of subordinates wrestle with the *Lucky Dragon* problem. Their tough stand was a product of political turmoil as hot as the Tokyo summer.[41]

Minister of State Ando Masazumi, who chaired the interministerial committee on the Lucky Dragon affair and spoke for the fishing industry, was in no hurry to accept Washington's offers. He wanted to await the return of the *Shunkotsu maru*, scheduled for July 4, which would provide independent data on the impact of thermonuclear testing on marine life and ocean currents; that information would substantiate still higher damage claims. Ando also sought advance notice of future test dates—a procedure the AEC opposed because it might help Soviet scientists determine the size and physical properties of the explosions. The former purgee and editor in chief of the *Asahi shimbun* may also have had personal political motives for publicly rejecting Allison's offers of more compensation. Standing up to the Americans could be interpreted either as aid to a Prime Minister criticized for toadying to Washington or as subtle criticism of Yoshida by an ally of his would-be successor, Hatoyama Ichirō. In either case, Ando's firmness commanded widespread praise.[42]

Foreign Minister Okazaki also had good reason to resist a settlement that might be construed as giving in to Washington. He faced mounting pressures to keep the nation safe from thermonuclear pollution. By early July, more than a million citizens had signed a petition calling for a ban on all nuclear weapons. On August 6, record crowds turned out for peace ceremonies at Hiroshima, and similar demonstrations took place at Tokyo and Yaizu, Yet Okazaki steadfastly refused to condemn nuclear testing. He may well have felt that firmness on compensation for the *Lucky Dragon* accident would compensate for softness on the larger testing issue. The Foreign Minister may also have shared socially conditioned views on alliance relationships expressed by Liberal Party Secretary General Ikeda Hayato. The man rumored to be Yoshida's preferred successor argued that America must act as a generous patron toward its Japanese client. Okazaki may have feared that niggardly damage payments would threaten the health of the alliance by implying that Washington lacked the breadth of vision and depth of understanding necessary to sustain it.[43]

Whatever the precise mix of motives for Japanese resistance to a quick settlement, it had a chilling effect on Ambassador Allison. By the late summer of 1954, he concluded that more money would not solve the *Lucky Dragon* problem. More time and political change in Tokyo were required. Enraged by Ikeda Hayato's suggestions to the effect that more dollars could buy better alliance relations, Allison concluded that Japan was a profligate that had wasted profits from Korean War military procurement orders. The ambassador also harbored serious doubts about Tokyo's trustworthiness as an ally; Japan, he warned, had "no basic convictions for or against the free world or communism." Worse still, Prime Minister Yoshida did not "shoulder responsibility" for difficult choices but blamed the United States for Japan's having to make them. Indeed, the more Allison reflected on Tokyo's handling of the *Lucky Dragon* affair, the more certain he was that Yoshida could not manage domestic politics in the manner necessary to preserve alliance harmony.[44]

The death of radioman Kuboyama Aikichi late in September 1954 pushed settlement of the *Lucky Dragon* affair still further into the future. His demise was not unexpected, for he had fallen into critical condition nearly a month earlier. State Department officials, who feared Tokyo would use the death to raise claims for compensation, hoped to prevent recurrence of earlier misunderstandings by prepreparing statements of regret at the death and warning the embassy not to debate its cause. Thus within hours of Kuboyama's demise, Ambassador Allison expressed deep regrets and offered his widow a one million yen consolation payment.[45]

But once again diplomats failed to control the situation. Medical and scientific discord helped produce radically American and Japanese reactions to Kuboyama's death. Cool geostrategic logic suffused American commentary. The *New York Herald Tribune* editorialized that it would be "doubly tragic" if the radioman's demise cast a shadow over friendship between the Japanese and American people. In Washington, chairmen of the Senate Foreign Relations Committee and of the JAEC's Subcommittee on Research and Development warned lest the "Red influence in Asia" place disproportionate blame on the United States for Kuboyama's death. In Tokyo, the press unanimously criticized America for conducting the thermonuclear tests; for "making light" of their consequences; for disregarding the "wrath and fear of the H-bomb" that suffused Japanese society; and for refusing to make sufficiently generous payment for the wrong that had been done. That the Japanese public believed Kuboyama's death increased American culpability was evident in Doshisha University students' behavior. When an American instructor there suggested that the radioman might have died from something other than irradiation, the students, like Chinese Red Guards a decade later, forced him to recant publicly.[46]

In this atmosphere, ceremonies for the internment of Kuboyama's ashes took on the color of a state funeral and a political demonstration. Ambassador Allison did not attend, but three of his subordinates, who invited the Foreign Ministry's chief negotiator to fly to the rites with them, were present. En route to the hillside temple in Yaizu where the internment was to occur, their car was surrounded by angry demonstrators who stuffed handbills inside. An audience of local citizens, priests, antinuclear activists, and fisheries committee chairmen from both houses of the Diet heard Minister Ando and an American embassy representative speak. When the ceremonies concluded, Ando approached members of the Kuboyama family and told them, with reporters and television cameras looking on, that the *Lucky Dragon* case might well have to go the International Court of Justice for final resolution.[47]

That remark publicized a diplomatic stalemate that each side blamed on the other. Four days earlier, Foreign Minister Okazaki had given Ambassador Allison a letter that put the burden of breaking it on the Americans. If Washington wanted to quiet fears generated by the *Lucky Dragon* affair, it would have to remove future tests to a more distant site; give advanced warning if that were not possible; and promise "sufficient compensation" for losses the fishing industry might sustain, "regardless of their location." The ambassador, on the other hand, faulted Tokyo. More than than a month had passed without response to his renewed offer of a $1 million settlement. Now, rather than repeating it or referring the case to a commission, Allison gave Washington sound practical reasons for waiting: Yoshida had departed on a world tour. Fifty-six Americans had died in the sinking of the ferry *Toya maru* three days after Kuboyama's death. Tokyo was responsible for settling claims arising from that disaster, and these claims might be used to make the Japanese resolve the *Lucky Dragon* affair for less.[48]

But the real reasons for the ambassador's counsel of inaction were political. Kuboyama's death had demonstrated, once again, that the Japanese and their leaders were out of control. The medical profession made mendacious statements about the radioman's death; the press amplified them; and the public fell victim to the rantings of "radicals, neutralists, and pacifists." What sense, if any, was there in trying to settle the *Lucky Dragon* affair with a government that did nothing to stop all of this? An ally without a responsible government was, in effect, no ally at all.[49]

SETTLEMENT

E xactly one month after Kuboyama's death, Foreign Minister Okazaki met Assistant Secretary of State for Far Eastern Affairs Walter Robertson to pave the way for Prime Minister Yoshida's imminent visit to Washington. Okazaki, who wanted summit results that would aid his politically beleaguered master, suggested that more money—between $1.5 million and $2 million—could settle the *Lucky Dragon* affair. Arguing that Kuboyama's death and fresh reports of contaminated tuna had changed the situation more than the loss of American lives in the *Toya maru* disaster, he insisted that settling for a mere million dollars "would really end the Yoshida government." Robertson politely responded that although the United States wanted to do "what is fair and equitable," it could not "set precedents which would be unfortunate." Two million dollars might be too much, but perhaps something more than $1 million would prove acceptable. After agreeing with Okazaki on the undesirability of a protracted legal inquiry into the *Lucky Dragon* case, he warned that a settlement at the higher figure might require congressional approval and prompt "bad reactions" among the American people.[50]

That conversation marked the beginning of the end of efforts to settle the *Lucky Dragon* affair. But Washington was not as eager as Tokyo to do so quickly. Money was not the source of American reluctance. State Department officials thought $2 million a cheap price to pay to end "this messy affair." Assistant Secretary Robertson and Ambassador Allison needed only two meetings with the Operations Coordinating Board to win approval for offering Japan up to that amount. The money would come from the $850 million in new Mutual Security Act funds, which Capitol Hill Republicans had given the President to spend in Southeast Asia and the Western Pacific. No longer required to justify such expenditures to congressional foreign affairs committees, Eisenhower could simply certify that they were "important to the security of the United States." Thus neither security-minded AEC officials nor tight-fisted Bureau of the Budget administrators had grounds for objecting to paying Japan more money.[51]

Politics and popular attitudes did not pose problems for the administration, either. Admiral Strauss would not stir up trouble so long as the settlement did not threaten future operations at the Pacific Island test site. Scientists and experts such as *New York Times* military affairs commentator Hanson Baldwin had educated the public to the dangers of fallout—a lesson Kuboyama's death seemed to confirm. Popular magazine articles suggested that Japanese-American relations were at a crossroads that could lead either to closer cooperation or a drift apart.[52]

But precisely because he recognized that the alliance was in crisis, John Foster Dulles vetoed a "quick fix" of the *Lucky Dragon* problem while Yoshida was in Washington. Probably influenced by Ambassador Allison, he concluded that the old Prime Minister must go. Consequently, it would be unwise "to pass out so much" that Yoshida would return to Tokyo demanding continuation in office "on the basis of what we do." Who one settled with, and what kind of ally he promised to be, were clearly more important to Dulles than how much one paid.[53] Thus despite Tokyo's desires to the contrary, the first Japanese-American summit conference ended without either side pressing for solution of the *Lucky Dragon* problem. Yoshida returned to Tokyo, fought one last unsuccessful battle to name his successor, and resigned.

The change of government in Tokyo set in motion forces that promised an early settlement of the *Lucky Dragon* affair. Anti-Yoshida conservatives and Socialist Diet members elected Hatoyama Ichirō, a former purgee and advocate of closer ties with Moscow and Beijing, Prime Minister. Although his accession worried CIA Director Allen Dulles, Hatoyama had compelling personal political reasons for striking a bargain with Washington to end the *Lucky Dragon* affair. On the one hand, he wanted to show Americans that his overtures to their enemies were not inconsistent with good alliance relations. Removing the irritant they evidently wanted to erase would help do so. On the other hand, his political allies had attacked Yoshida for being too soft with Washington, and the old Prime Minister had probably not paid enough attention to popular objections to thermonuclear testing. Thus Hatoyama had to get a settlement that would appear "obviously to the advantage of Japan" and redound to his credit in elections set for March 1955.[54]

His new government moved quickly to end the *Lucky Dragon* affair. Personnel changes shunted aside Minister Ando and senior bureaucrats who had the greatest personal stakes in the outcome of the negotiations. The new Foreign Minister, Shigemitsu Mamoru, put settlement of the incident at the top of his list of urgent issues when he met Ambassador Allison for the first time. Ambassador Allison revealed Washington's willingness to settle for $1.5 million. But Shigemitsu brushed aside Allison's time-worn and fallacious arguments about the dangers of having to ask Congress for more money. He insisted that Japan could not settle for less than $2 million.[55]

In the wake of this conversation Tokyo and Washington moved rapidly toward agreement. Hatoyama advanced in crablike fashion. He stood firm on principle, letting it be known that he was considering protesting against continued nuclear testing to both Moscow and Washington. He promised to cooperate with "ban-the-bomb" advocates who presented him with a petition bearing more than twenty million Japanese signatures. His Cabinet also agreed to make additional interim disbursements for damages caused by the Bikini II-bomb test. But at the same time Tokyo officials played down its consequences. The interministerial committee investigating the *Lucky Dragon* affair first announced that tuna could be safely eaten, then stopped random testing of tuna trawlers' catches. Health officials also allowed seven of the twenty-one hospitalized crewman to return home for the New Year's holiday. That gesture signaled to the public that they were not likely to meet radioman Kuboyama's fate.[56]

In the waning days of 1954, the Eisenhower administration proceeded with unusual dispatch toward a settlement. Favorably impressed by Shigemitsu's words and Hatoyama's deeds and convinced that haggling over the amount of compensation should end, Ambassador Allison advised that it would be "most helpful" to reach and announce a settlement by New Year's Eve, the traditional time for settling debts in Japan. His superiors in Foggy Bottom agreed, and on December 29 they persuaded the Operations Coordinating Board to take the necessary steps to obtain a presidential determination that payment of $2 million to Japan served the security interests of the United States. Six days after Eisenhower made that determination, Allison and Shigemitsu announced terms for final settlement of the *Lucky Dragon* claims.[57]

Prime Minister Hatoyama welcomed that news from the Grand Shrine at Ise, where he was paying traditional New Year's respects to the Shinto deities. In words that constituted his opening speech in the coming election campaign, he claimed that the settlement gave proof of American good will toward his new government.[58] Hatoyama spoke the truth. Rather than striking a cheaper bargain with a Cabinet it perceived as weak and untrustworthy, the Eisenhower administration paid more to a ministry that had some promise of becoming a stronger, more stable, and genuinely cooperative ally.

FALLOUT

The January 1955 compensation agreement formally ended the *Lucky Dragon* affair. Four months later, the last of the ship's crew were released from hospitals. Repaid in small measure for their sufferings, they returned to Yaizu, to obscurity, and to the task of rebuilding their lives. Thirty years later, all but three were living, and despite their fears of ostracism and sterility, most had married and fathered children. Time disproved their worst fears and healed their wounds. Time also cast their ship into obscurity for nearly a decade. The Japanese government renamed it, refitted it as a training vessel for the Tokyo Fisheries College, and eventually consigned it to a manmade island of garbage in Tokyo Bay euphemistically called the "Isle of Dreams."[59]

But the *Lucky Dragon* incident generated fallout that influenced relations between the United States and Japan for decades to come. The "ashes of death" that rained down on March 1, 1954, formed part of the antinuclear mantle in which Japan wrapped itself. The thermonuclear accident revealed the Japanese people's anguish and anger at being three-time victims of nuclear weapons. For a decade and more, annual "Bikini Day" commemorations at Kubuyama's grave and demonstrations in Tokyo and other major cities proclaimed their feelings. The League Against Atomic and Hydrogen Bombs (Gensuikyo) made the *Lucky Dragon* incident a powerful symbol of popular, nonpartisan opposition to the cardinal instrument of American national security policy. The incident also strengthened Japan's claim to speak out with special force in the United Nations for nuclear arms control. Fifteen years later, the antinuclear protestors of 1954 began a campaign to buy and restore the *Lucky Dragon*. In 1976, with the help of Tokyo's Socialist mayor, Minobe Ryokichi, they enshrined the ship in a handsome museum.[60]

The *Lucky Dragon* incident had far less dramatic effects on Americans. Most of them quickly forgot about the unfortunate Japanese fishermen and continued to support Washington's arguments for strategic nuclear arms competition with Moscow. Eisenhower administration officials insisted that national security demanded continued nuclear testing and believed they could control physical and diplomatic damage resulting from it. But the incident did plant seeds of doubt about administration policies, and these in time bore fruit. The accidental disclosure of information about thermonuclear weapons prompted some scientists to insist upon their control. One among them, Dr. Ralph E. Lapp, went to Japan in 1957 to interview the fishermen and those who had treated them. He returned to testify on the dangers of thermonuclear fallout before a congressional committee and wrote several widely read articles and a book on the *Lucky Dragon* incident. In this way, the 1954 accident laid foundations for the Nuclear Test Ban Treaty of 1963.[61]

The *Lucky Dragon* incident also revealed a great deal about the character, purpose, and balance of influence within the U.S.–Japan alliance. It demonstrated that security was both the heart of and the greatest irritant within the pact. Security-centered crises similar to the *Lucky Dragon* incident recurred with increasing intensity during the remaining Eisenhower years. In 1957, when an American soldier accidentally killed a Japanese woman on an army firing range near Mount Fuji, Prime Minister Kishi Nobusuke barely succeeded in quelling popular emotions, and President Eisenhower found it nearly impossible to convince Americans of the fairness of the Japanese court that tried the soldier. In 1960, despite diplomats' success in revising the U.S.–Japan Security Treaty, massive protests in Tokyo felled the Kishi government and forced cancellation of Eisenhower's visit to Japan. Pentagon opposition to Okinawa's reversion to full Japanese control for another dozen years thereafter fueled still more security-related discord within the alliance.[62]

Diplomats kept these crises from destroying the alliance, but their successes cloaked fundamental differences in American and Japanese understandings of its nature and purpose. For Washington, the alliance was above all else an instrument of control—a means of containing Soviet and Chinese power, of keeping the Pacific an American lake, and of insuring that friendly conservatives managed Japanese politics. These preeminent purposes ruled out serious reconsideration of the relationship between nuclear weapons and alliances in 1954, justified giving in to Tokyo's demands for higher damage payments, and guaranteed that the settlement would be timed so as to influence who occupied the Prime Minister's residence.

For Tokyo, the alliance was a tool for recovery of full independence, prosperity, and power within the Asia-Pacific region. While it demanded subordination to American global strategy and provoked resistance when, as in 1954, Washington appeared to trample on Tokyo's interests and sensitivities, it in fact allowed Japanese bureaucrats and politicians considerable freedom of choice. In the *Lucky Dragon* incident, they chose not to challenge, but rather to acquiesce in American security policies. That decision, repeated many times over by their successors, while it acknowledged the force of popular criticism of Washington's nuclear policies, tacitly accepted the reality of Japan's reliance upon American atomic and hydrogen bombs for defense.

In 1954 Yoshida Shigeru insisted that no other choice was possible because Washington was the overwhelmingly stronger alliance partner. That posture freed him from the political onus of acknowledging dependence on the very weapons that had been used against Japan less than a decade earlier. But it also allowed Yoshida and his successor to outmaneuver and extract much of what they wanted from their supposedly stronger American protector. By simultaneously professing loyalty to that ally and insisting that domestic forces opposed to their policies must be placated, they compelled Washington to pay a higher than intended price for their continued cooperation.

That end to the *Lucky Dragon* affair was not unique. Time and again during the Eisenhower years, supposedly weak clients driven by strong nationalism would outlast, outmaneuver, and outperform a "strong" America determined to control Asia-Pacific international relations. Manila and Seoul, Saigon and Taipei, all demanded and received larger than intended American compensation—ranging from alliance itself through arms and payments for basing rights to political support and preferential tariff agreements—in return for their continued acceptance of the linkage between alliance and nuclear weapons. In that sense, then, the *Lucky Dragon* affair was much more than an incident in the history of U.S.–Japan relations. It portended changes in the balance of influence in American–East Asian relations that would not become fully evident for another thirty years.

NOTES

Research for this essay was made possible, in part, by financial assistance received from the American Council of Learned Societies, the Institute of War and Peace Studies of Columbia University, and Yokohama National University. I wish to acknowledge my gratitude for that support and my sole responsibility for the opinions and arguments put forth in this essay.

1. John Foster Dulles, "A Policy of Boldness," *Life*, May 19, 1952, pp. 146–160.

2. Office of the Historian, Dept. of State, *Foreign Relations of the United States, 1952–1954* (Washington, D.C.: GPO, 1984), (hereafter cited as *FRUS*).

3. 694.00/9-1054, Tokyo 336 to Secretary of State, September 10, 1954, Dept. of State Decimal File, Record Group (RG) 59, U.S. National Archives (documents from these files will hereafter be cited simply by number, place of origin, and date); Robert Sherrod, "Grim Facts of the H-bomb Accident," *Saturday Evening Post*, July 17, 1954, p. 21.

4. The name of the ship in the text hereafter will be shortened to *Lucky Dragon* to correspond with contemporary usage. Ralph E. Lapp, *The Voyage of the Lucky Dragon* (New York: 1958), pp. 1–26; George T. Mazuzan and J. Samuel Walker, *Controlling the Atom: The Beginnings of Nuclear Regulation, 1946–1962* (Berkeley: 1985), p. 42; Edwin J. Martin and Richard H. Rowland, *Castle Series, 1954* (Washington, D.C.: Defense Nuclear Agency, 1982), p. 204. A brief account of the Lucky

Dragon incident also appears in Robert A. Divine, *Blowin' in the Wind* (New York: 1978), pp. 5–13.

5. Martin and Rowland, *Castle Series, 1954*, pp. 201–5. I have followed the more accurate current usage for identifying Enewetak given in this source rather than the conventional "Eniwetok."

6. *Ibid*, pp. 210–30; Bernard J. O'Keefe, *Nuclear Hostages* (Boston, 1983), pp. 165–96 provides a graphic account by the chief detonator of the BRAVO shot of its immediate aftereffects.

7. Lapp, *Lucky Dragon*, pp. 27–40, based upon 1956 interviews with the *Lucky Dragon*'s Fishing Master Misaki Yoshio and other crew members. See Japan interview journal, Ralph E. Lapp papers; Kawai Ryūsuke and Togasawa Hidetoshi, *Suibaku jiken to no sōgū* (Encounter with a Hydrogen Bomb Test) (Tokyo, 1985), pp. 27–30.

8. Robert H. Ferrell, ed., *The Diary of James C. Hagerty* (Bloomington, 1983), pp. 13–23 (hereafter cited as Hagerty diary); Divine, *Blowin' in the Wind*, p. 5; 711.5611/ 2-1554, Strauss to Smith, February 15, Smith to Strauss, February 20, 1954; Generalization on political debate in Tokyo in this and subsequent paragraphs are based on reading of *Asahi Shimbun* and *Nippon Times* January 10–February 28, 1954; No indication of earlier Japanese objections to proclamation of a danger zone around the Pacific Islands test site in September 1953 has been found.

9. *New York Times* January 22, 1951. The *Nautilus* was launched at 11 A.M. January 21, which was early the morning of January 22, Japan time.

10. In 1954, there existed a Fisheries Agency within the Ministry of Agriculture and Forestry with an administrative section that could have been used to regulate the fishing industry more closely. Fujinaga Motosaku, "Japanese Fishery," *Contemporary Japan* (1955), 23:711–25. For evidence of the lingering dispute over the so-called "Rhee line" in the Sea of Japan, see *FRUS, 1952–54*, vol. 14: (Washington, D.C: GPO, 1985), pp. 1486–87; and Taguchi Shinji, "Japanese-Korean Fishing Dispute," *Contemporary Japan* (1953), 22:392–415.

11. *FRUS, 1952–54*, 2:1321–68, passim; *FRUS, 1952–54*, 14: 1406–8, 1412–15, 1438–40, 1448–52, 1497–1502, 1572–73, 1616; 794.00/3–1254, Tokyo 1280, March 12; /3–2554, Tokyo 2300, March 25; UN, Bureau of Statistics, *United Nations Yearbook of International Trade Statistics, 1954* (New York, 1955), pp. 313–53; Okita Saburo, "Japan's Trade with Asia," *Contemporary Japan* (1955), 23:711–25, attests to the reasons for Washington's concern; *New York Times*, March 9, 1954.

12. My "Reconsiderations: The United States–Japan Security Treaty," *Pacific Community* (July 1976), 7:471–93; Hosoya Chihiro, *San furanshisuko kōwa e no michi* (The Road to the San Francisco Peace Settlement) (Tokyo, 1984), esp. ch. 7; and Igarashi Takeshi, *TaiNichi kōwa to reisen* (The Japanese Peace Settlement and the Cold War) (Tokyo, 1986), esp. chs. 2 and 3 provide insights into Tokyo's motivations in concluding the U.S.–Japan Security Treaty; William S. Borden, *The Pacific Alliance* (Madison, Wis., 1984), pp. 166–76.

13. Lapp, *Lucky Dragon*, pp. 45–54; Sherrod, "Grim Facts," p. 42; Kawai and Togusawa, *Suibaku jiken to no sōgū*, pp. 142–43, 159–61.

14. Eleanor Schoenebaum, *Political Profiles: The Eisenhower Administration* (New York, 1977), pp. 586–88; Lewis Strauss's autobiography, *Men and Decisions* (New York, 1962), chs. 1–11, and Richard Pfau, *No Sacrifice Too Great: The Life of Lewis L. Strauss* (Charlottesville: University of Virginia Press, 1984) chs. 1–7 detail his career before 1954; Strauss daily appointments schedule, March 9, AEC Secretariat files, 1951–1958, RG 326, U.S. Dept. of Energy; *New York Times*, March 2, 7, 14, 1954.

15. Lapp, *Lucky Dragon*, pp. 55–67, 77–79; Kawai and Togasawa, *Suibaku jiken to no sōgū*, pp. 39–41; *Yomiuri shimbun*, March 16, newspaper clipping collection, Daigo Fukuryū maru tenjikan (*Lucky Dragon #5* Exposition Hall) archives (here-

after cited as Lucky Dragon archives); frontespiece photograph of later *Yomiuri shimbun* edition, March 16, in Miyake Yasuo, Hinokiyama Yoshio, and Kusano Nobuo, eds., *Bikini suibaku hisai shiryo shū* (Documents on Sufferings from the Bikini Hydrogen Bomb), (Tokyo, 1976); *Asahi Shimbun, Mainichi shimbun, Yomiuri shimbun*, March 17; 711.5611/3–2154, Tokyo 2261, March 21, 1954.

16. *New York Times*, March 2, 11; Strauss schedule, March 11–12, minutes of AEC mtg. 967, March 16, 1954, Secretariat Files 1951–1958, MH & S, Radiation vol. 1, box 4928, RG 326; Divine, *Blowin' in the Wind*, p. 5; *Public Papers of the Presidents: Dwight D. Eisenhower, 1954* (Washington, D.C., 1960), pp 346–47 (hereafter cited as PPS); FRUS, *1952–54*, 14:1622; Dulles wanted Commander Naval Forces, Far East, headquartered in Yokosuka, to take over the ship.

17. *Ibid; New York Times*, March 18; *Asahi Shimbun*, March 23; Martin and Rowland, *Castle Series, 1954*, p. 35; Preliminary Report: Atomic Bomb Casualty Commission, March 26, DBM 326–78–3; AEC 730/4, Energy History Files, RG 326. Lapp, *Lucky Dragon*, p. 113 says that Tokyo University officials requested ABCC aid, but evidence now available suggests that the initiative came from Washington. Report on Radiological Activities of the Food and Drug Administration, item 6720, MH & S, vol. 1, Bugher to AEC Commissioners, March 31, 1954, AEC Secretariat Files, 1951–1958, MH & S, 3, Radiation vol. 1, box 4928; Martin and Rowland, *Castle Series, 1954*, p. 220.

18. John M. Allison, *Ambassador from the Prairie*, (Tokyo, 1975), pp. 3–8, 140–72; *New York Times*, March 18, 25; FRUS, *1952–54*, 14:1622; 711.5611/3–2154, Tokyo 2261, March 21; /3–2254, Tokyo 2264, March 22; /3–2354, Tokyo 2264, March 23; /3–2454, Tokyo 2279, March 24; /3–2454, Tokyo 2289; AEC mtgs. 967–969 minutes, Secretariat Files, 1951–1958, March 16–19, MH & S 3 Radiation, vol. 1; Nichols to Strauss, March 24, 1954, MR & A 7, CASTLE 3, folder 33, RG 326.

19. *New York Times*, March 17–25; PPS, p. 346; *Who's Who in Japan, with Manchukuo and China, 1939–1940* (Tokyo: Japan Who's Who, 1939), p. 737; *Japan Biographical Encyclopedia and Who's Who*, (Tokyo: Japan Biographical Encyclopedia, 2nd ed, 1960), p. 1164; 711.5611/3–2654 Tokyo 2324, March 26; FRUS, *1952–54, vol. 14*, p. 1622; *Asahi Shimbun*, March 17–24, 1954.

20. 711.5611/3–2254, Tokyo 2264, March 22; *New York Times*, March 18, 21, 26, 1954; Lapp, *Lucky Dragon*, 99–100, 127–30; Miyake, Hinokiyama, and Kusano, eds., *Bikini suibaku hisai shiryo shū*, pp. 668–69. Kondo Yasuo, ed., *Suibaku jiken to Nihon gyogyō* (The H-Bomb Incident and Japan's Fisheries) (Tokyo, 1958) exhaustively treats the impact of the March 1 incident on Japan's fisheries generally and the industry at Yaizu in particular.

21. Lapp, *Lucky Dragon*, pp. 101–2, 121–23; Sherrod, "Grim Facts," p. 49; 711.5611/3–2154, Tokyo 2261, March 21; /3–2354, Tokyo 2279, March 23; /3–2354, /3–2454, Tokyo 2284, March 24; AEC 730/4 Final report on Relations between Japanese and American Scientists, May 27, 1954, Energy History Files; n.d. 1954 Eisenbud to Bugher report: Contamination of the Fukuryu Maru and Associated Problems in Japan: Preliminary Report, Energy History Files, RG 326; *New York Times*, March 26, 1954.

22. 711.5611/3–2954, Tokyo 2347, March 29, 1954; Lapp, *Lucky Dragon*, p. 148.

23. 794.00/3–2654, Tokyo 1329, March 26; 711/5611/3–2454, Tokyo 2294, March 24; /3–2654, Tokyo 2324, March 26; /3–2954, Tokyo 2346, March 29; /3–3054, Tokyo 2360, March 30; /3–3154, Tokyo 2372, 2373, 2374, March 31; *Asahi, Yomiuri*, and *Mainichi* clippings, March 17–31, 1954, clippings collection, *Lucky Dragon* archive. Miyake, Hinokiyama, and Kusano, eds., *Bikini suibaku hisai shiryo shū*, pp. 506–7 lists articles concerning the incident that appeared in Japanese popular weekly magazines during this period.

24. FRUS, *1952–54*, 2:1379–80; *New York Times*, March 30, 1954.

25. *New York Times*, March 20, 28, 30; Holifield to Cole, March 18, Holifield

speeches "Tell the People the Facts about the Atomic-Hydrogen Weapons" and "Survival," March 29, 1954, box 79, Chet Holifield papers, Regional Cultural Historical Collection, University of Southern California Library, Los Angeles, Calif.; Strauss appointments schedule, March 30, 1954, AEC Secretariat Files, 1951–1958, RG 326.

26. Hagerty diary, pp. 36–37; *New York Times*, April 1; PPS, pp. 364–70; Strauss photographs, March 31, oversize files, Hearst/INS Photographic Morgue, Regional Cultural Historical Collection, University of Southern California Library.

27. Hagerty diary, pp. 36–37; *Time* (April 5), 63:17, (April 12), 64:21–24; *Newsweek* (March 29), 47:19–22, (April 5), 48:28–34; (April 12), 49:27, 46; *Life* (April 12), 36:38; *New York Times*, April 1–2, 4; 711.45611/4–254 Tokyo 2399, April 2; *Yomiuri Shimbun*, April 3, clippings collection, *Lucky Dragon* Archive; *Asahi Shimbun* and *Nippon Times*, April 1–3, 1954.

28. 711.5611/3–2154, Tokyo 2261, March 21; /3–2354, Tokyo 2279, 2289 and 2293, March 24; /3–2954, Tokyo 2347, March 29; /3–3154, Tokyo 2374, March 31, 1954.

29. 711.5611/3–3154, Tokyo 2374, March 31; /4–954, Tokyo 2462, April 9; *Asahi Shimbun*, April 12, 1954.

30. 711.5611/4–254 Tokyo 2402 and 2403, April 2; /4–554, Tokyo 2423, April 5; /5–1554, Tokyo unnumbered, May 1, 1954; *New York Times*, March 17, 30–31, April 11, 21–22, 29; Miyake, Hinokiyama, and Kusano, eds., *Bikini suibaku hisai shiryo shū*, pp. 489–90, 673–74; Ubuki Satoru, "Gunshuku to shimin undo: Nihon no gensuibaku kinshi undo o megutte," (Disarmament and Citizens: On the Movement against A- and H-Bombs in Japan," *Kokusai seiji* (International Relations) (October 1985), 80; 114.

31. 711.5611/3–2454, Tokyo 2293 and 2294, March 24; /3–2654, Tokyo 2654, March 26; 3–2854, Tokyo 2334, March 28; /4–854, Tokyo 2448, April 8; /5–2154, State 2510, May 21; /5–1421, Tokyo 2803, May 14; /5–2054 State 2579, May 20; 794.00/6–454, Tokyo 1632; *Asahi Shimbun* April 10, May 14, 20; *New York Times*, April 17; AEC mtg. 984 of May 12, MH & S, 3 Radiation, vol. 1, box 4928, RG 326.

32. Lapp, *Lucky Dragon*, 113–14, pp. 138–39; Sherrod, "Grim Facts," p. 46; Preliminary Report of Atomic Bomb Casualty Commission, March 26, Final Report on Relations between American and Japanese Scientists, May 27, DBM box 326–78–3, box 3, RG 326. The difference in tone and substance of these two reports provides the most striking evidence of conflict between American and Japanese medical personnel.

33. 711.5611/3–3154, Tokyo 2374, March 31; /4–1154 Tokyo 2471 and 2476, April 11; /4–1354, Tokyo 2497, April 13; /4–1654 Tokyo 1428, April 16, /4–2654 Tokyo 2613, April 26; /4–3054, State 2394, April 30, 1954.

34. 711.5611/5–1454, Tokyo 2806, State 2562, May 14; /5–2254, Tokyo 2881, May 22; /6–454 Tokyo 1631, June 4, 1954; *FRUS, 1952–54*, 14: 1651–52.

35. *Ibid.*, pp. 1643–48.

36. *Ibid.*, p. 1648; *Asahi Shimbun*, June 1, 1954.

37. 711.5611/2–654, McClurkin to Allison, memo, June 2; /6–1654 Finn to Hemmendinger, June 16, 1954; *FRUS, 1952–54*, 14:1648–53, 1661, 1665–67; Schoenebaum, *Eisenhower Administration*, pp. 446–47; Minutes of AEC mtg. 1012, June 30, MH & S, Radiation vol. 1, AEC Secretariat Files, 1951–1958, RG 326; *Asahi Shimbun*, June 21, 1954.

38. Hagerty diary, p. 61; *FRUS 1952–54*, 2:1470–71; Pfau, *Lewis S. Strauss*, ch. 11; *New York Times*, May 29; MH & S, 3 Radiation vol. 1; Minutes of AEC mtg. 995 of May 28, 1954, MH & S, Radiation, vol. 1, AEC Secretariat Files, 1951–1958, RG 326.

39. *FRUS, 1952–54*, 2:1425–29, 1472–73; Hagerty diary, p. 76.

40. *FRUS,1952–54*, 14:1653, 1662–63; Hagerty diary, p. 70; PPS, p. 587; *New*

York Times, July 15, 1954. Dulles and Eisenhower's concern for the alliance mirrored trends in American domestic opinion. Polls showed that popular faith in Japan as an ally had dropped precipitously. At Occupation's end, more than two out of three trusted Japan would cooperate with the United States; in the wake of the *Lucky Dragon* incident, scarecely half thought Tokyo would do so. Popular Attitudes toward Japan, February 7, 1955, box 39, Schuyler Foster Files, RG 59.

41. *FRUS, 1952–54*, 14:1653–54, 1666; 794.00/7–2054, Tokyo 97, July 20; /8–1854, Tokyo 230, August 18; /9–1454, Tokyo 350, September 14, 1954; Masumi Junnosuke, *Postwar Politics in Japan, 1945–1955*, trans. Lonny E. Carlile (Berkeley, 1985), pp. 298–301.

42. *Asahi Shimbun*, July 4; Miyake, Hinokiyama, and Kusano, eds., *Bikini suibaku hisai shiryo shū*, pp. 675–76; *New York Times*, July 10, 26, August 14; 1954; 794.00/9–1454, Tokyo 350, September 14, 1954; *Japan Biographical Encyclopedia and Who's Who*, p. 40; *Who's Who in Japan with Manchukuo and China, 1939–1940*, p. 29; 794.00/11–2254, Tokyo 1243, November 22; *Asahi Shimbun*, July 10; *New York Times*, June 8, July 10, 26, August 14, 1954.

43. Miyake, Hinokiyama, and Kusano, eds., *Bikini suibaku hisai shiryo shū*, pp. 676; 711.00/8–254, Consul General Nagoya 4, August 2; 794.00/7–2754, Tokyo 217, July 27; Chūgoku shimbun sha, *Hiroshima no kiroku: Kakubaku sanjūnen shashin shū* (The Record of Hiroshima: A Thirty-Year Photographic Collection) (Hiroshima, 1975), p. 114; *Asahi Shimbun*, August 6; 711.5611/8–654, Tokyo 299, August 6, 1954; *FRUS, 1952–54*, 14:1658–59.

44. *Ibid.*, 1704–7; 1714–15. Allison would have smiled and agreed with the *Asahi* cartoon of July 27, 1954, which lampooned Ikeda by depicting him as a hippopotamus with its mouth open to catch a bag full of dollars.

45. Miyake, Hinokiyama, and Kusano, eds., *Bikini suibaku hisai shiryo shū*, p. 677; *New York Times*, August 30, September 25; Tokyo 530, September 2, MH & S, Kuboyama File, 78–3–box 2, RG 326 (hereafter cited as AEC Kuboyama File); *Nippon Times*, September 25, 1954.

46. AEC press spokesman to Bugher, et al, September 3, C. L. Dunham to press spokesman, September 10; Tokyo 559, September 4, Tokyo 720, September 24, AEC Kuboyama File; *Asahi Evening News* September 24; Report of Dr. Ohashi's Press Conference, English Language materials file, *Lucky Dragon* archive; *Nippon Times*, September 25, 1954. Tokyo 712, September 24, AEC Kuboyama File; *New York Times*, September 26; *Asahi Evening News*, September 24; Bugher speech to 7th Industrial Health Conference, Houston, September 23, MH & S 3 Radiation, vol. 1, box 4928, RG 326. August 31; *Asahi Shimbun* and *Nippon Times*, September 24–26; *New York Times*, September 26; 794.00/11–854, Consul General Kobe 135, November 8, 1954. The American professor was Otis Cary.

47. 711.5611/11–554, memo on Kuboyama Funeral Ceremony, enclosed with Tokyo 571, November 5. The reporting American diplomat described the students as Communists and their handouts as "doggerel." *Asahi Shimbun*, October 9, 1954.

48. 711.5611/10–854, Tokyo 849, October 8; Tokyo 729, September 29; Tokyo 776, September 30, 1954, AEC Kuboyama File.

49. Allison must have been especially furious about the Japanese medical doctors' statements, for William Leonhart had informed him of American physicians' conferences with them that indicated uncertainty as to the course of treatment they were following. He could not have missed the differences between what Lt. Col. James Hansen, the American observer at the autopsy, reported Dr. Tsuzuki as saying and the translated and toned-down version of the Japanese scientist's remarks that appeared in the September 29 *Asahi Evening News*. See Leonhart to Allison, memo, September 1–2, Tokyo 449, September 4; Tokyo 793, October 1, 1954, AEC Kuboyama File.

50. *FRUS, 1952–54*, 14:1748–50.

51. State 530, September 3, State 749, September 23, 1954, AEC Kuboyama File; *FRUS 1952–54*, 14:1758–59, 1815; U.S. Cong., House of Rep., Committee on Foreign Affairs, *Selected Executive Sessions Hearings of the Committee, 1951–1956* (Washington, D.C.: GPO 1980), 9:190, 12:510, 526.

52. Strauss's views can be inferred from the absence of any discussion of the issue in available AEC records or in the press; Miyake, Hinokiyama, and Kusano, eds., *Bikini suibaku hisai shiryo shū*, p. 681 report Strauss's early December reaffirmation of continued intent to test in the Marhalls. That policy, it should be noted, mirrored the desires of the American public; the only Gallup poll taken on testing in 1954 showed 71 percent of the respondents favored continued testing. See George H. Gallup, *The Gallup Poll: Public Opinion, 1935–1971* (New York, 1972), 2:229–230; see also *FRUS, 1952–54*, 14:1568ff. for continued discussion of the nuclear sharing program and its relationship to the *Lucky Dragon* incident; *New York Times*, November 7, 9; "Japan's U.S. Ties Loosen," *Business Week*, August 28, 1954, pp. 96ff.; Robert Sherrod, "How Can Japan Ever Survive?" *Saturday Evening Post*, (October 9, 1954, 227:32–33ff. Richard L–G. Deverall, "H-Bomb Creates Japan–U.S. Fission," *America*, November 6, 1954, 92:34–36; Arthur Dean, "Japan at the Crossroads," *Atlantic Monthly* (November 1954), 194:30–35.

53. *FRUS, 1952–54*, 14:1769, 1785; *New York Times*, November 28, December 5–7; *Asahi shimbun*, December 5–7, 1954.

54. Masumi, *Postwar Politics in Japan*, pp. 301–5; *FRUS, 1952–54*, 14:1796, 1805; 794.00/11–2254, Tokyo 1243, November 22, /12–1754, Tokyo 1436, December 17; /12–2354, Tokyo 774, December 23; 611.94/12–2754 Tokyo 1502, December 27; *New York Times*, December 7, 10, 1954.

55. Tsuji Kiyoaki and Hayashi Shige, eds., *Nihon naikaku shiroku 5* (A Historical Record of Japanese Cabinets, vol. 5) (Tokyo, Daiichi hōki shuppansha 1981), p. 278; 611.94/12–2754, Tokyo 1502, December 27; *Asahi Shimbun*, December 27–29, 1954.

56. Miyake, Hinokiyama, and Kusano, eds., *Bikini suibaku hisai shiryo shū*, p. 681; *New York Times*, December 23–24, 1954; Office of Public Affairs, U.S. Dept. of Energy, Nevada Operations Office, Announced Foreign Nuclear Detonations through December 31, 1978, USSR, 1.

57. *FRUS, 1952–54*, 14:1815–16; *New York Times*, 4–5, 1955.

58. *Nippon Times*, January 5, 1955.

59. Miyake, Hinokiyama, and Kusano, eds., *Bikini suibaku hisai shiryo shū*, p. 683; Lapp, *Lucky Dragon*, p. 184; Kawai and Togasawa, *Suibaku jiken to no sōgū*, pp. 59–163; "The Lucky Dragon—the 5th Fukuryū-maru: A Witness of the Bikini Tragedy March 1st 1954," (Tokyo, Peace Society for the 5th Fukuryū-Maru, n.d.).

60. Kawai and Togasawa, *Suibaku jiken to no sōgū*, pp. 6–11. For an example of public information materials used in the commemoration of "Bikini Day," see *Gensuibaku kinshi nyuzu*, March 1957, item 56, file 1, box 5–3; items 1956–2, 1959–1, 1959–2, 1960–3, 1963–1, 1963–2, 1964–1, Bikini taiki shiryō, box 6, Hirota Jūdō papers, Kanagawa Prefectural Library, Yokohama. I am indebted to Professor Amakawa Akira of Yokohama National University for calling my attention to this massive and valuable collection. Hirota Jūdō, *Daigo fukuryū maru hozon undo shi* (A History of the Movement to Preserve the Lucky Dragon Number 5) (Tokyo, 1981) describes the preservation movement in detail.

61. *FRUS 1952–54*, 2:1576–77; Ralph E. Lapp interview, June 27, 1987; Lapp reported that the Japanese were "hyperallergic to atomic radiation." See Lapp to Ramey, May 4, 1957, 1957 Fallout Hearings Expert Witnesses File, General Correspondence, box 713, Records of the Joint Committee on Atomic Energy, RG 128; Lapp, "The Voyage of the *Lucky Dragon*," (December 1957), 215:27–36, (January 1958), 216:48–55, (February 1958), 217:72–79. A shortened version of the article also appeared in the most widely circulated magazine in the United States, *Read-*

er's Digest (May 1958), 72:114–20; "The Voyage of the Lucky Dragon," film script in Lapp papers; Richard Hudson, *Kuboyama Aikichi and the Saga of the Lucky Dragon* (New York, 1965); Divine, *Blowin' in the Wind*, chs. 2ff. provides the most recent history of the nuclear test ban movement.

62. George Packard, *Protest in Tokyo* (Princeton, 1966); Michael R. Beschloss, *Mayday: The U-2 Affair* (New York, 1986), pp. 319–21; Watanabe Akio, *The Okinawa Problem: A Chapter in United States–Japan Relations* (Melbourne, 1970).

11

U.S. China Policy in the Eisenhower Era: A Soviet View

P. M. IVANOV
Institute of Oriental Studies
Soviet Academy of Science

A merican policy toward China in the 1950s, during the presidency of Eisenhower, was influenced, first of all, by the cold war. Imperialism, led by the United States, opposed the international socialist system that had emerged in the immediate postwar years. This tension was the central element of international relations in the Eisenhower era.

After World War II, the United States, acting out of self-interest as well as altruisim, undertook responsibility for the rehabilitation and restructuring of the capitalist world. This role, combined with its hostility to socialist countries, led quite logically to American commitments to many reactionary, antidemocratic regimes in different parts of the world.

In Asia, the People's Republic of China became the primary socialist opponent of the United States. The removal of China from the imperialist sphere of influence meant more than great material loss for the American and West European bourgeoisie. The victory of the People's Revolution in China hastened the growth of national liberation movements and intensified the anticolonial struggle in Asia.

The government of the United States perceived the Chinese Communists as the main proponents of the expansion of socialism in Asia. To contain the Chinese, the Americans created a propagandistic image of China as the "red menace" in the Asia-Pacific region and gave China one of the leading roles in the domino theory.

Despite the American myth of an aggressive, expansionist China, China was hardly a credible rival to American power. The United States had nuclear weapons and established a series of bilateral and multilateral alliances on China's periphery. China, still very weak, struggling with internal problems and limited resources, could rely only on the high morale of its revolutionary army. Moreover, China could not offer decisive material assistance to antigovernment forces in the neighboring countries and territories. And certainly from a Chinese perspective, Chinese military action in Korea and the Taiwan Straits did not constitute aggression or expansion. In Korea, the Chinese acted primarily in selfdefense, as the enemy approached the Yalu and secondarily to demonstrate socialist solidarity. In the Taiwan Straits, China sought to resolve an internal problem inherited from the civil war.

In the 1950s, East Asia became an arena for the advance of socialism and national liberation, from Korea to Indochina. To counter this development, the United States built up its peripheral defense system, relying on close cooperation with the regimes of South Korea, the Philippines, Thailand, and Taiwan. Relations with Japan acquired new strategic importance because of the growing role of American military bases on its territory. The possibility, even the inevitability, of confrontation with Communist China was offered as one of the main motives for strengthening the American military presence in the region.

The war in Korea served as a catalyst for anti-Chinese elements in the United States. At the same time, the American government recognized the necessity of taking the Chinese Communists seriously, which lead ultimately to diplomatic contacts in Geneva. But developments during the Korean War had primarily negative consequences for the bilateral relationship between the United States and the People's Republic of China, especially American-inspired international sanctions against China and the U.S.–Taiwan rapprochement.

The Kuomintang (KMT) had lost its credibility entirely during the period of its rule on the mainland, but growing hostility between the United States and the PRC led to closer ties between Washington and Taibei. Strategic control over Taiwan offered the United States an unbroken chain of communications from Japan to Southeast Asia. The island of Taiwan became a base for military preparations for the anticipated armed confrontation with the Chinese Communists. The 1954 Mutual Defense Treaty between Taibei and Washington, congressional adoption of the "Formosa Resolution" in 1955, and statements by Eisenhower and John Foster Dulles about the possible use of atomic weapons against the PRC testify to American unwillingness to consider normalization of relations with Beijing. On the other hand, Washington was not eager for war, as evidenced by exclusion of the offshore islands from the sphere of application of the Formosa Resolution.

It would be wrong to assume the U.S.—KMT partnership was without tensions. The government of the United States was unwilling to give full support to the "return to the mainland" slogan. Condescending verbal support from Washington was not followed by readiness to be involved in hostilities. Before the United States would agree to a bilateral defense treaty, it forced Chiang Kai-shek to acknowledge that the treaty did not apply to Jinmen and Mazu. Moreover, Chiang had to guarantee that he would not start the war without preliminary consultations with the United States. American proposals for negotiation with the Chinese Communists were absolutely unacceptable to the Kuomintang, as were Washington's various efforts to institutionalize the idea of "two Chinas"—rejected by Beijing as well as Taibei.

Chiang and his followers were also unhappy with the American position on Taiwan's internal development. For several reasons, including international acceptance and consolidation of the division of China, the United States preferred liberal bourgeois democracy to the KMT dictatorship based on a repressive police apparatus. But all attempts at paving the way for pluralism met desperate resistance from Chiang and his son. They could not forgive American courting of Taiwan separatists or the contempt of American military advisers for the political commissars who exercised the KMT's will in the army.

Despite failure to obtain the desired political reforms, the United States continued to render Taiwan considerable military and economic aid. With American funding, intensive development of the island's economy on the foundation laid by the Japanese provided visible results by the end of the 1950s. The United States was able to advertise the positive experience of "its China" as opposed to the grave problems of the PRC during the "great leap forward." The division of China had resulted in the emergence of two competing social systems in one nation.

Whatever the relations between the United States and Taiwan, Americans worked hard to turn their conception of "two Chinas" into a political reality for which they hoped some day to gain international recognition. Clearly, the U.S. military presence on Taiwan and in the Straits was the principal obstacle to defeat of the KMT by the Communists, to completion of the civil war. Signing of the 1954 Defense Treaty had followed sharp attacks by the PLA against Jinmen and

Mazu and implied American participation in any future conflict involving Taiwan. Keeping the PRC out of the United Nations, preserving the KMT's status as the sole legal representative of all China, and the diplomatic isolation of the Beijing government were all devices by which the United States protected the regime on Taiwan, exerting considerable pressure on the international community to win support.

The Soviet stand on the Taiwan issue has always been consistent and based on the principle of the territorial integrity of China. More than once the Soviet Union supported China's condemnation of American interference in China's internal affairs and China's demands for the demilitarization of Taiwan and reunification of the country. On December 15, 1954, the Soviet Ministry of Foreign Affairs declared that "the aggressive treaty concluded 2 December between the United States and the Chiang Kai-shek clique is aimed at finding a pretext for the preservation of the American military presence on Taiwan and the Penghu islands, of the occupation of these territories by the United States. The conclusion of the treaty . . . is a rude violation of the sovereignty and territorial integrity of the People's Republic of China." Even when the Chinese government aggravated tension in the Taiwan Straits in February 1958 (only in order to draw attention of the world community to the problem of Taiwan, as now admitted by Chinese scholars), at a time when the Soviet Union was actively pursuing detente with the West, the Soviet Union unconditionally supported the PRC. The Soviet government asked the American President to "show wisdom, and prevent action, which could be followed by irreparable consequences." It warned that China "had loyal allies, who were ready to come to the rescue at any moment in order to deter the aggressor with the common effort, and the Soviet Union was among them."

In addition to cold war pressures, there were historical factors that affected American policy toward China in the 1950s. The victory of the people's revolution was perceived in the United States as a loss of China. There were several reasons for American embitterment on this occasion. First, beginning in the nineteenth century, the United States pretended to have its own approach, more constructive than that of the European powers, to modeling relations between China and the West. One manifestation of this thought in the mid–twentieth century was an attempt to play mediator in the KMT-CCP conflict. Failure in China meant that American policy there was bankrupt. Second, the loss of China was especially bitter because the Americans understood long before 1949 that it was erroneous to be allied with the KMT. But as the years passed, billions of dollars in military and economic aid formed an iron bond between the United States and Chiang. On the other hand, the Americans had no choice. The latest Chinese publications argue convincingly that there was no lost chance for the Americans in their contacts with the Chinese Communists during World War II or in the late 1940s or early 1950s. Rapprochment was possible only if one side sacrificed its national interest.

Another important result of the failure in China was severe psychological frustration of social consciousness. The Chinese Communists evoked a high level of animosity. Accusations that the socialist system was violating human rights, destroying the economic machine, and demolishing the eternal values of Chinese culture were spread by the anti-Communist media and widely accepted. The anti-Communist propaganda was supported by missionary groups long active in China and industrial, merchant, and financial capital, which had long prospered by exploiting the Chinese economy. Many influential groups in American society considered China to be their sphere of influence, whether ideological, educational, religious, or economic. Suddenly they lost their status in a country they had perceived as a half-colony rather than as a potential great power. Many responded with shock, disappointment, irritation, and the will for revenge.

A number of elements in American political life channeled these emotions into a strong campaign against recognition and in favor of the containment and isolation of the PRC. The wave of McCarthyism caught even American sinologists with realistic understanding of China. They were accused of Communist leanings. In the midst of anti-Communist hysteria, which was intensified by thwarted imperial ambitions, China became for a considerable part of the society one of the main enemies of American democracy and of peace and stability, especially in Asia. These fears were fanned by the politically and financially powerful Taiwan lobby, which had great influence in Congress, the executive branch, and the press.

There were also, however, restraints on American policy toward China in the 1950s. Among them were unwillingness to be involved in a new war; growing opposition to the containment policy in its extreme forms; humanitarian concerns, such as the desire to exchange POWs; uncertainty of allied support on the Taiwan and offshore island issues; and relations of the administration to the electorate, especially during the campaign period. These restraints, however, were outweighed by the hostility most Americans felt toward the People's Republic of China.

It should also be noted that American and Chinese leaders were influenced by different political cultures, different internal political contexts, and different levels of political and diplomatic experience.

Consequently, each side was often confused by the action and rhetoric of the other. The difference between expectations and real results was often disagreeable. Policy was rarely effective. In this context it is important to draw attention to the counterproductive effects of certain foreign policy moves of the Chinese leadership, most notably the way in which the crises in the Taiwan Straits resulted in further deterioration of relations instead of the positive improvements expected.

It should also be remembered that relations between the United States and China in the 1950s were essentially unilateral. Contacts were minimal, and each side had difficulty obtaining reliable information about the other. Visits of correspondents became possible only at the end of the decade. Private trips were forbidden, and there was no trade or cultural exchange. From Beijing's perspective, its every initiative was rebuffed by the Americans. Bilateral contacts were limited to ambassadorial talks first in Geneva and then in Warsaw. The results were not very encouraging except for the issue of prisoners of war and measures of restrictive character concerning the Taiwan Straits. During the decade, the value of the talks as a medium for exchanging information diminished. American policy might be understood best as being not toward China but rather about China—responses not to China but to domestic politics and American relations with third parties.

In this context the Soviet Union played the role of powerful and loyal ally to the People's Republic of China from the very beginning of its existence. Contemporary Chinese writings demonstrate that Chinese leaders perceived no alternative in the face of American hostility but to cling to the Soviet Union. American assistance to Chiang, subversion against the new regime in Beijing, and the humiliating conditions offered to the PRC as a price for recognition alienated China and precluded efforts to cooperate. If, as seems unlikely, pragmatic Chinese leaders once faced a moment of choice between the Soviet Union and the United States, then widespread anti-American sentiment in the society and in the party dictated the decision. The Soviet Union, on the other hand, was popular among the masses as a socialist power that had always helped the Chinese in their struggle for liberty. The Sino-Soviet alliance was a constant source of American anxiety. Knowing that any clash with the PRC meant confrontation with the Soviet Union, the United States responded to the alliance as an incentive for limited rapprochement with the Chinese side, as evidenced by the contacts of the late 1950s.

How strong was Sino-Soviet unity? To what extent was China dependent on the Soviet Union for its foreign policy decisions? To find answers to those questions, the Americans hoped the ambassadorial talks with the Chinese would help. They watched carefully for signs of imbalance, of deteriorating Sino-Soviet relations. If the friendship turned to animosity, it would mean the weakening of the positions of the two main opponents of the United States. It would be too naive to suppose that the United States waited for the rift to offer its partnership to China.

In sum, the policy of the Eisenhower administration toward China had several characteristic features. It was a policy of temporizing and observation, lacking reflective elements. There were no attempts at a critical analysis of the position of the United States. It was a policy of indirect aggression, of military and economic blockade, of encircling alliances, of an American military presence on Taiwan based on the experience of open confrontation in Korea. This policy ruled out any positive response from China. It was a policy of pragmatic myth-creation oriented to the utilization of the idea of a "China menace" for the purpose of strengthening the strategic position of the United States in the Asia-Pacific region.

Sino-American contacts in the 1950 were extremely important for the future development of the bilateral relations. During the presidency of Dwight Eisenhower, the United States faced the impossibility of dealing with the PRC on any but an equal footing—and without the use of force. China also proved that it would never permit the humiliation of its sovereignty or surrender of the territorial integrity of the country.

12

The Evolution of the People's Republic of China's Policy toward the Offshore Islands

HE DI
Institute of American Studies
Chinese Academy of Social Sciences

J inmen and Mazu are two island groups off the coast of China's Fujian Province. Since 1949 they have remained under the control of the Kuomintang Army. Twice during President Eisenhower's term in office these offshore islands were the focus of intense Sino-American diplomatic and military tension. During these two crises, the Chinese government continuously modified and adjusted its policies, eventually arriving at a coherent "offshore islands policy," which remains, to this day, the basis of China's Taiwan policy.

An examination of how China formulated its Offshore Islands Policy affords important insights into early PRC perceptions of America (and America's China policy), as well as insights into how — and why — these perceptions changed over time. Most importantly, an examination of these historical events clearly reveals that the Americans and the Chinese had a low level of mutual understanding. This led to repeated misinterpretations of motivation and behavior on both sides, chronic misjudgments of how the other side would react under pressure, and thus to the escalation of what should have been small-scale, localized conflicts into major international crises.

MAKING TAIWAN THE KEY ISSUE: THE TAIWAN STRAITS CRISIS, 1954–1955

To "liberate Taiwan and its offshore islands of Penghu, Quemoy and Matsu" was the established national policy of the newly founded People's Republic of China, designed to preserve its right of sovereignty and territorial integrity. In October 1949, a People's Liberation Army unit under the command of the East China Military Region Headquarters launched an offensive to take over Jinmen but did not succeed. In June 1950, the Korean War erupted, and soon thereafter the U.S. Seventh Fleet began to patrol the waters of the Taiwan Straits, which forced the Beijing government to delay its offensive campaign to recover the offshore islands.

In Korea, the military situation in the summer of 1952 was favorable to the North Korean and Chinese forces. At the same time, within China the people were experiencing a newfound unity and stability under the Communist government. Under these favorable internal and external conditions, Chinese leaders began to take a fresh look at the offshore island question. Chen Yi, Commander of the PLA Armed Forces in the East China Military Region, instructed his Chief of Staff, Zhang Aiping, to draw up plans for the liberation of the offshore islands along the coastal Fujian and Zhejiang provinces. A proposal was submitted by the Central Military Commission and approved by Mao Zedong. Zhang Aiping was put in charge of the mission.[1]

In formulating the concrete battle plan the Chinese leaders reviewed two important considerations: relaxed international tensions and the PLA's capacity to cross the Taiwan Straits. After the cease-fire agreement in Korea in 1953 and the Geneva Conference from April to July of 1954, which led to the cease-fire agreement for Vietnam, for the first time in decades the flames of war in the Far East had been dampened. Taking note of this trend, the Chinese leadership deemed it inappropriate to launch a large-scale campaign across the Taiwan Straits, but rather focused its attention on the KMT-occupied islands, which were a great threat to offshore communications and fishing. At that time, however, China lacked the experienced navy, air, and army forces to operate across the Taiwan Straits. So it was decided to choose the weakest point to make a breakthrough and to accumulate experience gradually. The strategy to recover China's offshore islands was therefore laid out: "from small to large, one island at a time, from north to south, and from weak to strong."[2]

In line with this policy, the Dazhens were chosen as the breakthrough point for they were the northernmost of the KMT-occupied islands. They were the weakest point on the KMT defense line, and they were a direct threat to Zhejiang—one of the most economically developed provinces in China. In August 1954, a Zhedong (East Zhejiang) Front Line Command Post of the East China Military Region was set up. On August 31, a conference was convened at Ningbo to formulate a battle plan. As adopted, the plan called for the attack on the Dazhens to begin with an assault on the Yijiangshan islands.[3]

The August 1954 battle plan evidently did not call for an early attack on either Jinmen or Mazu. Hence, an important question arises: how can the bombardment of Jinmen, which commenced on September 3 and raised the curtain on Eisenhower's first Taiwan Straits crisis, be accounted for? Scholars and policy analysts have long debated this puzzling question—with little apparent success. To begin to solve this riddle, it is necessary to approach the Jinmen bombardment not from a purely military standpoint, but from the broader strategic perspective of a rapidly shifting international diplomatic situation. Viewed from such a global perspective, it quickly becomes evident that the Jinmen bombardment, apart from constituting a possible feint (or diversionary action) in preparation for the planned attack on Yijiangshan and the Dazhens, had a deeper meaning — a meaning that was at once both highly symbolic and inherently political.

The Beijing government welcomed the relaxation of tensions after Geneva and hoped conditions were right for an end to the American diplomatic quarantine of China, which would enable the PRC to reenter the international community.[4] China played an active role in negotiating the Geneva accords and took the initiative in discussing the return of U.S. prisoners of war interned in China following the Korean cease-fire. At the same time China reduced the scope of its military plan to encompass only the first stage of the original plan— the attack on the Dazhens.[5]

However, China's leaders were not convinced that their self-restraint would have the desired effect on the U.S. government. Such doubts were not without foundation, for President Eisenhower had stated, soon after taking office in 1953, that the United States would no longer remain neutral on the question of the status of Taiwan. Emboldened by such statements, Chiang Kai-shek stepped up his anti-Communist activities, and in his 1954 New Year's address he publicly advocated the slogan "Recover the Mainland." In the eyes of Beijing's leaders, Eisenhower appeared to be playing the role of "unleashing Chiang." America had already begun stepping up its efforts to establish a network of mutual security alliances in Asia. With the signing both of a mutual defence treaty with South Korea and the protocol creating the Southeast Asia Treaty Organization the U.S. government entered into negotiations with the Kuomingtang to form a mutual defense treaty—the last link in the ring of encirclement of China.

Beijing was not aware of the differences between the United States and the KMT government in the negotiations on the subject of whether the agreement should refer simply to the island of Taiwan or to the whole of China and as to whether the KMT would be obligated to renounce the use of force to return to the mainland. Nor did Beijing know that the United States did not want to take the responsibility for the defense of the offshore islands. The Chinese leaders worried that a U.S.–Taiwan defense treaty would permanently separate Taiwan from the mainland, as had previously been the case with the division of North and South Korea as well as North and South Vietnam.

To prevent such separation from occurring, the Chinese government placed renewed emphasis on the Taiwan question in the forum of world opinion. In late July 1954, while Zhou Enlai was en route back to China from the Geneva Conference, Mao Zedong cabled him:

> In order to break up the collaboration between the U.S. and Chiang, and to keep them from joining military and political forces, we must announce to our country and to the world the slogan of the liberation of Taiwan. It was improper of us not to raise this slogan in a timely manner after the cease-fire in Korea. If we were to continue dragging our heels now, we would be making a serious political mistake.[6]

China sought to publicize the Taiwan question in a variety of ways. First, a massive propaganda campaign was initiated. On July 23 — the same day that Mao sent the cable about liberating Taiwan — the *Renmin Ribao* published an editorial entitled "We Must Liberate Taiwan." This was followed shortly by a speech given by PLA Commander in Chief Zhu De on August 1 (Army Day) and by Zhou Enlai's "Government Work Report" to the National People's Congress—both of which stressed that since a cease-fire had been reached in Korea and Vietnam, the Taiwan Straits area appeared to be the next trouble spot. And the mutual defense treaty negotiation confirmed that America intended to separate Taiwan from the mainland permanently. This would not be tolerated by the Chinese people.[7]

Taking the issue into the international arena, on October 10, 1954, Zhou Enlai sent a cable to the Ninth Session of the United Nations denouncing U.S. military intervention in China's sovereign territory of Taiwan. Zhou's protest was supported by members of the Soviet bloc.[8]

The most efficient, though controversial of all China's measures was undoubtedly the bombardment of Jinmen. Mao Zedong had long believed in using warfare to secure political objectives. The bombardment of Jinmen was a case in point: a military tactic employed to regain the initiative in the struggle to achieve a favorable diplomatic resolution of the Taiwan question and to focus world attention on the Taiwan issue as rapidly as possible—while at the same time avoiding, if possible, a direct military confrontation with the United States. (There were no known U.S. forces in the vicinity of Jinmen.)

By the time of the first Jinmen bombardment, in early September 1954, America had already initiated its policy of isolating and blockading China and had prevented the PRC from being seated in the United Nations. Only twenty countries had established diplomatic ties with the PRC—half of which were members of the socialist camp. Under these circumstances, the Chinese government was hard-pressed to gain favorable international attention for its stand on the Taiwan question. Thus the Chinese leaders had no other means but to resort to limited military action and shell Jinmen in order to make a statement to the world, and to Washington in particular.

The initial bombardment of Jinmen occurred on September 3 and lasted for twelve days. The Chinese People's Liberation Army launched the attack on Yijiangshan according to schedule, on November 1.[9] But the objective of this attack differed from the goal of the earlier Jinmen-Mazu bombardment. While the bombardment served to attract world attention and thus served China's political objectives, the Yijiangshan action was a purely military operation that China's leadership hoped would not increase tension or lead to conflict with the United States.

The Central Military Committee specifically modified its battle plans and limited the scale of conflict with the following measures. It admonished its forces not to provoke the Americans. In order to carry out this policy, the Zhedong Front Headquarters briefed its officers and men on the seriousness of this issue and explained to them the rules of engagement. For example, the battlefront Air Force commander, Nie Fengzhi, instructed his pilots not to engage the Americans without obtaining express prior approval from headquarters. This would avoid any accidental engagement with American military forces.[10]

The Zhedong Front Line Command Headquarters had decided to seize Yijiangshan on January 18. However, the central government decision-makers in Beijing had a somewhat different calculus, one that stressed overall strategic and political considerations rather than local, short-term military costs and benefits. On January 17, a day before the scheduled attack, the Zhedong Front Line Command Headquarters received a phone call from the Chief of Staff, requesting the Commander to postpone the launching date. This was done to avoid the possibility of a failed action, which might adversely affect China's diplomatic position.[11] The battle commander, Zhang Aiping, nevertheless insisted on maintaining his original assault schedule. Peng Dehuai reported this to Mao Zedong, Liu Shaoqi, and Zhou Enlai and was authorized to make the final decision. Peng gave his approval to Zhang Aiping's proposed timetable, and on January 18 the PLA attacked and seized Yijiangshan island.[12]

According to Zhang Aiping's plan of battle, the PLA was to rest for one week after securing Yijiangshan and then seize the Dazhens. However, Peng Dehuai and the Central Military Commission, taking cognizance of the shifting international diplomatic environment and noting reported movement by ships of the U.S. Seventh Fleet in the Taiwan Straits, passed on an order to postpone temporarily the attack on the Dazhens.[13]

On February 5, the U.S. State Department asked the Seventh Fleet and other U.S. armed forces in the region to assist the KMT in the evacuation of the Dazhens. Wishing to "strike while the iron was hot," the Zhejiang Front Line Command Headquarters proposed attacking the KMT forces during evacuation. Peng Dehuai again intervened, instructing Zhang Aiping to cancel the attack on the Dazhens. Peng emphasized that since the evacuation was being carried out with international assistance, it was best to leave things alone.[14] On February 14, following the KMT evacuation, units of the PLA entered and garrisoned the Dazhens.

China had at first wanted to focus world attention on the Taiwan issue by shelling Jinmen. Once this had been accomplished, Beijing then wished to reduce those tensions heightened by the Yijiangshan campaign. However, events did not always follow China's anticipated scenarios. Other factors often intervened. As a result, some developments met China's initial objectives, while others were contrary to its expectations.

For instance, it was very hard for the Americans to tell the difference between the two military actions, the result for them being the same. Eisenhower said that Chinese actions had "threatened a split between the U.S. and nearly all of its allies, and seemingly carry the country to the edge of war, thus constituting one of the most serious problems of the first eighteen months of my administration."[15]

American public opinion became more hostile towards the People's Republic. Congress was also incensed, leaving little room for the possibility of a shift to a more flexible American policy towards China (if such a possibility existed). Dulles' hard line towards the PRC enjoyed wide public support and helped the Eisenhower administration gain the willing approval of Congress for its China policy.

The U.S. government, for its part, wished to publicly demonstrate its support for Taiwan and accelerated the negotiations on the Mutual Defense Treaty. In January 1955, President Eisenhower submitted the Formosa Resolution to Congress. This gave the President the right to order military aid for the defense of Jinmen and Mazu.

The Formosa Resolution also brought some unexpected results for the United States. It not only provided an excuse for Chiang Kai-Shek to link the offshore islands to Taiwan on the issue of military defense, but it also provided an unanticipated future opportunity for the People's Republic to link the offshore islands issue to its Taiwan policy.

From Beijing's perspective, the entire military campaign should have come to an end once the PLA had liberated the Dazhens. China, in fact, halted further military activities by the end of January 1955 and expected the situation in the Taiwan Straits to calm down. This, however, did not happen. With no lines of communication and little mutual understanding between China and the United States, the atmosphere of hostility between the two increased as a result of the Taiwan Straits crisis.

In this situation, the American government grossly misjudged China's intentions and motivations. On February 22, 1955, Dulles stated at a SEATO meeting in Bangkok that there existed a real military threat from China. To meet this hypothetical threat, the U.S. government was seriously considering a nuclear strike against China. At a White House meeting on March 3, Eisenhower and Dulles confirmed that the American government might have to use nuclear weapons to guarantee the security of Jinmen and Mazu.[16] In the many press conferences that followed, Dulles, Eisenhower, and Vice President Richard Nixon all gave verbal hints concerning the possible use of such weapons. Thus, tensions in the Taiwan Straits area heated up again rather quickly.

The American nuclear threat produced two important consequences. First, it stimulated China's leadership to launch its own nuclear weapons program to meet the American nuclear threat. Because Eisenhower had stated that he would use nuclear bombs to end the war in Korea and had threatened China with nuclear warfare over the Taiwan Straits crisis, Mao Zedong himself began a discussion during the middle of January 1955 on developing China's own nuclear industry.[17]

Second, it increased the anxiety of the Asian nations towards the tense situation in the Taiwan Straits. During the April 1955 Bandung Conference of nonaligned Afro-Asian nations the Asian states questioned Zhou Enlai on the situation in the Straits and on the mounting crisis in Sino-American relations. Though the Chinese representatives were not prepared to talk about these issues on the floor of the conference, Zhou Enlai did make a public statemant on April 23 explaining China's position. "The Chinese people," he said, "are friendly to the American people. The Chinese people do not want to have a war with the United States of America. The Chinese government is willing to sit down and enter into negotiations with the United States government to discuss the question of relaxing tension in the Far East, and especially the question of relaxing tension in the Taiwan area."[18]

The U.S. government took note of this communication. After several months of considering options, on July 13 Washington sent a message to Beijing via the British suggesting that Chinese and American representatives hold ambassadorial-level talks in Geneva. China agreed to the proposal and the crisis in the Taiwan Straits began to ease.

Writing in 1956, Zhou Enlai drew the following conclusion about the crisis:

> 1954 and 1955 saw tensions mount along the Taiwan Straits. . . . It wasn't until after the Geneva and Bandung conferences, from the end of last year to early this year, that we began to see an actual relaxation of world tension.[19]

In order to further promote this relaxation of tension, the Chinese government opened the August 1 session of the Geneva ambassadorial talks by releasing eleven alleged American spies. On September 10, the Chinese and American sides concluded an agreement "Concerning the Return of Expatriates to the United States." At the same time, Chinese leaders reiterated their previously expressed wish to achieve the reunification of China by peaceful means, if possible.

By 1955, Chinese leaders had also become increasingly aware of the existence of significant conflicts of interest between Taiwan and the United States, as well as between the United States and its Western allies. Beijing sought to take advantage of such "contradictions in the enemy camp" in order to achieve its objective of reunification.

On July 30, 1955, Zhou Enlai formally proposed that representatives of the PRC and the KMT enter into consultations for the purpose of seeking a peaceful, negotiated resolution of the Taiwan question.[20] Soon afterwards, three unrelated events added new fuel to the growing rift between the United States and its KMT ally. The first was the case of Sun Liren, a pro-American KMT general arrested in Taiwan and accused of involvement in an anti-Chiang coup attempt. The second was the 1957 killing of a Taiwanese civilian, Liu Ziren, by an

American soldier stationed in Taiwan. And the third was the highly publicized creation of a Taiwanese independence movement in exile in Japan—the "Ad Hoc Government of the Republic of Taiwan—by Liao Wenyi, an anti-KMT Taiwanese expatriate, a movement encouraged by the United States. Spurred on by these signs of mounting KMT-American tension, China's leaders pushed their propaganda campaign into high gear.

At the same time, China's leaders began to perceive that the growing disunity of the enemy camp and the limitations in America's ability to control the policies and behavior of its allies might provide a conducive climate for the cultivation of closer relations with America's erstwhile Asian allies and "running dogs," including Japan, Thailand, the Philippines, and Malaya. From 1955 to 1958 the PRC initiated people-to-people diplomacy, trade relations, and other bilateral agreements with a number of these countries. In 1956, in comparison with 1955, China's foreign trade partners increased from forty-seven to sixty-two, while the volume of trade increased more than 28 percent.[21]

Chinese leaders had also become aware by 1955–56 of the existence of divergent trends within U.S. public opinion concerning America's role in the Taiwan Straits. With an increasing number of Americans expressing opposition to U.S. military intervention in the offshore islands dispute, Beijing sought to exploit such opposition to further its own political interests. In August 1956 the Chinese government announced the unilateral cancellation of the longstanding ban on U.S. reporters entering China. China also issued invitations to fifteen major press agencies to visit China. In the fall of the same year the Chinese government proposed several new bilateral agreements, including one on the embargo, and one on cultural exchanges.

Although China failed in the first Taiwan Straits crisis to bring its comprehensive offshore islands policy to fruition, the crisis nonetheless served to advance Chinese foreign policy interests in several ways. First, by opening up a new channel for dealing directly with the United States, the crisis led to the creation of an important new diplomatic venue for PRC participation in world affairs. Second, the crisis provided Chinese leaders with valuable experience in the design and execution of complex foreign policy maneuvers, including the coordination of limited acts of war with bold acts of political initiative ("da da, tan tan"). The Jinmen crisis also comprised an important watershed in China's search for strategic leverage: the bombardment of Jinmen demonstrated—at relatively low risk—China's determination to reunify the country, which served to increase the urgency of bilateral Sino-American contacts and led to the elevation of the Geneva talks to the ambassadorial level, which in turn added to Beijing's international visibility and prestige. Finally, the Jinmen bombardment could be used to exacerbate rifts within the opposition camp. The Jinmen experience thus provided an important lesson in the pursuit of political interest through military means—a lesson the Chinese leaders were to apply in later years.

By early 1955 the offshore islands crisis had subsided. It was not until August 1958 that the Taiwan Straits once again turned into a combat zone. In the interim, great changes took place in the international situation as well as within China itself.

USING THE OFFSHORE ISLANDS AS A LINK: THE TAIWAN STRAITS CRISIS OF 1958

D espite the relaxation of world tensions after 1955, the United States persisted in pursuing its rigid two China policy, with no hint of flexibility. On several occasions Dulles reiterated the three principles underlying America's China policy: the United States would not recognize the People's Republic of China; it would oppose the PRC occupying the Chinese seat in the United Nations; and it would uphold its blockade and trade embargo against China.[22]

Following their initiation at Geneva during the first Taiwan Straits crisis in the summer of 1955, the U.S.–China ambassadorial talks continued for more than two years, through seventy-three meetings, and officially terminated on December 12, 1957. The termination of the talks gravely disappointed the Chinese leaders, who had sought to demonstrate their good faith by agreeing at the first meeting to release twelve alleged American spies. Following this initial gesture, the Chinese side had proposed various initiatives in the hope that through negotiation and consultation Zhou Enlai could establish a direct dialogue with U.S. Secretary of State Dulles to resolve essential problems in Sino-American relations—including the long-standing Taiwan issue.

But the Eisenhower administration had its own reasons for continuing the talks. The primary item on the U.S. agenda was the desire to get back American POWs being held in China; a secondary objective was to persuade the Chinese government to renounce military force in its proclaimed policy of liberating Taiwan. In the Chinese view, Dulles' real purpose in seeking a renunciation of force agreement was to delay a final resolution of the Taiwan Straits question until the pressure of world opinion could be brought to bear on Chinese leaders, forcing them to accept the existence of Taiwan as a separate, independent entity whose existence the PRC, having renounced the use of force, would be unable to effectively challenge. In the end, this U.S. hidden agenda would have resulted in a situation similar to the one that had already emerged in the post–World War II divided states of Germany, Korea, and Vietnam—i.e., there would have been, in fact if not in law, two Chinas—an outcome the PRC simply could not accept.[23]

Zhou Enlai had repeatedly said that the military confrontation between China and the United States caused by America's stationing armed forces in Taiwan was an entirely different matter from the military confrontation between the mainland and Taiwan. In Zhou's words, "how the Chinese people liberate Taiwan is an internal Chinese matter, in which the U.S. government has no right to interfere, nor has it any right to request us not to use force."[24] Because of this deadlock on the renunciation of force issue, no further visible progress was made in the Geneva ambassadorial talks following the initial 1955 Sino-American agreement on the exchange of POWs and expatriates.

In addition to these policies, the United States continued to support Taiwan with substantial political and military assistance, which greatly worried the Chinese leadership. From 1955 to 1958, the American government signed numerous treaties and concluded more than fifteen official agreements with Taiwan. Of special significance was the United States' 1957 strategic positioning of Matador missiles in Taiwan and construction of an airport with an extra-long runway that could accommodate B-52 strategic bombers. During the same three-year period, various commanders of the American forces stationed in Taiwan made a number of provocative statements concerning U.S. support for Taiwan in its struggle against the Chinese Communists.[25] With at least tacit American approval, the Kuomintang Army stepped up its sabotage activities on the Chinese mainland.

In light of these developments, China's leaders grew increasingly distrustful of U.S. government intentions: They questioned the sincerity of the Americans' professed dedication to peace and tranquility in the Taiwan Straits area. In this context, the 1954 U.S.–Taiwan Mutual Defense Treaty was seen by Beijing as posing a potential offensive military threat to China and raising questions about the nature of the ultimate American objective in the Taiwan Straits.[26]

In the face of KMT and American provocation, Chinese leaders had serious reservations about the wisdom of continuing their established policy of flexibility and compromise. Perhaps confrontation ("da da") would prove more fruitful than conciliation ("tan tan") as a means of achieving the ultimate goal of national reunification.

From later-published materials on the Sino-Soviet dispute, it is clear that there were also increasing differences between the Chinese and the Russians in the late 1950s concerning how (and whether) to peacefully coexist with America.

After Stalin's death, his successor, Khrushchev, encountered external challenges from Eastern European countries, notably Poland and Hungary, and pressure from an internal opposition. A series of events placed the international Communist movement in a weakened and divided state. Faced with such difficulties, the Soviet Communists urgently needed the support of a major party such as the Chinese Communist Party (CCP). This shift in intrabloc status and prestige caused China's leaders to devote added attention to global problems and issues and increased their desire to play a more active role in confronting U.S. "imperialism" throughout the world. It was this change in China's global-strategic orientation—reflecting the PRC's increased stature and self-confidence in international affairs—that made the second Chinese bombardment of Jinmen and Mazu in 1958 different from the first in 1954–55.

The Chinese decision to bombard Jinmen and Mazu for a second time in 1958 was in part a reflection of these growing differences, and it signaled the end of—and the tacit Chinese dissatisfaction with—a three-year period of attempted Chinese diplomatic negotiation and compromise with the United States.

Within China, the newly adopted national plan for socialist construction—the "Great Leap Forward"—called upon the Chinese people to advance with high spirits and supreme confidence to "overtake Britain and catch up to America." To promote this objective, the government sought to break down widespread popular belief in the omnipotence of the United States.

World tensions heightened considerably in the summer of 1958. The Middle East, in particular, was in a state of turmoil. In July, U.S. and British military forces landed in Lebanon and Jordan, respectively; Iraq also felt the heat of Western military pressure. In the Far East, the KMT regime continued to build up its armed forces on Jinmen and Mazu, with the total number of troops involved reaching 100,000 — representing fully one-third of the total number of Chiang's ground forces. At the same time, Kuomintang forces continued making military forays across the Straits against the coastal regions of Fujian province.

On August 11 the U.S. State Department issued a public memorandum stating that "the U.S. does not recognize the People's Republic of China."[27] A few days later, on August 17, the United States transferred six warships and two thousand combat troops to Singapore.[28] These actions were of grave concern to China's leaders, who felt that the United States was not only ignoring the existence of China, but also preparing for new military operations. Under these circumstances, China's leaders reasoned that they must not appear to the Americans as weak or lacking in determination. Later, Mao Zedong likened this need for boldness in the face of a fearsome enemy to the situation of overcoming an irrational fear of ghosts: "Do not be afraid of ghosts," he urged. "The more you are afraid of ghosts, the more likely you are not to survive, to be eaten up by them. We are not afraid of ghosts; that is why we bombard Jinmen and Mazu."[29]

It was against this background that the second Taiwan Straits crisis took shape. The preparations for the second bombardment of Jinmen began early in the summer of 1958. The shelling this time was aimed at recovering Jinmen and Mazu.[30] In this respect, the Jinmen-Mazu bombardment constituted a resumption of the offshore islands battle plan, which had been suspended following the seizure of Yijiangshan and the Dazhen islands in 1954–55.

The PLA sought to bring overwhelming firepower to bear in order to cut off the enemy supply lines to Jinmen and Mazu, thus blockading the two islands and making it difficult for the KMT forces there to hold out. It was anticipated in Beijing that the blockading of the two offshore islands would intensify friction between Taibei and Washington over the scope of U.S. treaty commitments in the Taiwan Straits and would lead to increased U.S. pressure on Taiwan to withdraw from Jinmen and Mazu. In subscribing to this view, China's leaders clearly recalled that in a similar situation during the first Jinmen crisis, the Kuomintang had abandoned the Dazhen islands in the face of American pressure.

To ensure the success of the operation, Mao Zedong postponed the assault date. On July 27, Mao instructed Peng Dehuai to let Taiwan fire the first salvo before striking back. The Chinese commander was also instructed not to attack without the assurance of success, to put "politics in command", and to plan things out thoroughly in advance so that he could ensure victory from afar.[31] Mao did not make the final decision to bombard Jinmen and Mazu until the enlarged meeting of the Politburo of the CCP Central Committee held from August 17 to August 30.[32]

Washington had not responded affirmatively to China's fifteen-day ultimatum on the resumption of negotiations, issued on June 30. As a result, tensions quickly mounted in the Taiwan Straits, and the United

States soon faced another catch-22 situation. On the one hand, the Americans were concerned that the fall of any coastal island might create a domino effect. The possibility that "a lost nail is a lost shoe" prompted the U.S. government to reconsider the necessity of maintaining Kuomintang control over Jinmen and Mazu as a "vital" American security interest.[33] On the other hand, the U.S. government was also afraid that Chiang Kai-shek might take advantage of mounting tensions in the Taiwan Straits to deliberately enlarge the scope of conflict and thereby drag the United States into an all-out war with China.

To guard against both of these possibilities, the United States deliberately refused to define in advance its territorial defense perimeter, while at the same time it suggested the possibility of nuclear attack against coastal targets in Fujian province.[34] In so doing, the United States hoped to achieve a resolution of the crisis without actually employing military force. To minimize the risk of military confrontation with China, the United States mapped out contingency plans for the evacuation of KMT forces from Jinmen and Mazu. Simultaneously, the U.S. government exerted pressure on the Taiwan regime to agree not to use force to recover the mainland without America's consent.

The bombardment began on August 23. Prior to that date, Eisenhower and Dulles had agreed upon the need to consider the use of tactical nuclear weapons against China. The U.S. leaders believed that superior weaponry could overcome the weakness of their geographical position. Three days after the initial bombardment, Eisenhower instructed American convoy ships to prepare to escort KMT supply ships. On August 27, Eisenhower made public a statement implying that he would exercise the power entrusted to him under the 1955 Formosa Resolution to assist Taiwan in the defense of Jinmen and Mazu. On August 29, he instructed U.S. naval forces to implement the convoy-escort plan.[35]

On September 4, Dulles and Eisenhower jointly announced their "Newport Declaration," stating that the U.S. would carry out convoy activities as authorized under the Formosa Resolution.[36] At the same time, the Americans reinforced their troops along the Taiwan Straits and ordered two aircraft carriers from the Sixth Fleet, previously stationed in the Mediterranean, to proceed to Taiwan. By mid-September, the United States had amassed in the Taiwan Straits area the largest single concentration of nuclear support forces in history. The UPI reported that the United States had its "nuclear fist" ready to deliver "a knock-out blow."[37]

The dramatic escalation of conflict in the Far East and the American threat to use nuclear weapons against China were a source of grave concern to Soviet leaders. As a sign of his rising concern, Khrushchev sent Gomulka on a fact-finding mission to Beijing in early September. At the same time, in order to honor its commitments under the 1950 Sino-Soviet Defense Treaty, the Soviet government made public a statement of support for China, which implied that Russia would supply China with nuclear protection. On September 7 and again on September 19, Khrushchev wrote to Eisenhower, expressing the view that if America launched a nuclear attack on China, the aggressor would face a well-deserved counterattack by weapons of the same type.[38] With the Soviet Union thus entering the picture, the situation in the Taiwan Straits became even more complex.

Mao Zedong had not fully anticipated the gravity of the worldwide repercussions that would flow from China's bombardment of Jinmen and Mazu.[39] Under the circumstances Mao was constrained to rethink his policy of confrontation with the United States. In early September the CCP Central Committee convened a meeting of the Politburo, which listened to a briefing on Sino-American relations given by Wang Bingnan, principal Chinese negotiator at the Geneva ambassadorial talks. Following this briefing, a proposal was adopted calling for renewed negotiations with the United States. Twice during this period—on September 5 and again on September 8—Mao Zedong personally reviewed the world situation at a meeting of the Supreme State Conference. In his remarks to that body, Mao revealed some interesting changes in his point of view.

First of all, Mao perceived that U.S. policy toward China and the Soviet Union was primarily defensive, rather than offensive, in nature. Employing the theory of the "intermediate zone," he argued that the imperialist camp's intensified worldwide anti-China, anti-Soviet campaign was only a pretext for expanding U.S. domination over the third world. Mao believed that the imperialists had taken the offensive throughout Asia, Africa, and Latin America in order to contain the indigenous rise of nationalism and communism there. Toward the socialist camp, however, the United States and its allies had, in Mao's view, taken essentially defensive actions.[40]

Mao's belief that the prime focus of the imperialists' offensive was no longer either China or Russia constituted a major shift for the Chinese Communist leader. Ever since the establishment of the People's Republic, Mao had viewed American aggression as the prime threat to China's national security. On several occasions he had speculated that the United States was making preparations to mount a final, decisive attack on New China from the three fronts of Korea, Taiwan, and Vietnam. America's intervention in the Korean War had served to confirm Mao's belief, and the two Chinese campaigns of bombardment against Jinmen and Mazu thus comprised Mao's response to the American challenge in the Taiwan Straits area.

But as the world situation changed and as the socialist camp gained strength, approaching global strategic parity with the imperialist camp, Chinese leaders formulated a new view of U.S. strategic intentions—and capabilities—in Asia. Mao thus affirmed in 1958, for the first time, that the current world situation was one in which "the East wind prevails over the West wind," with the imperialist camp in a clearly defensive position. Having thus revised his basic assessment of the global situation, Mao asserted that the offensive military threat to China posed by the U.S.–Taiwan Mutual Defense Treaty was no longer as grave or as immediate as had previously been assumed; rather, the treaty was now seen to be essentially defensive and constrictive in nature, serving mainly to restrain Chiang Kai-shek, rather than to "unleash" him.[41]

Mao's reassessment of America's overall strategic situation carried with it a revised projection of the likelihood of the outbreak of war between China and America. Mao now asserted that both China and America were afraid of war, but that "they" (i.e., the United States) were "more afraid than we are." Hence, war was unlikely to break out.[42]

Mao reasoned that since the United States was ostensibly in a strategically defensive posture and was unwilling to risk a direct war with China, America's policy would have to be to "get out of Jinmen and Mazu." Mao believed that the American government really wanted to abandon the islands and that public opinion in the United States also favored evacuation. In physical terms, Mao reckoned, this would mean pulling 110,000 Kuomintang troops out of Jinmen and Mazu.[43]

Prior to Zhou Enlai's announcement, the Politburo of the CCP Central Committee held a meeting, which specifically discussed the state of Sino–U.S. relations and the guidelines for the ambassadorial talks. The meeting produced two decisions. First, previous experience had convinced Chinese leaders that a piecemeal approach to negotiating with the Americans was not fruitful. The CCP Politburo decided that all future negotiations should be conducted on the basis of the principle of "one lump sum."[44] In adopting this principle, the CCP leaders argued that if the Taiwan question could not be resolved, there was simply no point in talking about other issues.[45] This clearly elevated the Taiwan question to the number one priority in Sino-American relations.

Second, China hoped to make the United States withdraw its armed forces from the vicinity of Jinmen and Mazu through the negotiations. Accordingly, Mao instructed Wang Bingnan, who was then preparing to go to Warsaw to represent China in the talks, to try to persuade the U.S. representatives to pressure Chiang to remove his troops from Jinmen and Mazu and to approach the settlement of the Taiwan problem from the broader perspective of Sino-American relations.[46] At this time, China had not integrated its offshore island policy with the Taiwan issue and was still trying through negotiations and continued military pressure to urge the United States to pressure Chiang to withdraw his forces.

On September 4, Beijing proclaimed that insofar as China's territorial waters extended twelve nautical miles off the coastline of Fujian province, it was the PRC's intention to exercise its sovereign rights by blockading those offshore islands lying within twelve miles of the Chinese coast. It was under these circumstances that on September 6 Zhou Enlai announced China's decision to reopen talks with America to seek the reduction of tension in the Taiwan Straits area. At the same time, Zhou stressed that the Chinese people would not tolerate a direct threat to their security so close to the continental mainland.[47] Throughout the remainder of September the Chinese propaganda network stressed over and over again that "nobody likes to lie down next to someone who snores"—i.e., that China could not tolerate a U.S. military presence so close to its own shores.

As the military situation in the Quemoy-Matsu area remained tense, relations between the United States and its allies, including Taiwan, became increasingly strained. The allies did not support Taiwan's position. Within America as well, a polarization of opinion was occurring on the question of the U.S. commitment to the offshore islands, with many dubious about supporting Taiwan. Even the Chairman of the Joint Chiefs of Staff—who had earlier supported the defense of the offshore islands during the first Jinmen crisis—now recommended to the President that American forces should be withdrawn from Jinmen and Mazu. The Chairman warned that Chiang Kai-shek was interested in enlarging the crisis in order to drag America into his war with China for the "recovery of the mainland."[48]

Faced with a difficult diplomatic and military dilemma, the U.S. government continued to give vocal public support to Chiang Kai-shek's position in the offshore islands dispute, while privately U.S. diplomats began to try to persuade the Taiwan authorities to withdraw from Jinmen and Mazu. This ostensible American duplicity added considerably to the rising tensions between Taibei and Washington.

The U.S. desire to have the Kuomintang forces retreat from the offshore islands was motivated by political as well as military considerations. Back in 1951, the United States had used the occasion of the signing of the Taiwan-Japan and U.S.–Japan peace treaties to pressure the Kuomintang regime to accept the American view that "Taiwan's status remains to be determined." In line with this view, neither of the peace treaties signed in that year explicitly supported Taiwan's territorial claim to the offshore islands. In Beijing's and Taibei's view this amounted to an indirect acknowledgment that Jinmen and Mazu were a part of Fujian province. By now quietly urging Chiang K'ai-shek to abandon the islands—which were the last remaining points of direct physical contact between two bitterly antagonistic Chinese regimes—the United States hoped to neutralize an inherently volatile source of armed conflict and eliminate an important military "stepping stone" in any future attempt to resume the Chinese civil war. By defusing the territorial rights issue, the United States could hope, in turn, to increase the physical security of Taiwan while at the same time promoting the emergence on Taiwan of a sovereign, independent state—thus bringing about a de facto two China solution to the Taiwan problem.

For the KMT, the political value of the offshore islands far exceeded their military worth. Chiang Kai-shek was fully aware that relinquishing the offshore islands meant severing Taiwan's last significant physical links with the mainland; and he was also painfully aware of the emerging two China strategy within the Eisenhower administration. For these reasons, the Kuomintang leader refused to bow to American pressures to evacuate Jinmen and Mazu; and he explicitly acknowledged that holding onto the islands as "sovereign possessions" symbolized the maintenance of political ties between Taiwan and the mainland.[49]

Under mounting pressure from the United States and its allies, Chiang held a press conference in which he publicly stated Taiwan's determination to retain Jinmen and Mazu. "Taiwan will not be coerced into changing its position because of the allied nations' attitude," he said. "If necessary, Taiwan will fight alone."[50] Dulles responded on September 30, noting that while the United States and Taiwan had maintained frequent and close contacts on defense issues, they had not been able to reach agreement on the offshore islands question. He stated that if a reliable cease-fire could be achieved, it would be foolish, unwise, and imprudent for the Kuomintang to continue to maintain a large number of troops there.[51] The next day, Chiang Kai-shek remarked that Dulles' recommendation had been "only a unilateral [American] declaration; therefore, our government has no obligation to follow it." Chiang resolutely refused to withdraw his armed forces from Jinmen and Mazu.[52]

The public revelation of major differences between the United States and Taiwan on the offshore islands issue attracted considerable attention in Beijing. In early October, Mao Zedong began to rethink China's offshore islands policy. On the one hand, it appeared to Mao that the Taiwan authorities wanted to drag America into an all-out war with China; on the other hand, America—though attempting to intimidate China with its superior air and sea power—seemingly did not wish to get directly involved in an expanded war in the Taiwan Straits. Thus caught up in a difficult situation, the Eisenhower administration would be forced to make a conditional tactical retreat. Mao speculated that the United States had three main alternatives: first, the United States could try to achieve a cease-fire agreement with China that would keep Jinmen and Mazu in Chiang's hands; second, the United States could step up pressure on Chiang Kai-shek to withdraw from Jinmen and Mazu in exchange for a stronger American commitment to defend Taiwan—including the establishment of a U.S. military base on Taiwan; and third, in the event that the first two alternatives failed, the United States could forcibly dislodge KMT troops from Jinmen and Mazu and physically escort them back to Taiwan—thereby creating a de facto two China situation.

Mao Zedong considered the pros and cons of taking military action to recover Jinmen and Mazu. He noted that several benefits would follow from recovery of the islands: the direct threat posed by the KMT to China's coastal areas would be removed; sea transport lanes would open up; and new economic construction along the Fujian coast could be undertaken. In addition, such a victory would naturally be good for China's national pride.

On the other hand, Mao realized that certain strategic costs would be incurred if China were to liberate the offshore islands. Thus, if Chiang's troops were to retreat from Jinmen and Mazu, there would be an eighty-mile body of water separating Taiwan from the motherland, effectively severing the last remaining links—or stepping stones—between the two sides. And this, in turn, would get the United States "off the hook" in the Taiwan Straits, permitting Eisenhower and Dulles to pursue their two China scheme.

After carefully considering such factors, Mao Zedong decided to postpone implementation of the plan to invade Jinmen and Mazu and to leave them in Chiang's hands.[53] On October 6, the *Renmin Ribao* published "A Message to our Taiwan Compatriots," drafted by Mao Zedong, which officially announced a unilateral seven-day cease-fire.[54]

Subsequently, the Chinese government announced that bombardment of the offshore islands would occur only on even dates. From that point on, tensions began to diminish in the second Jinmen crisis.

By the early autumn of 1958, China had completed the adjustment of its offshore island policy. Viewing Jinmen and Mazu as an integral part of the Taiwan reunification question, PRC leaders had decided to permit these islands to remain temporarily in Kuomintang hands as a means of affirming Taiwan's ties with the mainland and as a special channel for signaling China's intentions to its adversaries. By early September, China had managed to elevate the Taiwan question to a central position in Sino-American relations, a position from which it would dominate the agenda of future U.S.–PRC negotiations. By October, the issue of the offshore islands had been effectively tied in with the Taiwan question.

By thus linking together China's offshore island policy, China's Taiwan policy, and China's U.S. policy, Mao Zedong effectively joined China's micropolitical and macropolitical objectives and interests. What had begun in 1954 as a rather narrow military campaign designed to recover one offshore island at a time had, by the fall of 1958, turned into a sophisticated, multidimensional approach that coordinated short-term military tactics with long-term diplomatic objectives. In the process, a piecemeal policy of territorial consolidation had evolved into a well-orchestrated, integrated strategy for confronting China's adversaries, across both the Taiwan Straits and the Pacific Ocean.

CONCLUSION

The evolution of China's offshore islands policy reveals how the "sovereign prerogative" of territorial unification and integration constituted the primary objective of Chinese foreign policy. To achieve the goal of national reunification, it was first decided to attack the offshore islands one by one. When unfavorable factors were encountered, this plan was modified. The shift from seizing Jinmen and Mazu to leaving them in Kuomintang hands typifies Mao's philosophy of subordinating immediate gains to broad national interests and making the means of policy serve the ends. Thus, although China was strongly motivated to occupy the offshore islands as a stepping-stone en route to the liberation of Taiwan, as soon as the United States pressed Chiang to abandon Jinmen and Mazu, PRC leaders, realizing that this would tacitly serve to advance America's two China scheme, altered their approach, noting that prematurely severing the offshore islands from Taiwan would be strategically counterproductive. And when Chiang Kai-shek opposed the American two China plan, proclaiming the indivisibility of Chinese sovereignty, a consensus emerged between the KMT and the CCP on the question of the existence of a singular, integral "one China."

Expressing this consensus in his "Message to Our Taiwan Compatriots" on October 6, 1958, Mao Zedong stated:

> There is but one China in the world; there are not two Chinas. On this point, we concur with each other. Americans are using their technique to try to force upon us a two China policy. All the Chinese people, including you and our overseas Chinese compatriots, will absolutely not let this materialize.[55]

Mao further argued in his "Compatriots" speech that to have Chiang Kai-shek—an ardent one China advocate—remain in power in Taiwan was preferable to having Taiwan fall under the control of liberals who might accede to the wishes of the American government and accept a two China solution.[56]

The principle of undivided sovereignty has consistently been upheld in China's foreign policy. This was true not only in China's relations with "enemy" states such as the United States, but also in China's relations with its allies, including the Soviet Union.

During the Jinmen crises Soviet influence over China's actions was minimal. China did not want to involve the Soviets in its offshore islands operations. China has consistently stated that the Taiwan question is an internal issue and rejected both American interference and Soviet assistance. If China had allowed Soviet involvement, it might have given others a pretext to make the Taiwan question an international issue. Also, in order to uphold its sovereign independence China had reached an agreement with the Soviet Union for the withdrawal of all Soviet troops in China in 1954–55 and for Chinese repossession of the Lu Shun naval base. Since that agreement, China's leaders have always been wary of any possibility of a Soviet effort to assert control over them.

Soviet specialists had participated in discussions leading to the formulation of a battle plan for the seizure of Yijiangshan in the winter of 1954–55, and prior to the second Jinmen crisis of 1958, the Chinese Ministry of Defense had informed Soviet specialists stationed in Beijing of the Chinese intention to resume bombardment of the offshore islands.[57] Yet the Soviet role in the design and implementation of China's offshore islands policy was negligible.

Fearful in 1958 that a Chinese attack on Jinmen and Mazu might undermine their own quest for detente with the United States, Soviet leaders sought to restrain China. At the same time, Russia also tried to impose certain controls on the autonomy of the Chinese military. Thus, in April and again in July of 1958, the Soviets proposed setting up a longwave radio station and a joint naval fleet—under joint command—in China. The Chinese government rejected this proposal.[58] After the battle sirens began to sound on Jinmen in late August, Khrushchev made a second proposal to PRC leaders on September 13 through the Chinese ambassador in Moscow, indicating that the Soviet Union would be willing to provide military assistance to China. Although this second proposal was ostensibly advantageous to China, PRC leaders refused Khrushchev's offer because of their concern over possible Soviet attempts to limit China's independence of action.[59] Mao's desire to safeguard Chinese sovereignty and autonomy represented an implicit challenge to the leadership of the Soviet Union and resulted in a rift that subsequently contributed to the open eruption of the Sino-Soviet split.

It is axiomatic that the establishment and preservation of national sovereignty and territorial integrity are the most fundamental strategic interests of any nation seeking to operate as an equal participant in international affairs. Like many other nations, China has struggled for much of the past hundred years to free itself from foreign domination and exploitation. Viewed in this context—as part of a vital struggle for national sovereignty and self-expression—China's antagonism to the United States in the 1950s can be understood as a natural reaction to America's China policy. The U.S. government had sought to isolate China, had stationed troops on Chinese territory (Taiwan), had interfered with China's unification operations on the offshore islands of Jinmen and Mazu, had deprived China of its seat in the United Nations, and had created a two China policy in foreign affairs. All these hostile measures posed significant obstacles to China's quest for equal, sovereign status in international affairs; and all, therefore, served to severely provoke China's leaders.

Throughout the 1960s, China maintained a firm posture on the question of national unification in all its dealings with the United States. Finally, by the early 1970s, after two decades of hostile interaction between the two countries, American leaders became convinced of two things: first, that the Communist government was more than a mere "passing phase" in China; and second, that no significant improvement of relations between the two countries would be possible without American acknowledgement of China's sovereign rights, including the recognition that Taiwan was an integral part of China. Such an American concession was eventually incorporated into the text of the historic Shanghai Communiqué in February 1972, which laid the foundation for the subsequent normalization of Sino-American relations.

NOTES

1. Nie Fengzhi et al., *The Three Armed Services Strike in the East China Sea* (Beijing: PLA Publishing House, 1985), p. 38.

2. *Ibid.*, p. 26

3. *Ibid.*, pp. 39–40

4. Wang Bingnan, *Review of the Nine-Year-Long Sino-American Ambassadorial Talks* (Beijing: World Knowledge Publishing House, 1985), pp. 5–6.

5. Certain participants in the actual policy-making process, personal conversation.

6. Wang, *Review*, pp. 41–42.

7. *Collected Documents of Sino-American Relations*, vol. 2, part 2 (Beijing: World Knowledge Publishing House, 1960), pp. 1942–43.

8. Ibid., pp. 2004–12.

9. Nie, *Three Armed Services Strike*, p. 12.

10. *Ibid.*, p. 16.

11. *Ibid.*, p. 51.

12. *Ibid.*

13. *Ibid.*, p. 57.

14. *Ibid.*

15. Dwight D. Eisenhower, *Mandate for Change, 1953–1956* (Garden City, N.Y.: Doubleday, 1963), p. 459.

16. Ibid., pp. 476–77.

17. Ministry of Nuclear Industry, PRC, *Modern China's Nuclear Industry.* (Beijing: Social Science Publishing House, 1987), pp. 13–14.

18. *Collected Documents*, pp. 2250–51.

19. *Selected Works of Zhou Enlai* (Beijing: People's Publishing House, 1983), p. 286.

20. *Collected Documents*, p. 2287.

21. *Ibid.*, pp. 2385–2404.

22. *Ibid.*, p. 2503.

23. Thomas E. Stolper, *China, Taiwan, and the Offshore Islands* (New York: Sharpe, 1985), p. 115.

24. Wang, *Review*, p. 58.

25. Chen Zhiqi, *U.S. China Policy in the Past Thirty Years* (Taibei: Zhongyang Ribao Publishing House, 1984), pp. 136–138.

26. *Collected Documents*, p. 2078.

27. *Ibid.*, pp. 2657–65.

28. *Ibid.*, pp. 2675–77.

29. Mao Zedong, "Talk at the Sixteenth Supreme State Conference," April 15, 1959.

30. See n. 5.

31. Mao Zedong, *Selected Works of Mao Zedong on Military Affairs* (Beijing: PLA Soldier Publishing House, 1981), p. 364.

32. Mao Zedong, "Conversation with Leaders of Zones of Coordination," December 12, 1958.

33. Dwight D. Eisenhower, *Waging Peace, 1956–1961* (New York: Doubleday, 1965), p. 294.

34. *Ibid.*, p. 295.
35. Stolper, *China, Taiwan, and the Offshore Islands*, p. 118.
36. *Collected Documents*, pp. 2681–82.
37. United Press International (UPI), September 5, 1958.
38. *Collected Documents*, pp. 2699–2778.
39. Mao Zedong, "Talk at the Supreme State Conference," September 5, 1958
40. Mao Zedong, "Talk with the Leaders of Zones of Coordination," December 12, 1958.
41. *Ibid.*
42. Mao Zedong, "Talk at the Supreme State Conference," September 5, 1958.
43. *Ibid.*
44. *Renmin Ribao*, September 9, 1958.
45. Wang, *Review*, pp. 70–71.
46. Ibid., pp. 72–73.
47. *Collected Documents*, p. 2686.
48. Eisenhower, *Waging Peace*, pp. 300–1
49. Shen Jiahong, *Eight Years of Ambassadorship in the U.S.* (Taibei: Limin Wenhua Publishing House, 1980), p. 186.
50. Chiang Kai-shek, *President Chiang's Speeches in 1958* (Taibei: Administration Information Bureau), pp. 48–56.
51. *Collected Documents*, p. 2816.
52. *Ibid.*, p. 2824
53. See n. 5.
54. *Collected documents*, p. 2838.
55. *Ibid.*, pp. 2889–91.
56. See n. 5.
57. Nie, *Three Armed Services Strike*, p. 45.
58. He Xiaolu, *The Marshal as a Diplomat* (Beijing: The PLA Publishing House, 1985), p. 70.
59. See n. 5.

13

British Policy in Southeast Asia: the Eisenhower era

✪

ANTHONY SHORT
Aberdeen University, Scotland

In the fading glow of imperial splendor it would be nice, by way of emotional compensation, to describe British policy in Southeast Asia during the Eisenhower years—by contrast, say, with a study of contemporary British policy in the Middle East—in terms of acumen, sensitivity, prescience, and restraint. Consider the vast experience, the counsels of wisdom, the mellow dignity, above all, the successful achievement. And, of course, the implied contrasts: Eden and Dulles; Slim, or Templer, and Admiral Radford; Macmillan, say, and Walter Robertson. Attlee perhaps, and Walter Judd, or even the early enthusiasms of Senator John F. Kennedy; and do not forget the Malcolm MacDonalds, Lennox-Boyds, Oliver Lytteltons, and Rob Scotts. In aggregate there is the epitome of difference between the boy scout simplicities of Edward Lansdale and the knowledge of Graham Greene that political verities are doubtful and certainly not eternal.

Nice, but not altogether convincing and not altogether true. In any event one would not really expect either the conception or application of British policy that for operational purposes, had its origins in the unhappy events of World War II, to be anything like immaculate. Neither, can it be considered apart from what Eisenhower and his administration defined not only in time but by character and connotation as well; and it is with this in mind that one may begin with the transformation of Southeast Asia, as far as Britain was concerned, from an area of colonial disengagement to a cockpit of the cold war and what, a week after the Geneva cease-fire, General John Wilson O'Daniel was suggesting might become a testing ground for anti-Communist warfare.[1]

France, it may be assumed, had become involved in the Vietnam War in 1946 in a fairly straightforward attempt to reimpose the essential structure of colonial rule. One might have assumed also that, as in similar nastiness, say in Madagascar or in Algeria on VE Day, the struggle would have been in the back alleys of international relations. The longer it went on, however, the greater was the French need to transform its presentation into a showpiece battle of the cold war in which France was standing firm against the hordes of Asian communism. To begin with, this may have seemed inherently less credible to the United States than to Britain, which was having comparable difficulties with an insurgency in Malaya that, for a time, combined the elements of communism and nationalism in the body of largely Chinese guerillas. But the perceived necessity of maintaining France as America's principal continental ally, as much as France's ability to project its Indochina struggle as the unmistakable containment of communism, produced the American commitment a month before the unexpected start of the Korean War. After Korea it was comparatively easy to argue that Korea and Indochina were part of the same war and that, in Marshal de Lattre de Tassigny for example, one beheld one of the paladins of the free world. One can argue, then, that Britain, too, became involved in the Eisenhower climax of cold war in Southeast Asia because of France. Although Britain and the United States could and would put the blame on France, it soon became a matter of mutual recrimination. One ought, thus, to look first at what the British and Americans seem to have understood and misunderstood about each other's purposes.

From practically all the papers and studies that have been published on the subject of American intervention at Dienbienphu, one conclusion stands out: if Britain had agreed, the United States would have engaged in some form of intervention in Vietnam in the spring or summer of 1954. Agreed to what? Here the range of possibilities narrows down to a particular sequence. Much of the confusion was caused by the collapse of the American plan for united action and the apparently ignominious part that was played by the British and, in particular, by Foreign Secretary Anthony Eden. Ignominious in that it might appear that before the going got rough, Britain and the United States not only had a common purpose in Southeast Asia, namely the containment of communism, but shared perceptions as well. Thus, it was not only the American Chiefs of Staff who had exaggerated ideas of the Communist threat and what to do about it:

they were common to the British Chiefs as well. The Chief Imperial General Staff (CIGS), for example, Field Marshal Sir John Harding, gave the conventional assessment—and enunciated a standard British concern—in his minute to the Minister of Defence: "If the French are defeated it will be a very severe blow to Western prestige throughout the Far East and may well set in motion a chain of events that would sooner or later have a serious effect on the situation in Malaya."[2] And the month before Dienbienphu fell there was more hope than prescience in the Imperial General Staff (IGS) appreciation that "provided weather continues to permit the dropping of essential supplies to French, they have a better than even chance of holding Dienbienphu."[3]

If this really was the professional assessment of French chances, why was it that, three days later, the British would not even allow the French a sporting chance and would, in fact, deny the United States an opportunity to turn stalemate into victory? The answer, complex though it is bound to be, will probably reveal the outline of British policy in Southeast Asia and in general terms is to be found in different assessments of China and communism. In its immediate focus, however, the British response was concerned with the texture of the war in Indochina and, whether or not the analogy was misplaced, the experience of more than six years of insurrection in Malaya, which suggested different perspectives and criteria for success.[4]

Thus, on the same day as the IGS were making their operational, and optimistic, forecast about the battle of Dienbienphu, Lieutenant General Sir Charles Loewen, Commander in Chief of the Far East Land Forces, on a tour of inspection was writing to the CIGS that Vietnam was a politicomilitary problem similar to Malaya. "This is now a civil war, Vietnam versus Vietminh, demanding civil war leadership and politico-military organisation such as was necessary to meet Malayan emergency. I could see no sign of this emerging, nor indeed any realisation by either Vietnamese leaders or by the French that this was the key to the problem." Perhaps it was the detailed map he enclosed showing how little French influence and control there was throughout Vietnam that prompted Lord Salisbury to minute: "Most depressing. I had no idea that the degree of Vietminh infiltration was so high."[5]

At Cabinet level Salisbury's comment reflected the change in British policy towards Indochina, which is described in Sir James Cable's admirable and superbly understated account of the Geneva Conference, written from official papers and personal experience.[6] After the totally inadequate Foreign Office brief for the Berlin Conference of Foreign Ministers in January 1954—that the French should be sustained in their refusal to negotiate except on conditions that would safeguard the independence of the Associated States—ideas, at least in that office, were beginning to change in February and March. Cable's paper for the South-East Asia Department, "Policy Towards Indo-China," rested on the premise that "the will to press on to military victory has quite disappeared in France." Although he concedes that he "exaggerated—thanks to the Chiefs of Staff, and most people then agreed with them—the dangers of global war,"[7] this was a question that was likely to turn on how the United States attempted to solve the problem. For the British, as Salisbury wrote, the situation in Vietnam was most depressing, and Cable's conclusion was that there might "no longer by any prospect of a really favourable solution . . . the most we can do is to strive for the adoption of the least disadvantageous course."[8] In practice, assuming the French were determined to reach a settlement (and with Bidault as Foreign Minister this was not yet certain), this meant the partition of Vietnam, while safeguarding the independence of Laos and Cambodia, might be best as a stop-gap.

For the Americans, however, as the British ambassador reported on April 3, partition had been considered and rejected, and if, as Dulles had told Sir Roger Makins on more than on occasion, Indo-China could not be surrendered to communism, the chances of arriving at a common Anglo-American negotiating position at Geneva seemed that much more remote. If there was to be a policy of "no surrender," then the obvious question is raised of whether Dulles, for one, was prepared to negotiate at all except from a position of strength. Since the French position at this time was one of manifest and growing weakness begged the further question of how this position could have been attained.

The key to Vietnam, for the United States, was China—or so they sought to persuade the British. If, said Dulles, it was made plain to the Chinese that continuation of aid to the Vietminh was dangerous for China, the Chinese would desist; and the Russians would use their influence in the same direction. The American account is somewhat different, but as Makins reported it to the Foreign Office, the American Chiefs of Staff, according to Dulles, believed that the allies had a military superiority in the Far East that they would not have in three or four years' time. The threat of action would itself be a sufficient deterrent, but if it wasn't, "We should be in a strong position to carry it out." This involved risks, but the risks of letting Indo-China go were greater, and the risks would be diminished if a group of countries joined in the warning. Not, said Dulles, that the Americans were thinking of 'anything silly'; rather they considered the *threat* of naval and air action against the China coast sufficient.[9] On Eden's behalf Makins said that action that might lead to an extension of the war had not been contemplated: a point that was well made since Dulles then went on to say that if the Chinese persisted in their intervention in the face of the warning of collective action, and if the warning had to be implemented, it would be impossible to restrain Syngman Rhee and Chiang Kai-shek. Not surprisingly, Makins followed up with a second telegram which warned that the Americans proposed to muster support for the necessary warning or threat of action against China and were ready to execute the threat if necessary.

This was the mood in which London was told to expect Dulles. Here, by contrast, is the British position as presented by Tahourdin of the South-East Asia Department for Eden, Lord Reading and the Permanent Undersecretary:

> US policy in Indo-China rests on the basic assumption that if it was made plain to the Chinese that continuation of aid to the Vietminh was dangerous to China they would desist. This is not our view. In the first place our own Chiefs of Staff have previously considered the blockade or bombing of China in connection with Korea, when they concluded that these measures would not have sufficient military effect to cause China to release her hold. The Chiefs of Staff then said that, with the possible exception of atomic bombing, there was no effective military action that could be taken against China. Secondly, there is a clear distinction between warning China that some specific further action would entail retaliation, which might be an effective deterrent, and calling upon her to desist from action in which she is already engaged. It is hard to see what threat would be sufficiently potent to make China swallow so humiliating a rebuff as the abandonment of the Vietminh without any face-saving concessions in return.

To underline the importance of Dulles' visit to London, Eisenhower sent a long personal message to Churchill. It seems unmistakable that its purpose was to persuade the British to join an alliance which, if it had failed to persuade the Chinese to abandon the Vietminh—'discreet disengagement' was the expression used—would have gone to war with China. Perhaps the threat would have been enough; but "the important thing is that the coalition must be strong and it must be willing to join in the fight if necessary."[10] The letter was suggested by Dulles just after he had met congressional leaders on April 3—'the day we didn't go to war'—with, it has been suggested, a joint resolution in his pocket that would have authorized presidential action. In the account he gave Eisenhower over the phone Dulles said the feeling was that Congress would be quite prepared to go along on some vigorous action if the United States was not doing it alone—and, he added, the position of "Britianh is what congressmen were thinking of."[11] Or, as the formal record has it, "It was decided that the Secretary would attempt to get definite commitments from the English and other free nations."[12]

As far as the United States was concerned, there could be no surrender to communism in IndoChina. A negotiated settlement at Geneva was impossible. Congress would give its authority for intervention on one principal condition: that America did not go in alone. And that condition meant, in effect, British support. As far as Britain was concerned, one part of this sequence was unknown, but the omens for Dulles' visit were alarming enough. Even more alarming, on April 7 the French Ambassador called on the Permanent Undersecretary, Sir Ivone Kirkpatrick, to tell him that because of certain possible unauthorized assurances given to General Ely by Admiral Radford, the French government had asked the U.S. government to intervene in the battle with a massive airstrike. After some delay, said Massigli, the American government had replied that it could not directly intervervene except as a member of a coalition in which the United Kingdom and Australia at least were members.[13]

Dulles' arrival in London on April 11 was, then, more of a visitation than a visit. Like Ho Chi Minh at Fontainebleau in 1946—although it is doubtful whether he would have appreciated the irony of the comparison—Dulles had to have something to take home with him. In the long account of the discussions on Southeast Asia,[14] Eden mentioned the Warning Declaration "that was produced outside the meetings for us to look at, but it was never produced in the formal discussions" and observed/complained that the Americans had no other prepared documents when they arrived. Eden had already told Churchill, "I have misgivings about certain aspects of Dulles' proposals, especially the wisdom of a minatory declaration before Geneva."[15] Whether one called it a "Warning Declaration" or, as Dulles did, a "Declaration of Common Purpose," when he circulated the paper in London, it looked rather like the prospectus for the South Sea Bubble: "Gentlemen are invited to subscribe to an enterprise the nature of which shall hereinafter be revealed." What it said was, that if the lands of any of the signatory governments in the Southeast Asia or West Pacific area fell under the domination of international communism, it would be a threat to the peace and security of them all; and that they would combine their efforts to prevent such a threat.[16] In the Reading-Eden presentation which covered the period from Dulles' "united action" speech of March 29th to the end of May a distinction is made between four quite separate, even if closely related, topics. The first was the long-term project to create a Southeast Asia Defense Organization "intended to be permanent in character and not devised merely to meet the immediate problem." The second were short-term proposals for active armed intervention in the Indochina war with the object of preventing the fall of Dienbienphu or at least averting its more disastrous consequences. Third, was a more curious assertion, which hardly takes in the United States, that there was consideration of measures "to furnish effective guarantees of any settlement in Indo-China which might be reached at Geneva" or in default of any settlement, to contain further Communist advances in Southeast Asia. The fourth—and, again, the grace note is added in the British account—was the institution of Five Power Staff talks *"without commitment to the countries participating"* (stress added) to recommend possible courses of action to check further communist aggression or infiltration in the region of Southeast Asia as a whole.

In June Lord Reading explained the problem that developed to Makins in Washington:

> This account covers, amongst other things, the misunderstanding between the United States Government and Her Majesty's Government of what had been agreed during Mr. Dulles' visit to London on April 11 to 13. Although the misunderstanding was unfortunate, it was aggravated by the publicity given to the intention of the United States Government to go ahead at once with ten members for the formation of a South-East Asia Defence Organisation without waiting for any preliminary confidential discussions about possible additional Asian membership. The prospect of repairing our differences was still further impaired by the publicity given to the proposals made by Mr. Dulles in Paris on April 25 and later for active intervention in Indo-China. In such circumstances any action to set up a South-East Asia Defence Organisation would have been taken as an acknowledgment that we had abandoned any hope of an arrangement at Geneva and would have ended the possibility of Asian association with the project or even benevolence towards it. Since Her Majesty's Government attach great importance to the successful establishment of such an Organisation, I decided that this aim should take precedence over any facile attempt to restore Anglo–United States unity at the expense of our objective.[17]

In rather loose historical terms, it might be argued, from a British point of view, that Dulles' draft declaration of policy sounded more like a multilateral Monroe Doctrine for Southeast Asia than for the sort of organization that would have been comparable to that of the North Atlantic Pact. Indeed, to continue the rather wavering parallel, it was not that far off the Holy Alliance, with its transposed fears of "international communism," and Eden's reaction was much the same as that of Castlereagh in 1820: "We shall be found in our place when actual danger menaces the System of Europe but the Country cannot, and will not, act upon abstract and speculative Principles of Precaution." As it was, Eden's familiar but unconscious endearments and Dulles' chronic halitosis would help to produce a notable noncongruence over the next few weeks when, as one observer recalls, they seemed simply to talk past each other. When the American draft was "informally" produced, the Foreign Office (Dennis Allen) "expressed great reserve" because "definitive action before the Conference began might foreclose the possibility of successful negotiation."[18] Dulles emerged from this encounter without the draft declaration but with Eden's signature on what could be assumed was a contract: a joint statement that said, "We are ready to take part with the other countries principally concerned in an examination of the possibility of establishing a system of collective defence."[19] And as Dulles, overlooking the setback to his draft declaration, told the French, it was a communiqué that fully satisfied the purposes he had in mind in coming to Britain.

Certainly it might be seen as the basis for some sort of united action. The only matters it had not settled were what, and most important, when. Taken in the context of what can be seen were British attitudes before the communiqué was issued—rather than after, when they could be regarded as excuses for escaping from unexpected or unwelcome commitments—it hardly looks as if Britain contemplated armed intervention of any kind before the Geneva Conference had had the opportunity of arriving at a diplomatic settlement. The communiqué could be understood to mean that. It could equally well be understood to mean that an armed coalition would be formed before the conference began; thus, the French would not only be supported but would even be able to call on power they were themselves unable to command and from this position of strength negotiate a settlement that might be acceptable to the United States. If, however, this proved, for whatever reason, to be impossible, France's opponents would at least have to reckon with an alliance in being.

Either course might have been tried; both were implied; and the Americans came away from their first British encounter believing, or claiming to believe, that they had secured British approval for the creation, announcement, and even deployment of the forces of an armed alliance.[20] One must, of course, concede, ruefully, that the slightest hint of equivocation gives a good lawyer as much as he needs. Did Eden renege, as Dulles subsequently claimed, on the agreement that had been made in London? Is it evidence of pusillanimous policy or Perfidious Albion? Is there anything surrounding the incident that illuminates British policy? And does it much matter?

The practical result was that Eden refused to permit British participation in Washington once Dulles returned and went ahead, publicly,
with what seemed to be preparatory talks for a coalition. But as far
as British policy was concerned, the context of discussions in Parliament and in the Cabinet shows, if nothing else, different perceptions
and a concern with different political factors.

Compared to the previous Labour government, Churchill's Conservative administration had a comparatively comfortable majority
of twenty-six. A back-bench revolt over Indo–China was unthinkable,
and, within the government, the principal but fluctuating and mostly
implicit dissent over aspects of British policy focused on Anglo-American relations—and the source was Churchill himself. As far as ministers were concerned, policy towards Southeast Asia was largely a
one-man affair—Eden—or two men—Eden and Lord Reading, at
most. Churchill's contributions may appear somewhat eccentric—
praise for French exertions in Indochina and their splendid work in
North Africa—at the Bermuda Conference in December 1953, even
though it was mostly a favorable in retrospective comparison with
the way the British had left India: "a colossal disaster." He also sent
a personal message of support for the French commander at Dienbienphu. And later, what Eden's biographer cites as a "blood row" between Eden and Churchill occurred over the entry of China into the
UN.[21] Eden, much more than Churchill, was ambivalent toward the
United States although Rhodes James says that at Bermuda "So
coarse was Eisenhower's language, and his threats of the use of atomic
weapons in the Far East and Indo-China in certain eventualities, that
even Churchill became concerned."[22]

After the Dulles visit to London, when the Cabinet were considering the joint communiqué, they made it plain that they should be
concerned only with establishing a system of collective defense that
was the equivalent of NATO: "otherwise it would have been interpreted as foreshadowing direct military intervention."[23] The following day in Parliament even this was too much for Bevan, on the
opposition benches, who said it was a surrender to American pressure
whose purposes would be to impose European colonial rule. Much
more substantial comment came from Attlee and two Labour "War
Ministers" (as they were plainly called in those days), Strachey and
Shinwell. Attlee, like Bevan, was concerned with the defense of obso-
lete colonialism, but for him it was vital that the collective defense
system would be open to all the peoples of Asia. Strachey, echoing
Attlee, said the very worst way of attempting to halt the advance of
communism in Asia was even to appear to support what certainly all
the nations of Asia, including Commonwealth members, would regard

as an untenable French colonialism in Indochina. But it was Shin-well's question "Have we got his assurance that he does not propose to proceed any further than the examination of the project and will not commit this House or this country definitely to any scheme which is unacceptable?" that gave Eden the opportunity to confirm that it was still the objective of Her Majesty's Government to go to the Geneva Conference in order to secure peace that was honorable to all the parties involved in the Indochina conflict. And he added, "I hope that those critics who thought that we were going to issue some fulminating declaration before the Geneva Conference took place will realise that we are as anxious as they are—and perhaps more so—to see the Geneva Conference succeed."[24]

Contextually, therefore, it would seem that Eden's policy—and this was certainly the account he gave of it—was to seek a diplomatic solution first at Geneva and then, if that failed, to join in some collective defense arrangement for the rest of Southeast Asia. Before that happened, the United States had come even closer to intervention, and Admiral Radford had sought to convince Churchill, if not the British Chiefs of Staff, that "allied intervention would at least allow the French to hold most of Indo-China even if they lost Dien Bien Phu." This, said Radford, was the critical moment to make a stand against China. He did not think that the Russians, who were fright-ened of war, would go openly to China's assistance. In any event, the situation would be much worse in five years time, and, as a tradeoff, "If we co-operated over this the US would be willing to help us in other spheres and he [Churchill] thought there would be no difficulty in revoking the present American policy of aloofness with regard to our difficulties in Egypt."[25] Churchill's response was to contrast the difficulty in influencing the British people by what had happened in the distant jungles of Southeast Asia with the knowledge that there was a powerful American airbase in East Anglia; and that war with China, which would invoke the Sino-Russian pact, might mean an assault by hydrogen bombs on these islands. The British could not, said Churchill, commit themselves at this moment, when all these matters were about to be discussed at Geneva, to a policy that might lead by slow stages to catastrophe.

There seems little doubt—whether or not they were as Dulles said, scared to death, that Eden, Churchill, and practically the entire Brit-ish Cabinet were gravely alarmed by what they considered to be the recklessness of American policy. Nor were they any less alarmed by the role that had been allotted to them. Dulles, for example, had told Prime Minister Laniel that on two conditions the United States would seek congressional approval for direct acts of belligerency. The second, which he thought had been substantially met, was that France would give the Associated States real and complete independence. The first was that the United Kingdom would agree to join in the military defense of Indochina.[26] Returning to London for emergency Cabinet meetings on April 25th Eden said "We were being pressed to join in a general declaration of readiness to fight Communism in South-East Asia in order to support a request to Congress for authority to employ naval airforces of the United States in an air-strike against the besiegers of Dien Bien Phu."[27] From which Churchill concluded, "What we were being asked to do was in effect to aid in misleading Congress into approving a military operation which would itself be ineffective and might well bring the world to the verge of a major war."[28] In the climatic year of 1954 it would seem, therefore, that the object of British policy in Southeast Asia was as much to restrain the United States as it was to contain communism. Certainly as far as the French predicament in Indochina was concerned there was a willingness to seek a negotiated settlement and, for various reasons, a corresponding reluctance to engage beforehand in what could have been a fighting alliance, even if its proclaimed purpose was prophylactic. Eisenhower, for one, thought the British *too* ready to negotiate, and there were one or two outbursts about their "miserable trading posts" in the Far East and the millstone of British colonialism around the American neck. Nevertheless there *were* considerable risks for Britain, and in the rather chilling account of contingency planning General Joseph Collins raised the delicate question of whether the United States would be able to bomb the outskirts of Kowloon and pointed out that Britain would undoubtedly "lose" Hong Kong. Paul Nitze, then of the Policy Planning Staff, replied that they might be sold the idea of at least accepting the risk, and the risk of war spreading to China, because of the importance of defending South-East Asia.

Even after the fall of Dienbienphu and the Indochina phase of the Geneva Conference had begun, plans for American intervention continued and provided an unusual background to what in one sense at least was supposed to be a peace conference. Eden's emergence, in the avoidable absence of Mr. Dulles, as, perhaps, the principal negotiator on the Western side, allows us to examine the ideas and organizing principle that he needed to bring forward and, in so doing, illuminate British thinking if not British policy on Southeast Asia. Eden thought in terms of the Locarno Conference of 1925. For him, Locarno meant a guarantee of any settlement that might emerge at Geneva, and the implication, moreover, of a guarantee that would apparently involve Russia and China as well as Britain and the United States. The original Locarno agreements were concerned with guaranteeing the frontiers and security of established states: France, Germany, and Belgium. Insignificant in themselves, the agreements had been guaranteed by Britain and Italy, and there had been a further guarantee by France alone of the even more doubtful frontiers of Poland and Czechoslovakia. It was seen, therefore, that neither Eden nor the Foreign Office had thought ahead to what this might involve at Geneva, whether the analogy was appropriate, or who would have signed what. But if Tahourdin, of the South-East Asia Department of the Foreign Office, is to be believed, "A Locarno-type guarantee was, in fact, in our minds throughout the first half of the Geneva Conference. Our hope was that the Colombo powers might be induced to assume the role of guarantor that had been played by Great Britain and Italy in the original Locarno Agreement."[29] So, it seems the British may have been thinking of, if not enunciating, something that would not, after all, have involved China and the Soviet Union. But in one respect at least the analogy was hopeful. The "Spirit of Locarno" engendered by the original agreements had been one of reconciliation between former enemies. It had also led to Germany's entry into the League of Nations, and even though Eden and Churchill seemed not to have mentioned the implication for China and the UN, there was nothing to stop the Americans from drawing this conclusion.

In the event some of them, such as Senator William Knowland, equated Locarno instead with Munich. Indignant members of the House Foreign Affairs Committee wrote to the President as soon as they heard of Eden's statement. "He advocates that the free world not only accepts communist conquests and gains but in fact guarantee them." When the House debated the Mutual Security Bill a few days later, an amendment was moved that provided that none of the funds for the Far East could be used "on behalf of governments which are committed by treaty to maintain Communist rule over any defined territory of Asia." Incredibly, with almost four hundred Congressmen present, it was passed unanimously.

Although he would hardly have put it like that, maintaining Communist rule over a defined territory of Asia was, however, almost exactly what Eden had in mind. Before the end of May he was looking for a *modus vivendi*. Negotiations would take time, and Eden had always recognized they would involve concessions to the Communists, probably entailing the creation of a buffer state on China's southern border. This would have to be excluded from the defense organization he envisaged; but the Americans, Eden said, appeared to contemplate an organization that would assist them into reconquering Indochina. "HMG for their part would not be prepared to participate in such a venture."[30] Foreshadowing the establishment of a Communist North Vietnam, Eden, by implication, was less sanguine about prospects in the South. For example, he circulated the following extract from the British Minister in Saigon to his Cabinet colleagues. "The mood of the country is difficult to determine but it would not be far wrong to say that most Vietnamese whine to the following tune 'Somebody will have to do something for us. We can't be expected to work out our own salvation.' A spineless people headed by a flabby octopus."[31]

Informing the Cabinet from Washington of the proposed joint declaration with Eisenhower, Churchill's cable also seemed to have some qualifications about self-determination: "where peoples desire and are capable of sustaining self-government and independent existence," —and, in any event, it sounded more like Eden, even if the reservations were not intended.[32] In spite of the joint declaration, there was scarcely a firm Anglo-American position and even though it was agreed that an armistice would have to meet seven criteria the incompatibility between points 4 and 5 was astounding—but apparently unremarked, except by the French. For an agreement to be acceptable under point 4) it would not contain political provisions which would risk the loss of the retained area to Communist control but point 5) would not exclude the possibility of the ultimate reunification of Vietnam by peaceful means.

Even though, in principle, they had accepted partition and other salient features in Vietnam, neither America nor Britain was looking even a short way ahead to consider how an agreement could be confirmed. Dulles was apparently convinced that there could be neither meaningful negotiation nor lasting settlement with Communist powers and found the prospect of signing an agreement with the Chinese Peoples' Republic morally outrageous and politically impossible. In spite of the Korean War—but perhaps, it might be said, because in effect Britain held Hong Kong hostage—the British attitude toward China, particularly in Southeast Asia, was based more on practical considerations than on ideological preconceptions. On the basis of operational experience China's aggressive intentions were discounted. The foundation of this experience was, of course, Malaya. With a prospect of winding down its own revolutionary war there, the British had no intention of becoming involved in a war which they thought the French had practically lost in Indochina. And certainly not if it was, as arguably it might have been, a prelude to World War III.

Before the prospect of American intervention provided a climax to the first Vietnam war British policy in Southeast Asia had centered on an acceptable form of independence for Malaya and a process of what they hoped would be successful decolonization. The premises of British policy toward Malaya were different from those of France in Indochina. Moreover, by 1954 when the war in Vietnam reached its peak, the insurrection in Malaya had been reduced to almost trivial dimensions. Thus, in the week when the cease-fire was concluded at Geneva, the Situation Report from Malaya recorded only nineteen incidents for the whole country, seven of which were regarded as major. Twelve guerrillas had been killed and one Gurkha. Thirty-eight guerrilla camps had been found, as well as ten supply dumps, and while only a handful of weapons had been recovered, none had been lost. Overall monthly average casualties were four for security forces and civilians combined and almost four times as many guerrillas killed, captured, and surrendered. One particular point of interest was that newspapers in China were claiming a hundred guerrilla attacks a month in 1953—but the source that was given was the Federation of Malaya annual report, presumably because they had no other sources of information.

Considering that something like 90 percent of the Malayan guerrillas were Chinese, even though many and perhaps most of them had been born in Malaya, and that they were organized by a Communist party, it is surprising how little help they got from China itself. Certainly there was no appreciable difference before and after the Communist victory of 1949. In 1954 the Malayan Communist Party still had ambitious plans to step up its military attacks as well as build underground organizations and a united front. Although it was trying to establish contact with China via Singapore the Party by this time was heavily penetrated by government intelligence and had difficulty enough communicating internally without being part of an international network.

Meeting Chinese face to face in Southeast Asia either as guerrillas or as colonial subjects at least gave them human rather than fantastic shape. International developments, and particularly Indochina, had improved party morale appreciably, but neither from experience nor in anticipation was Britain faced with an unmanageable Chinese problem in Malaya. Nevertheless with things so obviously improving in 1954 it comes as a considerable shock to read "Military Government will be set up in Songkhla." Songkhla lies across the northern border of Malaya, and this, even though it was hardly on the scale of the Cambodian incursion of 1970, was the third version of a British plan to invade Southern Thailand. The project had begun as a means of defending Malaya on the Kra Isthmus in January 1953, when it was assumed there would only be negligible Thai opposition to a

British advance. Now, it was thought possible that, in the event of a Communist coup in Thailand, the armed forces or part of them might throw in their lot with the new government; but Operation Warrior, like its predecessors Ringlet and Irony, was little more than a contingency plan even if it revealed that considerations of sovereignty were unlikely to stand in the way of a *sauve qui peut* strategy. In any case, while it was extremely unlikely after Geneva, and not all that likely before, that there would be a conventional "Communist" invasion of Thailand from the North or East, "subversion," essentially a political problem, was recognized as a strong possibility. In Malaya, with the elections of 1955 putting the country only one step or so away from independence, the problem of subversion was more or less under control, although it was identified in SEATO as common to Southeast Asia as a whole. Most of Asia was now at least nominally independent, and while it can be argued that Britain, since the Colombo Plan of 1950, was more interested in international economic cooperation in Southeast Asia, from the political and defense point of view it wanted very little to do with the principal object, at least for the United States, of the SEATO exercise—namely, Vietnam.

After Geneva and in spite of the assumption of "cochairmanship" a good deal of British policy toward the fulfillment of whatever was decided at Geneva was itself uncertain and implicit. Whatever it was, it was sufficient to bring another letter from Eisenhower to Churchill, exactly one year after Dulles' "united action" speech, that was written more in anger than in sorrow. There was, said Eisenhower, "an apparent difference between our two governments that puzzles us sorely and constantly. Although we seem always to see eye to eye with you when we contemplate any European problem our respective attitudes towards similar problems in the Orient are frequently so dissimilar as to be almost mutually antagonistic." He responded:

> The conclusion seems inescapable that these differences come about because we do not agree on the probable extent and the importance of further communist expansion in Asia. In our contacts with New Zealand and Australia we have a feeling that we encounter a concern no less acute than ours; but your own government seems to regard Communist aggression in Asia as of little significance to the free world future.

> As I once explained to you, we are not interested in Quemoy and Matsu as such. But because of the conviction that the loss of Formosa would doom the Philippines and eventually the remainder of the region, we are determined that it should not fall in the hands of the Communists, either through all-out attack or, as would appear to be far more likely, through harassing air-attacks, threats and subversion.

There was a note about sustaining high morale among Chiang's forces—and how Eisenhower personally would be very happy to see him withdraw voluntarily from the offshore islands—before Eisenhower reverted to Southeast Asia:

> Another apparent difference between us that added to our bewilderment occurred in connection with Foster's recent visit to the Far East. He urged the Government of Laos, while it still has the ability to do so, to clean out the areas in that country where Communist elements are establishing themselves in some strength. The Laos Government is fully justified in taking such action under the terms of the Geneva Agreements. When Laotian officials expressed to Foster some concern lest such action on their part provoked attack from the Vietminh and the Chinese Communists he assured them that aggression from without would bring into play the Manila Pact. This would mean assistance from the other signatories of the Pact to preserve the territorial integrity of Laos.
>
> Sometime after this conversation, we heard that both the British and the French Ambassadors in Laos informed that Government that under no circumstances could Laos expect any help against outside aggression, under the terms of the Manila Pact, if such aggression should result from their own efforts to rule their internal affairs.'

Eisenhower followed this with another argument:

> If the Chinese Nationalist government should disappear the emigré Chinese (in the Far East) will certainly deem themselves subjects of the Chinese Communist Government and they will quickly add to the difficulties of their adopted countries. Indeed where their numbers are quite strong, I believe that their influence might become decisive and that no outside aid that any of us could bring to bear could prevent these regions from going completely communist. Do not such possibilities concern you?
>
> As we consider such developments and possibilities, it seems to me we cannot fail to conclude that the time to stop any advance of Communism in Asia is here, now.[33]

The President again invoked the Grand Alliance—"I do believe that all of us must begin to look these unpleasant facts squarely in the face and meet them exactly as our Grand Alliance of the '40s met our enemies and vanquished them"—but the Communist sweep over the world since World War II had been much faster and much more relentless than the 1930 sweep of the dictators. And he argued, in what might have been an ominous comparison, "Two decades ago we had the fatuous hope that Hitler, Mussolini, and the Japanese War

Lords would decide, before we might become personally involved, that they had had enough and would let the world live in peace. We saw the result."

As an academic exercise, based on textual analysis, should one conclude from this letter that Eisenhower was writing in anticipation of another world war? Or was he holding out the prospect of some "free world" coalition that would deter the aggressors so that war would be averted? Probably the latter, but both then and later a consolidation of Anglo-American policies would turn on a definition and appreciation of "aggression." In the meantime and before the case could be argued that it was the aggression of one Vietnam against the other, it is worth looking at what it was the British thought had been agreed at Geneva, how they thought things would develop, and what, if anything, they did to influence events in Indochina.

Explicit in the note that the South-East Asian Department (Tahourdin) sent the Foreign Affairs Committee was that an agreement had been reached at Geneva because for different and probably temporary reasons the interests of the various parties pointed in the same direction. As far as Vietnam was concerned, Tahourdin noted, two days earlier, his understanding was that elections would be held in July 1956, supervised by Canada, India, and Poland, with the object of unifying Vietnam. A year later, Cable minuted: "Article seven of the Formal Declaration says 'Consultations will be held on this subject (General Elections) between the competent representative authorities of the two zones from July 20 1955 onwards." This seems clear enough to me, but I should be grateful for Mr. Sinclair's confirmation that this does mean that consultation should start on July 20."[34] Mr. Sinclair was not so sure. And from Washington, Makins reported, "State Department have re-examined Geneva Agreement and say that in answer to an unwelcome French request for a clarification of their views they have been compelled to state that from a strictly legal point of view they do not see that Vietnam is compelled to start discussions on July 20." On which Cable, in turn, minuted "This telegram suggests a deplorable backsliding by State Department from the view previously expressed by Mr. Dulles that Vietnamese should be urged to take part in these preparatory talks: a deplorable instance of the degree to which the Americans have become involved in the Vietnamese obsession with their quarrel with the French."[35] The Foreign Office (Allen) suggested that Macmillan might want to mention the matter to Dulles when he was in America. "The American attitude shows no sense of urgency. A provision that talks should begin after July 20 this year is an integral part of the Geneva Settlement . . . a major breach of an important provision of the Settlement, which must be regarded as a whole, could jeopardise the other provisions, including eventually those relating to a cease-fire." Allen continued:

> Unless Mr Diem shows a forthcoming attitude towards the beginning of consultation (once they start he can within the wide limits set by Geneva be as stubborn as he likes) there is a danger a) the Vietminh will capture the initiative b) such international support as he now has will be dissipated c) there may even, sooner or later, be a breach of the precarious peace which Indo-China now enjoys. But it would probably be useless and even dangerous to say anything to Diem about elections unless we were certain of the full backing of the US.[36]

By this time Eden had been succeeded as Foreign Secretary by Harold Macmillan and although, as Prime Minister, he continued to take a very close interest in Indochina there were, nevertheless, significant differences between them both of opinion and approach. Before the Geneva Conference ended, Eden thought the most important thing was to reach an agreement that was acceptable to the United States. Obviously, it was not and the device of listing the Conference participants in order to underpin the Final Declaration, not to mention their unilateral statement, had only concealed American disagreement. Eden seemed to assume, however, that at least a basic agreement had been reached, certainly with respect to the responsibilities of the government of Vietnam in the South. When, for example, Macmillan had met Dulles and Faure at a Foreign Ministers' meeting in Paris in 1955 it had been agreed that officials should draft parallel instructions to be sent to U.S. and French representatives in Saigon. These instructions would have provided for support for Diem's government but also for joint pressure on him to prepare for the meeting with the Communist government in the North about elections. In the event the officials failed to agree, and the instructions that were sent, although similar, were not identical. Eden minuted: ("This could be very dangerous . . . the matter cannot be left as it is. If US will not play we will have to give Diem a solemn warning ourselves whether it is effective or not."[37] A fortnight later, on July 1, Macmillan responded to Eden's question of "whether the obstinate and unsuccessful American support of Diem has to continue whatever the price." "Our answer," said Macmillan "is that we have not found an effective reply to the American question 'Who else?' " Apart from that, Macmillan was obviously more impressed than Eden with Diem's performance. "In the recent struggles Diem has displayed considerable ability as a revolutionary politician, and his firm handling of the Sects, although it may yet lead to serious complications, has strengthened his internal position. It is true that he has yet to demonstrate that he can run an effective administration; but for the present there is no serious rival for power in South Vietnam."[38]

Macmillan's position was, therefore, much closer to that of the United States at this time. Indeed, his arguments for giving Diem a chance were practically identical, and he told Eden that he saw no point in trying to persuade the Americans to change their minds.

Nevertheless, both Macmillan and Lord Reading, the Minister of State, *were* prepared to put considerable pressure on the Diem government in the person of M. Chau, the minister without portfolio, when he called at the Foreign Office in July. First of all, Reading emphasized that in the view of HMG the provision that electoral consultations should begin on July 20 was an integral part of the Geneva Agreements and the failure to give effect to it would constitute a major breach of them. If such a breach could be laid at the door of the government of Vietnam one consequence would certainly be that it would forfeit much of the international sympathy and support it otherwise might expect to receive. Furthermore, the Vietminh, for their part, would feel free to flout the provisions of Geneva. It was possible that they would not take any sudden dramatic step, but guerilla attacks would probably begin leading to a steady deterioration of the whole position. The important thing, said Reading, was that the consultations should start. Once the Vietnamese had agreed to begin, HMG would be happy to discuss tactics.

M. Chau was then turned over to Macmillan, who said that all that the Vietnamese were being asked to do at this point was to arrange for some sort of *prise de contact* with the Vietminh no later than July 20. They could, of course, insist on every kind of safeguard. But if July 20 came and Vietnam had shown no disposition to start consultation, a serious situation would arise. And in case M. Chau had not got the point, Macmillan added, "If fighting did recommence as the result of what would appear to the world to be the breakup of the Geneva Agreement on the part of Vietnam it would be impossible for HMG to give any support to the Vietnamese Government. World public opinion was very powerful and the Government of Vietnam would be well advised not to flout it."[39]

Eden's view of elections in Vietnam, particularly in response to Makins' opinion that he did not think they would be held, was his minute: "We must not be afraid of this," and, he continued, "If US take this responsibility they will have to shoulder it before the world."[40] The following day in another minute he wrote: "Foreign Secretary. This continues v. grave." After Diem had specifically rejected pre-election negotiations with Hanoi and his position had been endorsed by Dulles, Eden's minute to Macmillan read: "Dulles moves further away from his position at Geneva every time he speaks. I hope we shall address the US government very seriously on this subject soon. If they are going to advise the wrecking of the Geneva Agreement—for that is what this amounts to—we should make it clear it is their sole responsibility."

Eden's sense of responsibility was obviously different, and in spite of the derogatory but second hand opinion of Nehru, which Cable attributes to Eden, there was close and almost intimate consultation between them in 1955 on Laos and Cambodia as well as Vietnam. For example, when he told Nehru that the government of Laos should be established forthwith in the Pathet Lao provinces, Eden said that if the International Control Commission (ICC) had to be split, it was as well that it should be on an issue that was not only fundamental but also where the Poles were clearly wrong.[41] Perhaps it was flattering to Nehru to be asked whether Indian chairmanship could bring the Commission into play in Laos—Eden suspected the Pathet Lao now had at least ten infantry battalions with equipment supplied by the Vietminh—and even more so to be told that in Cambodia the apprehensions of both sides might be quietened if India were to assume a greater role.[42] The reference here was to the possibility of India's sending a military training mission. In the event and after what the Foreign Office called a number of misunderstandings, the Americans stepped in at the last moment. Even if India had provided the men, the United States would still have to have found the money, but at least the Foreign Office hoped that India could eventually assume the responsibility for training the Cambodian Army.[43]

For both Nehru and Eden South Vietnam was quite a different matter. Nehru had taken a particular dislike to its representatives at the nonaligned conference at Bandung—about which he gave Eden another confidential report, states that these representatives were "Productive of more good to our common cause than perhaps we dared to anticipate." At the conference, perhaps to Nehru's surprise, they had made a "violent attack" on his resolution, hoping that the Geneva Settlement would be carried out. They, or rather their government, had followed this up in July 1955 with a "spontaneous" attack on Indian and Polish members of the ICC in Saigon. Nehru's response had been to give notice that the time had come to approach the two cochairmen (USSR and UK) and, if necessary, all the Geneva powers.[44]

The U.S.S.R, which provided the other cochairman, was apparently not anxious to reconvene the Geneva Conference even if South Vietnam were to be considered in breach of an agreement that they had not signed (General Giap had told the French that they were responsible for carrying out the agreement). With the French on their way out, Macmillan told Molotov, when they met in New York in September 1955: "We are now in a better position to argue that Diem had succeeded to the obligations of his predecessors." Macmillan wanted to let Diem know, by way of extra pressure, that he and Molotov had met and would be meeting again. On this occasion, at dinner with Molotov, and with an echo of Churchill's slight misquotation to Stalin at Yalta about the eagle and the small birds, Macmillan noted, "After a course or two I said I thought it very important that we should keep the small countries quiet in South-East Asia and everywhere else so as not to interfere with our serious negotiations. Molotov agreed." *A propos* Egypt, Molotov said, "We all have friends whom we have to help. This is not always very convenient."[45]

The Geneva Conference was not reconvened in 1955, and when Lord Reading and Gromyko, as cochairmen, met in London in May 1956, Reading thought they would be able to avert what he called the immediate threat of another conference. Ten years on, when Eden published his proposal for "Peace in Indo-China" and a limited retrospective, he described 1956 as, by coincidence, perhaps Diem's best year and the worst for the Communists and those under their rule in North Vietnam.[46] It was this state of affairs, Eden thought, that might have accounted for the relatively moderate pressure from Communist sources for the election. But if the pressure was relatively minor, the British concession was absolutely major. For the first time, and although it was obviously too late for elections in 1956, Britain committed itself publicly to free, nationwide elections for the reestablishment of the national unity of Vietnam and to the validity of the Final Declaration. It was an astonishing if unremarked announcement, and, addressed by the cochairmen to both the Vietnamese governments, it "strongly urged" them to ensure the implementation of the political provisions and principles the Final Declaration embodied. Afterwards, the Foreign Office said that the announcement was "the unavoidable price of Russian support for the cease-fire." At least they had not given in to the Russian proposal, which echoed Giap, that the cochairmen should announce that the only parties concerned in Vietnam were the Vietminh and the French. By 1956, therefore, it seemed that Vietnam at least was going off the boil. By then Britain was facing what looked like a more urgent and at least potentially critical problem: the future of its base in Singapore. At the beginning of the year a constitutional conference was held in London to determine the conditions of Malayan independence, which, by comparison with Singapore, would be quite straightforward. As far as future defense was concerned, which also meant the defense of Britain's considerable economic as well as strategic interests, it was recognized that there would be a continuing need for Commonwealth forces (the response to the amnesty for guerillas had been disappointing). In its electoral platform the Alliance Party had declared that Ms150m per annum would be a fair share of the total cost of the emergency—and the rest would be met, they suggested, "by other nations interested in fighting world communism."[47] In practice, this meant the Commonwealth Strategic Reserve, created in 1955, which reflected Australia's interest in Malaya, described by Prime Minister Menzies as Australia's northern frontier. At least in Malaya there was a coincidence of political purpose. After the failure of talks in 1955 between Chin Peng, the Communist guerrilla leader, and the political leaders of Malaya and Singapore had apparently convinced Tungku Abdul Rahman of the impossibility of compromise with the Communists, the way was clear to establishing a Malayan-Commonwealth defense partnership and alliance. But in Singapore, although Mr. Marshall's more moderate Labour Party had won the 1955 municipal elections, there was a highly volatile situation with rioting Chinese middle school students (in which the American UP correspondent was killed), strikes, and a left-wing People's Action Party that was demanding immediate independence.

Singapore had all the makings of a classical British colonial problem overlaid with strategic considerations of the first order.[48] For the governor of Singapore, decolonization was a process that could not now be halted. In London, the Colonial Secretary, Alan Lennox-Boyd, provided the Cabinet with a memorable presentation of the dilemmas that were facing them:

> Marshall, unstable and emotional as he is, is the only political leader in Singapore who has a chance to rally popular support against communism and who can meet on terms of ability and popular appeal to leaders of the extreme Left-wing groups.
>
> We cannot but recognise that over the last ten years Asian nationalism has created such pressures that it would be idle to think we could control them at will. At the same time HMG have to take grave account of the importance of Singapore as part of the defence system of the free world and as the logistic base for Commonwealth troops in the Federation of Malaya.
>
> The Chiefs of Staff regard Singapore as indispensable as a naval, military, air base to the support of allied forces in the Far East. They are essentially of the opinion that under no circumstances must Singapore be given its independence except possibly as a member of the Federation of Malaya. They consider that even if we remained responsible for external defence and had the right to bases in Singapore, under arrangements giving Singapore independence, we should have no more

than paper safeguards and should be in Singapore only so long as it suited the Chinese. They conclude that we should aim at a policy of union with Malaya when both sides are ready for it, and until then give Singapore full power of self-government other than internal security and the direction of prosecutions, defence, foreign affairs, franchise and of nationality. They state that the transfer of control over internal security should not take place until Singapore has adequate local forces to prevent a communist takeover and to maintain law and order without outside aid.

It appeared that Britain's Commissioner-General in Southeast Asia, Sir Rob Scott, largely concurred in the Chiefs of Staff opinion. But the High Commissioner in Malaya did not. He agreed that the logical future of Singapore lay with the Federation, but it was an illusion to assume that union of the two would offer Singapore political stability or save it, as he put it, from the clutch of Communist China. Moreover, Malay opposition in the Federation (and, it will be remembered, the government of independent Malaya would be dominated by Malays) was more solidly and strongly against any form of political union with Singapore in the immediate future than perhaps ever before. Malay opposition derived from a combination of things. First, with Singapore added on, Chinese numerical superiority would endanger Malay supremacy. Second, it might delay independence for Malaya. Third, there were fears that communism would spread from Singapore.

As Lennox-Boyd pointed out to the Cabinet, Singapore had all the elements of another "Cyprus"; but a refusal could quickly lead to a "Saigon" situation in the Island. Internal security, and the control thereof, was the key and Lennox-Boyd wanted authority to negotiate a settlement that a) did not concede complete independence (i.e., sovereignty) and b) went as far as possible toward meeting the demands of the people of Singapore, "provided it leaves us in a position to resume effective control if things go wrong."

When things did go wrong in Singapore, it was not until 1963, and then, with the carefully constructed mechanism of the Anglo-Malayan-Singaporean Internal Security Council, left-wing opponents of Mr. Lee Kuan Yew were detained. In the meantime, both Singapore and Malaya had become independent, but the British still had their bases, their investments, and even, perhaps, their respectability. The price in Malaya had been the Anglo-Malayan Defense Agreement, perhaps the most tightly constructed of all Britain's postwar security alliances, which before long would engage Britain, under a Labour government, in a small war at a financial cost no British government was prepared to pay again. In Malaya, the British had been more than fortunate to find an amiable and delightful Prime Minister; and in Singapore they had been doubly lucky—at least compared to American misfortunes with Diem. First, with Mr. David Marshall, although one would never have guessed from the Commissioner-General's "appreciation":

> The strains and excitement of the last twelve months have told heavily on Marshall, now a sick man with a persecution complex and a touch of megalomania. Clever, vain, ambitious, temperamental and inconsistent, in money matters of doubtful integrity, with acute complexes about his race and colour, he is a very lonely man, almost psychopathic. Without roots, basically irresponsible, almost recklessly fatalistic.[49]

In spite of this notable absence of British confidence, they were after all, fortunate in having an acceptable if adversarial relationship with him and, then, with the dynamic Lee Kuan Yew who, as he put it, was trying to ride a Communist tiger within his party. That was obviously something that coincided with British interests, and, with considerable if temporary mutual mistrust, Lee and the colonial government maneuvered in very close conflict, like bull and matador, although it was by no means obvious who was which. Until the climax, and the abortion, of Malaysia, Britain had faced in Singapore potentially one of the most violent manifestations of Chinese communism in Southeast Asia:

> Full self-government is likely to lead to growing unemployment, a strong communist movement and an incompetent and corrupt administration. The city would first be ruined and then transformed into a focus of communist infection for all South-East Asia, a spearhead of Chinese expansionism menacing the Indian Ocean, Indonesia, and Australia.[50]

But in spite of the echo of falling dominoes, the similarity with Vietnamese communism, perhaps, is that it was indigenous communism—and this was the difference between American and British understanding. The other difference between America and Britain in Southeast Asia during the Eisenhower era was the immense advantages that Britain had in being a genuine rather than a neocolonial power.[51] Allegorically, one may see two ships passing, one taking the British colonial civil servants home, and the other bringing the American military advisers in. As an epilogue, an episode from the Sumatra affair will serve. When the news arrived in Singapore on a Sunday morning that one of the CIA pilots flying in support of the rebels against Sukarno (one of the Dulles' brothers' adventures in destabilization) had been shot down, after accidentally bombing a church, the CIA liaison officer with British MI 6 ("found it painful to watch their cool, professional equanimity. . . . The CIA was in a full scale flap, officers pulled in from home, people running about. The British attitude was implicit but clear: by the time an operation is blown its too late to do anything about it: why all the excitement?"[52]

Or, as they might have said of Vietnam as well, "Not my show, old boy."

NOTES

1. Foreign Relations of the United States (FRUS), 1952–1954, vol. 13; *Indo-China*, Washington, D.C.: GPO, p. 1885. O'Daniel, Chief of the U.S. Military Assistance Advisory Group, thought that Vietnam-type warfare would be used by Communists everywhere, including, he added darkly, the United States.

2. March 19, 1954, PREM 11 645 Public Record Office (PRO).

3. *Ibid.*, April 9.

4. An account of the Malayan "experience" may be found in Short, *The Communist Insurrection in Malaya, 1948–1960* (London and New York: 1975). A much briefer account, "The Malayan Emergency" is in Ronald Haycock, ed., *Regular Armies and Counter-Insurgency* (London and New Jersey: 1979).

5. PREM 11 645.

6. Sir James Cable, *The Geneva Conference of 1954 on Indo-China* (London, 1986).

7. Cable, *Geneva Conference*, p. 45.

8. *Ibid.*

9. FO 371 122049. Makins had been under pressure to declare the British position since February. The Foreign Office responded: "Sir R. Makins cannot expect a snap reply on this fundamental question."

10. April 4, *FRUS, 1952–54*, 13:1238–40.

11. *Ibid.*, p. 1230

12. *Ibid.*, p. 1225. Which presumably meant the Scots didn't matter—or else they were one of Mr. Dulles' "captive nations."

13. FO 371 112050.

14. June 12, CAB 129/68.

15. FO 371 112050, April 5.

16. FO 371 112052, April 12.

17. CAB 129/68.

18. *FRUS, 1952–1954* 13:1311.

19. *Ibid.*, p. 1321.

20. The French ambassador in London had told the Foreign Office, according to the American ambassador, that when Dulles had dinner with Churchill and Eden assurances had been given that Britain was willing to join in a military contribution to Indochina. Eden denied, as did Churchill, that they had said anything of the kind. FO 371 1071, April 15.

21. Robert Rhodes James, *Anthony Eden* (London; 1986). In reality, says Rhodes James, in this instance Eden had grasped the big point, while Churchill, obsessed with keeping in with the Americans and more than sympathetic to their continuing veto of Communist China's entry into the world organization, took the small view. P. 381.

22. *Ibid*, p. 374.

23. PREM, 11 645, April 12.

24. HC Deb Vol. 526, April 13.
25. FO 371 112057.
26. *FRUS, 1952–1954* 13:1395.
27. CAB 129/68.
28. *Ibid.*
29. FO 371 112087.
30. FO 371 112085 (bound volume *Geneva Conference, April 26–July 21*).
31. CAB 129 68, June 18, 1954.
32. *Ibid*, July 1. This drew a spirited reply from the Chancellor of the Exchequer: "We have consistently refused to acknowledge anything so vague as a 'right of self-determination.' This Wilsonian doctrine has caused enough trouble in its time and we would not have thought that a Republican Administration would insist upon it"(!).
33. PREM 11 1310, March 29, 1955.
34. FO 371 117142, June, 11 1955.
35. *Ibid*, July 13.
36. *Ibid.*
37. PREM 11 1310, June 16.
38. *Ibid*, July 1.
39. *Ibid*, July 1955.
40. *Ibid*, March 25, 1955.
41. *Ibid*, May 13.
42. *Ibid*, June 27. Nehru, who kept rather an avuncular eye on Sihanouk, was particularly pained about Cambodia's obligation in the U.S. aid agreement to contribute to the defense of the free world. Sihanouk sent a disarming reply.
43. PREM 11 1310, September 10.
44. *Ibid*, September 30. Speaking in the same debate as Nehru, Krishna Menon, Nehru's roving ambassador, had said it was the job of the ICC to promote agreement between North and South Vietnam to hold elections. Eden disagreed. He, and much of the Foreign Office, regarded Krishna Menon as an infernal nuisance. On another occasion Eden penned the quintessential personal minute: "I had a difficult discussion with Krishna Menon at intervals in the Royal Tent at tea-time yesterday." The subject was Laos. Again Eden demurred.
45. PREM 11 1210, May 5.
46. Anthony Eden, *Towards Peace in Indo-China* (London, 1966). See also *Documents Relating to British Involvement in the Indo-China Conflict 1945–1965*, Cmnd. 2834 (London: HMSO, 1965).
47. Chin Kin Wah, *The Defence of Malaysia and Singapore* (Cambridge, 1983), p. 24.
48. CO 1030, February 18, 1956. In Washington the House Committee on Un-American Activities excited itself with a print, "International Communism (Communist Penetration of Malaya and Singapore)." It was the result of a small "staff consultation" with a Chinese sports editor of the Colorado Springs Free Press who had worked in Singapore for six years.
49. *Ibid.*
50. *Ibid.*
51. It could, for example, suspend the Singapore constitution—something the United States must have longed to do in Vietnam.
52. Thomas Powers, *The Man Who Kept the Secrets: Richard Helms and the CIA* (New York: 1979), p. 114.

14

The American Search for Stability in Southeast Asia: The SEATO Structure of Containment

◉

GARY R. HESS
Bowling Green State University

At both the beginning and the end of the Eisenhower administration, the United States faced crises in Southeast Asia. Indochina, which officials in Washington considered vital to the preservation of a strong Western position in the region, was the center of the crises of 1953–54 and 1960–61. It was in response to the military and political gains of the Vietnamese Communist movement that the Eisenhower administration increased significantly the level of the U.S. political, military, and economic commitment in Southeast Asia. The cornerstone of the effort to stabilize the region was the Southeast Asia Treaty Organization, which was established at the Manila Conference of September 1954—less than two months after the Geneva Conference had produced an Indochina settlement that was commonly seen as a major victory for the Soviet Union, the Chinese People's Republic, and their Vietnamese allies.

The Eisenhower administration's approach to Southeast Asia, as in other areas of the world, reflected an essential continuation of the fundamental objectives of the containment policy while introducing important changes in its implementation. The cold war decisively shaped the U.S. definition of its Southeast Asian interests, meaning that political developments in individual countries were interpreted within an analytical framework based almost solely on whether they seemingly benefited the Sino-Soviet bloc or the Western alliance. During the systematic review of national security policy that President Eisenhower initiated during his first months in office, officials of the new administration embraced without question the twin assumptions that the preservation of pro-Western governments in Southeast Asia was vital to U.S. interests and that the outcome of the French–Vietminh War would determine the future not only of Indochina, but of the region.

Such reasoning had been at the base of U.S. policy in Southeast Asia since the Truman administration had redefined America's Asian interests in 1949–50. Undertaken in response to the Communist ascendancy in the Chinese civil war, that policy review had given high priority to securing Southeast Asia. A Policy Planning Staff study, which formed the basis of NSC 48/2, held that "with China being overwhelmed by communism, Southeast Asia represents a vital segment on the line of containment, stretching from Japan southward to the Indian peninsula." U.S. security and the survival of India, Japan, and Australia necessitated "denial of Southeast Asia to the Kremlin."[1] Drawing the line also was considered essential to the revitalization of the Japanese economy and to the stabilization of sterling area economies. A series of special diplomatic, military, and economic missions to Southeast Asia called for a significantly enlarged U.S. role in the region. The outbreak of the Korean War reinforced the imperative of strengthening the Western position on China's southern frontier. This led to the military assistance agreements with Thailand in 1950, and with the Philippines in 1951, and economic assistance programs to those countries as well as Indonesia and Burma.[2]

The most important commitment to emerge from the 1949–50 policy review was U.S. support of the French in Indochina. By endorsing the Elysée Agreement which established the State of Vietnam and the kingdoms of Laos and Cambodia as "Associated States within the French Union," the United States completed an often-anguished transition from official neutrality in the French-Vietminh War to formal embrace of French policy. After extending recognition to the Bao Dai government in February 1950, the United States began direct aid to the French military effort. The Korean War linked French and American interests, as the United Nations intervention there and the French struggle in Indochina came to be seen as two fronts of the same battle to preserve the Western position in Asia. Comparing the two wars in a 1950 article, Jacques Soustelle wrote that "each results from the expansion of Soviet power . . . pushing its satellites ahead, and exploiting against the West the nationalism, even xenophobia, of the Asiatic masses."[3]

As the Eisenhower administration formulated its "New Look" strategy, that French presence in Indochina seemed essential. If the United States was to reduce its defense expenditures and thus enhance its domestic economic strength, it needed to reinforce the determination of those allies resisting Communist movements. In addition, security, it was assumed, could be enhanced without substantial U.S. commitments; instead, bilateral and multilateral alliances could be increasingly relied on to achieve deterrence. Mutual security arrangements and increased economic and military assistance, especially in third world areas, became increasingly important, as did reliance on covert operations to undermine unfriendly governments.[4]

These subtle shifts in the tactics of containment from the Truman administration's approach to national security had special relevance in Southeast Asia. NSC 153, which was a preliminary policy overview completed in June 1953, the reports of the Project Solarium task forces, and NSC 162/2, which was the comprehensive national security statement Eisenhower endorsed on October 30, 1953, all recognized the importance of the French and other allies for the American position in Asia. "In the Far East," NSC 162/2 held, "the military strength of the coalition now rests largely on U.S. military power plus that of France in Indochina, the UK in Malaya and in Hong Kong, and the indigenous forces of the Republic of Korea, Vietnam, and Nationalist China." Allies were vital to American security, for "the military striking power necessary to retaliate depends for the foreseeable future on having bases in allied countries . . . [and] the ground forces required to counter local aggressions must be supplied largely by our allies."[5]

The outcome of the Indochina War, officials assumed without question, would be the principal determinant of U.S. interests in Southeast Asia. As NSC 162/2 was being completed, the United States was cautiously sanguine about the prospects in Indochina. A change in French political and military leadership paralleled the coming to power of a new administration in Washington. General Henri Navarre was appointed commander of French forces in Indochina, and, in Paris, the new Cabinet headed by Joseph Laniel promised to "perfect" the independence of the Associated States. The French enlisted American support for an ambitious military initiative; the Navarre Plan called for strengthening the Vietnamese army, sending additional regular French troops, and concentrating these forces against the Vietminh's power base in the Red River delta. Despite reservations about the Navarre Plan's feasibility, the United States agreed in September 1953 to provide $385 million in support of the French effort.

The association with the French military effort seemed imperative, for its failure would undermine America's global position. A comprehensive overview of U.S. interests in Southeast Asia—NSC 5405, which Eisenhower endorsed on January 16, 1954—saw Indochina as the point where "the Communist and non-Communist worlds clearly confront one another on the field of battle" and concluded that a French loss "in addition to its impact in Southeast Asia and South Asia . . . would have the most serious repercussions on U.S. and free world interests in Europe and elsewhere." Because of the "interrelationship of the countries in the area," Communist ascendancy in any country would lead others in the region to align with communism; that would be followed by India and the Middle Eastern countries succumbing to Communist pressures. Moreover, the U.S. security position in the Pacific, centered in the offshore island chain, would be jeopardized. The resources of Southeast Asia and its value as a market for industrialized countries would be lost to the Soviet bloc. "With continued U.S. economic and material assistance," it was predicted, "the French-Vietnamese forces are not in danger of being militarily defeated unless there is a large-scale Chinese invasion."[6]

If the French were the key to holding the line in Southeast Asia, they also constituted a large part of the American problem. Differences over military and colonial policies had strained Franco-American relations. The French failure to grant genuine independence led to increasing resentment among the non-Communist nationalists; thus, when the Laniel government discussed its promised liberalization of colonial policy, it found the Vietnamese to be distrustful, demanding an end to the French presence altogether. American officials understood the Vietnamese position, for they had ample evidence of the remoteness and ineffectiveness of the French-supported State of Vietnam; in sum, the "Bao Dai solution" had failed. More importantly, the Navarre Plan quickly unraveled. Seizing the initiative, the Vietminh Commander, General Vo Nguyen Giap, took advantage of the ill-conceived French defense of the remote outpost at Dienbienphu, thus setting the stage for the decisive battle of the eight-year war. In France, war-weariness became chronic, leading to demands for a negotiated end to the conflict. The Soviet Union, as part of the post-Stalinist leadership's program of "peaceful coexistence," called for reduction of tensions and championed Indochina negotiations. In early 1954, Britain and France — despite U.S. objections — accepted inclusion of Indochina on the agenda of the conference that was to meet at Geneva in the spring to consider outstanding Asian issues.

The United States, fearing that the Western allies would be bargaining from a position of weakness, reluctantly accepted negotiations. Yet it could not alienate Britain and France, for both were vital to American interests in Europe and Asia. Indeed, ever since the beginning of the Southeast Asian nationalist struggles against the European colonial powers after World War II, the importance of its allies to cold war strategy in Europe had limited American options in dealing with Asian nationalism. Thus, throughout the French-Vietminh War, the United States had been able to exert only limited influence on French colonial and military policy. The substantial U.S. contribution to the French military effort had brought no significant leverage. France's capacity to defer American suggestions on Indochina policy continued, for a priority of U.S. global strategy in 1954 was enlisting French participation in the European Defense Community.[7]

During the Indochina crisis of the spring and summer of 1954, the United States, in the words of Secretary of State John Foster Dulles, engaged in "holding action" diplomacy to prevent the Vietminh from gaining control of all of Vietnam. This came to mean a strategy of: a) strengthening the French resolve in Indochina; b) assuming an ambivalent position during the Geneva negotiations, thus assuring the option of dissociation from an unacceptable settlement; and c) planning for a system of collective defense in Southeast Asia. This approach thus calculated that U.S. military power—evident in the option of military intervention in Indochina and in the potential collective defense arrangement—would strengthen America's allies and deter the Communist powers.

Ultimately, however, the effort to sustain the French failed, and the settlement reached at Geneva constituted, in the view of American officials and leading congressional spokesmen, a Western defeat. Without an effort to draw the line against further Communist advances, the settlement, it was widely assumed, would lead to Sino-Soviet domination of Indochina, and perhaps of all Southeast Asia. Those developments made the collective defense program vital to the realization of U.S. objectives.

In the prolonged French-American dialogue over the war in the spring of 1954, the French made continuation of their struggle against the Vietminh conditional upon U.S. military intervention. Eisenhower, in turn, made U.S. intervention conditional upon congressional and allied support. That led to the first public expression of the idea of collective defense. In a speech of March 29, Dulles proposed "United Action" in Southeast Asia. Linking the Vietminh with the "Communist imperialism" of the Soviet Union and China, Dulles stated that" "the imposition on Southeast Asia of the political system of Communist Russia and its Chinese ally, by whatever means, would be a grave threat to the whole free community. The United States feels that that possibility should not be passively accepted but should be met by united action." While vague in certain ways, United Action anticipated that agreement among the U.S., Britain, France, Australia, New Zealand, the Philippines, Thailand, and the Associated States would deter Communist expansion. At the NSC meeting of April 6, the Secretary held that the outcome in Indochina would be determined largely by such a coalition; "if we could effect a real political grouping, the Communists might well give up their intent to seize the area." Eisenhower added that the coalition "must go forward as a matter of greatest urgency."[8]

That urgency, however, was not shared by the British; Prime Minister Winston Churchill and Foreign Secretary Anthony Eden insisted that priority had to be given to a negotiated settlement. In the end the United States had to accept delaying movement on collective defense. Even as the French capacity to hold Dienbienphu eroded, Eisenhower still firmly opposed unilateral intervention. At his April 29 press conference, Eisenhower stated the need to steer "a course between two extremes, one of which . . . would be unattainable, the other unacceptable."[9]

As the Indochina phase of the Geneva Conference began on May 8 —the day after the fall of Dienbienphu—American officials could foresee only the "unacceptable extreme." Any compromise settlement, it was assumed, would lead inevitably to the Vietminh's domination of Vietnam. A coalition government was the "most dangerous possibility," for by enhancing Ho Chi Minh's prestige it would lead to the consolidation of Communist control "with the subversion of all of Southeast Asia to follow." The partition of Vietnam would be such a "catastrophic settlement" that it would be best if "responsibility [were] borne by the French alone." To forestall those alternatives, the United States pressed France to stand firmly while itself assuming an anomalous role at Geneva. Undersecretary of State Walter Bedell Smith headed the U.S. delegation during the Indochina negotiations, Dulles' conspicuous absence serving as a reminder of the U.S. attitude. Dulles instructed Smith that he represented an "interested nation" that was not a "principal in the negotiations"; the United States would not be associated with a settlement that meant losing Indochina to the "Communist bloc of imperialistic dictatorship." An acceptable settlement had to embody international control machinery and evacuation of Vietminh forces from Laos and Cambodia, but could not include any provisions that would lead to Communist control.[10]

The Geneva Conference negotiations, however, fulfilled American forebodings. The United States exerted some influence through the continuing option of intervention and the advocacy of United Action.

The Laniel government eventually despaired of the conditions attached to intervention, and with its fall on June 12, the French momentum to withdraw from Indochina became irresistible. The new Premier, Pierre Mendès-France, dramatically established a deadline of July 20 to reach an acceptable settlement. The Soviet Union and China quickly offered important concessions on the issues of the composition of an international control commision and the withdrawal of Vietminh forces from Laos and Cambodia. When Churchill and Eden arrived in Washington for conversations on the weekend of June 25–27, the British and American positions on an Indochina settlement seemingly converged. In essence, the U.S. accepted the partition of Vietnam in return for British support of a united effort to hold the non-Communist areas of Indochina. A joint seven-point statement on "minimum terms," while deliberately ambiguous and inconsistent on issues that still defied agreement, clearly anticipated the partition of Vietnam, but also stipulated that no provisions in the final settlement should risk the loss of southern Vietnam, Laos, and Cambodia to Communist forces.[11]

When the conference resumed, Dulles declined to have Smith return to Geneva, using the threat of U.S. nonparticipation in the final negotiations as a means of influencing that process as well as of appeasing right-wing Republican critics of the conference. This posturing, however, annoyed the British and French. At Eisenhower's insistence, Dulles went to Paris, where he met with Eden and Mendès-France, both of whom left Geneva to plead for U.S. participation. Dulles agreed to Smith's return, while insisting that France acknowledge the U.S. reservations about the negotiations and the Anglo-American seven-point agreement. Dulles' Paris mission may have been evidence, as he boasted to the NSC, that "when it really comes down to something important, the United States is the key nation." Eden and Mendès-France had rushed to Paris, leaving the Soviet and Chinese foreign ministers "cooling their heels." The evidence of Western solidarity likely influenced the Soviet Union and China to pressure the Democratic Republic of Vietnam (DRV) to accept a compromise on the partition line and other issues. Moreover, the cause of collective defense in Southeast Asia had been advanced; Dulles told Eisenhower on July 15 that the British and French now understood that "we did not particularly like the idea of partition of Vietnam but would go along with it if they agreed to support the American effort to form promptly . . . a Southeast Asia Treaty Organization."[12]

As the negotiations at Geneva moved quickly toward a settlement, the United States sought, above all, to assure that its program of collective defense would not be restricted. The "U.S. position," Dulles instructed Smith, "is still that it will not negotiate and sign with Communist bloc any multilateral declaration on Geneva Conference or any agreement issuing therefrom." In an effort to involve the United States in the settlement, Molotov and Eden worked out the device of listing the conference participants in the preamble to the Final Declaration (which complemented the French-DRV armistice). Rather than signing the declaration, each participant was to give an oral statement. The U.S. declaration—"a calculated ambiguity"—offered a conditional promise to support the agreements while maintaining freedom of action.

Upon his return to Washington, Smith accurately described the agreement as "the best that could be expected under the circumstances. . . . Diplomacy is rarely able to gain at the conference table that which cannot be gained on the field of battle." In many ways, however, the West had gained more than the military situation would have dictated, for the DRV had been obliged by the Soviet Union and China to accept not only the division of Vietnam, but the seventeenth parallel as the line of demarcation; that was a significant concession, considering that the initial French-Vietminh proposals on demarcation had been the eighteenth and thirteenth parallels, respectively. The DRV also had to withdraw its troops from southern Vietnam, Laos, and Cambodia, and it was denied a role in the political settlement in Laos and Cambodia while having to accept a delay until 1956 of Vietnamese unification elections. Dulles conceded privately that the "Communist demands had turned out to be relatively moderate in terms of their actual capabilities."[13]

Yet in other ways, the DRV gained significantly from the Geneva settlement. The legitimacy of the DRV in northern Vietnam was given international recognition. Assuming that the provisions for French withdrawal and for the nonintroduction of other outside military forces were fulfilled, the Vietminh would be in a position to achieve its objective of national unification. It was that prospect, and its ramifications for neighboring countries, that led to the immediate U.S. dissociation from the Geneva settlement. The United States, Eisenhower said on July 21, "had not itself been party to or bound by the decisions taken by the Conference." The important task must be "the rapid organization of a collective defense in Southeast Asia." Two days later Dulles asserted that the "important thing was not to mourn the past but to seize the future opportunity to prevent the loss in northern Vietnam from leading to the extension of Communism throughout Southeast Asia and the Southwest Pacific." The time was now opportune, the Secretary went on, "to bring about the collective arrangements to promote the security of the free peoples of Southeast Asia." At an NSC meeting, Dulles defined the American task: "the great problem . . . is whether we [can] salvage what the Communists had ostensibly left out of their grasp in Indochina." NSC 5429—the post-Geneva policy review endorsed by Eisenhower on August 20— held that the "Communists have secured an advance salient in Vietnam from which military and nonmilitary pressures can be mounted against adjacent and more remote non-Communist areas. . . . The situation must be stabilized as soon as possible to prevent further losses through (1) creeping expansion and subversion, or (2) overt aggression."[14]

However important Southeast Asia was in terms of U.S. security, the Eisenhower administration assumed that it could not make significant military commitments in the region. Dulles wrote that "we do not envisage a security pact developing into NATO-type organization with large permanent machinery under large forces-in-being to which [the United States] would be committed [to] contribute forces for local defense." That limited involvement reflected not only the general reluctance to increase conventional military expenditures, but also grew out of the recognition that the American capacity to influence developments in the area was limited and that the long-term prospects were not especially favorable. "I expressed my concern [to Eisenhower] with reference to projected [Southeast Asia] Treaty," Dulles recorded, "on the ground that it involved committing the prestige of the United States in an area where we had little control and where the situation was by no means promising. On the other hand, I said that failure to go ahead would mark a total abandonment of the area without a struggle. . . . The President agreed we should go ahead." Hence, the unfavorable prospects for the region that provided the imperative for SEATO also limited the level of commitment, for the greater the American involvement, the greater the risk to American prestige.[15]

Beyond avoiding a military commitment, the Eisenhower administration also discouraged suggestions that SEATO would involve any special claims on U.S. economic assistance programs. Not only would that encounter congressional opposition, but it would also alienate Asian countries that did not participate. Yet the Asian nations that were prepared to associate themselves with the American-led defense system expected that it would be accompanied by a large-scale program of economic assistance. The Philippines, which had long resented the levels of American economic assistance to Europe and the priority given to Japan's economic revitalization, especially championed the idea of an Asian Marshall Plan as part of SEATO.

The American insistence that SEATO be established quickly after the Geneva Conference brought attention to the fragile basis for a collective defense system. Differences with the British over Asian priorities, which had been evident throughout the Indochina crisis, combined with difficulties of enlisting Asian support to plague the development of the defense system. The British defined their Southeast Asian interests much more narrowly than the Americans and did not share the sense that Indochina was critical to the future of the region. Any British contribution to a defense system, Churchill wrote Eisenhower on June 21, had to be limited; "our main sector must be Malaya." Yet the British also refused to play second-fiddle to the Americans. Shortly after Dulles' initial United Action proposal, Sir Roger Makins, the British ambassador in Washington, warned the Foreign Office that allowing the United States to champion a coalition would enhance its influence throughout Southeast Asia as well as with Australia and New Zealand. Reflecting the long-standing British resentment over the ANZUS agreement, Makins added that the British had to "work for a security system in which we shall have our rightful place." The British were also sensitive to pressures from the newly independent Asian countries, especially India, not to be part of an international arrangement that suggested a resurgence of Western imperialism. To Eden and other British officials, it was essential to accommodate the Colombo powers (India, Pakistan, Ceylon, Burma, and Indonesia), which in the spring of 1954 had called for an Indochina cease-fire and a negotiated settlement. Given the close economic and cultural ties of those nations to the West, the British and Americans agreed that it was essential to secure, if not their participation, at least their benevolent neutrality.

The issue of Asian membership gave the British leverage in dealing with the United States, which wanted to involve a number of Asian countries in SEATO. With the Philippines and Thailand as the only Asian countries initially inclined toward participation, the United States risked sponsorship of a regional defense arrangement in which most of the participants would come from outside the area to be protected. Moreover, the Philippines and Thailand were already closely tied to the United States, so that the defense arrangement was not increasing Asian association with the West.

The Philippines and Thailand had special interest in the regional defense proposal. Philippine leaders had for years championed a Pacific security pact, seeing in it a means by which their country could play an enlarged role internationally and enhance its claims on more American economic and military assistance. Philippine-American relations improved in November 1953, when the Filipinos elected Ramon Magsaysay to the presidency. U.S. officials had long considered

Magsaysay to be the type of vigorous leader desperately needed in the Philippines; as Defense Minister from 1950 to 1953, he had led the military campaign against the Communist-led Hukbalahap movement. That effort had been strongly supported by U.S. military assistance and the advice of the CIA counterinsurgency operative Edward G. Lansdale. Lansdale and other American officials had supported Magsaysay's emergence as a presidential candidate, seeing him vastly preferable to the discredited Elpidio Quirino. In the opinion of most American observers, Quirino's political posturing, pettiness, and incessant demands were all too reminiscent of Chiang Kai-shek. In sum, Magsaysay's prestige gave his calls for a Pacific pact greater credibility than those of his distrusted predecessor.

Among the countries of Southeast Asia, Thailand most closely shared the American apprehension over the prospects of a Communist-dominated Indochina. Pibul Songgram, whose return to power in 1948 had brought political stability at the price of constitutional government, consistently supported U.S. policy in Asia. As the French position weakened in Indochina, Thailand pressed the United States for increased military and economic assistance. While the Eisenhower administration was generally sympathetic, it was reluctant to commit the level of military aid sought by the Thais. To Bangkok, SEATO thus offered a means of moving closer to a military alliance with the United States.

British influence in the former European colonies, U.S. officials believed, was the instrument for enlisting wider Asian support. Eden may have exploited that connection by exaggerating his concern over Asian membership in order to enhance the British bargaining position. Certainly he used the argument that the Asian countries could not be rushed into making a decision to justify delaying consideration of the collective defense proposal until after the Geneva Conference.[16]

By the time the Geneva settlements had been reached, the United States pressed for immediate action on collective defense. Indeed, Washington's planning was well advanced; by July 9 the State Department had completed a draft treaty. The proposal reflected the determination to hold the area with a minimal American commitment. By the terms of the proposed Article II, members would develop "individual and collective capacity to resist armed attack, and Communist subversion and infiltration." Article III-1 provided the groundwork for including Laos, Cambodia, and southern Vietnam in the treaty area; it stipulated that each member would recognize that "an armed attack . . . on any of the Parties, or on any states which the Parties by unanimous agreement would so designate" endangered its own security and would "meet the common danger in accord with its constitutional processes." In an effort to deal with subversion and guerrilla warfare, article III-2 added that if the security of any member were "affected by an aggression which is not an armed attack," the others would consult on the appropriate means of collective defense.

The other prospective members strongly opposed the American proposal, and in the six weeks between the Geneva and Manila conferences, the United States reluctantly accepted a series of compromises. Great Britain, Australia, and New Zealand objected to several provisions in the July 9 draft treaty; they argued that "Communist subversion and infiltration" lacked any treaty precedent; and "aggression which is not an attack" lacked not only precedent, but meaning as well. In addition, they sought inclusion of a provision for economic cooperation.[17]

The American planning was further complicated by the unexpected and unwelcome decision of Pakistan to seek membership. Britain, at Washington's request, had solicited the Colombo powers, but this seemed a futile gesture since India and Indonesia—the two most influential members of the group and the largest countries in South and Southeast Asia, respectively—had indicated their unwillingness to participate. The British entreaties had been intended principally to gain the "benign neutrality" of the Colombo nations, which, it was hoped, might lead to their membership in the future.

Pakistan was not a Southeast Asia country and was not covered in the proposed "treaty area." Its prospective membership foreshadowed the prospects of drawing SEATO into the defense of Pakistan's fragile frontiers with India. In addition, Pakistan looked upon membership as a means of enhancing its economic and military relationship with the United States—a program of military assistance having been initiated earlier in 1954—which it sought principally as a means of redressing its power imbalance with India. Thus, Pakistan's membership would add to the already serious strains in Indo-American relations. Even Dulles, who had little tolerance for Indian nonalignment, acknowledged that it would be very difficult to include Pakistan unless India also agreed to join.

The United States endeavored to dissuade Pakistan. State Department officials pointedly asked Pakistani Ambassador S. Amjad Ali whether his country's interests would be enhanced by membership. Did Pakistan not need to strengthen its domestic economy before undertaking more substantial military commitments? Did Pakistan want to be isolated from the other Colombo powers? In response to this not very subtle indication of American reluctance to welcome his country into SEATO, Ali replied that Pakistan would attempt to enlist

Ceylon's participation. That possibility altered the American attitude, for having both Pakistan and Ceylon in SEATO would place India on the defensive. The U.S. ambassador in India, Richard V. Allen, observed that if Pakistan could prevail upon Ceylon to join or even to adopt a benevolent attitude, then Burma might not be hostile. As a result, Indian criticism would be muted, for as Allen wrote, "Nehru could hardly lash out against all his neighbors." U.S. officials even considered moving the SEATO conference to Colombo as a means of encouraging Ceylon's participation.

The Pakistan-Ceylon link, however, failed. Ceylon's Prime Minister, Sir John Kotewala, told the U.S. ambassador that he personally supported SEATO, but pointedly added that he would have to consult with other Colombo nations before reaching a decision. On August 12 Ceylon formally declined an invitation to the Manila Conference. U.S. officials blamed India for Ceylon's disaffection. While the Indian position unquestionably influenced Ceylon's decision, Ceylonese officials later indicated that nonparticipation reflected their country's resentment over being presented with a *fait accompli*. Regardless of the reasons for Ceylon's nonparticipation, the United States was left with Pakistan as the third, and least welcome, Asian member of SEATO.[18]

Hence, as the State Department revised its draft treaty, it sought not only to accommodate the Western allies' criticisms of the July 9 draft, but also to avoid further alienation of the nonaligned bloc. A revised proposal added an article on economic cooperation "with each other and other like-minded states," thus meeting the Asian members' concerns about the lack of economic cooperation but without limiting economic and technical assistance programs to the alliance. And in deference to other criticisms of the July 9 draft, the State Department relented on article II, substituting "subversive activities from without" for the objectionable "Communist subversion and infiltration."

Yet in other ways, the United States was uncompromising. State Department officials and the Joint Chiefs of Staff feared that SEATO would draw the United States into colonial disputes and rivalries between non-communist states. Those concerns were reinforced by congressional leaders, who opposed any treaty that involved ill-defined commitments. Hence, the State Department sought to retain a clear anti-Communist objective. The revised draft of August 24 proposed a preamble in which members would declare "their sense of unity, so that any potential Communist aggressor will appreciate that the Parties stand together." Moreover, in Article IV (formerly III) members were to recognize that "Communist aggression by means of armed attack against any of the Parties or against Cambodia, Laos, or

the territory under the jurisdiction of the free Vietnamese government
. . . would endanger its own peace and security, and . . . would . . .
meet the common danger in accord with its constitutional processes."
Meeting with Douglas MacArthur II, the State Department Counselor
who would serve as the U.S. representative on a preconference working group that was to meet in Manila beginning on September 1,
Dulles was adamant that the United States "hold fast" to the references to Communist aggression in the preamble and article IV.[19]

As the August 24 draft was sent to the Manila Conference participants, it became immediately evident that the American approach
was destroying the limited coherence of the coalition. By August 28,
all of the prospective members, except Thailand, had objected to the
"Communist aggression" provisions. Such restrictive language, they
observed, was without treaty precedent and would alienate further
the nonaligned nations, thus foreclosing the prospects for additional
Asian membership in the future. MacArthur put it bluntly to Dulles:
"if the Manila Conference is to result in the initialling of a Treaty, we
are going to have to agree to eliminate the word 'communist.' " Dulles
charged that the other parties were "more interested in trying not to
annoy the Communists than in stopping them." The British and French
were "blocking everything we want to do." Eden's role in coordinating the objections to the American draft treaties especially annoyed
Dulles. The Foreign Secretary's last minute decision not to head the
British delegation at Manila compounded Dulles' irritation, but was
perhaps an appropriate British retaliation for the equivocal American
role at Geneva. Angered by the behavior of the wayward allies, Dulles
privately threatened not to attend the Manila meeting.[20]

In the end Dulles went to the Manila Conference because he had no
choice. SEATO was so clearly an expression of U.S. strategic interests
that his absence would have undermined the substantial realization
of Dulles's call for collective defense. At length Dulles agreed to eliminate the "Communist aggression" references, again because he had
no choice. That was the price for building this most fragile of coalitions. Dulles' opening address to the conference underscored the am-
biguities and limitations of the treaty structure. If the Communist
powers considered their victory in Indochina a bridge to further advance, the United States and its allies were warning any aggressor
that an attack on the treaty area would provoke a reaction "so united,
so strong, and so well placed" that the aggressor would "lose more
than it could hope to gain." Yet Dulles acknowledged that subversion
and infiltration posed the mostly likely challenges to regional stability and conceded that "no simple and no single formula" could withstand such pressures.

Despite the compromises, U.S. interests were substantially recognized in the Southeast Asia Collective Defense Treaty. The elimination of the "Communist aggression" provisions was offset by a U.S. "understanding" that accompanied the signing of the treaty to the effect that the United States interpreted Article IV as applying "only to Communist aggresion." In addition, at American urging, a treaty protocol declared that Cambodia, Laos, and "free territory of Vietnam under the jurisdiction of the State of Vietnam" were included into the provisions of Article IV. Under pressure from the Asian participants, the United States eliminated reference to the "like-minded states" in the economic cooperation article, but at the same time the Americans refused to incorporate any commitment to large-scale economic assistance. Finally, the U.S. delegation resisted pressures for an elaborate administrative and military organization on the scale of NATO, with the result that the SEATO structure was limited to a council with vague consultative responsibilities.[21]

The weaknesses of SEATO were obvious from the outset. It not only lacked substantial Asian support, but in fact alienated the largest and most influential countries in South and Southeast Asia. That alienation was exploited by China, in ways that enhanced its prestige and influence. In a sense, then, SEATO ironically gave greater influence to the very power it sought to isolate. Moreover, the lack of provision for economic cooperation and the limited capacity to deal with aggression and subversion restricted SEATO's effectiveness. Shortly after the conference, Vice Admiral A. C. Davis, a member of the U.S. delegation, observed that SEATO served "more a psychological than a military purpose. The area is no better prepared than before to cope with Communist aggression."[22]

Yet that type of defense system substantially fulfilled American objectives. SEATO served as a means of deterrence but without commitment. When combined with American nuclear capacity and other instruments of containment, it offered a means of revitalizing the American position in Southeast Asia. SEATO integrated existing ties with the Philippines and Thailand with the support of the South Vietnamese government. "For the United States," Russell Fifield has written," the Manila Treaty of 1954 was designed to deter overt armed aggression from Communist China . . . and provide a shield to buy time for American and related programs of aid which might lead to the economic and social advance of the people, to greater stability in their governments, and to the reduction of Communist appeal."[23]

A vastly expanded program of military and economic-technical assistance was a critical instrument of the redefined containment structure. Toward the objective of building larger armed forces among the regional allies, the United States substantially increased military assistance to the Philippines and Thailand; those countries received military support valued at $218 million and $229.4 millions, respectively, between 1953 and 1961. The commitment to Thailand was especially significant, considering that U.S. military assistance to that country between 1950 and 1952 had totalled $17 million. The most substantial military assistance effort—approximating $800 million—was for building the army of South Vietnam. Relatively modest levels of military aid were also given to Cambodia and Laos, with the objective of supporting (at least initially in the case of Laos) the capacity of neutral governments to withstand insurgency.

While the Eisenhower administration resisted pressures for an Asian Marshall Plan, its effort to stabilize the region included increased reliance upon economic and technical assistance. Addressing representatives of the Colombo Plan nations meeting at Ottawa in October 1954, Harold Stassen, director of the Foreign Operations Administration, proposed a broad multilateral regional development program, to which he pledged increased U.S. economic assistance. Stassen may have characteristically overstated the administration's case, but not the essence of its thinking. Eisenhower stated in December that the Asian situation demanded a new plan for economic development and that he would propose a special Asian economic fund.

The Eisenhower administration's foreign assistance programs consistently encountered stiff opposition in Congress, especially from the conservative wing of the Republican Party. The President's plea for a $200 million special Asian economic development fund was pared to $100 million in fiscal year 1956 and was eliminated entirely the following year.

Despite continuing executive-congressional tensions over economic assistance manifested in the persistent congressional reductions of presidential requests, the United States' economic and technical assistance programs in Southeast Asia increased significantly. The principal beneficiaries were those governments linked to the U.S. containment strategy. Thailand, whose economic and technical assistance from the United States totaled about $31 million between 1951 and 1954 (all references in discussing assistance programs are to fiscal years), received $107 million over the 1955–1957 period. Even in the Philippines, which traditionally had a high claim on U.S. assistance, U.S. aid increased from an average of $19.9 million per year from 1951 to 1954 to an average of $26.7 million during the next three years. The most dramatic commitment was in Indochina. Economic-technical assistance programs, channeled through the French, had averaged $23 million per year from 1951 to 1955. The United States, now engaged in direct assistance, provided $41.53 million in 1956 and $65.88 million in 1957.[24]

Economic assistance also came to be seen, more so than earlier, as a means of solidifying relations with the nonaligned Asian nations. The initiatives of the Soviet Union and China in identifying with the strong anti-Western sentiments in Asia added to the pressures to improve relations with such influential countries as India and Indonesia. Indeed, the approach to the nonaligned countries reflected greater sophistication than the rhetorical outbursts of Dulles about the immorality of neutralism implied. Eisenhower, despite his suspicion of any type of leftist nationalism, recognized that the United States had to reach accommodation with the nonaligned, socialist-oriented world. Lecturing a recalcitrant Republican senator who opposed aiding neutral countries, Eisenhower observed that he "want[ed] to wage the war in a militant, but reasonable, style whereby we appeal to the people of the world as a better group to hang with than the communists." He approved of neutrality because it served not only the interests of the countries themselves, but of the United States as well. The United States could not reasonably guarantee the defense of India, for instance, but it could provide economic assistance; Eisenhower repeatedly argued that foreign aid was America's "best investment." In a 1956 letter the President elaborated: "for a long time, I have held that it is a very grave error to ask some of these nations to announce themselves as being on our side. . . . Such a statement on the part of a weak country like Burma, or even India, would at once make them our all-out ally and we would have the impossible task of helping them arm for defense." Moreover, a Communist attack upon any country allied with the United States would "be viewed in most of the world as a more or less logicial consequence . . . the reaction . . . would be 'Well, they asked for it.' On the other hand, if the Soviets attacked an avowed neutral, world opinion would be outraged."[25]

Despite the objections of many outspoken Republicans in Congress, the Eisenhower administration carried forward its effort to expand assistance programs with the nonaligned countries. In the process, it generally "outspent" the Sino-Soviet bloc. The United States responded quickly when Burma indicated its willingness to receive assistance after a lapse of three years. In 1953 the Burmese government had curtailed U.S. assistance programs out of concern that its neutrality was being compromised. It had been apprehensive over the implications of having economic assistance allocated under the Mutual Security Act. More importantly, the American support of the Chinese Nationalist government at a time when Kuomintang forces were still in northern Burma had threatened Burma's relations with the People's Republic. In 1957 the United States resumed economic and technical assistance, allocating $25 million—which almost equaled the total assistance between 1951 and 1953. Similarly, the United States indicated its interest in expanding assistance efforts in Indonesia, with the result that U.S. economic and technical assistance, which had averaged about $6 million per year between 1951 and 1955, was increased to $11 million in 1956 and to $26.7 million in 1957.[26]

The sense of crisis that led to the U.S. policy review of 1954 gradually gave way to the conviction among American officials, congressional leaders, and others that the regional initiatives were working. Developments in the Philippines and South Vietnam seemingly confirmed the potential for developing pro-Western, democratic political and economic systems. In both cases, dynamic leadership seemingly offered the key to resisting Communist insurgency.

American officials saw in Magsaysay's election to the Philippine presidency in 1953 the promise of leadership that could not only stabilize that country but also strengthen anti-Communist forces throughout Asia. Magsaysay's role in the prolonged battle against the Huks, his pro-American position on international issues, and his strong support among the Philippine elite meant, in the words of Ambassador Raymond A. Spruance, that "the United States must do everything possible [to] make [his] administration [a] success . . . [for] after he has achieved such success domestically and so has prevented any substantial reduction in his current prestige and popularity with [the] mass of [the] Filipino people, he should assume [a] natural position of leadership in Southeast Asia, perhaps in Formosa, Korea."[27] Reflecting such assessments of Magsaysay's potential role, the United States urged a program of land reform as vital to internal stability and offered concessions on two issues—the tariff and military bases —that had troubled U.S.–Phillipine relations since independence.

American officials believed that only a program of land reform would forestall a resurgence of rural radicalism. Magsaysay, as a presidential candidate in 1953, had appealed to the landless peasants. After some prodding from Washington, a land tenure reform program was enacted in 1955.

At the same time, in the negotiations leading to the Laurel-Langley Agreement, the United States agreed to eliminate certain of the inequitable aspects of the U.S.–Philippine Trade Agreement of 1946. In particular, the Philippines was given some tariff protection against U.S. imports, and Philippine exporters were offered greater access to the U.S. market; the pegging of the value of the peso to the dollar was ended; quotas on all Philippine exports except sugar and cordage were also ended; and parity rights in investment were made reciprocal. The Eisenhower administration told Congress that the compromises in the Laurel-Langley Agreement were a necessary reward for the Philippine government's anticommunism. The State Department urged approval, not on economic grounds, but "in light of the present situation in the Far East."

Besides the trade issue, the United States also dealt with the troublesome questions arising from the Military Bases Agreement of 1947. The large U.S. military presence, combined with the trade issue, underscored the neocolonial relationship. The sprawling Clark Air Base, which occupied 130,000 acres, including the city of Olongapo, symbolized the American military position, which included numerous other air and naval facilities. Compromise on these matters was more difficult than in the trade area, but negotiations eventually led to the joint statement issued in 1956 by Magsaysay and Vice President Richard Nixon acknowledging Philippine sovereignty over the bases. Carlos Romulo proclaimed that this statement was "the most effective refutation of all the Communist prattle that the United States has mercenary motives or aggressive designs." In another gesture to Philippine sensitivity, the United States in 1959 relinquished control over some of the unused base areas and the city of Olongapo.

The American initiatives of the Magsaysay era, despite their aura of "reform" and "compromise," did not fundamentally alter the symbiotic relationship of American political-military-economic interests with those of the Philippine elite. The land reform measures were modest, intended to maintain the wealth and status of the elite. Little land was redistributed, and the tenancy rate actually increased. The Laurel-Langley Agreement did not harm U.S. concerns, nor did it help the Philippines break its dependence on the American market. In fact, the Philippine industries that were able to expand their exports in the U.S. market were mostly American-capitalized. The elimination of the peso-dollar valuation was meaningless, for the Philippine currency was still subject to International Monetary Fund control, in which U.S. influence was predominant. The reciprocity of parity rights did not eliminate the American investment opportunity in the Philippines, but in fact expanded it into all areas of enterprise. Filipinos gained the same rights in the United States, but they lacked the capacity to invest substantially.

In sum, the American response to Magsaysay's leadership continued the neocolonial relationship. Yet the sense of American accomplishment in the Philippines survived Magsaysay's death in early 1957. His successor, Carlos Garcia, may have lacked Magsaysay's charisma, but not his commitment to preserving the close ties with the United States.[28]

If Magsaysay was "America's Boy" in the Philippines, then Ngo Dinh Diem was "America's Mandarin" in South Vietnam. From Washington's perspective, South Vietnam's development under Diem's leadership amounted to a "miracle." Indeed, during the year after the Geneva Conference, Diem emerged from obscurity into the unquestioned leader of the government responsible for the administration of Vietnam south of the seventeenth parallel. Diem's success depended, in large part, on American support; but it also reflected a good deal of luck and poor judgment on the part of his opponents.

The American connection with Diem strained Franco-American relations. From the time of Diem's appointment as Prime Minister in June 1954, the French regarded him with contempt—a result, in large part, of his strong animosity toward French colonialism—and sought to find a more pliable leader. American officials recognized Diem's shortcomings; no less than the French, they saw Diem as a man of narrow vision, pettiness, remoteness, and complacency. He lacked popular support, not having been associated with the struggle against the French. Diem won American backing only because he appeared to be better than any other leader in the South. Those supported by the French were generally Francophiles, who faced even greater obstacles than Diem in gaining public favor. Hence throughout the tense months of late 1954 and 1955—when a chaotic political and economic situation prevailed in the South—the United States stood by Diem against the intrigues of the French and his domestic opponents, principally the Cao Dai and Hoa Hao religious sects and the gangsterish Binh Xuyen. Edward Lansdale of the CIA, fresh from his role in helping to suppress the Huks, provided critical support. In the spring of 1955, Diem's army dramatically withstood its most serious challenge from the sects, thus securing his position. The United States took the occasion to force France's hand once and for all, and shortly thereafter the French began a phased withdrawal of their forces and other official personnel. Buoyed by his success, Diem called for a national referendum, winning an astounding 98 percent of the vote. However fraudulent that election, Diem had built an impressive political base by the summer of 1955.

Over the next six years, the United States undertook a major commitment in South Vietnam. It provided over $1 billion in assistance (nearly 80 percent of which was military), making South Vietnam the fifth largest recipient of U.S. aid. The U.S. mission in Saigon became the largest in the world, and some 1,500 Americans worked in South

Vietnam. The evidence of political stability, affluence in Saigon, and increased rice production suggested that a "miracle" was indeed occurring.

In fact, the American–South Vietnamese collaboration had serious shortcomings. The "miracle" was restricted to the cities, for in the countryside, where 90 percent of the population lived, economic conditions had not improved. Moreover, despite consistent American prodding, Diem failed to broaden his political base; in fact, he undertook measures in the rural areas that further alienated his government from the peasantry. And despite his lip service to democratic ideals, Diem countenanced no political opposition, effectively suppressing all criticism. In sum, the government of South Vietnam was so dependent politically and economically upon the United States than any lessening of the American commitment threatened its collapse.

By the end of the Eisenhower administration, the shortcomings of the "miracle" were becoming evident. Opposition to Diem's repressive measures slowly developed, being hindered initially by Diem's success in destroying much of the Vietminh network and by the North Vietnamese reluctance to intervene in the South. By 1960, however, the dissidents in the South—now typically called the Vietcong—were supported by the North and had begun a campaign of terrorism against government officials.[29]

Yet the immediate crisis in 1960–61, as the Eisenhower presidency was ending, was not in Vietnam, but in neighboring Laos. The unraveling there of an effort to build an anti-Communist bastion seemed to threaten the entire SEATO structure. The central U.S. objective in Laos had been to prevent the Communist Pathet Lao movement from gaining political influence. The United States had given military and economic assistance to the neutralist government so long as it resisted pressures for a coalition government that would include the Pathet Lao. When Prime Minister Souvanna Phouma pursued a policy of national unification, the United States curtailed aid and worked to repace him. In the summer of 1958, a pro-American government under Phoui Sannikone came to power, due in large part to CIA machinations, but even with a resumption of U.S. aid, it survived only until December 1959. After several months of instability, Souvanna Phouma returned to the premiership in August 1960. By that time, U.S. policy in Laos was in disarray and that obscure country had become a focus of East-West differences.[30]

That the political status of Laos had become a major issue spoke to the limitations of the Eisenhower approach toward Southeast Asia. The unquestioned assumption that the "loss" of any country would have ramifications throughout the region reflected an unwillingness to examine the political, social, and economic developments in the region except through cold war terms. Looking upon Southeast Asia in a "zero sum" manner gave equal importance to all countries. The Laotian situation also underscored a central dilemma of U.S. policy as it took shape in 1954–55: if Southeast Asia was so vital to U.S. global interests, how could the United States place limits on its power? Eisenhower never had to reconcile the problem of coordinating ends with means. Eventually the Kennedy administration accepted a compromise in Laos, but neither it nor the Johnson administration was prepared to compromise in Vietnam. As South Vietnam faced collapse in 1965, Johnson at length resolved the inconsistency that had been central to U.S. policy since 1954. In sum, the SEATO structure brought a temporary, but not inconsequential, coherence to U.S. policy.

NOTES

1. "U.S. Policy toward Southeast Asia," Policy Planning Staff (PPS) Paper, (March 29, 1949, State Dept. Files, PPS Files, box 2.

2. On the 1949–50 policy review, see William S. Borden, *The Pacific Alliance: The United States Foreign Economic Policy and Japanese Trade Recovery, 1947–1954* (Madison, Wisc., Univ. of Wisconsin Press, 1984); Andrew J. Rotter, "The United States, Southeast Asia, and the World," Ph.D. dissertation, Stanford University, 1981; Michael Schaller, "Securing the Great Crescent: Occupied Japan and the Origins of Containment in Southeast Asia," *Journal of American History* (1982), 69:392–414; Gary R. Hess, *The United States' Emergence as a Southeast Asian Power, 1940–1950* (New York: Columbia University Press, 1987), pp. 333–65.

3. Jacques Soustelle, "Indochina and Korea: One Front," *Foreign Affairs* (1950), 29:56–66; Gary R. Hess, "The First American Commitment in Indochina: The Acceptance of the 'Bao Dai Solution' 1950," *Diplomatic History* (1978), 2:331–50.

4. John Lewis Gaddis, *Strategies of Containment: A Critical Appraisal of Postwar American National Security Policy* (New York: Oxford University Press, 1982), pp. 127–97; Blanche Wiesen Cook, *The Declassified Eisenhower: A Divided Legacy* (New York: Macmillan, 1981), pp. 149–216; Richard A. Melanson, "The Foundations of Eisenhower's Foreign Policy: Continuity, Community, and Consensus," in Richard A. Melanson and David Mayers, ed. *Reevaluating Eisenhower: American Foreign Policy in the 1950s*, (Urbana, Ill. University of Illinois Press, 1987), pp. 31–66.

5. Report to NSC (NSC 162/2), October 30 1953, *Foreign Relations of the United States, 1952–1954 (FRUS)*, vol. 2: *National Security Affairs* (Washington, D.C.: GPO, 1984), pp. 577–97.

6. Report to NSC (NSC 5405), Jan. 16, 1954, *FRUS, 1952–54*, vol. 12: *East Asia and the Pacific* part 1, pp. 366–81.

7. George C. Herring, *America's Longest War: The United States and Vietnam, 1950–1975*, 2nd ed: New York: 1986, pp. 18–29.

8. Kitchen, memo, March 1, 1954, *FRUS, 1952–54*, vol. 16: *Geneva Conference*, pp. 427–28; *Dept. of State Bulletin*, April 12, 1954, p. 539; Robert F. Randle, *Geneva 1954: The Settlement of the Indochinese War* (Princeton; Princeton University Press, 1968), pp. 62–67; George C. Herring and Richard H. Immerman, "Eisenhower,

Dulles, and Dienbienphu: 'The Day We Didn't Go to War' Revisited," *Journal of American History* (1984), 71:343–63; NSC mtg., memo of discussion, April 6, 1954, *FRUS, 1952–54*, vol. 13: *Indochina*, pp. 1250–65; NSC mtg., memo of discussion, April 13, 1954, *ibid.*, pp. 1323–26; discussion (Bowen), memo, April 20, 1954, *FRUS, 1952–54*, 16:535–38.

9. *Public Papers of the Presidents of the United States: Dwight D. Eisenhower, 1954* (Washington, D.C.: 1960), pp. 427–28; Richard H. Immerman, "Between the Unattainable and the Unacceptable: Eisenhower and Dienbienphu," in *Reevaluating Eisenhower*, pp. 120–54.

10. Gullion to Bowie, February 24, 1954, *FRUS, 1952–54*, 16:417–23; Bonsal, memo, March 8, 1954, *ibid.*, pp. 437–42; Wilson to Dulles, March 23, 1954, *ibid*, pp. 471–79; Dulles to Smith, May 8, 1954, *ibid.*, pp. 731–32; Dulles to Smith, May 12, 1954, *ibid*, pp. 778–79.

11. Randle, *Geneva*, pp. 274–83; Francois Joyaux, *La Chine et le Réglement du premier conflit d'Indochine (Geneve 1954)* (Paris: Publications de la Sorbonne, 1979), 205–9, 226–36; governments of U.K. and U.S., minutes, June 27, 1954, *FRUS 1952–54*, 12:580–81; Robert H. Ferrell, ed., *The Diary of James C. Hagerty: Eisenhower in Mid-Course, 1954–55* (Bloomington: Indiana University Press, 1983), pp. 74–81.

12. Conversation (Johnson), memo, July 13, 1954, *FRUS, 1952–54*, 13:1819–26; conversation (Johnson), memo, July 14, 1954, *FRUS, 1952–54*, 16:1359–661; conversation (Dulles), memo, July 14, 1954, *ibid.*, pp. 1361–67; NSC mtg., memo of discussion, July 15, 1954, *FRUS, 1952–54*, 13:1834–40; Ferrell, ed., *Hagerty Diary*, p. 91.

13. Dulles to Smith, July 16, 1954, *FRUS, 1952–54*, 16:1396–97; Randle, *Geneva*, pp. 332–44; Joyaux, *La Chine*, pp. 275–98; James Cable, *The Geneva Conference of 1954 on Indochina* (New York: St. Martin's Press, 1986), pp. 115–28; George McT. Kahin, *Intervention: How America Became Involved in Vietnam* (New York: Knopf, 1986), pp. 61–65.

14. *New York Times*, July 23–24, 1954; *Dept. of State Bulletin*, August 2, 1954, p. 163; NSC mtg., memo of discussion, July 22, 1954, *FRUS, 1952–54*, 13:1867–71; Note to NSC (NSC 5429), August 20, 1954, *FRUS, 1952–54*, vol. 12, part 1, pp. 769–76.

15. Dulles to London embassy, July 28, 1954, *ibid.*, pp. 680–81; conversation (Dulles), memo, August 17, 1954, *ibid.*, p. 735.

16. FO 371/112051, Makins to Foreign Office, March 29, 1954, (Public Records Office, London); FO 371/112050, Makins to Foreign Office, April 8, 1954; Churchill to Eisenhower, June 21, 1954, *FRUS, 1952–54*, 12:569–70; Russell H. Fifield, *Americans in Southeast Asia, Roots of Commitment* (New York: Crowell, 1973), pp. 96–99, 200, 225–33; Stephen R. Shalom, *The United States and the Philippines; A Study of Neocolonialism* (Philadelphia: Institute for Study of Human Issues, 1981), pp. 68–93; Cable, *Geneva Conference*, pp. 51–60; Hess, *United States' Emergence as Southeast Asian Power*, pp. 342–52; NSC mtg., memo of discussion, May 6, 1953, *FRUS, 1952–54*, vol. 12, part 2, pp. 667–70; Moyer to Stassen, December 1, 1954, *ibid.*, pp. 738–40.

17. Draft Southeast Asia Collective Security Treaty, August 2, 1954, *FRUS, 1952–54*, vol. 12, pp. 686–94.

18. Hildreth to State Dept., August 4, 1954, *ibid.*, pp. 704–5; minutes of State Dept. mtg., August 5, 1954, *ibid.*, pp. 705–8; Allen to State Dept., August 9, 1954, *ibid.*, pp. 713–15; conversation (Thacher), memo, August 19, 1954, *ibid.*, pp. 758–60; conversation (Metcalf), memo, July 27, 1954, *ibid.*, pp. 676–77; Allen to State Dept., July 28, 1954, *ibid.*, pp. 678–79; Crowe to State Dept., July 29, 1954, *ibid.*, p. 682; State Dept. mtg. minutes, August 5, 1954, *ibid.*, pp. 705–8; Crowe to State Dept., September 9, 1954, *ibid.*, pp. 901–2; *New York Times*, August 14, 1954.

19. Revised U.S. Draft Treaty, ca. August 24, 1954, *FRUS, 1952–54*, vol. 12, part 1, pp. 784–87; State Dept. mtg., minutes August 24, 1954, *ibid.*, pp. 787–89.

20. British embassy to State Dept., August 27, 1954, *ibid.*, pp. 799–800; MacArthur to Dulles, August 28, 1954, *ibid.*, pp. 806–8.

21. Spruance to State Dept., September 4, 1954, *ibid.*, pp. 839–45; meeting of U.S. Delegation, September 5, 1954, *ibid.*, pp. 845–48; NSC mtg., memo of discussion, September 12, 1954, *ibid.*, pp. 903–8; *The Signing of the Southeast Asia Collective Defense Treaty . . . Proceedings* (Conference Secretariat, 1954), pp. 41–42.

22. *U.S.–Vietnam Relations*, 1945–67, (Washington, D.C.: GPO, 1971) bk. 10, p. 747.

23. Fifield, *Americans in Southeast Asia*, p. 236; Herring, *America's Longest War*, pp. 44–45.

24. Burton I. Kaufman, *Trade and Aid: Eisenhower's Foreign Economic Policy, 1953–1961* (Baltimore; Johns Hopkins University Press, 1982), pp. 49–73; John D. Montgomery, *The Politics of Foreign Aid: American Experience in Southeast Asia* (New York: Praeger 1962), pp. 11–61, 281–89; Charles Wolf, Jr., *Foreign Aid: Theory and Practice in Southeast Asia* (Princeton Princeton University Press, 1960), pp. 75–243, 390, 403–4; Roger M. Smith, *Cambodia's Foreign Policy* (Ithaca: Cornell University Press, 1965), pp. 68–73, 122–39.

25. Gaddis, *Strategies of Containment*, p. 154.

26. Montgomery, *Politics of Foreign Aid*, pp. 31–35; Wolf, *Foreign Aid*, pp. 209–24; Cook, *Declassified Eisenhower*, pp. 326–27.

27. Spruance to State Dept., Nov. 24, 1953, *FRUS, 1952–54*, vol. 12, part 2, pp. 565–66.

28. Shalom, *The U.S. and the Philippines*, pp. 86–144; Milton W. Meyer, *A Diplomatic History of the Philippine Republic* (Honolulu University of Hawaii Press, 1965), pp. 165–87.

29. Herring, *America's Longest War*, pp. 43–72.

30. Charles A. Stevenson, *The End of Nowhere: American Policy Toward Laos since 1954* (Boston: Beacon, 1972), pp. 28–128; Martin E. Goldstein, *American Policy toward Laos* (Rutherford, N.J.: Farleigh Dickson University Press, 1973), pp. 102–78.

15

Breakthrough to the East: Soviet Asian Policy in the 1950s

Steven I. Levine
Duke University

O n March 5, 1953, the shape of the world changed. On that day, Joseph Stalin, America's quintessential cold war adversary, died in Moscow. At a news conference in Washington just a few days later, Secretary of State John Foster Dulles triumphantly proclaimed, "The Eisenhower era begins and the Stalin era ends. . . . A new era begins in which the guiding spirit is liberty."[1] Indeed, for President Eisenhower, who had taken office just six weeks earlier, the death of Stalin came as a belated inaugural present from the Soviet Union. It was a gift that conveyed the hope for a less confrontational American relationship with the Communist world than that which had prevailed since the beginning of the cold war. Not a little of the tension between Washington and Moscow at that time focused on Asia, where the United States was pitted against Moscow's Chinese ally in the stalemated war in Korea and the Communist Vietminh were gradually besting the French in the accelerating war in Indochina.

Despite the hopes in Washington aroused by Stalin's death, the challenges that the Soviet Union presented to American interests, in Asia as elsewhere, intensified as well as changed character during the 1950s. Led by a shrewd, vigorous, and resourceful statesman, Nikita Khrushchev, the new Soviet leadership displayed a bold and innovative diplomacy that availed itself of many opportunities to advance Soviet interests in Asia. In the course of the decade, the Soviet leadership undertook significant initiatives vis-à-vis China, Japan, India, Vietnam, Indonesia and other Asian states. Since Washington saw Moscow as its chief global adversary, it is important to grasp what the Soviet Union was attempting in Asia and what it actually accomplished in order to comprehend American policy in Asia during this period.

By the time of Khrushchev's fall from power in 1964, the Soviet Union's Asian policy scorecard had registered some notable successes as well as some monumental failures. On balance, despite the failures —China policy being the most conspicuous example—the 1950s and early 1960s was a time when the Soviet Union considerably strengthened its credentials as a major actor in Asian politics. This period was a kind of dress rehearsal for the Soviet Union's contemporary superpower role in Asia. Indeed, in important respects postwar Soviet influence in Asia peaked during the midpoint of the Khrushchev years only to ebb during the subsequent Brezhnev era. Notwithstanding Dulles' proclamation that the 1950s would be the Eisenhower era, the international relations of the post-Stalin decade bore the imprint of Nikita Khrushchev more clearly than that of Dwight Eisenhower. Unlike the cautious Stalin, Khrushchev, with the soul of a riverboat gambler, went for high stakes in Asia, as he did everywhere else, and he played his hand daringly, mixing skill and bravado in equal portions.

This chapter surveys Soviet policy in Asia during the part of the Khrushchev era that overlapped the administration of President Eisenhower. After sketching the general background of Soviet domestic and foreign policy, the chapter discusses Soviet crisis management in Indochina from 1954 to 1961; examines the Soviet breakout to non-Communist Asian states (India and Indonesia); charts the evolution of Soviet relations with China; and summarizes Soviet relations with Japan and North Korea.

THE SOVIET CONTEXT

The post-Stalin decade was a time of enormous upheaval in Soviet and Communist-bloc politics. In Moscow, the death of the "Kremlin mountaineer" with his "cockroach whiskers" intensified a succession struggle in which power passed to the "rabble of thick-skinned leaders" who had quite literally danced attendance on the tyrant.[2] After purging the dread NKVD boss, Lavrenty Beria, Stalin's surviving lieutenants invoked the principle of collective leadership as a form of self-protection. From the political struggle, Nikita S. Khrushchev gradually emerged as the primus inter pares, ousting such rivals as Malenkov, Kaganovich, and Molotov and eventually outmaneuvering erstwhile partners like Bulganin and Zhukov. To his initial post of First Secretary of the Central Committee of the Communist Party of the Soviet Union, Khrushchev added that of Prime Minister in 1958. Although his early Asian initiatives were undertaken in tandem with then Premier Nikolai Bulganin, Khrushchev himself was effectively in charge of Soviet foreign policy, using the Foreign Ministry and the Central Committee apparatus to implement ideas that originated with him or his entourage.

His American counterparts viewed Khrushchev as a formidable adversary. Earthy and blunt (like his sometime comrade Mao Zedong), Khrushchev more than made up in energy and wit what he lacked in polish and manners. In his presidential memoirs, Eisenhower summed up Khrushchev as "shrewd, tough, and coldly deliberate even when he was pretending to be consumed with anger. Certainly he was ruthless."[3] Khrushchev's unflattering assessment of Eisenhower confirmed Ike's judgment. Comparing him unfavorably with John F. Kennedy—the other American President with whom he dealt—Khrushchev referred to Eisenhower as a man with "something soft about his character," a mediocre military leader and a weak President excessively dependent upon advisors such as Dulles.[4] (One supposes that Khrushchev would have scoffed at the notion of a "hidden-hand presidency.")

Even as the Soviet succession struggle unfolded, the new Kremlin leaders, reflecting in part their feelings of uncertainty and vulnerability, rapidly implemented a policy of relaxing international tension. They sanctioned a New Course in their East European empire, moved to repair Stalin's rift with Yugoslavia, sought a modus vivendi with the Western bloc in Europe, and took steps to terminate the festering wars in Korea and Indochina. These attempts to promote a more relaxed international environment were connected with the post-Stalin leaders' need to transform the strained domestic order, rooted in terror, that the late dictator had bequeathed them.

Domestic changes, therefore, were no less profound. To the dismay of many of his more cautious and conservative colleagues, Khrushchev attacked some of the most repressive features of Stalinism, most dramatically in his impassioned but incomplete denunciation of Stalin's crimes at the Twentieth Congress of the CPSU in February 1956.[5] Schemes to reorganize the Party and the state apparatus, liberalize cultural policy, revamp the stagnant agricultural sector, energize the consumer economy, and so forth proliferated under the constant goading of the ebullient Nikita Sergeyevich. Unfortunately, the spirit of experimentation and innovation that Khrushchev sought to foster engendered massive resistance from the hidebound Soviet bureacracy and its Politburo patrons. Moreover, like all innovators, Khrushchev undoubtedly made his share of errors and miscalculations, and his opponents eventually seized upon these mistakes to justify their ouster of him in October 1964.

Soviet foreign policy in the post-Stalin decade inevitably focused on relations with the United States, the Communist bloc, and Western Europe, in that order. What was relatively new in Khrushchev's diplomacy was his sympathetic attention to the third world, particularly the new states of Asia that had emerged from the wreckage of European colonialism. (In a sense, like much else at this time, Khrushchev's third world diplomacy was a return to Lenin, who, already in the early days of the Soviet republic, had grasped the significance of the anti-Western, anticolonial nationalist movements of his time.)

Although himself not much of a theorist, Khrushchev nevertheless rooted his policies toward the West and the third world in two important concepts. The first — peaceful coexistence — sanctioned the Soviet attempt to reach an accommodation with the West. The second — the possibility of peaceful transitions to socialism — rationalized Moscow's efforts to forge new links with Asian and other nationalist leaders. Such leaders, while eschewing the Marxist-Leninist label, were said to have embarked upon a noncapitalist path of development that would eventually lead them to socialism.[6] Under this favorable interpretation of postcolonial Asia, the Soviet Union began to engage in normal state-to-state relations with a variety of regimes, using such diplomatic instruments as high-level meetings with foreign dignitaries, arms transfers, economic aid, student scholarships, and cultural and scientific exchanges. Khrushchev's diplomacy revolutionized the conduct of Soviet foreign affairs. After decades as a city secluded from view behind its Stalinist purdah, Moscow gradually loosened its inhibitions and joined the ranks of the world's capitals.

Khrushchev's foreign policy initiatives produced mixed results. In Eastern Europe they contributed to the explosions in Hungary and Poland that rocked the Communist camp and precipitated a crisis of authority in the international Communist movement. Relations with the United States careened from the relaxed atmosphere of the Geneva summit and the Austrian State Treaty of 1955 to the collapsed Paris summit of 1960 and the Cuban missile crisis of 1962, only to right themselves again with the Test Ban Treaty of 1963. Khrushchev's West European policy, although perhaps best remembered for various

Berlin crises and the Berlin Wall, laid a rough foundation for the regularization of state relations with West Germany and the Helsinki Accords of 1975.

This bare summary of Soviet foreign and domestic affairs during the post-Stalin decade may suffice to indicate the instability and volatility of the environment in which Khrushchev pursued his policies toward Asia as well as the complexity of the factors with which he had to contend. In a period of rapidly declining European imperial power, Soviet opportunities for advancement in Asia were nevertheless still constrained by considerations of European politics. Khrushchev's policies toward China and Japan were linked willy-nilly to his relations with the United States. Soviet relations with Vietnam were affected by the emerging Sino-Soviet rivalry and involved the ideological-strategic question of peaceful transition to socialism versus revolutionary wars of national liberation. In all these issues, a key factor was the rapid development of strategic nuclear weapons systems, which allowed Moscow and Washington to hold each other hostage. Stalemated in Europe, both countries looked to the third world as an arena in which they could maneuver more freely and seek opportunities to improve their global position vis-à-vis each other. In sum, for the Soviet Union, as for the United States, the transition to the status of a world superpower vastly complicated the conduct of diplomacy and intensified the already existing tendency toward the conflation of regional and global issues.

INDOCHINA: WAR TERMINATION AND CRISIS MANAGEMENT

The Soviet leadership was closely attuned to one of the major historical currents of the 1950s—namely, the emergence of a postcolonial order in Asia and Africa and the growing Afro-Asian political consciousness that accompanied it. In Indochina, the struggle for independence from France took the form of a war of national liberation led by the Communist-dominated Vietminh, who had been battling the French since 1946. Parallel movements, each with its own peculiar characteristics, were developing simultaneously in Laos and Cambodia. Soviet policy toward Indochina during the Khrushchev era demonstrates a clear linkage between Moscow's global and regional policy concerns.

The Soviet Union had accorded recognition to Ho Chi Minh's Democratic Republic of Vietnam (DRV) on January 31, 1950 (following the lead of the People's Republic of China). Keeping a low profile, the Soviets covertly supplied substantial quantities of military equipment and materiel to the Vietminh using China as a conduit.[7]

At the 1954 Geneva Conference on Indochina, Moscow favored its own objectives of pursuing detente with the United States and dissuading France from approving the European Defense Community over the Vietminh's goal of national unification. Foreign Minister Molotov joined Zhou Enlai in persuading the Vietnamese Communists to accept a divided Vietnam as a way station along the road to their ultimate objective. Khrushchev asserts in his memoirs that despite their victory at Dienbienphu, the Vietminh were on the verge of military exhaustion in mid-1954 and that the Geneva settlement served to consolidate their gains.[8] Be that as it may, Vietminh officials resented Soviet and Chinese pressures.[9] On the other hand, China's presence at Geneva, the first international conference in which the PRC participated, owed much to Moscow's insistence and could be seen by the Chinese as a tangible benefit of their alliance with the Soviets.[10]

In the decade after Geneva, Moscow provided diplomatic and political support to the DRV and contributed substantially to Hanoi's efforts to build socialism in the northern half of Vietnam. The first economic aid agreement, dating from July 18, 1955, and valued at about $100 million, provided Soviet equipment, specialists, and financial assistance to help develop an industrial and transportation infrastructure in the North. By 1961, Moscow had provided Hanoi with between $.5 billion and $1 billion of aid. Over a thousand Soviet specialists had worked on scores of major and minor projects while an estimated 7,000 Vietnamese had been trained at Soviet universities and technical institutes. At the same time, much more modest amounts of military aid were provided to the DRV.[11]

In July 1955, Ho Chi Minh visited Moscow, where he was accorded the honors of a head of state. Soviet Deputy Premier Mikoyan visited Hanoi in April 1956, followed by President Voroshilov in May 1957. The DRV, largely isolated from the Western world, became a functioning member of the socialist international system.

By 1960, Soviet relations with Vietnam were increasingly influenced by the emerging Sino-Soviet conflict and by the lack of any progress towards the unification of Vietnam. With respect to the first of these, the Vietnamese Workers Party (VWP), always reserving to itself the right to chart its own strategy, initially drifted away from the Soviet position and edged closer to the Chinese side on several of the key issues in the ideological dispute within the Communist world.[12] Its revolutionary victory blocked by American support of South Vietnam, Hanoi was unpersuaded by Khrushchev's ideas of peaceful co-existence and peaceful transformation. But the Soviets appear to have used their economic aid to lure the VWP back into the fold by the time the 1960 Moscow Conference of Communist and Workers' Parties took place.[13] (Later, the Vietnamese, in a display of Asian Communist solidarity, again drifted closer to Beijing.) At the Third Congress of the VWP (December 1960), the Soviets endorsed Hanoi's goals of carrying out the socialist revolution in the North while promoting the liberation of the South. With respect to the latter goal, however, Khrushchev limited his support to diplomatic means and wound up alienating Hanoi.[14] It was left to Brezhnev and Kosygin to arm Hanoi in 1965 for its confrontation with Washington.

In a regional context, the parallel Laotian conflict was a subordinate element in the Indochina story, but it achieved the status of a full-fledged international crisis due to American cold war machinations. Mistrusting the neutralist, middle ground represented by Prince Souvanna Phouma, U.S. officials in Laos backed a series of hapless right-wing generals and politicians in order to avert the "loss" of Laos to the Communist-controlled Neo Lao Hak Sat and their fighting arm, the Pathet Lao.[15]

Captain Kong Le's neutralist coup d'état of August 1960 provided an opening for Soviet diplomacy. Premier Souvanna Phouma, hard-pressed by the Laotian right-wing backed by the CIA and economically blockaded by Thailand's military regime, turned to Moscow for assistance. In October 1960, a Soviet embassy was established in Laos and a massive Soviet airlift of supplies, fuel, foodstuffs, ammunition, etc., was undertaken in December to bail out both Kong Le's neutralist forces (who supported Souvanna Phouma) and the Pathet Lao forces. (The bulk of Soviet supplies actually was trucked overland into northern Laos from Vietnam.)

By the winter of 1960–61, the Soviet Union, which had not even been an onlooker in Laos earlier, had become a major player, thanks to the United States' policy of backing the rightists. The Soviet ambassador in Laos, Aleksandr Abramisov, sardonically thanking the United States for its unwitting assistance, was quoted as saying, " 'Had the Americans been our best friends, they could not have acted otherwise.' "[16] A Soviet diplomatic note of December 1960 accused the United States of "flouting the sovereign rights of the Laotian Government headed by Prince Souvanna Phouma" and said that the Soviet Union could not ignore the threat to peace and security in Southeast Asia.[17]

As the waning Eisenhower administration reined itself in on the brink of military intervention in Laos, Washington's military clients in Laos suffered one defeat after another at the hands of Kong Le's neutralists and the Pathet Lao with whom they were cooperating. Both of these forces were armed by the Soviet Union. Rather than push for the military humiliation of America's clients (as Beijing and Hanoi might have preferred), Moscow urged North Vietnam and the Pathet Lao to accept a ceasefire in Laos and a negotiated settlement. Perhaps Khrushchev did not wish to start off on a bad footing with the incoming Democratic administration of John F. Kennedy and sought to demonstrate his reasonableness in an area of tertiary importance. In any case, after persuasive consultations in Moscow on April 16, 1961, with Prince Souphanouvong, the nominal leader of the Pathet Lao, Khrushchev secured Hanoi's and Beijing's support for a ceasefire and the convening of an international conference on Laos, which opened in Geneva in mid-May.

At their frosty June summit meeting in Vienna, Kennedy and Khrushchev endorsed the concept of "a neutral and independent Laos chosen by the Laotians themselves."[18] But because of the contentiousness of the Laotian factions, it took another year to hammer the elements of a Laotian coalition together. Once this was accomplished, in November 1962, Moscow terminated its airlift in Laos and faded into the background.

The significance of this story is that, on the whole, Moscow played a moderate and constructive role in the Laotian crisis. Its original involvement in Laos, in the words of one scholar, was "chiefly an investment in goodwill in Hanoi," the prime patron of the Pathet Lao.[19] But Khrushchev was well aware of the divergence between Soviet and Vietnamese interests in Laos. As in Geneva in 1954, Khrushchev acted so as to minimize Soviet-American confrontation, but he paid a price in terms of reduced confidence on the part of Hanoi.

THE SOVIET BREAK-OUT TO
NON-COMMUNIST ASIA

The post-Stalin Soviet leadership's embrace of Asian nationalism contrasted sharply with the Eisenhower administration's standoffish attitude. Combining ideological flexibility with diplomatic adroitness and making excellent use of economic aid programs and concessionary military sales, the Soviet Union under Khrushchev achieved some significant successes in its diplomacy toward non-Communist Asia. Soviet relations with Indonesia and India are two cases in point, even though the first proved to be only a transient success while the latter remains a core element of Soviet Asian diplomacy.

Moscow's presumed instigation of the Indonesian Communist Party's (PKI) brief but bloody Madiun revolt of 1948 dissipated much of the initial Indonesian sympathy towards the Soviet Union deriving from Soviet support for Indonesian independence. Although the Soviet Union recognized the Indonesian Republic in January 1950, diplomatic missions were not exchanged until 1954. Even contacts between the PKI and the Soviet Communist Party were virtually nonexistent during the twilight of the Stalin era.[20]

Under their new leader, D. N. Aidit, the Indonesian Communists adopted a broad, national united front policy that, by the mid-1950s, had gained for the PKI the status of a valued partner of President Soekarno. In the complex and shifting political environment that lasted until 1965, the phenomenal growth and substantial influence of the PKI demonstrated the apparent validity of a popular, mass-based, peaceful road to socialism such as Khrushchev had endorsed.

Cooperation between Soekarno and the PKI smoothed the path for Soviet official diplomacy towards Indonesia. As early as 1954, Moscow expressed its approval of Indonesia's independent foreign policy, which spurned SEATO and condemned the establishment of military alliances in Southeast Asia. President Soekarno's September 1956 journey to Moscow, where he was greeted effusively, initiated a series of high-level visits that included President Voroshilov's pilgrimage to Jakarta in May 1957 and a visit from Khrushchev himself in February 1960.

Soviet political and military support for Indonesian national objectives added substance to these symbolic exchanges. Moscow championed Jakarta's claim to West Irian and joined Indonesia in denouncing Western imperialism at the UN and other international forums.[21] In 1956, the Soviet Union extended its first long-term credit to Indonesia (a twelve-year low-interest $100 million loan) to be used for arms purchases. Over the next five years, the Soviet bloc (Poland and Czechoslovakia as well as the Soviet Union) provided over $1 billion of military assistance to the Indonesian armed forces.[22] Soviet-bloc transport ships, MiG 15s and 17s, submarines, destroyers, troops carriers, and other heavy equipment helped the Indonesian armed forces suppress the Sumatran revolt of 1958. Khrushchev, meanwhile, echoing charges of CIA involvement in the revolt, in a May 1958 speech stated that "the Soviet people cannot be indifferent to the imperialist machinations in Indonesia."[23]

Very soon, however, Soviet influence in Indonesia faded almost as quickly as it had flowered. As the Sino-Soviet dispute sharpened, the Indonesian Communists, in a show of Asian solidarity much like the Vietnamese, sided with the Chinese Communist Party against the CPSU. The Indonesian armed forces, recipient of Soviet military largesse, remained on guard against domestic communism and were wary of external support for the PKI from any quarter. Meanwhile, President Soekarno, his megalomania encouraged by Mao Zedong (who may have sensed in him a kindred spirit), voiced a species of third world Islamic socialism that echoed Chinese anti–status quo views and that left little room for the Soviet Union as a white, European superpower. Khrushchev's comments in his memoirs that "we were cautious toward people who adopted the word Socialism but who seemed mostly interested in getting military aid from us" was wisdom after the fact.[24] Moscow's initiative toward Jakarta ended in failure.

Things turned out very differently in India. There, too, the post-Stalin Soviet leadership saw a major opportunity to forge friendly relations with a non-Communist Asian power that was emerging as a leader of the nonaligned world. Premier Malenkov, in an August 1953 speech to the Supreme Soviet, said, "The position of so large a state as India is of great importance for strengthening peace in the East. ... We hope that relations between India and the Soviet Union will continue to develop and grow with friendly cooperation as the keynote."[25] Malenkov's rather bland rhetoric quite accurately forecast the future of Moscow–New Delhi relations not only through the rest of the 1950s but right up to the present.

Peace and development were the watchwords of Soviet policy towards India in the post-Stalin decade. Raising Indian hopes that the cold war era might be fading, Soviet leaders embarked on a peace campaign that defined India as part of a "zone of peace" said to embrace the Communist bloc countries and the third world. Nehru and his ambassador in Moscow, K. P. S. Menon, an apostle of Soviet-Indian friendship, were both very favorably impressed by the post-Stalin liberalization of Soviet domestic politics and inclined to give the benefit of the doubt to Soviet foreign policy as well, even with regard to such outrages as the crushing of the Hungarian revolution in 1956.[26] Soviet overtures toward India benefited from New Delhi's identification of imperialism with the West and its tendency to view the Soviet Union as a partner in anti-imperialist and anticolonialist causes. The fact that Soviet imperialism focused on Europe rather than Asia may have contributed to India's perceptions.

Personal diplomacy was a vital element in building friendly Soviet-Indian relations. Prime Minister Nehru, who, along with his daughter

Indira Gandhi, was warmly greeted during his first trip to the Soviet Union in June 1955, reportedly told his Soviet hosts upon his departure from Moscow, "I am leaving my heart behind."[27] Nehru's considerable vanity as well as India's national amour propre were gratified by the attention the Soviets lavished on him and on India's position in global politics. In another exercise in personal diplomacy, Nehru despatched two unusual Indian emissaries to Moscow—baby elephants named Ravi and Shashi—as a gift to the children of the Soviet Union.[28]

In November 1955, Khrushchev, accompanied by his then sidekick, Marshal Bulganin (who could have passed muster as a Soviet Colonel Sanders), barnstormed through India, playing to huge and enthusiastic crowds. Khrushchev backed New Delhi's stance on the Portuguese enclave of Goa (which India finally annexed in December 1961), and in Srinigar, the capital of Kashmir, he endorsed India's position in its unresolved dispute with Pakistan.[29]

Entering the arena of foreign aid diplomacy, the Soviet Union extended a $130 million credit to India in 1955 for the construction of a large steel plant at Bhilai, which went into operation in 1959. At a time when Washington was still chary of assisting state-controlled heavy industrial projects, Moscow invested in such projects, realizing that India, like other developing nations, gave priority to the public sector. India's development as a modern industrial power in such areas as steel, oil-refining, machine-manufacturing, and so forth, owed much to Soviet assistance beginning in this period. In the summer of 1960, as Soviet technicians were yanked out of China, Moscow upped its pledge of economic assistance to India's third Five Year Plan to $500 million. Trade between India and the Soviet Union also grew rapidly, although for both nations it remained a miniscule part of their overall trade through the end of the 1950s.[30]

Khrushchev's courtship of India occurred during the same period when serious problems began to emerge in Soviet-Chinese relations. When Sino-Indian conflict flared along the disputed Himalayan border in August 1959, Moscow, reluctant to take sides between an established ally and a new friend, adopted a neutral stance, deploring the outbreak of violence and urging a peaceful resolution.[31] Nehru appreciated the Soviet position, while the Chinese fumed at what they considered an act of betrayal by their fraternal socialist ally. Khrushchev's attempt to play the role of go-between in the Sino-Indian dispute (like Kosygin's mediation between India and Pakistan in 1965) was unsuccessful. Soviet arms transfers to India belong to a later period, commencing in 1961 and picking up momentum in the years following.[32]

Unlike the case with Indonesia, the Soviet-Indian friendship that began in the Khrushchev era served as the foundation for the full-fledged cooperation between the two countries that developed in subsequent decades. As Sino-Soviet relations deteriorated further in the 1960s and Sino-Indian relations became frozen in a cold war pattern after 1962, India and the Soviet Union became for each other important partners in their parallel strategies of containing the PRC. By the time this happened, of course, Khrushchev and his successors had suffered the "loss of China."

THE SOVIET UNION AND CHINA: THE COLLAPSE OF ALLIANCE

Looking back from the vantage point of his involuntary retirement, Khrushchev reflected bitterly upon Mao Zedong, his archrival in the Communist world. "Politics is a game and Mao Tse tung has played politics with Asiatic cunning, following his own rules of cajolery, treachery, savage vengeance and deceit. He deceived us for a number of years before we saw through his tricks."[33]

Nikita Sergeyevich might be forgiven his biliousness. China represented the greatest failure of Khrushchev's foreign policy, not only in Asia but throughout the world, and the consequences of that failure shaped global politics for a score of years thereafter. The irony was that during the post-Stalin decade, Soviet-Chinese relations first attained their peak of cooperation only to plunge by the early 1960s into a vortex of recrimination, accusations, ideological disputes, and crude power politics, from which there seemed no escape. Within the limitations imposed by his position and personality, Khrushchev had started off by attempting to rectify the inequality in Soviet-Chinese relations that was the legacy of the Stalin era. Yet he wound up reviled by the Chinese as the symbol of all that was wrong with the Soviet Union, its leadership of international communism, and its foreign policy. The struggle against "Khrushchevism" became China's battle cry within international communism, and Mao indicated the intensity of his animus towards Liu Shaoqi, whom he destroyed during the Cultural Revolution, by dubbing him "China's Khrushchev."

Built into the Sino-Soviet alliance that Mao negotiated with Stalin in 1949–50 and the actual system of relations that developed down to 1953 were elements of inequality that chafed against Chinese sensibilities. Among these were the Soviet-Chinese joint stock companies that were an instrument of Soviet economic penetration of China, the continuing Soviet leases on the Port Arthur naval base and the port of Dalian, Soviet co-ownership of the Chinese-Changchun Railway (the old Chinese Eastern Railway), as well as the subordination of China's revolutionary experience to the universalist pretensions of the Bolshevik model of revolution. This is not to suggest, however, that the Chinese were somehow dragooned by force of circumstances into entering a relationship with Moscow they would have preferred to avoid—an argument that does not stand up to scrutiny. Nor do these facts prove that Stalin treated China as a satellite state. He did not. It must be recognized that the PRC derived important security, political, and economic benefits at this time from its membership in the socialist bloc.

Soviet policies in the early post-Stalin years, both towards China and more broadly, accorded with Chinese interests in several important respects. First, the new Soviet leadership moved swiftly to eliminate major irritants in the Sino-Soviet bilateral relationship. The joint stock companies, which Khrushchev himself called "an insult to the Chinese people," were abolished in 1954, and the Soviets also returned the Chinese-Changchun Railway to China.[34] The following year, Dalian and Port Arthur, along with their Soviet-built installations, were handed back. The liquidation of these vestiges of Russian imperialism assuaged Chinese national sentiments.

Second, the Soviets significantly stepped up their contribution to Chinese economic development. By 1960 about $2 billion worth of Soviet credits had been extended to China. Soviet-assisted industrial projects in such fields as machine-building, motor vehicles, energy development, and transportation formed the heart of the first Five Year Plan (1953–1957). Thousands of Soviet and East European technicians, blueprints in hand, helped supervise the construction projects and train Chinese personnel, while additional thousands of Chinese students (including the current Chinese premier, Li Peng) were educated in the Soviet Union. Soviet heavy equipment and machinery flowed into China.

Third, the relaxation of international tensions that Moscow strived for diminished the threat to China's security while facilitating China's entrance into the global political arena. Although a competition for influence perhaps existed in embryonic form, it is more accurate to stress Soviet-Chinese foreign policy cooperation and coordination, up until at least 1957. Moreover, the relaxation of Moscow's grip on Eastern Europe and the upheavals of 1956 in Hungary and Poland enabled China to play a mediating role in the socialist bloc and to make progress toward a position of coleadership. (Similarly, in the post-Stalin succession struggle, Chinese support was solicited by the

Soviet contenders for power who realized the prestige and authority that Mao and his colleagues enjoyed in the international Communist movement. Unable to wield the authority of the late dictator, Stalin's successors needed China's approval to legitimize their own positions.) The status gap between Soviet elder brother and Chinese younger brother narrowed considerably in this period.

Fourth, the Soviets enhanced their military-security cooperation with the PRC, providing China with modern tanks, artillery, aircraft, and naval vessels. In 1957 the signing of an agreement for nuclear technology cooperation promised to speed China along the road toward acquisition of its own nuclear arsenal. Sino-Soviet military cooperation was epitomized by the adoption in 1955 of a Soviet system of ranks and military uniforms, which, as one scholar wryly noted, meant that officers of China's revolutionary army began wearing the tsarist epaulettes that the Red Army had adopted as its own.[35]

Finally, the Soviet Union accorded a high priority to its relations with China, symbolized by Khrushchev's and Bulganin's journey in October 1954 to Beijing, where they helped celebrate the fifth anniversary of the PRC. It was on that occasion that the Soviet leaders undertook to abolish the unequal aspects of the Stalinist legacy and pledged to increase their economic assistance to the PRC.

In his retrospective account, however, Khrushchev claims that when he returned from China in 1954, he told his Politburo colleagues that, on the basis of various remarks made by Mao Zedong, "conflict with China is inevitable."[36] Whether or not one trusts this recollection, it is certain that by 1956 signs of Soviet-Chinese discord were emerging. Here it may suffice simply to recall a few of the issues that, by 1960, had produced not only bitter Sino-Soviet polemics but also an escalating conflict that within three years led to a rupture of party relations and a determination on each side to achieve the humiliation of the other.

Both substance and process must be considered in order to understand the breakdown of Sino-Soviet relations that occurred between 1956 and 1963. With respect to the former, the issues may be listed as follows: intrabloc authority; foreign policy coordination; general strategy and tactics; security cooperation; and economic development issues.

Khrushchev's unexpected attack against Stalin at the Twentieth Congress of the Soviet Communist Party (February 1956) created significant short-term problems for all Communist parties and Communist party regimes. More than that, it was an arrogation of authority within the Communist world by a leader whose position even within his own party was still far from secure. The CCP leadership, and Mao

Zedong in particular, deeply resented this. In the wake of the Polish and Hungarian traumas of October–November 1956, the Soviet leadership endorsed principles of equality and mutual respect among socialist states that amounted to a new charter for the international movement. But in practice, once the crisis had abated, Soviet leaders seemed unable or unwilling to stop acting as masters.[37]

Beginning in 1958, China's Bandung-era diplomacy, whose watchword was "peaceful coexistence," gave way to much more assertive policies with respect to the United States and Taiwan as well as Japan, India, and other countries. Misreading the significance of Soviet missile technology, Mao proclaimed that the East Wind was prevailing over the West Wind, and he urged upon the Communist bloc a forward policy of challenging imperialism. Intoxicated, as well, with the moonshine of his own Great Leap Forward, in 1958 Mao taunted the United States in the Taiwan Straits before finally backing away from confrontation.

None of this sat well with Khrushchev. Having bested his domestic rivals in 1957 and restored a semblance of order to the socialist camp, the Soviet leader was loath to allow the Chinese to destroy the fragile detente he had nurtured with the West. Khrushchev's second trip to Beijing in September 1959 failed to persuade a sceptical Mao Zedong of the desirability of coexistence with the United States.[38] The Chinese leadership dismissed as the fearfulness of small-minded men the caution that the Soviets believed nuclear weaponry imposed on the conduct of diplomacy.

Soviet and Chinese disagreements multiplied over the question of what policies the Communist movement should pursue towards "revisionists" like Tito and the Yugoslavs and toward third world "bourgeois" nationalists. This took the form of a bitter ideological polemic in which each side invoked the authority of the Marxist-Leninist classics to undermine the arguments of the other. Thunderous polemical volleys reverberated through the halls of international Communist meetings at this time.[39]

Already disenchanted with his Chinese comrades, in 1959 Khrushchev reneged on the nuclear cooperation agreement that had been signed just two years earlier. For their part, the Chinese refused Soviet requests for the establishment of a submarine base in China and for the opening of a Soviet naval communications center on Chinese soil.[40] Jealous of Chinese sovereignty, Mao was unwilling to expand the sphere of military cooperation to the point where, from his perspective, it might eventually jeopardize his control of the People's Liberation Army (PLA). Mao's brutal response to Defense Minister Peng Dehuai's temperate challenge to the Great Leap Forward at the

Lushan Plenum in August 1959 may also be germane, for Peng was accused of maintaining illicit relations with a foreign power—namely, the Soviet Union.[41]

Finally, the Soviet model of development that China had adopted in its first Five Year Plan was jettisoned in the Great Leap Forward, which embodied the utopian fantasies of Maoism divorced from both reality and rationality.[42] Khrushchev's sneering comments about the Great Leap (addressed to bourgeois politicians like Hubert Humphrey) wounded Chinese pretensions. In the summer of 1960, the Soviet Union, trying to choke China into submission, exacerbated a worsening economic situation in China by precipitously withdrawing the remaining Soviet technical personnel, who, it was said, were unable to work in the bizarre conditions created by the Great Leap Forward.

If these are some (though not all) of the substantive issues, what, then, of the procedural questions? Two points may suffice. First is that the original conception of the Sino-Soviet alliance was unrealistic and flawed. Rather than being seen as a limited partnership embodying overlapping interests in the realms of security, economics, and so forth, it was conceived as what might be called a "meta-alliance," deriving from the fictive identity of interests that socialist states supposedly shared. This contributed to the creation of a structure of unfulfillable expectations on both sides.

Second, because of the presumed congruence between the interests of both parties, no effective means of conflict resolution had been built into the relationship. Disagreements, rather than being handled at the working levels, escalated rapidly into questions of good faith, fundamental belief, and personal power. Accustomed to destroying their domestic rivals by the application of force and guile, Khrushchev and Mao tried without success to apply the same techniques to their own increasingly hostile encounters.

In sum, through a combination of factors, including Soviet habits of leadership, Chinese assertiveness, and domestic and international circumstances, Khrushchev's China policy ended in disaster. His failure was invoked by his domestic opponents as one of the reasons to remove him, but they had no better luck with the Chinese than he had. Searching for a major partner in Asia to replace China, Moscow happened upon India, which, by this time, was locked in its own bitter stalemate with the PRC.

NORTH KOREA AND JAPAN

S oviet–North Korean relations during the Khrushchev era repeated in a minor key many of the same themes that characterized Soviet-Chinese relations. Like Mao Zedong, North Korean leader
Kim Il Song saw Khrushchev's de-Stalinization campaign as a threat
to his own paramount position. At the same time, the concept of
peaceful coexistence and Khrushchev's opening to the West contradicted Pyongyang's continuing struggle against the U.S.-supported
government of South Korea. By the time of Khrushchev's fall from
power, the Soviet Union and North Korea had drifted far apart, but
no cataclysmic break occurred between them.

Following the Korean armistice agreement in July 1953, Moscow
used economic assistance to try to regain some of the influence it had
lost in Pyongyang to the Chinese, whose military intervention into the
Korean War in 1950 had rescued the North Korean regime from
certain extinction. The Soviets extended a 1 billion ruble loan (ca.
$250 million) to North Korea on the occasion of Kim Il Song's visit in
September 1953 and provided substantial further assistance through
loans and debt forgiveness in 1956 and 1960. The assistance was used
to reconstruct and develop the industrial plant and infrastructure of
the war-devastated North Korean economy. In 1955 four-fifths of North
Korea's foreign trade ($85 million) was with the Soviet Union, though
this dropped precipitously to only 35 percent five years later.[43] In
1963–64, when Soviet–North Korean relations had already drastically deteriorated for political reasons, Khrushchev tried to pressure
Kim Il Song by withholding military as well as most economic aid.[44]
As in the case of China, this served only to exacerbate an already
badly strained relationship.

In late 1955, Kim Il Song began sounding the themes of Korean
nationalism, and he promoted the de-Sovietization of North Korean
culture as well as of politics. Moving to consolidate his own power, in
1956 Kim purged intraparty opponents, some of whom had ties to
either Moscow or Beijing. When Soviet Deputy Premier Mikoyan interceded directly with Kim on behalf of the targeted individuals, the
North Korean leader temporarily retreated, but he completed the
purge two years later and never forgave this intervention. Thereafter,
even while proclaiming his loyalty to and admiration for the Soviet
Union, Kim emphasized the idea of *chu ch'e* or self-reliance which
functioned like a "No Trespassing" sign warning off his larger Communist neighbors.[45] In economic terms, however, self-reliance remained a slogan rather than a reality.

Between 1956 and 1961, Kim personally visited the Soviet Union on five separate occasions, participating in the international Communist meetings and congresses that marked the early stages of the Sino-Soviet dispute. By 1958, Pyongyang edged toward a pro-Chinese position on the ideological and strategic issues that divided Moscow from Beijing, and the Korean Workers Party maintained its links with the Albanian Labor Party even after Khrushchev's verbal assault on Albanian leader Enver Hoxha at the Twenty-Second Soviet Communist Party Congress in October 1961. Kim Il Song paid lip service to the idea of collective leadership, but he never said so much as a critical word about Stalin.

In sum, during the first post-Stalin decade, the Soviet Union witnessed the consolidation in Pyongyang of a North Korean leadership that, however indebted it may have been to the Soviet Union for its original accession to power, was no longer inclined to follow Soviet wishes. With increasing assertiveness, paralleling the growth of his own cult of personality, Kim Il Song proclaimed a Korean path to socialism and pursued interests that diverged ever further from those of the Soviet Union.

K hrushchev-era Soviet diplomacy toward Japan foundered on the hard rock of the U.S.–Japan security relationship and the conservative political orientation of Japan's political elite. Soviet leaders tended to view Japan in the 1950s as a semisatellite of the United States, bound to Washington by economic, security, and political ties that rendered its independence as nominal as that of Moscow's own East European client states.

The Soviet Union's sour view of U.S.–Japan relations was enhanced by the San Francisco Peace Treaty of September 1951. Moscow denounced the treaty as an aggressive instrument that kept Japan in thrall to the United States and harbored the seeds of future conflict. For good measure, the Soviets vetoed Japan's application for UN membership in June 1952.

Post-Stalin Soviet leaders expressed an early interest in normalizing relations with Japan, but not until mid-1955 did the negotiations that eventually produced the Joint Declaration of October 19, 1956, begin. This agreement ended the state of war between them, restored diplomatic relations, pledged Soviet support for Japan's entry into the UN, and envisioned commercial and other economic relations. In addition, Moscow agreed to transfer the islands of Shikotan and the Habomais to Japan after a Soviet-Japanese peace treaty was signed.[46] (Now, more than thirty years later, such a treaty has still not been signed, and the Japanese insist on the return of all of their northern territories included Etorofu and Kunashiri as well as Shikotan and the Habomais.)

Despite what seemed like a promising beginning, rather little developed thereafter in the way of substantive Soviet-Japanese relations. Meanwhile, Khrushchev continued to refer to Japan disparagingly as a country that lacked true independence. During the joint Socialist- and Communist-led struggle against revision of the U.S.– Japan Security Treaty in 1959–60, the Soviets cheered the leftist-populist forces, apparently hoping that the goal of an unarmed and neutral Japan lay within reach. When the opposition did not succeed in prevailing over Kishi and the Liberal Democratic Party majority, the Soviets announced that the return of Shikotan and the Habomais would now be contingent upon the prior withdrawal of all foreign (i.e., U.S.) forces from Japan. This, in effect, was reneging on their promise.[47] Khrushchev, like earlier as well as later Soviet leaders, treated Japan rather contemptuously and allowed historical animosities and prejudices to hold sway in this area of Soviet policy.

CONCLUSION

From this summary of Soviet policy in Asia during the Khrushchev era, several major points emerge that bear comparison with American policy during the same period: the attitude toward the emergence of Asian nationalisms; the question of policy instruments employed in the quest for influence; the management of crises; and the linkage between regional and global issues.

Khrushchev and the Soviet leadership grasped more quickly and viewed more sympathetically than did the United States the significance of Asian nationalism in the postwar global transformation. Heirs to the Leninist tradition, the Soviets adapted first their practice and then their theory with the aim of befriending a broad range of Asian nationalists, including Soekarno and Nehru in the non-Communist world and Ho Chi Minh and Mao Zedong iin the Communist world. Moscow viewed Asian nationalism as a natural ally of the socialist bloc in the struggle against Western imperialism.

In the post-Stalin period, Moscow realized that working with existing nationalist leaders was a more effective means of expanding Soviet influence than supporting small and isolated Communist parties in quixotic quests for power. So the Soviets began employing the same arsenal of diplomatic means that the United States used in Asia. Political support for key national objectives, economic aid programs, cultural diplomacy, arms transfers, and so forth, all figured in Moscow's Asian diplomacy. Khrushchev's outgoing personality, the natural ebullience of a born politician, was also an asset for the most part. His frequent travels—including visits to India, Indonesia, Burma, Afghanistan, and China—projected the image of an active leader of a great power who was not afraid to expose himself to varied circumstances.

As noted above, Soviet diplomacy during the Khrushchev era focused on Europe and the United States, where the major interests of the Soviet Union were engaged and where threats to Soviet security originated. For this reason, Soviet diplomacy toward Asia sought to dampen rather than enflame regional hot spots that had become or threatened to become international crises. This was particularly true if the United States was involved. However, this did not imply a policy of abstinence. In 1960, as I have noted, Moscow intervened effectively in Laos, but the thrust of its policy was to promote a negotiated political settlement rather than a Communist military takeover. Six years earlier in Geneva, the Soviets had acted in a similar fashion. The objective in both cases was to head off a threatened U.S. military intervention. On the other hand, where only the interests of smaller Western powers were involved (e.g., the Dutch in Indonesia), Moscow gave full political support and military assistance to Jakarta.

As a country just moving onto the stage of global politics, where it was competing with a more developed and more powerful American rival, the Soviet Union was acutely aware of the need to defend its own security and protect its primary interests in Europe before becoming too deeply engaged in secondary theaters in Asia. During this period, Moscow avoided the pitfall of extending its commitments in Asia beyond its capabilities. Such successes of the decade as Soviet relations with India enabled later leaders to build upon Khrushchev's foundation. The failure to consolidate Soviet influence in Indonesia carried with it no long-term burdens.

China, of course, was a special case. In part, there was a personal dimension to the historic falling out of the Soviet Union and China. Khrushchev and Mao were exceedingly ill matched as partners, however well matched they were as rivals. Although the alliance breakdown was the result of an interactive process, the evidence clearly suggests that it was Mao who wanted to rid China of its supposed Soviet yoke. Other Chinese leaders such as Liu Shaoqi might have gained distance from Moscow without effecting a rupture. Since neither side had experience in dealing with an ally on an equal basis, each tried unsucessfully to force the other's submission. As in America's "loss of China," domestic Chinese political factors were more responsible for the Soviet "loss of China" than was Khrushchev's China policy.

American and Soviet leadership cycles do not neatly coincide, of course. In 1961, when Dwight D. Eisenhower moved out of the White House, Nikita Khrushchev was still at the acme of his power in the Kremlin. In the eight years after Stalin's death, Khrushchev and his colleagues had taken the Soviet Union a good distance down the road toward the status of a global superpower. By its policies toward both Communist and non-Communist Asia, the Soviet Union had effectively demonstrated its claims to be a major actor in the region. Riding the crest of the Asian nationalist wave, Moscow had friends in New Delhi and Jakarta as well as in Hanoi and Pyongyang. Relations with Beijing were already seriously strained, but probably not as yet judged to be irredeemable. In sum, as the Soviets entered the decade that was to bring about political upheavals in China and Indonesia and wars in Indochina, South Asia, and along the Sino-Indian border, they had reason for feeling satisfied with the results of their efforts. Their position in Asian affairs was no longer confined to the Communist world or dependent upon the goodwill of one or two partners. Across the length and breadth of the continent, from Afghanistan to Japan and from Korea to Indonesia, they were now a factor to be reckoned with not only by the states within the region but by the new men in Washington as well, who picked up the burdens of leadership at the end of the Eisenhower era.

NOTES

1. *Department of State Bulletin*, March 23, 1953, vol. 28, no. 717, p. 430.

2. The quoted phrases are from Osip Mandelstam's famous poem about Stalin. Osip Mandelstam, *Selected Poems*, trans. David McDuff (New York: Farrar, Straus & Giroux, 1975), p. 133.

3. Dwight D. Eisenhower, *Waging Peace, 1956–1961* (Garden City, N.Y.: Doubleday, 1965), pp. 557–58.

4. Nikita S. Khrushchev, *Khrushchev Remembers*, trans. Strobe Talbot. (Boston: Little, Brown, 1970), p. 397.

5. For a sympathetic appreciation of Khrushchev and his accomplishments, see Roy Medvedev, *Khrushchev*, trans. Brian Pearce (Garden City, N.Y.: Anchor Press, 1983).

6. For the Soviet reevaluation of third world regimes, see the discussion in Richard B. Remnek, *Soviet Scholars and Soviet Foreign Policy* (Durham: Carolina Academic Press, 1975), pp. 127–70.

7. Douglas Pike, *Vietnam and the Soviet Union: Anatomy of Alliance* (Boulder: Westview Press, 1987) p. 13, 107–8.

8. Khrushchev, *Khrushchev Remembers*, pp. 482–83.

9. Melvin Gurtov, *The First Vietnam Crisis* (New York: Columbia University Press, 1967), p. 129.

10. *Ibid.*, pp. 72ff.

11. Pike, *Vietnam and the Soviet Union*, pp. 109–139.

12. See William Smyser, *The Independent Vietnamese: Vietnamese Communism between Russia and China, 1956–1969*. (Athens, Ohio University, Center for International Studies, 1980), pp. 7–14.

13. P. J. Honey, *Communism in North Vietnam: Its Role in the Sino-Soviet Dispute* (Cambridge: MIT Press, 1963), p. 81.

14. Pike, *Vietnam and the Soviet Union*, pp. 43–44; Smyser, *Independent Vietnamese*, p. 29.

15. Charles Stevenson, *The End of Nowhere: American Policy towards Laos, since 1954.* (Boston: Beacon Press, 1972); also Bernard Fall, *The Anatomy of a Crisis* (Garden City: Doubleday, 1969); and Arthur Dommen, *Conflict in Laos: The Politics of Neutralization* (New York: Praeger, 1971), rev. ed.

16. Fall, *Anatomy of a Crisis*, p. 190.

17. *Ibid.*, p. 198.

18. *Ibid.*, p. 80.

19. Pike, *Vietnam and the Soviet Union*, p. 44.

20. See Donald Hindley, *The Communist Party of Indonesia, 1951–1963* (Berkeley: University of California Press, 1963), p. 31, p. 314, n. 5. This section also draws from a paper by J. Soedjati Djiwandono, "Indonesia's Changing Perceptions of the Soviet Union and Its Policy Implications," presented to a workshop on Soviet Policy in Asia, East-West Center, Honolulu, March, 1987.

21. Justus M. Van Der Kroef, "Soviet and Chinese Influence in Indonesia," in Alvin Z. Rubinstein, ed., *Soviet and Chinese Influence in the Third World* (New York: Praeger, 1975), pp. 57–58.

22. Uri Ra'anan, *The USSR Arms the Third World: Case Studies in Soviet Foreign Policy* (Cambridge: MIT Press, 1969), p. 237.

23. *Ibid.*, p. 213.

24. Khrushchev, *Khrushchev Remembers*, p. 433.

25. Cited in Robert Horn, *Soviet–Indian Relations: Issues and Influence* (New York: Praeger, 1982), p. 3.

26. Arthur Stein, *India and the Soviet Union: The Nehru Era* (Chicago: University of Chicago Press, 1969). For Menon's observations see his Moscow diary published as *The Flying Troika* (London: Oxford University Press, 1963).

27. Stein, *India and the Soviet Union*, p. 67.

28. K. P. S. Menon, "India and the Soviet Union," in B. R. Nanda, ed., *Indian Foreign Policy: The Nehru Years* (Honolulu: University Press of Hawaii, 1976), pp. 131–32.

29. Stein, *India and the Soviet Union*, pp. 72–76. Khrushchev's second venture in personal diplomacy in India—his brief visit of February 1960—was a good deal less successful.

30. *Ibid.*, pp. 125–26, 194–96.

31. See William J. Barnds, *India, Pakistan, and the Great Powers* (New York: Praeger, 1972), pp. 156–58.

32. Stein, *India and the Soviet Union*, pp. 203–6.

33. Khrushchev, *Khrushchev Remembers*, p. 461.

34. *Ibid.*, p. 463.

35. Witold Rodzinski, *The People's Republic of China: A Concise Political History* (New York: Free Press, 1988), p. 38.

36. Khrushchev, *Khrushchev Remembers*, p. 466.

37. The memoirs of the Yugoslav ambassador to Moscow for much of the 1950s and 1960s provide vivid evidence of this. See Veljko Mićunović, *Moscow Diary* (Garden City, N.Y.: Doubleday, 1980).

38. Medvedev, *Khrushchev*, p. 149.

39. See Donald S. Zagoria's classic *The Sino-Soviet Conflict, 1956–1961* (New York: Atheneum, 1964).

40. Khrushchev, *Khrushchev Remembers*, p. 472.

41. See Roderick McFarquhar, *The Origins of the Cultural Revolution*, vol. 2: *The Great Leap Forward* (New York: Columbia University Press, 1983.

42. See Carl Riskin, *China's Political Economy* (New York: Oxford University Press, 1987).

43. Joseph Sang-hoon Chung, *The North Korean Economy: Structure and Development* (Stanford: Hoover Institution Press, 1974), pp. 112, 118–19. See also E. A. Konavalov, ed., *Koreiskaya Narodno-demokraticheskaya Respublika* [Democratic People's Republic of Korea] (Moscow: Nauka, 1975), pp. 51ff.

44. Ralph Clough, *Embattled Korea: The Rivalry for International Support* (Boulder: Westview, 1987), p. 248.

45. See Robert Scalapino and Chung Sik Lee, *Communism in Korea* (Berkeley: University of California Press, 1972), 1:500–635; Dae-Sook Suh, *Kim Il Sung: The North Korean Leader* (New York: Columbia University Press, 1988), pp. 137–75.

46. Rajendra Kumar Jain, *The USSR and Japan, 1945–1980* (Atlantic Highlands, N.J.: Humanities Press, 1981), pp. 235–38. For the Japanese domestic context of this agreement, see Donald C. Hellman, *Japanese Domestic Politics and Foreign Policy: the Peace Agreement with the Soviet Union* (Berkeley: University of California Press, 1969).

47. For full discussions of Soviet-Japanese relations in this period, see Savitri Vishwanathan, *Normalization of Soviet-Japanese Relations, 1945–1970* (Tallahassee: Diplomatic Press, 1973); Rodger Swearingen, *The Soviet Union and Postwar Japan: Escalating Challenge and Response* (Stanford: Hoover Institution Press, 1978).

INDEX

Abramisov, Aleksandr, 302
Acheson, Dean, 36
Activists, revolutionary, 16
Administration of revolutionary states, 21
Advisers to Dulles, 39–41, 55, 57n26
AEC, *see* Atomic Energy Commission
Afro-Asian politics, Soviet Union and, 300
Aggression, Anglo-American policies, 262
Aidit, D. N., 304
Aircraft carrier task forces, 67
Air defense system, Japan, 71–72
Air Force, U.S., policy development, 77
Air power, Taiwan Straits crisis, 78
Ali, S. Amjad, 283–84
Allen, Dennis, 253, 262–63
Allen, George V., 52
Allen, Richard V., 284
Alliances, 187; containment policies, 274; Japanese-American, 207–8; U.S., Communist China and, 224–25
Allied occupation of Japan, Great Britain and, 173, 176, 182nn9,14
Allies: and embargo of China, 126; and Taiwan Straits issues, 238; U.S. foreign policy and, 46, 87, 274
Allison, John M., 180; and *Lucky Dragon* incident, 192, 193, 196–205 *passim*

Ambassador-level talks, U.S.–China, 8, 148–50, 229, 231–32
American prisoners in China, 53, 229, 231
Ando Masazumi, 200, 202, 204
Anglo-Malayan Defense Agreement, 268
Anglo-Malayan-Singaporean Internal Security Council, 268
Anticolonialism in Asia, 215
Anti-Communism, U.S., Soviet view, 219
Anti-Communist warfare, Southeast Asia, 247
Antinuclear movement, Japan, 196, 200, 206
ANZUS treaty, Great Britain and, 172, 173, 174, 281
Appeasement policies, Eisenhower's view, 92
Armed Forces Policy Council, 68
Army, U.S.: policy disagreements, 76; strategies, 67; troop deployment, 80
Asian fund proposal, 107, 108, 112–15
Atomic bomb, *see* Nuclear weapons
Atomic Energy Commission (AEC), and nuclear test accident, 192–93
Attlee, Clement, Asia policy, 171, 254
Australia, interest in Malaya, 267; and SEATO draft, 283
Austria, Soviet withdrawal, 165